THE
HISTO

CW01500087

OF THE

BALTIC CAMPAIGN

OF

1854

FROM DOCUMENTS AND OTHER MATERIALS FURNISHED BY

VICE-ADMIRAL SIR C. NAPIER, K.C.B.

EDITED BY

G. BUTLER EARP

The Naval & Military Press Ltd

published in association with

FIREPOWER
The Royal Artillery Museum
Woolwich

Published by
The Naval & Military Press Ltd
Unit 10 Ridgewood Industrial Park,
Uckfield, East Sussex,
TN22 5QE England
Tel: +44 (0) 1825 749494
Fax: +44 (0) 1825 765701
www.naval-military-press.com

in association with

FIREPOWER
The Royal Artillery Museum, Woolwich
www.firepower.org.uk

The Naval & Military
Press

MILITARY HISTORY AT YOUR
FINGERTIPS

... a unique and expanding series of reference works

Working in collaboration with the foremost
regiments and institutions, as well as acknowledged
experts in their field, N&MP have assembled a
formidable array of titles including technologically
advanced CD-ROMs and facsimile reprints of
impossible-to-find rarities.

*In reprinting in facsimile from the original, any imperfections are inevitably reproduced
and the quality may fall short of modern type and cartographic standards.*

TO

LIEUT.-GEN. SIR WILLIAM NAPIER, K.C.B.

COLONEL OF THE 22ND REGIMENT OF FOOT,

ETC. ETC. ETC.

THIS VOLUME,

FORMING AN ADDITIONAL RECORD OF INJURY TO A RACE OF WARRIORS

WHICH HAS EFFECTED MUCH

FOR THE GRATITUDE OF THEIR COUNTRY,

AND SUFFERED MORE FROM OFFICIAL INJUSTICE THAN ANY OTHER RACE

WHOSE WORLD-WIDE ACHIEVEMENTS RANK AMONGST THE

PROUD PAGES OF ENGLISH HISTORY,

Is Inscribed,

BY

HIS OBLIGED AND OBEDIENT SERVANT,

G. B. EARP.

EDITOR'S PREFACE.

A SHORT time ago, on perceiving the reiterated and virulent attacks made on SIR CHARLES NAPIER, by members of the Government under which he had served, and that even these, skilfully devised, and pertinaciously resorted to, failed to remove from the public mind an impression that not the Admiral but his employers were to blame for the conduct of the first Baltic campaign, the Editor of this volume represented to Sir Charles that he should make known all the material circumstances connected with the campaign, not by way of defence, but in a clearly connected historical narrative, whereby all classes might satisfy themselves as to the conduct of the war in the Baltic, so far as he was concerned, and thus draw their own conclusions as to whether blame existed; and if so, where, and upon whom it really lay. Thus, he considered, a stop would be put to such attacks, and justice done to the Admiral's previous fame, no less than to the naval profession, in-

stead of tamely submitting to the attacks made upon
him, from time to time, in the newspapers, — upon
which attacks alone public opinion was founded.

The Editor offered, moreover, if the necessary materials were placed at his disposal, to produce such a
work as the one indicated. The great number of documents inseparable from the management of a fleet,
although formidable, presented no insuperable difficulties which a little time and patience could not
readily surmount; provided that, should real difficulty arise, the Admiral himself would aid the
Editor in unravelling it, by pointing out the precise
nature of the subject in question.

This proposition being warmly seconded by a member of Sir Charles Napier's family, the Admiral gave
the desired access to his private documents and
papers, as well as to the books and papers of the
fleet. He at the same time intimated to the Editor,
that if he thought it worth while to wade through
such a mass for the purpose of preparing a continuous history of the campaign, he had no objection,
as he had nothing to fear from such publication,
being fully conscious that he had done his duty, and
indifferent as to what opinion might be formed respecting the course he had pursued when in command
of the Baltic fleet.

The present Volume is the result. The time occupied in the task has been, however, by no means

commensurate with the magnitude of the subject, so
that marks of haste as regards composition may
doubtless abundantly be found, though the Editor
trusts none will be found as regards matters of fact.
The principle of the work has been, that, for every
assertion made, a confirmatory document shall be
produced, in case of question. These remarks are not
made in any deprecatory spirit, than which nothing
can be more contemptible. When an author gives his
work to the public, it must stand for what it is
worth, and no more. If its object be truth, no
amount of adverse or party criticism will check it;
if to mislead, no critic is so acute as the public, to
whom it is addressed.

Nothing, however, could more proudly stamp the
confidence of the Admiral in having thoroughly performed his duty, than the publication of documents
by which alone this can be established. This has
been done in defiance of red-tape routine, which imperatively insists that a commander shall sustain any
amount of injury from his superiors and remain *si-
lent*. The moral courage which can fly in the face of
this arbitrary rule must rest on a pretty secure basis.

When a portion only of these documents was
made public, the Board of Admiralty stood aghast at
the proceeding, and many naval men, with the fear
of the Board before their eyes, though fully aware of
the injustice committed towards the Admiral, shrank

instinctively from the challenge thus thrown out by him to back his acts against the abuse of Government power which had so foully aspersed them. They did not see, though the nation was well aware of it, that the quarrel of Sir Charles Napier was not with the Government, but with one or two Lords of the Admiralty only, who were making unfair use of their power to ruin an Admiral's reputation, in order to cover the deficiencies of their own department.

No man of any eminence in the Government has found fault with Sir Charles Napier; but, on the contrary, they have highly praised him, not only throughout the war, but ever since. This will appear from their own letters here published; and this has recently been manifested in the instance of Lord Palmerston, who, only a few days ago, bestowed upon Sir Charles the highest eulogium on the whole conduct of the Baltic Campaign, as a set-off to the aspersions of his own colleague, Sir Robert Peel; Lord Palmerston thus nobly preferring division of opinion to the sacrifice of truth.

Even the Board of Admiralty, which had aspersed Sir Charles Napier, afterwards recommended Her Majesty to confer upon him the highest naval distinction, for his services in the Baltic, viz., the *Grand Cross of the Bath;* and to this recommendation Her Majesty promptly assented. The Admiral, however, felt bound to decline this honour,— respectfully towards Her Majesty, inasmuch as he was still labouring under the imputation of failure in the object for which he had been sent to the Baltic, — firmly towards the Admiralty, as refusing to receive compensation for the deliberate and unjust attacks on his reputation by a sop, whilst those imputations still remained as a blot on his escutcheon.

The refusal of the Grand Cross of the Bath, under these circumstances, is one of the noblest acts of Sir Charles Napier's self-denying career. Such an instance of honourable self-respect is almost unique. He would have felt it a degradation to wear an outward mark of honour on his breast, whilst his inward soul must have told him, that not only he, but his unthanked officers and men, were labouring under the imputation of failure — nay almost of cowardice. He had been censured and degraded — was denied the opportunity of clearing his reputation — but was offered the *Grand Cross of the Bath* to cover his tarnished fame! Had the investigation which he asked for been accorded, no more appropriate reward could have been bestowed on him ; for it must have shown — not only the great services for which his accusers had so highly praised him during the campaign, but that, had he followed the advice of the First Lord of the Admiralty, he might not have brought half his ships back to England, instead of bringing back the whole fleet safe and sound. With-

out being confronted with his accusers, who can say
the Admiral is not more honoured by declining the
proffered decoration than he would have been by
accepting it ?

It has been said by the accusers of Sir C. Napier,
that "*he has lost his nerve.*" Let the stand which he
has made against Admiralty opprobrium, from which
younger men would have shrunk—let the masterly
despatches contained in this work—reply to this unworthy assertion. Let naval men weigh well these
despatches, full of professional wisdom. Let them
observe, that many were written in the very gall and
bitterness of unmerited obloquy ; some when betrayed,
insulted, and dismissed from his command by a corrupt cabal against him. Let them see, that, even
under this deep sense of injury, there is not a word
too much, and every word in its right place. There
is no "loss of nerve" here ; but there must have been
a sad *want* of nerve in those who recommended him
to honour, in very fear of what his nerve might
accomplish if a *quietus* were not administered.

But these despatches caused his dismissal. They
"were not respectful to authority." Who, thoroughly
experienced, could be respectful to such authority ?—
Yet to the authority itself he was not disrespectful,
but only to the ignorant assumptions of authority in
directing his every movement as an Admiral. What
respect, for instance, could be due to an authority

which told him to make use of the "vertical fire of his line-of-battle ships?"—what to an authority which could deliberately recommend him to "*risk*" (*lege*, "lose") four line-of-battle ships, with their brave crews, to satisfy public clamour? What respect could there be for an authority which was always pestering him with advice of this kind, instead of supplying him with means to get at an enemy who would not come out to meet him; whilst the same authority was at other times cautioning him "not to run his head against the stone walls" behind which the enemy's ships lay? What respect could there be for an authority which, when he asked for gun-boats, offered to send him a "dredging machine"? when he asked for mortars, told him to try "diving bells" to get up the Russian piles before Cronstadt? when he asked for rockets, informed him that there was nothing like breaking a trench in the ice round the island of Oesel, to keep the Russians off? and which, when the Admiral asked for small steamers as indispensable, recommended him to "*hire them from Sweden, as nothing would be so economical in the long run?*"

It is a disgrace to the naval power of England, that, with the experience of Sir Charles Napier before the Admiralty, Sweaborg was not afterwards destroyed. The *Times* clearly pointed out the defect. When Admiral Dundas bombarded Sweaborg

the *Times* triumphantly wrote " *Sweaborg is no more.*"
A day or two, however, sufficed to prove that the
fortress was untouched. Then wrote the same journal:
"We are defeated by our own triumphs, *and all for
want of mortars.*" Sir Charles Napier *never had a
single mortar in his fleet!* and it was for urging the
necessity of mortars, &c., that he was superseded, as
will plainly appear in these pages. The *Times* has
been a very bitter enemy to Sir Charles Napier. Let
it at length do him justice from the text just quoted
from its own columns. Admiral Dundas *had* mortars,
but so worthless that they burst from firing; he had
also a fleet of enormous magnitude as compared with
that of Sir C. Napier, when the latter was ordered
by the Board of Admiralty to attack Sweaborg; still,
Admiral Dundas no more took Sweaborg *with* mortars
than Sir Charles Napier did *without* them. The *Times*
afterwards called Admiral Dundas's bombardment " *a
boasted victory; we have not silenced the enemy's
batteries, but we have silenced our own!* " Sir Charles
Napier had no batteries of his own to silence. The
Times can never show to greater advantage than when
retracting injustice. Here is a fitting opportunity.

But, unprofessional criticism apart, let us turn
for a moment to the opinions of an officer, whose
deeds have now become well-nigh historical, ranking
amongst the most brilliant achievements of the most
brilliant periods of our history, — the contemporary

and survivor of the Nelsons and St. Vincents of the days of our fathers, viz., the Earl of Dundonald, the Lord Cochrane, whose name in days long past struck terror into our European foes, and whose prowess has since liberated half the Western World from the thraldom of its European oppressors. No man knows better than Lord Cochrane — we prefer the name attached to the noble Earl's exploits — what fleets can do, and no man knows better the power of a Board of Admiralty to crush gallantry when opposed to its own petty political interests. His own glorious early life was itself clouded by Admiralty hatred, for no better reason than that his inflexible though dangerous honesty would persist in denouncing official dishonesty. The uncompromising enemy of naval abuses, stupidities, and atrocities, he himself had been deprived of his honours, as the surest way to get rid of a stumbling-block; but only to have them restored to him at an advanced age by a sailor King, who knew his merits no less than the official demerits which, in evil times, had marked him out as a victim. The noble Earl, seeing the determined injustice heaped on Sir Charles Napier by ignorance the most palpable, shrouded in the garb of official power, recently made known his opinions as follows : —

" The honourable testimony officially given by the First Minister of the Crown (Lord Palmerston) in regard to the conduct of a late Commander-in-Chief of Her Majesty's Naval Forces in the

Baltic (Sir Charles Napier) having been subjected to severe non-professional criticism, I feel it a duty to the Crown and to our country, as a naval officer, to submit the following observations to the judgment of the whole naval profession. Admirals as enterprising and brave as any whose deeds are recorded in history were employed during the long war between 1793 and 1815. Yet hostile fleets were *passively* blockaded by superior force in bays and roadsteads having wider entrances, deeper water, and more capacious anchorages, less effectually protected by forts and batteries, than those of Cronstadt ; nevertheless, there is not one instance of an enemy's fleet having been destroyed, or *even assailed*, in such positions under these more favourable circumstances. The attack on Algiers, garrisoned by inexperienced barbarians, is not a case in point; neither was the capture of the Danish fleet at Copenhagen, previous to a declaration of war; nor the naval action in the Bay of St. Domingo (ill-provided with means of offence), nor the battle of the Nile, any proof of the practicability of combustible ships successfully contending with red hot shot. No, nor did the practicable success at Basque Roads induce even the most sanguine officer there present to anticipate greater good fortune than to escape without material damage from the batteries of Aix, whilst running through a channel half a league in width, into an anchorage nearly three leagues in circumference, on the distant side of which the enemy's squadron (driven on shore by fire vessels) lay in a helpless condition.

Great blame has been imputed by *self-constituted naval critics* to the disclosure made of the inefficient state of the crews of the Baltic fleet ; but I respectfully submit to the judgment of my brother officers whether the fact ought not to be *pressed* on public attention with a view to the safety of our country, by promoting an unanimous call for a recurrence to our former truly judicious navigation laws, thoughtlessly abolished. Better would it have been had the legislature indemnified influential corporations, and the suffering shipping interest, out of the public purse, and by the remission of taxes on timber, hemp, and on all that is used in shipbuilding and navigation, than to have lowered the pay of our gallant tars to a parity with that of continental navigators, who (with their families) can subsist on the most costless food — on stockfish and train oil. I announced six years ago * that 80,000 " blue jackets

---

* " Observations on Naval Affairs," published by Ridgway.

had resorted to a foreign land, where the absence of exaction ensures remunerative freights without resorting to the diminution of wages. Since that period our coasting trade (once highly prized as a nursery for seamen) has been thrown open to alien navigators. How many more of our gallant defenders have thus been forced to follow the example of their Transatlantic brethren it would be important to ascertain, in order with greater zeal to promote an unanimous expression of public opinion in favour of liberal wages, and against the fatal expedient which might otherwise be adopted —that of a Naval Foreign Enlistment Bill.

Having thus publicly requested a verdict from my brother officers, I deem it proper to express my own opinion, namely, that red-hot shot from half a hundred cannon, directed at the bows of ships advancing through a narrow channel, independent of carcasses and shells showered from a thousand artillery around, would, in a few minutes, destroy any number of vessels. It is true that means of setting these hitherto formidable methods of defence at defiance have been communicated at various times to Government; but it is equally true that these important means have failed to obtain impartial consideration by minds preoccupied by party or political objects, pressed by powerful influence — such as produced the expatriation of our *unrepresented* seamen, and thus caused the vital interests of our country to be overlooked. Thirty-three noble ships of the Spanish line have I seen under weigh.* Their naval power is now no more. Yet the causes of its downfall were not so manifest as those which threaten our Naval Service, and consequently our national independence.

                                                    " DUNDONALD.
"London, Dec. 27."

It is a singular yet incontrovertible fact, that every British Admiral of eminence, when in command of a fleet, has been subjected to the marked enmity and insult of the Board of Admiralty. The reason is plain enough, viz., that Admirals of eminence rarely possess political interest enough to obtain a seat at the Board; and whilst they are else-

---

* Ibid.

where performing distinguished services, the Board is using its petty jealousies to keep them down.

Let us take the instance of Lord Nelson after the Battle of the Nile. Notwithstanding the honours showered upon him by a grateful country, he was not allowed the class of smaller vessels, which he wanted to complete the destruction of the French force in the harbour of Alexandria; hence, by the subsequent escape of Bonaparte, his work at Aboukir might as well not have been done. This was precisely the case with Sir Charles Napier. But this was not all. Another Commander-in-Chief (Lord Keith) was placed over Nelson's head in the Mediterranean! How bitterly Nelson felt this treatment is evident from his letters: —

"Having a Commander-in-Chief, I cannot come on shore till I have made *my manners* to him. *Times are changed.*" (*Feb.* 3. 1800.)

"Lord Keith sailed from Spithead, *to take from me all opportunity of rewarding merit.*" (*March* 11. 1800.)

"My task is done — my health lost— and I have wrote to Lord Keith for my retreat. May all orders be as punctually obeyed! but never again, an officer at the close of what I must, without being thought vain (for such I am represented by my enemies), call a glorious career, *be so treated.*" (*April 6th,* 1800.)

When Lord Nelson was afterwards sent to Copenhagen, he was, notwithstanding his victory in Egypt, put under the orders of Sir Hyde Parker, a man whom history has pronounced to have been unfit to command a fleet under such circumstances, and still more so to command Nelson, who only gained his victory by direct disobedience to the orders of his Chief, the latter literally hoisting a signal which would have led to the loss of the battle. Let us see what was Lord Nelson's opinion of this treatment: —

" The difficulty was to get our Commander-in-Chief *either to go past Cronenburg or through the Belt ;* because, what Sir Hyde Parker thought best, and what I believe was settled before I came on board the *London, was to stay in the Cattegat,* and there wait the time when the whole naval force of the Baltic might choose to come out and fight ; a measure, in my opinion, disgraceful to my country." (*May* 12. 1801.)

The reader will in the following pages find the exact parallel to this, where it had " *been settled* " that Sir Charles Napier was to " *watch in the Cattegat,*" and he was actually reprimanded for quitting it! The Board of Admiralty is not at all altered since Nelson's time.

Sir Charles, however, had not a Chief put over his head, but was dismissed from his command for services which throughout had been most highly applauded by those who dismissed him!

The public is not generally aware that, on the dismissal of Sir Charles Napier, the command of the Baltic fleet was offered to another eminent Admiral, who promptly refused it on the ground of Sir Charles Napier's treatment, and also on the ground that he would not command a fleet in which the officers were set to criticise their Admiral.

a

This point calls for more than passing remark. A short time since, when addressing his constituents at Gloucester, Admiral Berkeley stated, that *" he was in correspondence with most of the officers "* in Sir Charles Napier's fleet. This is no new thing in the conduct of fleets. Let us see what was Lord St. Vincent's opinion on the matter; for no Admiral suffered more from it than he did; nearly all his officers denouncing him to the Board either as a tyrant or an old woman, according as they suffered from his discipline, or disapproved of his acts.

"I have no doubt of bringing the fleet to as great perfection of discipline as it can be, *serving so immediately under the Admiralty Board.* (*25th July*, 1800.)

"H.M.S. *Ville de Paris*, near Ushant, 14th October, 1800.
" MY DEAR NEPEAN,
" I have no objection to the correspondence of the whole world being conveyed under cover to me, *with the exception of that which passes between Puisne Lords of the Admiralty and subordinates of the fleet under my command,* and I hope in future no letters so sent will compel me to write to you as enclosed. A hint to your clerks will remedy *what I will not endure.*
" Yours, &c.
(Enclosure.) " ST. VINCENT."

" H.M.S. *Ville de Paris*, 14th October, 1800.
" Having positively forbidden in public orders any *surreptitious correspondence* upon the individual subject of any ship, or relative to the fleet, *between members of the Board of Admiralty and the officers under my command,* so derogatory to the discipline and subordination thereof, *I cannot submit to be the vehicle of such correspondence ; I therefore return this letter to ——, which came under cover of the despatches I received to-day.*
" I am, &c.
" ST. VINCENT."

Sir Charles Napier never did anything half so dis-respectful to the Board of Admiralty as *to return the letters from members of the Board to his officers*, as a piece of impertinent interference with the management of his fleet. Yet the Board's private letters to Sir C. Napier's officers came through his hands in abundance, and were replied to by the officers in shoals, according as the spleen or the ignorance of the writers might dictate. The Board durst not kick at Lord St. Vincent's reproof, because it knew that the country would uphold him'; as, if it desire the proper conduct of its navy in future, the country will uphold Sir Charles Napier, notwithstanding that he did wrong in not adopting Lord St. Vincent's precedent of sending the Board's letters back. Lord St. Vincent was obliged to adopt stronger measures before he could put a stop to the evil. On the 17th of December, 1800, he thus wrote to the Secretary of the Admiralty :—
" *The next impertinence I receive will make room for Sir Hyde Parker.*" And again, on the 18th of September, 1856 :—"*I pity the exposure of the weakness of some of your Lords, whose dulness I have long been acquainted with ; but I did not conceive it possible they could be so thoroughly unacquainted with the chart of the ocean as to express such an opinion.*" There is no lack of room for similar remark in the present volume.

Admiral Berkeley could not have read these letters of Lord St. Vincent when he made the statement at

Gloucester, that he was in communication with the officers of Sir Charles Napier's fleet. On the dismissal of Sir C. Napier, even Admiral Berkeley himself did not accept the Baltic fleet, though on its first equipment he stated in the House of Commons, that "he had run an honest race with Sir Charles for the command." It has been said that Admiral Berkeley again sought the command, but the request was not complied with. This looks very much as though the fleet had literally gone a-begging after Sir C. Napier had been ordered to strike his flag. Two Admirals had, in one way or other, declined it before Admiral Dundas took it.

It is a trite remark, that history recurs in cycles. The remark is in a great measure true, as it ever must be, when the same mischievous causes are productive of the same ruinous effects. In proof of this, we need scarcely refer to the ancient Admiralties of Greece and Rome, the more scholastic mode of proceeding; but will simply go back to Alison's History of Europe*, where he narrates the condition of the navy in 1804, exactly fifty years before Sir Charles Napier's fleet sailed for the Baltic. His description of the navy at that period so nearly coincides with the following narrative, that, after citing Sir A. Alison's conclusions, it is almost a work of supererogation to say another word on the matter : —

* Vol. viii. chap. xxxvii. p. 293.

" During this interval of doubt and alarm, the minds of the great majority of men throughout the nation became convinced of the necessity of placing the helm of the state under firmer guidance. On the 15th of March, 1804, matters came to a crisis. (Sir Charles Napier sailed on the 13th of March, 1854.) The trifling nature of the success which had been gained, notwithstanding such costly efforts, during the first year of the contest, produced a very general conviction that ministers, whatever their individual respectability and talents might be, were unequal as a body to the task of steering the vessel of the State through the shoals and quicksands with which it was surrounded; and in particular did not possess that weight and eminence in the estimation of foreign states, which was necessary to enable Great Britain to *take her appropriate station as the leader of the general confederacy.*

" This feeling was much increased by the complaints which strongly broke out as *to the reduced and inefficient state of the navy;* and it soon became painfully evident, from a comparison of the vessels in commission, at the close of the former and commencement of the present war, *that this important arm of the public defence had declined to a very great degree during the interval of peace; and that, under the delusion of a wretched, and in the end most costly economy, the stores on which the public salvation depended, were dissipated to an extent in the highest degree alarming. The consequence was, that when war broke out, the navy was in an unprecedented state of dilapidation.*

" Mr. Addington (*lege,* Modern Ministries) boasted during the peace, that if war broke out, fifty ships of the line could be equipped in a month. But when this declaration came to be put to the test, it was discovered that the Royal arsenals were almost emptied! Neither vessels could be procured for the King's squadron, nor convoys for the merchant service. When the Royal message was delivered in Parliament, on the 8th of March, *there was hardly a* ship of war ready, or in a state of forwardness. The consequence was, that notwithstanding the utmost efforts to repair the ruinous economy and dilapidations of preceding years, the ships in commission on the 5th of January, 1804, only numbered seventy-five of the line; whereas, at the commencement of 1801, there were 100 of the line."

This is an exact description of the state of the

fleet in 1854, varying in one particular only. Suppose, in 1854, we had been suddenly engaged in war with France instead of Russia, where would then have been the convoys to protect our merchant vessels? Even before we were at war with Russia, the Government exhibited very unseemly alarm lest the Russians should get out of the Baltic, whilst we had no ships to protect our coasts or commerce; and, what is more, none could be got to protect either, for up to the end of the campaign, the constant instructions to Sir C. Napier were, to be sure not to let any Russian ships slip past him into the North Sea. The bravery of English power had, by the fault of our rulers, degenerated into imbecility, those who wielded that power being the first to give vent to their fears.

In 1804, says the historian, the navy had fallen so low that we had *only* seventy-five ships of the line. But at the commencement of the war in 1854, we could not muster even half seventy-five ships of the line! Sir Charles Napier sailed from Portsmouth with *four* sail of the line only, four block-ships, four frigates, and three steamers, whilst, in the Black Sea, Admiral Dundas had only *ten* sail of the line and a few frigates; and on the declaration of war, there were only *eight* at home, destined for the Baltic. The bad armament of 1804 would have been a perfect godsend to the Admirals in 1854. What will be our armament in 2004, if England should survive so long the cheeseparing of Parliamentary economists, the foes most to be dreaded both by the nation and the navy? The enormous waste of money and life which these men have caused to the nation for no purpose, ought to figure in the national accounts as a separate item. Then the public will be enabled fairly to estimate the cost of economy,—incomparably the dearest of all national acquisitions. Let us put this broadly: the naval economy of, say, five millions, has cost us at least fifty millions, besides failure in our object as compared with the result of former wars. Nay, more than this; we are now openly branded by our Continental allies as a " second-rate power."

This naval economy is nothing new, any more than are the disasters arising from it. Two hundred years ago, Sir Walter Raleigh thus wrote of the Humes and Cobdens of his day, as regarded their pernicious interference with the navy:—

"Contrary spirits may say, why should the State be troubled with this needlesse charge of keeping so great a navy in such exquisite perfection and readinesse, the times being peaceable? To this I answer, that this may stand for a prettie superficiall argument, to bleare our eyes, and make us negligent of those causes from whence the effect of peace grows, and by the virtue whereof it must be maintained. For well may we be assured, that if we could not again, upon occasion, readily assume the use and benefit of those powerful means whereby we reduced them to seek us, those proud mastering spirits would be more ready and willing *to shake us by the ears as enemies, than to take us by the hand as friends.* (*Sir Walter Raleigh,* " *Observations on the Navy and Sea Service.*")

The writings of Sir Walter Raleigh are so singularly prophetic of the state of the navy in 1854, that a few more extracts may well be subjoined : —

"Many times the men goe with a great grudging to serve in His Majestie's ships, the case being clean contrarie in merchant service.

"The greatest ships are the least serviceable, are of marvellous charge, and fearful cumber, less nimble, less maineable, and seldom employed ; overpestred and clogged with great ordnance, which only serves to overcharge the ships' sides in foule weather."

Sir Charles Napier, in a letter to Lord John Russell, written in 1849, had, in an equally prophetic spirit, warned the Government of the same thing :—

"We seem to have quite forgotten that there are such seas as *the North Sea and the Baltic*, where small ships of two or three decks, with a light draught of water, are indispensable. Unless we can produce a larger class of men, they will never be able to furl the canvass."

Sir Walter Raleigh, moreover, hit on the precise cause of the inefficiency of the navy in his day, and, strange to say, as regards the really governing powers of the Admiralty, it remains unchanged to our own times :—

"I will first begin with the Admiralty officers, and therein crave pardon if, speaking plainly in a matter of so great importance, I doe set aside all private respects and partiality. In affairs of this nature every good subject is deeply interested, and bound in conscience and duty both to say and doe his best.

"It is to be wished that the chiefe officers under the Lord Admiral should be men of experience in sea service, as well as of judgement and practise in the utensils and necessaries belonging to shipping, even from the batt's end to the very kelson of a ship ; and that *no kind* of people should be preferred to *any* of these offices but such as have been *thoroughly practised,* and be very judiciall in either kind of the above-named services ; but we often-times see it to fall out otherwise."

The chief ruling power of the Admiralty is in our day a civilian ; his first Secretary, a soldier ; and the financial Lord, Sir Robert Peel.

One more extract from Raleigh is too apposite to be omitted : —

" I have lost my sonne and my health, and endured as many sorts of miseries as ever man did, in hope to do His Majestie acceptable service. An unfortunate man I am, and it is to me a greater loss than all I have lost, that it pleaseth His Majestie to be offended for the burning of a Spanish town in Guiana."

In this respect the case of Sir Charles Napier differs in the latter part of the preceding sentence only. It " pleaseth " the Admiralty to be offended with him, because they did not supply him with the means of burning a Russian town in the Baltic, and because it was expedient for them to endeavour to avert popular wrath from themselves, and throw it on him.

In these historical parallels, we must not omit one more from Alison : —

" Nor was the ability and energy of Lord Melville less conspicuous in the rapid restoration of the navy from a state of unexampled decrepitude and decay. Every thing was to be done, for such was the mutilated and shattered state of the fleet, and to such an extent had the disastrous spirit of parsimonious reform been carried, that when stores and timber were offered at comparatively moderate rates, they were refused by the late Admiralty, and suffered to be sold rather than deviate from their pernicious economy, even in the purchase of those articles which were in daily consumption. The consequence was, that Lord Melville was compelled to accept the offer of timber, stores, and masts at whatever price the contractors chose to demand, and the savings of one naval administration entailed a quadruple expenditure upon that which succeeded it." (Page 297.)

Did our space permit, it would be easy, from Parliamentary returns, to prove the exact parallel to this in 1854. It is a trite remark amongst naval men, that Tory Governments invariably look to the navy, and accumulate stores of every description; whilst the moment a Whig Government comes into office, they dissipate them, and then boast of the economy with which they have conducted the navy. In this respect 1854 had learned nothing from the disasters of 1804.

We will here adduce the opinion of a man whose writings are more esteemed throughout Europe than are those of Raleigh or Alison, admirable as these may be. It was anonymously published in December, 1854, when Sir Charles was on his return from the Baltic. Its author is Lieut.-General Sir William Napier: —

"Public opinion in England is a myth, presenting the *Arimanes* and *Oromanes* of Zoroaster — the principles of good and evil. The *good* is the influence of the thoughtful, sound-judging men in the community, which percolates, slowly indeed, but generally surely, through the outward crust of folly to the national intellect. The *evil* is the loud obstreperous cry which on every great event bursts forth, overpowering sense and facts. It might be typified by a high donkey with cloven hoofs planted in dogged semblance, tail stretched out stiffly behind, and long ears poked forward to catch every flying falsehood,— something of devil and ass combined, braying with such full satisfaction and contentment with its own ridiculous perceptions that the voice of reason cannot be heard. A woodcut of his at once ridiculous and malignant figure would form an appropriate heading for the *Times*.

" When the Baltic fleet was first assembled, how loudly, how fiercely, did this donkey, *Arimanes*, bray ! 'Never were there such ships afloat ; they could of themselves, like the groom's favourite horse, *do anything but speak and clean knives.'* They were not indeed to sail overland to Moscow ; but they were to screw through Cronstadt to St. Petersburg. The Czar was sick — was panic stricken — was mad ; his Ministers, his Generals, his public servants were all knaves and fools ; his soldiers (if he had any, which was doubtful, and he certainly had no seamen) were more than half starved, without shirts or shoes, and entirely indisposed to fight ; his fortresses were built only to crumble from the shaking of their own guns ; and his artillerymen were doomed to be stifled by smoke in their own casemates before the masonry fell.

" Great was *Arimanes'* discontent to find that his brays were not bullets, nor the sails of the ships wings. ' Why were not Sweaborg and Cronstadt laid in ashes ? Everybody, except the Admiral, knew — especially the midshipmen — that it was only necessary to shout before them, and, like the walls of Jericho, they would tumble down. Granite was a poor contemptible material ; a finger might be thrust through it. Look at Bomarsund ! that settled the question of granite against ships. Behold, also, how Sebastopol is going to be taken — it has not, indeed, yet fallen, and there is an army besides the fleet before it — but it will be reduced immediately by a fleet and an army, and, of course, Sweaborg and Cronstadt can be at once taken by a fleet without an army. The Baltic ships could go through such flimsy structures as ducks go through foam on a pond.' Such was substantially, and nearly textually, the language of the *Times*, that most potential of *Arimanes'* voices ; but truly it would try the strength of ducks to plough through the foam of that journal.

" Time wore on. Sebastopol did not fall. Our ships failed before its walls, which, by the way, are not granite, but limestone ; and *Arimanes'* bray having subsided for the moment, the voice of *Oromanes* may be heard. Let us take advantage of the lull to give a calm statement of facts.

" The Baltic fleet was a magnificent one, so far as ships and guns went, but the manning of it was defective to a much greater extent than the public were permitted to know — *Arimanes'* bray was too loud. The men were brave and willing, although not very well treated ; for they were refused pea-jackets to protect them from the cold of the North Sea, to which they were certainly sent a month too soon : but they were not *men-of-war's men*, nor even seamen, for the greater part, and presented a heterogeneous mass, demanding much care, skill, and practice to make them work together efficiently. The Admiral, well aware of this deficiency, and of the difficulties in the way of a brilliant campaign, was not elated by the cry of the moment above a regard for reason ; and when maudlin Ministers at the Reform Club Dinner shouted, ' *Go it, old Charley*,' his answer was a model of sarcastic wisdom. He heard the bray, knew that it was no lion's roar, and told them — not that he would take St. Petersburg with his fleet, but that if they came to his farm he would teach them ' how to *rear young lambs.*'

" The fleet sailed by order, too soon, as aforesaid ; and, beset with gloomy weather, fogs, currents, and rocks, oftener than once escaped destruction by a supreme fortune against probability. However, fine weather came at length : the Russian fleet, although at first more than double the number of the British, was blockaded ; explorations were made, soundings were taken ; and a knowledge of the navigation — suppressed by the removal of lighthouses and buoys — restored and enlarged, while the crews of the fleet were exercised in gunnery and seamanship without cessation. What then was to be done ? ' Assail Cronstadt and Sweaborg, certainly,' quoth *Arimanes ;* ' they were only built for show.' It did not strike him that so active a monarch as Nicholas was not likely to let Cronstadt, covering his Capital and within forty miles of his Palace, be rendered useless by corrupt superintendence ; or that Sweaborg was not a Russian-built fortress, having been constructed under a Swedish Government by a celebrated engineer, who superintended the details himself, and rested his reputation on them. Part of it is cut out of the living rock, indeed ; but what then ? That precious young gentleman, Mr. Oliphant, had informed the world that Sebastopol was all rubbish ; and there-fore Sweaborg could not resist the broadside of a single man-of-war.

" Logical *Arimanes !* It did not occur to him that neither Cron-stadt nor Sweaborg could be approached by ships, except through narrow channels rife with sunken rocks, where not more than three vessels abreast, if so many, and in some places only one, could pass, exposed to an overwhelming fire before they could get near enough to batter the walls. It did not occur to him either, that behind those fortresses were many powerful ships of war, drawing less water than ours, and better fitted for the shallow waters, ready to come out and fall upon our battered and dis-mantled fleet after its fight with the fortresses should be decided. No. All that was nonsense. Bomarsund had been taken by troops, and therefore the others could be taken *without troops.* Granite was weak against wood—the question was decided. Stop, *Ari-manes !* If the question between wood and granite were decided, that between heavy ships and shallow narrow channels studded with sunken rocks had not been so. Granite above water was crumbled under your bray, but granite below water remained intact. Moreover, Bomarsund did not even touch the question of granite above water. It was not a granite fortress : it was of rubble cased with granite ; and even then, when the shot struck the centre of a slab no harm was done ; it was only by striking the jointings that an impression was made, for then the rubble behind gave way, and the granite slab, turning round, fell out. Pooh! said the braying one, it is only Admiral Napier's want of resolution and dash that saved Cronstadt and Sweaborg. Indeed! How, then, did it come to pass that Lord Nelson, Lord St. Vincent, and Lord Collingwood never attacked Brest or Toulon? They are not so strong as the Russian fortresses. Oh! the ships of the present day are ten times as powerful for offence as the ships of those days. But they were far better manned, and the artillery for defence has progressed in the same proportion as that for attack.

" The Baltic fleet is now coming home, and the services of its veteran commander may be thus summed up —

" He has caused the thirty sail composing the powerful Russian fleet to shrink like rats into their holes ; he has taken Bomarsund, caused Hango to be blown up, interrupted the Russian commerce ; and for six months has kept in a state of inaction, certainly, eighty or ninety thousand good troops, viz., —twenty thousand at Helsingfors, fifteen thousand at Abo, and forty thousand at Cronstadt, besides smaller corps protecting Revel and other places. He has restored and enlarged the knowledge of the Finland Gulf to navigation ; has ascertained what large vessels can do there, and what they cannot do; when they can act alone, when with troops, and when gun-boats can be used with effect. He carried out an ill-manned, undisciplined fleet ; he will, if not assailed by storms, bring back unharmed a well-organised, well-disciplined one, with crews exercised in gunnery and seamanship,—in fine, a fleet now really what it was falsely called when it started ; that is to say, one of the most irresistible that ever floated on the ocean for all legitimate purposes of naval warfare."

These extracts may well be concluded with the opinion of a writer of still greater celebrity than any of the writers quoted : —

" I shall just give you the summary of my opinion. You should raise supplies. You should keep up your present forces, and reform what abuses may be found in them. But, above all things, let those corrupt ministers feel the severest punishment. Let them at all times, and in all places, be the objects of your abhorrence. If you act thus, if you shake off your indolence, perhaps even yet we may promise ourselves some good fortune. But if you only just exert yourselves in acclamations and applauses, and when anything is to be done sink again into your supineness, I do not see how all the wisdom in the world can save the State from ruin. I have given you such counsels as have sunk my reputation ; but such as, if pursued, must raise the reputation of my country." (*Demosthenes on the state of Chersonesus.*)

One remark more is necessary. In the present volume will be read the plans of Sir Charles Napier for destroying both Sweaborg and Cronstadt as a *matter of certainty*, when means were supplied in the following year. No Admiral could be found to carry out these plans. When the dockyard of Sweaborg was afterwards destroyed by gunboats, the fleet was at Cronstadt ! In the Black Sea, nothing worthy of our naval armaments was effected. In neither place was any victory achieved. Let the nation beware lest, under Admiralty guidance, its fleets do not one day achieve a defeat.

CONTENTS.

CHAPTER I.

CHAP. II.

b

CHAP. III.

DIPLOMACY OF THE GERMAN AND NORTHERN COURTS, AS RELATING TO THE WAR IN THE BALTIC.

CHAP. IV.

CHAP. V.

CHAP. VI.

TRANSACTIONS OF THE SQUADRON FROM ELGSNABBEN TO HANGO.

CHAP. VII.

TRANSACTIONS OF THE SQUADRON AT HANGO.

CHAP. VIII.

CHAP. IX.

CHAP. X.

THE RECONNAISSANCE OF CRONSTADT.

CHAP. XI.

CRONSTADT AND ITS DEFENCES.

CHAP. XII.

RETURN OF THE FLEETS TO BARO SOUND.

CHAP. XIII.

PREPARATIONS FOR ATTACKING THE ALAND ISLES.

CHAP. XIV.

BOMARSUND.—ALAND.—FINLAND, ETC.

CHAP. XV.

THE SIEGE OF BOMARSUND.

CHAP. XVI.

EVENTS CONNECTED WITH THE DEMOLITION OF BOMARSUND.

CHAP. XVII.

CHAP. XVIII.

CHAP. XIX.

CHAP. XX.

CHAP. XXI.

CHAP. XXII.

THE SQUADRON AT KIEL. VOYAGE TO SPITHEAD. ADMIRAL
ORDERED TO STRIKE HIS FLAG. CORRESPONDENCE WITH THE
ADMIRALTY.

CHAP. XXIII.

SIR C. NAPIER'S NOTES ON RUSSIA.

NAVAL CAMPAIGN IN THE BALTIC.

ERRATA.

Page 314., line 3 from bottom, for " eighteen " read " fourteen."

  ,,   328., line 5 from top, for " waiting " read " watching."

  ,,   407., line 21, for " I came down here last night in the middle watch. The " read " I came down here last night. In the middle watch the"

  ,,   470., line 17 from bottom, for "western" read "south western."

  ,,   475., line 18, for " Gulf of Finland " read " Baltic."

  ,,   476., line 2, for thirty-one " read " forty."

NAVAL CAMPAIGN IN THE BALTIC.

CHAPTER I.

ON the 5th of July, 1853, Sir Charles Napier addressed a letter to Lord Aberdeen, then at the head of Her Majesty's Government, in which letter he pointed out to his Lordship the all but certainty

B

of war with Russia, and at the same time the ill-defended condition of our coasts, in case of war. He apprised his Lordship that Russia had in the Gulf of Finland twenty-seven sail of the line, besides frigates and smaller vessels, and that she had also a large disposable army at St. Petersburg—with all, or any of which forces, she might, in the event of war, menace the English coast at a moment when we had no available force to oppose to her. The Admiral pointed out to his Lordship that, as our trained fleet was in the Mediterranean, the only available force, to meet any sudden demonstration on the part of Russia, was little more than the guard-ships, block-ships, and ordinaries, at the various naval ports, whilst these were between three and four thousand men short of their complement. He represented to his Lordship that the Emperor of Russia was a bold man, who was playing a great game; that, if he were aware of our want of means of defence, he might as easily make a dash at England as we could send the Mediterranean fleet to Constantinople; and that, should he do so, the confusion on our coasts would be extreme. It was thus evident that in the event of sudden war, this country was not safe; that if Russia lost her fleet in a sudden attack on our shores, she would care nothing for the loss; but that if we lost the few ships which could be opposed to her, the nation would be ruined.

Sir Charles further represented to Lord Aberdeen that, in the event of sudden war, and with a fleet so inadequate to the purpose, the Admiral commanding would be expected by the Government to keep our

entire coast from being insulted, and by the nation
to fight and conquer, as he no doubt would, if his
fleet were properly manned and disciplined,—but that
this was not to be done in a day. He begged of his
Lordship to take the opinions of other officers on the
subject, and to see whether their opinions did not
coincide with his own. Sir Charles, moreover, told
his Lordship that he himself was no alarmist, but
that he knew what ships could do, and ought to do,
as well as what would be expected from them. He,
therefore, urged upon Her Majesty's Government the
necessity of putting the small force at command in
the highest state of discipline and completeness, as a
matter of justice to whatever Admiral might be
selected to command it, as well as a matter of the
first importance to the country at large.

To this communication Lord Aberdeen replied that
he highly appreciated the Admiral's caution, and considered that his opinion must always be valuable; but
that he did not by any means abandon the idea of
an early and pacific settlement of Eastern affairs. A
short time would, however, enable him to see more
clearly, so that he would be in a position to form a
more correct opinion.

Failing to impress on Lord Aberdeen a sense of the
inadequateness of our naval power at home to the
protection of the coast, to say nothing of aggression
on our part, should aggression become necessary,
and convinced of the hopelessness of eventual peace,
as even the chances of present peace diminished, Sir
Charles addressed other Cabinet Ministers on the
subject, both by letter and by personal interviews.

His remonstrances, however, failed to impart to them the impulse by which he was himself prompted ; and the hope of peace appears to have supplanted that vigorous effort on the part of the Government, which, had it been made, might even then have proved the most effectual peace-maker.

Whilst Englishmen rested secure in the belief that they were efficiently protected by their wooden walls — though no fleet was ready — Russia was preparing to use her means to the best advantage.   Nay, more : whilst England slept — Russia was making the most energetic preparations for war.   So far from intending peace, that power pursued her object steadily and energetically ; not fearing war, but, by the magnitude of her preparations, rather courting it.

This, of course, became apparent to our Ambassadors, who lost no time in making known the preparations of Russia.   On the 22nd of November, 1853, when it was becoming evident that peace could no longer be maintained, Sir James Graham, spontaneously and unexpectedly, apprised Sir Charles that he should not appoint him to the North American station, then about to be vacated by the retirement of Sir George Seymour, for that, " in present circumstances, *it would be as well to have him near at home ready to meet any emergency.*"   Sir James added : " Even if the peace of Europe should be preserved, I should like to see you *hoist your flag nearer home ;* and in the course of the next six months a fitting opportunity may present itself, when a Vice-Admiral's command is vacated."

This letter from Sir James Graham was very remarkable. Sir Charles Napier had not solicited the command of the North American station, nor would he have accepted it had it been offered to him. The letter, therefore, can only be regarded as a feeler as to whether he would take the command of the Baltic fleet in case of war.

The letter, of course, drew forth the Admiral's intentions on this point, and he replied : " In the event of war, I conclude you intend sending me to the Baltic, and in the event of peace, I fear you destine me for Sheerness. In the first case, I am ready and willing to serve my country, as long as I have health and strength, even on that station, which will be an important and serious one. Had I been in the Mediterranean now, I could have rendered good service. I should have had considerable influence with the Turks, as having before led them to victory; and they have not forgot me."

At the commencement of the year 1854, matters began to wear a more serious aspect. In place of wishing for peace, Russia was ready for war, and, to judge from her exertions as regarded her marine, it became equally evident that she contemplated meeting an English fleet, and that even the fears of Sir Charles Napier as to the unsafe condition of our coasts might not prove unfounded.

At the latter end of December, our Government was apprised by its representative at St. Petersburg that the Russian Government had ordered the provisioning of the fleet for six months. On the 15th of January, Sir Hamilton Seymour warned the Ministry not to think too lightly of the Russian fleet.

On the 24th of January, our Consul at Copenhagen apprised the Government that the spring promised to be unusually early, and that a Russian squadron might quit Sweaborg or Revel when the lower part of the gulf became passable. On the 31st of January, our representative at New York ascertained that Russian agents had arrived there for the purpose of buying steamers. On the 4th of February, Sir Hamilton Seymour stated that the Russian Government had contracted for a vast quantity of coal. To these instances it would be easy for us to add many others, were not those adduced sufficient to show that Russia, so far from desiring peace, meant mischief.

There was evidently no time to be lost. Danger was imminent; and we were scarcely more prepared to meet it than when Sir Charles Napier had addressed Lord Aberdeen on the subject.

On the 23rd of February, 1854, Sir Charles Napier was sent for by Sir James Graham, and informed that the Cabinet had decided on appointing him to the command of the fleet, though this had to be formed as well as manned. Of the leading ships which were to compose it, many were at Lisbon, viz. the *Duke of Wellington, St. Jean d'Acre,* and *Prince Regent,* of the line; *Impérieuse, Arrogant, Tribune, Amphion, Odin,* and *Valorous,* steam-frigates. Others had to be collected at the various naval ports. There were at Portsmouth, the *Princess Royal and Cæsar,* of the line; the *Neptune,* ordinary guard-ship; and the *Edinburgh* and *Blenheim,* block-ships. It had been the intention that these block-ships should remain in port for defence, but now they had suddenly to be taken for the impending war, leaving Portsmouth and the other ports unprotected.

At Plymouth were the *Royal George*, *James Watt*, and *Nile*, of the line, just commissioned; the *Hogue*, block-ship, and the *St. George*, ordinary guard-ship, bearing the pendant of the Commodore-Superintendent. At Sheerness were the *Cressy* and *Majestic*, of the line, just commissioned, and the *Monarch*, ordinary guard-ship. At Cork was the *Ajax*, flag-ship. At Chatham, the *Boscawen*, which had been commissioned for the flag-ship in the West Indies. These were all the ships; and when they were appropriated for the Baltic fleet, nothing was left for the defence of the whole coasts of England but the *St. Vincent* and *Royal William*, ordinary guard-ships, at Portsmouth and Plymouth, and the *Waterloo*, flag-ship, at Sheerness. The *Hannibal* was commissioned at the latter port a week after the squadron had sailed. Such were our inadequate resources for defence, had the Russians been able to get out of the Baltic, so as to throw a squadron on our coasts.

The difficulty lay in manning the ships thus hastily got together. Notwithstanding the previous remonstrances of Sir Charles Napier, nothing whatever had been done towards training men, or even procuring men to train. The public voice had decidedly pronounced against the old system of impressment, and, to obviate this, Sir James Graham had very wisely passed a Bill through Parliament, empowering Her Majesty to issue, in case of war, a proclamation, offering ample bounty to all seamen who volunteered promptly when called upon; a step which, had it been acted on, would in all probability have supplied men almost as fast as ships could have been brought forward for manning.

In his interview with the First Lord, the Admiral therefore urged the necessity of issuing this proclamation forthwith, as the only way to get men quickly. He pointed out, also, that a considerable number of good seamen were to be found on board the numerous yachts belonging to various gentlemen ; and that, if Her Majesty would consent to transfer the men from her own yacht to the flag-ship, English gentlemen would follow her example, — would forego their summer's amusement at sea, and would lay up their yachts. By simply adopting these two measures, a good class of seamen would be at once secured ; whilst, if they were not adopted, the fleet must of necessity be badly manned, as, without an offer of bounty, inexperienced men could alone be obtained.

The suggestions of the Admiral met with a decided refusal from Sir James Graham, who, in a letter of the 24th of February, informed him that he looked upon his suggestions in the light of " *signs of distress*," which he considered impolitic and unnecessary, and which he could not sanction.

It could scarcely have been a " sign of distress " to adopt the best means of manning the fleet promptly and efficiently, seeing that it was immediately and imperatively required. The real reason for the refusal lay deeper. In the passage of the Bounty Bill through Parliament, it had been so framed that the men already on board the fleet could also have claimed the offered bounty, which would thus have amounted to nearly half a million of money. For this half million Government would have had to apply to the House, in the face of the fact that, in 1847, Sir Charles Napier, when in Parliament, anticipating the difficulty which would arise, and which now had arisen, endeavoured, but in vain, to amend this want of foresight in Sir James Graham's Bill. The First Lord's position was a delicate one; but still it is to be regretted that the efficiency of the fleet at its formation should have been sacrificed to the consideration of even half a million of money, and the more so as its non-efficiency at the outset of the war has cost the country many millions.

This refusal to give bounty to seamen, of whom there were considerable numbers waiting in expectation of its being offered, is the more singular, as the Government was most lavish of bounty to militiamen, and still more so to the utterly useless Foreign Legion,— a body of men who have reflected far more discredit on themselves than credit on our arms. These men received ample bounty, were abundantly petted whilst in training; their comfort was carefully studied; and at the close of their non-service they have been rewarded in a way that no Englishman would expect or hope for even for real service. To our seamen no bounty was offered. Any one who presented himself had to be accepted. No provision was even made to clothe them in the manner which an Arctic climate required; and such as could afford it had afterwards to clothe themselves, or go without. Yet England prides herself on being a naval nation!

Accompanying this refusal to adopt the suggestions of the Admiral as to manning the fleet, was an intimation from the First Lord that, in the conversation which he had with him on the subject, a painful impression had been left on his mind that Sir Charles appeared to consider the means which the Admiralty had provided for fitting out and manning the fleet insufficient for the occasion, and unequal to the purpose desired. If he were really dissatisfied with what had been done, and if he had not entire confidence in his force, Sir James urged that he had better decline to accept the command than undertake it with any such misgivings; and the more so, as, without cordial concurrence between himself and the Board of Admiralty, they could hardly work well together.

This was, at any rate, candid. The Admiral had his misgivings about the future fleet, and had told Sir James what those misgivings were, viz., that raw men were not fit to fight, and that they ought not to be entered in such an emergency, when, by offering bounty, seamen could be got. But be the materials of the fleet what they might, he had no misgivings as to his ability to reduce them eventually to the requisite state of discipline. What he wanted was trained and disciplined men at once, in the event—as the Admiralty itself considered probable—of the Russians meeting him with a well organised fleet of thirty sail of the line.

The Admiral therefore replied, that he had merely pointed out what he thought was the best way of manning the fleet to ensure a speedy success, in case the enemy came out as was expected. He stated that he should consider himself unworthy to hold Her Majesty's Commission, were he to decline any service, however desperate. With the means at his disposal, he would do all he could for the honour of his Queen and country, which should not be tarnished in his hands.

Sir James Graham, in reply, assured the Admiral that his explanation had removed all doubt and apprehension; that when he offered him the command he felt certain that the honour of the country and of the flag might safely be confided to him, and that he did not anticipate that he " *should ask him to undertake any desperate service.*"

On receiving his appointment, Sir Charles hoisted his flag on board the *Fisguard*, at Woolwich, shortly afterwards transferring it to the *Princess Royal*, at Spithead, which ship he found, from some accident, ashore on the Middle Bank. Commodore Seymour was appointed by the Board of Admiralty Captain of the Fleet, and Captain Gordon was nominated by the Admiral to the command of the *Duke of Wellington*, she being destined for the Flagship on her arrival from Plymouth.

Great exertions were made by the Admiralty to get together a squadron for sea, since, from intelligence which continued to be received as to the early breaking up of the ice within the Baltic, fears were entertained that a Russian squadron might take advantage of it, slip out, and inflict damage on our coasts and commerce. The people of England were, as usual, relying on the protection of their wooden walls, the

condition of which we have already spoken of. It
was more to the purpose of the nation that there were
ice walls in the Baltic which prevented any movement
of the Russian fleet to take advantage of our insecurity,
which could scarcely be unknown to the Czar, though
our own Government, notwithstanding that it had
its Ministers and Consuls all over the Baltic, was
entirely ignorant of the position of the Sweaborg fleet,
and had to despatch Captain Lyons in the *Miranda*,
to force his way through the ice, in order to obtain
that very necessary information.

The Board of Admiralty, now in earnest to get the
squadron away as quickly as possible, soon found out
the evil of having neglected the Admiral's previous
warnings with regard to manning the fleet; which,
had those warnings been accepted, would have long
before been completed, and the men in a state of
tolerable discipline. Now that the last moment had
arrived, it became evident that to man a fleet without
offering bounty was no easy matter. Good seamen,
many of whom were known to be waiting for the
offer of bounty, — especially in the north of England,
— according to the custom in former wars, would
not come forward. The men who had been entered
at the Tower were so inferior, that Admiral Berkeley,
who had the charge of manning the squadron, deemed
it expedient to request of the First Lord of the
Admiralty that two other Lords might be sent to
examine them. This was done, but with instructions
to the examiners *not to be over particular*. The consequence was that men of all descriptions were entered,
even to butchers' boys, navvies, cabmen, &c., and

men destitute of clothing; not " *men of the standard of.the Guards,*" as Admiral Berkeley afterwards stated in the House of Commons.

Fortunately there were some old seamen available, who had been employed as riggers in the Dockyard, as well as some coast-guardsmen ; but many of these were too old for such an arduous expedition, whilst some had never been to sea before. Still all were an improvement upon the mass casually picked up. The officers were, for the most part, inexperienced in the movements of a fleet; whilst of mates and midshipmen, one could scarcely be found on a watch. Of such materials was the Baltic fleet composed.

The Admiralty, conscious of the bad state of the ships from the raw and inexperienced hands who had been hurried on board in order to fill up the complement, issued an order for leave to be stopped, throughout the fleet, to the ship's companies. Directions were also issued that the captains and officers must use every exertion to train the men. The Commander-in-Chief, immediately on his appointment, sent orders to Admirals Chads and Corry to use their utmost exertions to bring the men on in gun-drill, &c., and not to limit the expenditure of powder and shot for exercise. These orders were zealously carried out; and Admiral Chads, who had been appointed on the 6th of February, nearly three weeks before Sir Charles Napier, had been indefatigable in his exertions to discipline the crews.

On the 7th of March, a most necessary order was issued by the Admiralty, viz., as they had not officers for their ships, the ships were to bear a *reduced number of mates and midshipmen!* First, second, and third rates were to have *eight* mates or midshipmen, in lieu of *twelve.* Fourth-rates were to have *six* in lieu of *nine*, and fifth-rates *six* in lieu of *eight.*

On the 3rd of March, Admiral Corry had shifted his flag from the *Prince Regent* to the *Neptune*, taking with him his former crew. On the 9th she was ordered to be completed with "newly raised men, and such landsmen as were most forward." The dockyard riggers and coast-guard men, before spoken of, were put in the fleet; but unfortunately, many of the latter, instead of being good seamen, had been placed in the coast-guard from interest, and knew little of seamanship. All these men behaved extremely well, and having themselves previously been subjected to a certain degree of discipline, were indefatigable in teaching the raw hands their duty.

The public, ignorant of these matters, and confident in that noble and favourite arm of defence upon which this nation so especially relies for security, — though too often without inquiry as to its real efficiency, upon which alone their security can be based, — was greatly pleased at the appointment of Sir Charles Napier to the command; whilst from his previous exploits, popular enthusiasm indulged in the most extravagant expectations as to what the squadron under his command would shortly accomplish. The utter insufficiency of his badly manned squadron, as compared with the Russian fleet and forts, — some of the latter far superior in strength to Sebastopol, — was not taken into account. The British fleet was a British fleet; and as its Commander had formerly beaten all opponents, he could do the same again. All this was regarded as a matter of course.

A farewell dinner was given to the Admiral by the members of the Reform Club, at which dinner Sir James Graham took great credit to himself for the selection of Sir Charles Napier; and for this selection Sir James really deserved great credit, as it had been made in opposition to strong family interest. One Lord of the Admiralty was already in command of the Black Sea fleet. Another, Admiral Berkeley, who had never commanded a fleet at sea, or, indeed, a line-of-battle ship more than a year or two, afterwards admitted in Parliament that he " had run with Sir Charles an honest race for the command." To the great credit of Sir James Graham he disregarded such influence, and conferred the much coveted honour on Sir Charles Napier, who never in his life did a more unwise thing than to accept the command of such a fleet, in such a sea, and under such circumstances. His patriotism must certainly have outweighed his interest.

At this Reform banquet some after-dinner jocularities were exaggerated by the press into serious statements as to what the fleet would shortly accomplish. Amongst these statements was one so ludicrous that it was surprising how it could have found its way into sober type, even in a newspaper, viz., that the Admiral would be at St. Petersburg in three weeks! the ice before that capital not breaking up till May, whilst the Admiral had not a ship of the line in his squadron which, from its great draught of water, would float within twenty miles of St. Petersburg, even when the ice had broken up. It would be needless to say that Sir Charles never made any declaration of the kind.

On the 9th of March, thirteen days only after his appointment, and with a squadron thus hurriedly got together within that brief period, the Admiral, whilst attending Her Majesty's levee, received orders to go to sea. He at once quitted London for Portsmouth, and after taking leave of his family, prepared for immediate departure.

On the evening of the 11th, the Corporation of Portsmouth, representing in this instance the national feeling, presented a congratulatory address to the Admiral, who warned them not to expect too much from the fleet. Shortly after having received this address, and amidst the acclamations of a vast concourse of people assembled from all parts to witness the departure of the ships, Sir Charles shifted his flag to the *Duke of Wellington*, at Spithead. In order to give *éclat* to a scene in which the whole nation felt the deepest interest, Her Majesty had announced her intention of leading the squadron to sea, and, as a preparatory formality, had publicly received the Admiral and his Captains on board her yacht, by way of farewell. The enthusiasm of the fleet, as well as of the multitude assembled to witness a scene *unique* even in the naval annals of England, was without bound, and high hopes were raised for the success of an expedition thus Royally inaugurated.

The squadron consisted of the following ships:—

SCREW-SHIPS OF THE LINE.

DUKE OF WELLINGTON
(Flag of Vice-Admiral
Sir C. Napier) . . Capt. Geo. T. Gordon.
ROYAL GEORGE . . Capt. Henry I. Codrington.
ST. JEAN D'ACRE . . Capt. Hon. Henry Keppel.
PRINCESS ROYAL . . Capt. Lord C. Paget.

BLOCKSHIPS.

EDINBURGH (Flag of Rear-
Admiral Chads) . Capt. R. S. Hewlett.
BLENHEIM . . . Capt. Hon. Fred. Pelham.
HOGUE . . . . Capt. William Ramsay.
AJAX . . . . Capt. Frederick Warden.

FRIGATES.

IMPÉRIEUSE . . . Capt. Randle B. Watson.
ARROGANT . . . Capt. H. R. Yelverton.
AMPHION . . . Capt. Astley C. Key.
TRIBUNE . . . Capt. Hon. S. T. Carnegie.

PADDLE-STEAMERS.

LEOPARD . . . Capt. George Giffard.
DRAGON . . . Capt. James Wilcox.
VALOROUS . . . Capt. Claude H. M. Buckle.

Total:—

Four Ships of the Line.
Four Block-ships.
Four Frigates.
Three Steamers.

C

The *Neptune*, bearing the flag of Rear-Admiral Corry, not being ready for sea, had to be left behind, as had also the *Prince Regent*, 370 short of her complement of men and officers; her former crew having been turned over to the *Neptune*. The *Boscawen* had also to be left, being 105 short of her complement. These were placed under the orders of Rear-Admiral Corry, with instructions to join the Admiral in Wingo Sound.

The squadron weighed anchor and proceeded to sea, accompanied by her Majesty in the *Fairy*, as far as the Nab Light. The First Lord eulogised, in Parliament, the masterly way in which it had set forth; but the Admiral, with a better eye for seamanship, declared that he saw nothing masterly in the proceeding. The seamanship had to be made, both as regarded the majority of officers and men. During peace, and chiefly to make way for the promotion of new men, many of our ablest captains had been shelved as Rear-Admirals on half-pay, and on the distinct understanding that they were not to be again employed, whilst the younger captains had acquired no experience in the management of a fleet, from the parsimony of the Admiralty in not incurring the expense of manœuvring fleets in time of peace, — parsimony to which they had, no doubt, been impelled by the Parliamentary rage for economy, — a false policy for which the nation has had to pay in an infinitely greater ratio than has been compensated by its savings.

Though few in point of numbers, never, perhaps, had finer ships left our shores; yet never before had a squadron sailed so deplorably manned. The subsequent testimony of one of the Lords of the Admiralty on this point was, unhappily, as true as significant: — "*If you find three hundred able seamen on board each ship I shall be agreeably surprised.*" Nor was the following, from the same source, more satisfactory: — "*The Emperor of Russia should try his strength with you while he musters double your numbers, and your hands are so miserably raw!*" This description of the squadron by those who manned it, as frankly recorded as it was true, was by Admiral Berkeley.

The fact is, that had it not been for the coast-guard men, the squadron could not have got to sea. Though themselves, as a body, inexperienced as regarded the operations of fleets, — many of them much too old to have been selected for service in such a climate, — all accustomed to the comforts of home, and suddenly thrown into a position in which no adequate provision had been made for their comfort, — the conduct and example of these men were beyond all praise, acting most beneficially upon the heterogeneous mass which had been scraped together from the streets of London and elsewhere, and thus supplying ready obedience and a will, where otherwise none would have been found.

Perhaps one of the strongest testimonies to the inefficient condition of the fleet in 1854, is the plan now being adopted by the Admiralty to create a permanent naval force to a certain extent by stationing ships at various ports,—which ships shall at the same time serve as head-quarters for the coast-guard, and

as a *nucleus* for the navy in case of sudden emergency.
It is a tacit admission that under the system which
obtained before the Russian war, this country was
not safe ; nor were its fleets in a fit condition to meet
an enemy. So far, so good. The fear is, that parliamentary economy will again be applied even to
this instalment towards the improvement of an arm
of defence, which, to be efficient, ought to be perfection. Yet the lesson taught by the late war
should, from the disparity between its costliness and
its results, show the nation that true economy consists in adequate preparation for all contingencies —
not in cheese-paring, the resort of minds incapable
of looking ahead.

There is, since the war, an affected prudery as
regards the navy. If anything is said relative to the
want of discipline in the fleet thus hastily got together, the cry is, " See! the navy is being traduced ! "
As though a fleet thus suddenly got together could
be any other than undisciplined ; and as though the
fact of its being so undisciplined were not of the
deepest importance to the public, in order that popular
remonstrance may be brought to bear on the Government in such a way that on a fresh emergency arising
the same thing may not again happen. If it do, such
another occurrence will be more serious than they
who place blind reliance on an undisciplined navy,
because it is a navy, may be willing to admit. Other
powers have now got an accurate measure of our
naval capability, and also of the Admiralty incapability which has so notoriously failed to make use of
it, from having provided ships, but not seamen or

other adequate means. This incapability, in case of another war, is to us the most important element of failure, and to our enemies the most important element of success. To show this, then, is *not* traducing the navy, but warning the country against the Board of Admiralty, which misdirects, and, in a critical moment, may paralyse, the strength upon which the nation mainly relies for safety.

There was no doubt great praise due to the Board of Admiralty for equipping the fleet at so short a notice. The blame was, that, with so many previous warnings, the exigency should not have before been provided for; or rather, that with the probability of such exigency looking the Admiralty in the face, the condition of the fleet should have been allowed to fall so low, that on the necessity actually arising, we should not have been prepared to meet it. Our foes will not again wait whilst we get together and drill a fleet. Every naval power, except ourselves, keeps its seamen ready drilled; and he must, indeed, have overweening confidence in our navy, who will assert that we can successfully meet a well trained fleet, suddenly thrown on our coasts, with no fleet at all! Yet this was precisely our condition at the commencement of the Russian war.

It is a singular feature in the British public, that, whilst they almost universally delight in abuse of the army, they exhibit the utmost impatience whenever the shortcomings of the navy are mentioned. The reason is, perhaps, plain, viz., that a standing army can hardly be an object of respect to any people, and is, more or less, always present amongst them; but the navy — removed from sight, and only viewed through the long-drawn vista of its former glories— is an object of universal esteem, as it most richly deserves to be. It is free from that abominable mercenary stigma which, in the army, creates an officer out of a banker's cheque; but if people would dispassionately look at the government of the army, they would find it wisdom itself as compared with the incapability which directs the navy — incapability, perhaps, not so much of men as of a system, which the most eminent Lords of the Admiralty have themselves desired to see abolished.

The army is beyond popular control; but surely the way to keep the favourite navy up to the mark, is by a jealous watchfulness of whatever may tend to deteriorate its fame or its efficiency, and by a determination to reprobate those shortcomings which may one day, upon some unforeseen emergency, paralyse, or even destroy it. It is amongst our national fallacies, that a British ship can beat a French or Russian one as a matter of course, but it would very much puzzle the assertor of such a fact to show why it should be so. Our former supremacy on the sea consisted in superior seamanship, but steam has very much altered this. A Frenchman or a Russian is just as brave as an Englishman. He can fire just as well and as fast. Indeed, at the commencement of the war in the Baltic, the Russian gunners could have fired much better, for they were well-trained, whilst many of our men were not trained at all.

Superiority in naval power will henceforth consist in keeping up a proper naval armament and discipline.

The first naval nation to fall will be the one which is first caught napping. So that, in place of resting on our former naval renown, it will be much more to the purpose to watch vigilantly that this renown is not made to suffer from the neglect of Governments to train fleets. Everything which tends to promote this watchfulness will tend to promote national safety. Assuredly, our naval armaments — the largest ever equipped — gained little renown in the late war. Yet this was not the fault either of the seamen or their commanders.

There is nothing like example to illustrate such matters. The late Admiral Pasco, Nelson's flag-lieutenant, was despatched with a corvette from Plymouth to join his illustrious chief. His crew consisted of raw hands, like those of the Baltic fleet. On emerging from the Channel, the corvette fell in with a French East Indiaman, so that, to use the words of the gallant Pasco, he "considered his fortune made." To lay the corvette alongside of the prize was but the work of a moment. But she had reckoned without her host. From the deck of the Indiaman up rose a body of troops and poured a deadly volley upon the decks of the corvette, whose "raw hands" bolted below like a flock of sheep! and the corvette dropped astern of the prize, which, thanks to their rawness, made the best of its way off without further molestation.

But mark the sequel. "In less than twelve months," said Admiral Pasco, "the exploits of these very men who had quailed before a French Indiaman, were, in cutting out and other operations, the wonder of

the fleet. Nothing was too hot for them." They
had a character to retrieve, and, under the effect of
discipline, nobly did they retrieve it. When they
encountered the Indiaman they were without self-
reliance or mutual reliance, which form the elements
of victory, and in the absence of which even natural
bravery goes but for little. This mutual and self-
reliance can only be imparted by discipline, which, it
is folly to say, can be either comprehended or prac-
tised by " raw hands."

When the Baltic fleet first sailed its hands were
thus raw and undisciplined, and it was consequently
unfit to meet a trained fleet as was expected. When
the fleet returned from the Baltic, the case was different; the " raw hands" had become highly disciplined
seamen. But where are they now? " Paid off," as it
is technically termed. Scattered to the winds by
order of the Board of Admiralty. When some few
years hence—or perhaps before—disciplined men are
wanted on an emergency, a fleet manned with raw
hands will have to be collected as before, but, it may
be, not again with an enemy ignorant of the fact, or
unable to take advantage of it. Let the nation rely
as much as it will upon its wooden walls, but as it
values its safety, let it not rely too much upon those
who man the wooden walls, unless these can be made
more fully to comprehend their duty and to fulfil it.

After Her Majesty had quitted the squadron, it
formed in order of sailing, and stood for the Downs,
where it arrived on the following day, and was joined
by the *Cressy*, Capt. Richard L. Warren.

It has been stated that the squadron was hurried

off to sea in this unfit condition, in consequence of intelligence received from the Baltic relative to the movements and intentions of Russia.   This haste was not without good reason, though the Government has never explained why the equipment of the squadron was delayed till almost too late.   It was even now a question of the ice breaking up earlier or later.   That this was so there is incontrovertible proof; and as the principle upon which this work is written is that of having authentic documents to fall back upon in case of question of the facts narrated, it is easy to supply the most ample information upon this point, as documentary evidence is fortunately as abundant as its authority is unquestionable.

The following is a synopsis of such evidence as bears more immediately on the subject of this chapter.

The Government was not at ease as regarded Sweden and Denmark.   The former power had not joined us, whilst it was more than doubtful if Denmark would not join Russia, should the Russian fleet get to Copenhagen before our own squadron arrived there.   It was known to the Government that Russia had some time before been negotiating with Sweden for a change of territory, being desirous to possess the Warranger Fiord and some other ports in Finmark, which were never closed by ice, and which would have therefore formed excellent places both for shelter and departure.   Shortly before the appointment of Sir Charles Napier to the command, and when war became imminent, Sweden had interdicted nearly all her ports to the belligerents, but Denmark interdicted one port only, in the Island of Bornholm, and that one which neither fleet was likely to make use of. There was nothing, then, to prevent the Russian fleet, could it get out of the ice before the British squadron entered the Baltic, from going into Copenhagen and lying there safe from attack in a neutral port, whilst Russian diplomacy was acting on Denmark — little loth — to persuade her to make common cause with Russia in the war. That this course was intended by Russia, whatever might have been its effect on Denmark, was so far apparent, that it was a matter of no slight importance to thwart it at the outset, as will presently be apparent when we come to consider the instructions given to the Admiral.

Mr. Buchanan, the British Minister at Copenhagen, had warned the Government that it was impossible not to see that there were many persons amongst the higher classes in Denmark whose sympathies were Russian ; whilst among the lower classes the events of 1801 and 1807 had left a feeling of distrust towards England, which might easily be excited into open animosity. The commercial classes, from fear of Russian dictation, were well inclined to England ; their interest being in unison with their sympathies. The hope of the Russian party in Denmark lay in the expectation that misunderstanding might arise between Her Majesty's fleet and the Danish authorities ; and, said Mr. Buchanan, " should such opportunity occur, it will not be neglected by the partisans of Russia."

The Danish authorities even disagreed amongst

themselves. The Minister of Finance objected to raise the Danish garrison to the strength recommended by the Minister at War, and the battalions in consequence were only raised from 240 to 300 men each. The garrison of Zealand was to be increased to 6000, but with recruits and men who had been already drilled, this could, on an emergency, have been raised to 20,000.

Col. Hodges, the British *Chargé d'Affaires* at Hamburgh, apprised the Government that an influential Russian merchant at Libau had sent his son to Altona for the purpose of making over to him seventeen Russian merchantmen, to be placed under the Danish flag. As the expenses of transfer, at the reduced rate, recently adopted by the Danish Government, were almost nominal, there was no difficulty in such an arrangement.

On the 10th of March, the day before the squadron sailed, it had become known to the Government that it was the intention of the Czar to station 30,000 troops in the vicinity of the Gulf of Finland, and that contracts were being entered into for conveying 300 heavy guns to Hogland, an island commanding the deep-water channel of the Gulf. The subsequent rapid movements of the British squadron appear, however, to have led to the abandonment of this plan, as when the squadron entered the Gulf no guns were found on the island.

Advices had been received that, in January, 1854, the Russian fleet in the gulf had been increased to twenty-seven sail of the line. Besides these there were eight or ten frigates, seven corvettes and brigs, nine paddle-steamers, fifteen schooners and luggers, and fifty or sixty gun-boats, or, according to one report of Sir Hamilton Seymour, 180 gun-boats. The main-deck guns of the Russian ships recently constructed, consisted of 48-pounders, with four shell 68-pounders. The upper deck was armed with 36-pounders. The whole naval force mounted 3160 guns, and the full complement of men for the ships was 33,750, but the actual number on board was 27,000, exclusive of the Finnish contingent, amounting to 1000 men, who were probably reserved for fifty gun-boats, in course of construction in Finland, for the most part at Abo, or its vicinity.

Of these ships, on the 10th of March, eighteen, carrying from 84 to 120 guns, were in harbour at Cronstadt, whilst another division, which was usually at Revel, was destined for Sweaborg. Her Majesty's Government was apprised that the Russians were devising means to break the ice, and so to get one of the divisions of the fleet, then at Cronstadt, down to Sweaborg; but, added the informant of the Government, "I hope the British fleet will be in the Gulf of Finland in sufficient time to prevent the realisation of this project. As to breaking through the ice, that, I think, is impracticable; but the season is likely to be an early one, and there is no doubt, the moment the navigation is open, an attempt will be made to get some of the best ships to Sweaborg, where they may *remain in perfect safety.*" This was done.

With regard to the capabilities of the Russian fleet, Sir H. Seymour, the British Ambassador at St. Petersburg, had, on the 15th of January, warned the Government that, decided as was the superiority of the English and French navies over that of Russia, the latter could not, with safety, be under estimated. " The bravery of the Russian seamen, too, was unquestionable, and though not equal to the seamen of the allies, they had the advantage of knowing their own waters, of which the allies knew nothing. The Russian seamen, moreover, would stand well to their guns, and though inferior in gunnery, they would be able to choose their distance in action." This was a mistake. The Russian gunners were all trained, whilst the majority of those in the British squadron was not so. Sir H. Seymour, moreover, apprised his Government that the Russians wished to get their best ships to Sweaborg, expecting that Cronstadt would be first attacked, in which case, calculating on the strength of the forts to resist attack, they could harass the disabled fleet as it returned, by fresh ships. No decided course, however, had been come to by the Russian Government, as to whether it should await an attack under the guns of Cronstadt, or whether it should defend the Gulf of Finland, by taking up a position between Dago and Hango. He, however, inclined to the latter opinion.

Sir H. Seymour emphatically warned the Government of the number of Russian gun-boats, *eighty* of which would be manned by Finns, about fifty in each boat. He told the Government that to clear the Gulf of these, *a number of light steamers, drawing as little water as possible, would be required*, the crews of which should be armed with *Minié* rifles.

On the 6th of March, it was ascertained that the

Russian Government had determined to station large bodies of troops at Viburg, Cronstadt, and Revel, viz. three divisions and a brigade of the Light Cavalry division. Another brigade was destined for Finland, under the command of Lieut.-General Konakouski, whilst the coast troops were to be under the order of General Von Berg.

On the 8th of March, intelligence was received by the Government that the ice was breaking up in the Gulf of Finland. At Revel the " fair water" had become free from ice on the 25th of February, so that there was no time to be lost in getting the British squadron to sea. Nor was any fault to be found with this hasty despatch ; but that the squadron should not have been in a fit condition for sea is anything but creditable to those who despatched it, and the more so after the warnings they had received.

On the 7th of March, the Hon. Mr. Grey notified to his Government the strength of the Swedish squadron intended for Gottland. It consisted of three ships of the line, two frigates, and two steam corvettes, under the command of · Admiral Crusenstjerna, with His Royal Highness Prince Oscar as Flag Captain. The squadron had orders to go to sea on the 20th of March, taking troops with it to Gottland. Twelve gun-boats were to follow as fast as possible. Six more squadrons of gun-boats, seventy-two in number, were being got ready for sea.

Between Aland and Abo, Mr. Grey reported the ice as still very strong, though there was less ice than usual in the Gulf of Bothnia. The probability was that the general navigation of the Baltic would be open early.

As frequent allusion will have to be made to Gottland or some of its harbours, it may here be stated
that this island lies about sixty miles from the Swedish
mainland, between 56° and 57° north latitude. Its
length is about seventy-five miles, and its breadth
about twenty-six miles. The island presents the
appearance of a huge plateau, rising some 150 feet
above the level of the sea. It contains several good
harbours or anchorages, the most important to the
British fleet being Faro Sound, the harbour of Slito
having been interdicted to the Allied forces. The town
of Wisby, on the west side of the island, was formerly a
factory of the Hanseatic League, and attained to considerable wealth and importance. It is now much
reduced, having a population of only 4000.

After Sir Hamilton Seymour had left St. Petersburg, Lord Bloomfield, our Minister at Berlin, apprised the Government that Mr. Lumley, who left
St. Petersburg after Sir Hamilton, had seen Baron
Plessen, the Danish Minister at the Court of Russia.
Baron Plessen informed him that in an interview
which he had with Count Nesselrode, the latter stated
the Russian Government to have learned that the
Allied Governments were engaging the services of
Danish pilots. If this was permitted by Denmark,
the Russian Government would regard the engagement of Danish subjects as an act of direct hostility
towards Russia. Mr. Buchanan alluded to this subject as one of great importance with regard to the
relations between Russia and Denmark.

The Hon. Mr. Grey, the British *Chargé d'Affaires*
at Stockholm, represented to this Government that

Baron Stjerneld had informed him that four battalions of infantry, two squadrons of cavalry (the Crown Prince's Hussars), and two battalions of artillery, were to be sent immediately to Gottland. These, added to the militia of the island, about 6500 effective and well-trained men, with three batteries of artillery, would make a total force of 10,000 men, with forty guns, exclusive of the guns on the fortifications of Slito. This force would be assembled in Gottland about the 25th of March, and was amply sufficient for the defence of the island. General Lowerhielm, who commanded the third military district, General Dahlström, Governor of Gottland, and Baron Oxenstjerna, Governor of Griselhamm, had received orders to proceed to their several posts without delay.

Mr. Grey at the same time received positive information that the buoys and lighthouses in the Gulf of Finland had already been removed or changed by the Russian authorities.

It was further intimated to Her Majesty's Government by Mr. Crowe, the British Consul at Christiania, that although Slito, in the Island of Gottland, was undoubtedly the best and most capacious harbour, there were two other available ports in the island. Mr. Crowe had ascertained that within the Island of Oland, on the coast of Sweden, there was safe anchorage for a fleet during the summer months. There were also several good harbours at the entrance of Stockholm, deep enough for ships of the *Duke of Wellington's* class; whilst for vessels drawing between twelve and twenty feet of water, there were other convenient harbours between Carlscrona and Stockholm.

On the 9th of March, Mr. Peto stated that he had obtained a concession from the King of Denmark to construct a railroad between Flensburg and Tonning, thereby connecting the German Ocean with the Baltic. The distance was thirty-six miles only, and the facility of communication with the fleet by this route would be of great importance to the Government. As Mr. Peto had the control as well as the construction of the railroad, he placed it at the disposal of the Government, as well as his express steamers in the Baltic, should it appear desirable. This latter offer was accepted.

The harbour of Flensburg is one of the finest in the world. It is completely land-locked, and has sufficient depth of water for the largest fleet. The town of Flensburg is of considerable importance, and contains 18,000 inhabitants. Supplies of provisions are abundant and cheap, and there is plenty of fresh water. Flensburg is situated at the entrance of the Belts, and has the largest trade of any port in Denmark.

Tonning, the other *terminus* of the railroad, is situated on the river Eider, which is navigable for large steamers up to the town. This is the nearest port in Denmark to Great Britain, being distant from Lowestoff 285 miles. By rail from London to Lowestoff, and by steamer thence to Tonning, Flensburg may be reached in from thirty-two to thirty-six hours.

CHAP. II.

TRANSACTIONS OF THE FLEET FROM THE DOWNS TO KIOGE BAY.

PROPER PILOTS NOT PROVIDED FOR THE FLEET. — ADMIRAL ORDERED
TO PUT TO SEA WITHOUT THEM. — DEPARTURE FROM THE DOWNS. —
ARRIVAL IN WINGO SOUND. — FOREIGN OFFICE INSTRUCTIONS.— AD-
MIRAL VISITS COPENHAGEN. — RETURNS TO THE FLEET. — PASSAGE OF
THE BELT.— CAPTAIN LYONS' RECONNAISSANCE OF REVEL. — INEX-
PERIENCE OF. THE MEN. — ADMIRAL TOLD TO ENTER SEAMEN IN THE
BALTIC. — ARRIVAL AT KIEL. — ANXIETY FELT AT HOME. — SQUADRON
REMOVES TO KIOGE BAY. — FURTHER INSTRUCTIONS FROM SIR J. GRA-
HAM. — ADMIRALTY INFORMATION OF RUSSIAN MOVEMENTS. — MUNI-
TIONS OF WAR SHIPPED TO RUSSIA FROM LUBECK. — RUSSIAN PLANS
FOR RECEPTION OF BRITISH SQUADRON.

IN the preceding chapter was detailed the force and
disposition of the Russian fleet in the Baltic, as far as
it was known to our Ministers and Consuls in the
vicinity; the anxiety of the latter that we should be
prepared to meet it before the ice broke up; their
cautions that a proper class of small vessels should be
provided to encounter it, and, above all, that the mistake of underrating our enemy should not be committed. To effect these purposes, the Admiralty,
by dint of great exertions, had got together a wretchedly manned squadron of five sail of the line, four
blockships, four frigates, and three steamers; the
whole forming, both in point of numbers and ef-

ficiency, a *burlesque* upon the naval operations of previous wars.

But this was not taken into account at home,—the press teeming with highflown descriptions of our magnificent fleet! without comprehending that it was scarcely sufficiently respectable for a squadron of evolution. Yet this inadequate fleet had to meet nearly the whole naval power of Russia, had it come out, as was expected by the Admiralty itself; whilst to encounter the portion of the Russia fleet in the Black Sea, was a well trained fleet of ten sail of the line, nine frigates, three corvettes, and eleven steamers; all more than two years in commission, and thoroughly up to their work.

Before leaving Spithead, the Admiral had his misgivings that proper pilots had not been provided for the fleet, and made a communication to the Admiralty to this effect. He was assured that he would find all in readiness in the Downs; but, in place of this, he found only eight pilots for the sixteen ships composing the squadron.

The eight pilots who were available had made a voyage in the *Hecla* through the Belt and Sound, but knew little of the former, and indeed were not employed when the squadron afterwards passed the Belt, as none were found competent for the service. There were no North Sea pilots whatever; and the First Lord apprised the Admiral of Captain Scott having informed him that the Thames and Humber pilots, with one or two exceptions, would be of no use; whilst, as regarded Baltic pilots, they must be obtained at Kiel or on the shores of Sweden.

No blame is, however, to be attached to the Admiralty for the deficiency of pilots, as strenuous exertions were made to procure them, but with no better result than the one narrated. The deficiency was only a consequence of the precipitancy with which the fleet had been got together. This hurried improvisation of fleets just at the moment they are required, or, more properly speaking, the neglect which delays their equipment till the last moment, is, strange to say, a characteristic of our naval system. Sir Charles Napier was not the first of our naval commanders who has had to contend with the consequences of such a system, and it was a knowledge of this which led him to urge upon the Government the necessity of placing the fleet in a state of perfect equipment before it was wanted. Now that other nations, having the fullest claim to the title of great naval powers, are adopting every possible means to render the equipment of their ships complete in time of peace, it will be well if a persistance in a contrary course do not one day plunge us in disaster.

Finding the deficiency of pilots, Sir Charles, on the 13th of March, wrote to the Admiralty that he had no North Sea pilots at all, and asked if he was to go to sea without them. He reminded the Admiralty that, in a former war, each ship had always two pilots on board. This appears not to have been thought of. Yet the total absence of North Sea pilots must, at this season of the year,—close, too, upon the equinox, —have been most dangerous to the safety of the squadron. He received for answer that the ships must go to sea without them. On receiving this reply he at once got under weigh.

The destination of the squadron was Wingo Sound, to which anchorage the Admiralty had given instructions to proceed, and there await further orders. Further instructions, accompanied by a sealed despatch, commanded that, after passing the 55th degree of north latitude, the Admiral was to open the despatch, and conform himself in all respects thereto.

Fortunately, no accident occurred on the voyage to Wingo Sound, though the weather was foggy, and the ships were much scattered, some reaching the anchorage before the Flag-ship. On the 16th, when the fog cleared away, there were only three ships, the *St. Jean d'Acre*, *Edinburgh*, and *Hogue*, in company. On the 18th, the whole squadron, with the exception of the *Royal George*, which arrived on the following day, was at anchor in Wingo Sound, where it was joined by Rear Admiral James H. Plumridge, who had embarked at Yarmouth in the *Leopard*. The *Dauntless*, Capt. Ryder, also joined the squadron at Wingo.

On reaching the 55th degree of north latitude, the Admiral opened the sealed despatch, which proved to be one from the Foreign Office, directing him, as the ports of the Baltic were represented to be now in a great measure free from ice, to take up such a position near the entrance of that sea as might, without loss of time, enable him to give prompt effect to further orders from Her Majesty.

He was moreover instructed that as the answer of the Emperor of Russia to the *ultimatum* of the Allies had not been received, though it was expected not to be otherwise than unfavourable, the squadron was not to assume an attitude of positive hostility against

Russia, nor to seek occasion for a conflict with the Russian fleet in their own ports. Notwithstanding this, he was to take care that no Russian ship of war should pass by him into the North Sea, on account of the injury which it might inflict on the British coast. At the same time he was instructed that great disappointment would be felt should any over-strained forbearance on his part allow any portion of the Russian fleet to place itself in a position to inflict injury on British interests.

He was therefore ordered so to dispose his fleet as to prevent this. Should any Russian ship attempt to pass him, he was to apprise their Commanders that he could not allow them to do so, and if they persisted he was to attack them; whilst, should they seek shelter in a neutral port, he was to watch them, so as to prevent them from getting out of the Baltic.

In addition to this the Admiral was instructed that he was to take the most effectual means for the protection of Danish or Swedish ships and territory from any hostile attack by Russia, in the event of an application to him to that effect being made by the Governments of Denmark or Sweden. He was to conform himself in all respects to these instructions, in the " possible contingency of an attack being made by Russia," either with or without a previous declaration of war — with the view of constraining either of those powers to adopt a course of policy favourable to Russian views, or of occupying a portion of their territory so as to enable the fleets of Russia to resist with greater effect the attacks of the British fleet.

It is thus evident from what has been narrated that

the British Government expected the Russian fleet to meet the Admiral at the entrance of the Baltic, and that an attempt would be made to pass ships into the German Ocean. The neutrality of Denmark, and even of Sweden was considered doubtful, in case the Russian fleet got into their waters ; whilst evidence has been given in the preceding chapter that Denmark was rather inclined to Russia than to the Allies — the leanings of the influential classes in Denmark being decidedly Russian. It was then the first duty of the Admiral to prevent this, and, failing in prevention, to frustrate such co-operation.

These orders from Her Majesty's Government were perfectly clear and distinct, and as clearly superseded the previous order of the Admiralty to remain in Wingo Sound, by ordering the squadron to take up such a position as would prevent any Russian ship from passing out of the Baltic, which could not have been done by remaining in Wingo Sound, as a glance at the map will show. Having no orders from the Admiralty as to his position, the choice of that position was as clearly left to his own unfettered judgment.

The Admiral at once saw that, in the foggy weather which accompanies the breaking up of the ice within the Baltic, nothing would have been more easy than for the Sweaborg squadron, did the state of the ice permit, to make a dash at Copenhagen, and to turn the neutrality of Denmark — even then wavering — into active co-operation with Russia. That the intention existed he well knew, and he interpreted the order from Her Majesty's Government, not to

allow the Russian fleet " to place itself in a position
to inflict injury upon British interests within the
Baltic," into an understood command not to permit
any such combination. He was ordered, moreover,
by the Admiralty, to conform himself in all respects
to the superior despatch, and at once determined to
take up the position which, in his judgment, these
joint instructions required.

He therefore decided upon passing the Belt, and
without loss of time proceeding to the vicinity of
Copenhagen, as the best position to carry out his
orders. Before doing so, he, however, deemed
it necessary to visit Copenhagen in person, in order
to gain the most authentic information possible
relative to the probable intentions of the Russian
fleet at Sweaborg. Previous to his departure for the
Danish Capital, he notified to the Admiralty that he
had opened the despatch from the Foreign Office,
and that, in obedience to it, as well as to the Admiralty order to conform himself to it, he should
use all expedition in getting through the Belt,—as,
should the Russian ships at Sweaborg get out before he had passed the Belt, they might, in the fogs,
slip past him through the Sound, or anchor at
Copenhagen.

As the British squadron was unaccompanied by a
single gun-boat, and as the Russians were known to
be well supplied with this class of vessels, so necessary in a war in the Baltic, the Admiral pointed
out to the Board the necessity of supplying the deficiency, and transmitted to them the plan of a gun-
boat which had been submitted to him. Before

quitting England he had repeatedly urged upon the
Board the necessity of small steamers, as being absolutely requisite for successful operations in the
Baltic.* Sir Hamilton Seymour had pointed out
the same thing, and the Admiral repeated his demand when at Copenhagen.

On the 19th of March, the day after the fleet had
reached Wingo Sound, Sir Charles hoisted his flag
on board the *Valorous*, and proceeded to Copenhagen, leaving the squadron in charge of Rear
Admiral Plumridge, who, during the absence of the
Commander-in-Chief, was diligently engaged in exercising the men at firing at a mark, a practice which,
from their inexperience, was much needed.

On reaching Copenhagen the Admiral learnt that
the Russian Government was making every effort to
effect a junction of a division of the Cronstadt fleet
with that at Sweaborg, as soon as the state of the ice
would permit ; and as the spring promised to be
unusually early, they expected to be successful. If
so, there would have been no difficulty in getting
from thence to Copenhagen in the absence of the
British squadron. Had this been strong enough —
or had it possessed in discipline and experience what
it wanted in numbers — it might have been matter
of congratulation had the Russian fleet attempted an
union with that of Denmark ; though, in the present

---

* "Captain Scobell has put the enclosed memorandum into my
hands, and I fulfil my promise in sending it to you. I told him
that the use of fire-vessels *had not been overlooked by you from
the first hour of your appointment to your present command.*"—
Sir J. Graham to Sir C. Napier, July 11. 1854. It is almost
needless to say, that not one was ever supplied.

condition of the British squadron, it would have been no easy matter to dispose of the two fleets when united.

As the British squadron had neither numbers nor experience, it was a paramount object to prevent any such movement of the Russian fleets, or, indeed, any other which could be checked. The great point was to anticipate such movement.

Whilst at Copenhagen the Admiral informed Sir James Graham that the Russians were still fast at Sweaborg, where he trusted they would remain till he could bring up the squadron to Kiel or its neighbourhood, by which he hoped to prevent any attempt on their part at reinforcing their ships. The Danes were much pleased at the vicinity of the British ships, as it would confirm the neutrality of their Government, and thus save them from war.

The Admiral apprised the First Lord that a number of small steamers was absolutely necessary for despatch boats and fire-vessels, as well as to protect the squadron; as, from all he could learn, the Russians were likely to be enterprising. Although the British squadron was lying in a neutral port, the Russians might not be very particular in case they came out, and at night they might start a number of fire-vessels amongst them, and then make their escape amongst the numerous islands. To guard against this, he had only four steamers.

On the 21st Sir Charles returned to Wingo Sound, and on the 22nd the squadron was again ordered to prepare for sea. On the following morning it was under weigh for its new position, which the Admiral informed the Board would, in all probability, be Kioge Bay, — an anchorage, in his opinion, preferable to that of Kiel ; as from Kioge Bay he should be able to command both the Sound and the Belt.

The squadron had not been able to procure any pilots at Wingo, nor were those in it competent to take charge of it through the Belt. The passage of this intricate navigation, with line-of-battle ships of great draught of water, may, therefore, be classed amongst the remarkable instances of modern navigation, and indeed was so regarded by the Government, being rightly characterised by Sir James Graham as " a most successful exploit," which in truth it was, and one which reflected the highest credit on the captains and masters of the several ships, especially considering the inexperience of their men.

It has been said that the *Hecla* made a voyage through the Belt. She was commanded by Mr. Peter Wellington, Master of the *Victory* flag-ship at Portsmouth, who had been selected for the service. Mr. Wellington arrived at Copenhagen on the 5th of March, having left Kiel on the 3rd. It was anticipated that he would have returned to England by the time the fleet sailed, and in this Mr. Wellington succeeded, having met the Admiral at the Downs. But in order to effect this, he had not been able to proceed to Bornholm, according to his instructions. The time allotted to him was, in fact, insufficient, considering the service he was upon.

On his arrival at Copenhagen he found that the

Danish Government had issued an order that no vessel was to be allowed within a certain distance of the Trekronen battery; so that the necessary operation of coaling had to be performed with great loss of time and much inconvenience. Mr. Wellington recommended that, in navigating the Belt, a steamer with six beacon buoys to mark the dangers would be of the greatest benefit, especially in passing Sprogo. Of the harbours seen by him, he preferred that of Christiania in Norway, Wingo Sound on the Swedish coast, Nyborg in the Great Belt, and Kiel in Holstein, as the best place of all for a general rendezvous; supplies of all kinds being as reasonable there as at Copenhagen.

There was not much in this report which could be of use in the navigation of the Belt, and the journals of the *Hecla* were not supplied to the Admiral. What he wanted to know was something of the dangers to be encountered in navigating the Belt, and in this respect he was nothing the wiser for the voyage of the *Hecla*.

The squadron weighed anchor soon after 6 o'clock on the morning of the 23rd of March; the rendezvous being appointed at Foreness. At 5 P.M. it was off Anholt, where it was joined by the *Neptune*, Capt. Frederick Hutton, and the *Monarch*, Capt. John E. Erskine. The *Neptune* bore the flag of Rear Admiral Corry, who, on joining, was directed to proceed to Foreness for the night, as it was blowing hard. The squadron anchored there in a strong gale, at 11 P.M.

On the 24th, at 7 A.M., the *Leopard* was sent forward to place vessels on the various shoals between Foreness and Kallundborg Fiord. This service was very judiciously performed by Admiral Plumridge, the squadron shortly afterwards following. At 4 P.M. the ships rounded Reefness Light, passing the *Dauntless,* at anchor between Reefness and the shoals. A little before sunset the squadron anchored in Kallundborg Fiord; but so badly manned were some of the ships that it was with difficulty they could furl their sails. This is hardly to be wondered at when the Admiral was afterwards officially apprised that, " *notwithstanding the number of landsmen entered, we are come nearly to a dead stand for seamen!* " This was from Admiral Berkeley.

At 10 o'clock on the following morning, the *Leopard,* bearing the flag of Admiral Plumridge, was sent forward to place steamers on the Sprogo and Vengeance shoals, which service was performed in a masterly manner. The morning had been overcast with drizzling rain, and this was accompanied by strong gales, which at 4 P. M. had so much increased as to induce the Admiral to order the squadron to strike topmasts.

The ships held on during the night, and early on the following morning the *Vulture* was sent forward to Copenhagen, in obedience to previous Admiralty order. In the course of this morning the squadron was joined by Capt. Lyons, who, in the *Miranda,* had been reconnoitring in the direction of Revel and Port Baltic. Capt. Lyons reported that there were no Russian ships of war in either port, both of which he had reached with great difficulty, having had to force his ship through fifty miles of ice in going, and nearly the same in returning. Less able officers might have shrunk from such a task; yet was the service as completely performed as though there had not been an ice-floe in the Baltic.

That Capt. Lyons had been able to force his way at all, was a proof that, with a further break up of the ice in the time which had elapsed since he quitted Revel, the Russians might, with a fair wind, be able to force their way also; and there was every reason to believe that they would do so the moment that the ice in the Gulf of Finland became practicable. When Capt. Lyons left the gulf, the ice had not broken up; but the Admiral felt that he would not be through the Belt any too soon to destroy the Russian hope of effecting a junction between their fleets, whatever might be the purpose of such junction.

That the rapidity of his movements did so deter them is certain. The Russians, believing the British fleet to be in a high state of efficiency, judged that it might follow in the track of Captain Lyons, and thus meet the Sweaborg division, if it left port. It did not therefore venture out, thus rendering any contemplated junction with the Danish fleet out of the question.

Capt. Lyons, whose ship had received considerable damage from the ice, proceeded, in pursuance of previous orders, to Sheerness. At 2 P.M. the *Leopard* rejoined the squadron, bringing with her Mr. Buchanan, the British Minister at Copenhagen. At 3 P.M. the squadron came to an anchor between Nyborg and Sprogo.

On this day the Admiral wrote to Sir James Graham, notifying the arrival of the *Neptune* and *Monarch*, but complaining that the *Monarch* was in a condition hardly fit to go to sea — certainly not fit to fight. He represented to the First Lord that it would be better to give such ships more time, as, in the state in which they joined the squadron, they were only a nominal force, whilst they gave him the credit of being stronger than he really was.

To this representation the First Lord subsequently replied, " *I hope to hear that you have been able to enter men in the Baltic.*" This is perhaps the first time in our history that an Admiral was sent forth to war, and told to find his men amongst foreign nations as he went along: nations, moreover, which, though now professedly neutral, would, as regarded some of them, have become hostile, had the chances of war been against us.   Yet this injunction to pick up foreign seamen was afterwards frequently and most anxiously repeated.   The only immediate hope held out by the First Lord was that the *Cumberland*, which had been three years in commission, would now join the squadron, and that probably many of her men would be found qualified for higher ratings ; in which case they were to be turned over as petty officers to ships in want of them, their places in the *Cumberland* being filled up by a draft of men from home.

On the morning of the 27th, the squadron having procured a few pilots, again weighed anchor, first saluting the Danish flag, which salute was duly returned from Nyborg.   At 6.15 A.M. it passed Sprogo in the Great Belt, and the rendezvous was appointed

at Kiel, where the Flag-ship anchored at 4.30 P.M. ;
a fortnight only after having quitted England, and
having conducted the squadron through a most intricate and dangerous navigation.   The Admiral
having preceded the squadron to the anchorage, it
was left in charge of Admiral Corry, who at 9 P.M.
brought the ships to an anchor in the outer roads of
Kiel.   No disaster of any kind had occurred during
the passage, beyond the temporary disablement of one
of the engines of the *Dauntless*.

On his arrival at Kiel, the Admiral wrote to Admiral Berkeley, on whom had devolved the charge of
manning the squadron, advising him of the bad condition of some of the ships.   "The *Monarch*," wrote
Sir Charles, "is in a most deplorable state ; she ought
not to have been sent to sea.   There is hardly a man
in her who knows a rope.   You may suppose I am
anxious to be reinforced, as, by all I hear, the Russians will be in great force, what with their ships and
gun-boats.   I warn you to beware that if accidents
happen to us from want of men it will be no joke:
especially *Ajax* and *Monarch* are badly manned, *Monarch* abominably so; none are fit to go into action
as they ought to be.   Be sure you send us powder
and shot to fill up."

Whilst, as regards the fleet, matters were in this
state, England was on the tiptoe of expectation
that some decisive blow would be at once struck,
though where, or by what means, it is difficult to
guess.   A blow had indeed been struck by the rapidity of the Admiral's movements, which had completely frustrated the plans of Russia, viz., by placing

the squadron between them and the Danish capital, and preventing the smallest chance of any of their cruisers getting out of the Baltic.

On the 22nd of March, when the Baltic was a mass of solid or broken ice, Sir H. Seymour, our late Ambassador at St. Petersburg, thus wrote to the Admiral : " I am doing all I can to moderate the expectations of my countrymen, and to explain to them that the fleet cannot sail on the ice, or take Cronstadt by the wasp's nest process; and that, even if Cronstadt were taken, the Winter Palace is too large to be packed up for erection in Trafalgar Square." No man better knew the strength and resources of Russia, or the difficulty of getting at her, than did Sir H. Seymour, who thus ridicules the inordinate expectation of what the Admiral was to effect *instanter*, though, unhappily, as will ere this have been gathered, without the means to effect anything.

It should have been enough, that in nineteen days after quitting England, the Admiral had, by his rapid progress, utterly paralysed the movements of Russia, and had not permitted a single ship of war to pass him into the North Sea, whereby the undefended coasts of England—then with scarcely a ship of war in her ports—would have been at the mercy of any that had escaped his vigilance. On the contrary, he had the whole of the enemy's force in front of him, enclosed, as it were, in the net of their own waters, beyond the power of external mischief either by action or political diplomacy. This fortnight's work alone, whether nationally or diplomatically considered, was worthy of a campaign.

E

On the 26th of March, the Board of Admiralty apprised Sir C. Napier that quarters were being prepared at Riga by the Russian Government for a garrison of 8000 men, and at Revel for a garrison of 32,000 men. Further information was sent to him respecting the movements of Swedish gun-boats. He was also apprised that extensive military defensive preparations were being made on the coast of Norway.

The Admiralty, acting on the information of Col. Hodges and Mr. Buchanan, at various times warned Sir Charles that the Russians were actively engaged in getting the *materiel* of war from the neutral ports. Col. Hodges reported considerable quantities of lead lying at Lübeck for shipment to Riga. The navigation was open, and great exertions were being made to get it away before the declaration of blockade. Mr. Buchanan ascertained that Swedish vessels were engaged in this object, and that one had already left hurriedly, in consequence of telegraphic instructions, in tow of a Lübeck steamer for Bornholm, whence she would be able to get to Russia. Mr. Buchanan moreover learned that several other vessels had left Lübeck for Russian ports ostensibly laden with cotton, but really with munitions of war, additional cargoes of which were in a state of active forwardness. The train of 23rd of March had brought from Hamburg 300 quintals of sulphur, to be shipped to Finland. Ten thousand muskets and thirty-two cases of Congreve rockets had also arrived at Lübeck on Russian Government account. It is remarkable, that although notifying this to the Admiral, the Board of Admiralty, throughout the whole campaign, never supplied the fleet with a single Congreve rocket! though it was no secret that numbers had been made in London for Russia, to whom they were of less use than to the British fleet, which could not well undertake any bombarding without them.

On the 29th of March, the squadron, having been joined by the *Odin*, Capt. Scott, again weighed, and left the outer roads of Kiel for Kioge Bay. It was shortly afterwards joined by the *Lightning*, surveying vessel, Capt. Sulivan, and was compelled to anchor at 5 P.M. on account of heavy fog.

On the 30th of March, Sir James Graham transmitted to the Admiral further instructions as to the course to be pursued, viz., that, when assured of having the whole of the enemy's force in front of him, and within the Gulf of Finland, his first object must be to shut them up there, and to see if they were disposed to measure strength with him. The First Lord thought that they would not now do so, but would more probably await his attack under cover of their fortresses. He doubted the prudence of any such operation, but inclined to the belief that the Admiral, having established his blockade, should rather look to Aland, which, from report, the Russians were about to evacuate. If not, it would be necessary to take steps for attacking it, and preparations must be made accordingly,—the Admiral's instructions being specially directed to this object, as the first success obtained in the Aland Islands would have a great effect both on Finland and Sweden. But if the Russians held their ground and meant to defend

Aland, the Admiral was to consider that, without the co-operation of " *a military force, at least equal to the enemy's garrison, success could not be secured,*" and it would not do to begin by risking a failure. However, the First Lord informed Sir Charles that he was disposed to leave to him the largest discretion. He would make him strong as rapidly as he could, and he must then turn the means placed under his command to the best account.

On the 30th of March the squadron was still detained at anchor off Langeland by the fog. On the 31st it again sailed, and anchored in Kioge Bay at noon on the 1st of April, having been joined by the *Gorgon*, Commander Arthur Cumming, which ship brought out from England Mr. G. Biddlecombe, Master of the Fleet. When at anchor the squadron was joined by the *Conflict*, Captain John Foote.

Whilst under way for Kioge, the *Princess Royal* and *Cressy* ran foul of each other, fortunately without sustaining greater damage than the loss of two of the *Princess Royal's* boats, and the fore-yard and flying jib-boom of the *Cressy*. Whilst regretting this accident, which was rather owing to inexperience than to neglect, the Commander-in-Chief congratulated the Admiralty on the successful passage of the Belt with so many large ships.

When at Kiel, a deputation of the British merchants at Hamburg waited on the Admiral, with an invitation to partake of a public dinner; but Sir Charles was compelled to decline accepting it, on account of the onerous duties of the squadron.

Whilst on his way to Kioge Bay, the Board of

Admiralty was indefatigable in communicating to him all the information they had obtained of the movements and resources of the Russians. On the 18th of March he was told that the Russians were fitting their gun-boats with disc steam engines; though the Board did not credit the report: why, is not stated. If so, it was small consolation to Sir Charles Napier that he had no gun-boats to meet them. Nor was it much more satisfactory to be told, on the 27th of March, that at Cronstadt the Russians had two floating batteries, each armed with four 98-pounder mortars, whilst he had not, then or afterwards, a single mortar in his fleet! He was also told that one of the Russian forts at Cronstadt mounted 128 guns, equally divided into four classes, of 112-pounders, 98-pounders, 74-pounders, and 48-pounders.

On the 30th of March, the Board of Admiralty transmitted to Sir Charles the preparations which the Russians were making for his reception. At Sweaborg, Cronstadt, and Revel they had laid down 70 mines and booms, for the purpose of destroying his ships. All the forts were supplied with red-hot shot. The Board also obtained the Russian plan of meeting the British squadron, which they felt assured would at once proceed to Cronstadt. The fleets were ordered to remain close in harbour and receive the attack, till our vessels were disabled, as it was calculated they would be. Whilst in this condition, the fire of the forts was to be seconded by that of the fleets, which would thus secure an easy prey. The Sweaborg division was then to be ordered, by electric telegraph,

to come to the support of the Cronstadt fleet, and
thus make sure of the whole of our ships. The plan
was not ill devised, and would, no doubt, have met
with more or less success, had the Admiral been unwise enough to fulfil the Russian expectation that he
would attack the forts at Cronstadt.

In case Revel should be attacked, the Russian mode
of meeting the attack has at least the merit of novelty. A number of large ships were to be lightened
and dragged into shoal water, so that it was expected
the British squadron would, by following them, have
fallen into the snare, and, when dashing at these ships,
themselves run aground, whereby they would have
become an easy prey !

It was also ascertained that an imperial ukase had
arrived at Riga, putting the provinces " *en état de
guerre.*" The supreme military command of Livonia was
entrusted to Prince Susaroff. Esthonia and Courland were to form separate commands, Prince Susaroff
retaining the civil command of the three provinces.

We have spoken of the defensive preparations of
Norway. It was now ascertained that, besides the
ships of war to be stationed on the coast of Finmark,
two engineer officers were deputed to prepare the
fortress of Wardehus on the island of Wardoe, at the
entrance of the White Sea, for the reception of troops.
The casemated fortress of Kaholmen, which commands the entrance to Christiania, was also to be put
in order. The naval stations of Horten and Christian-
sand were being prepared for any contingency. The
Swedish fortified ports generally were to be closed to
ships of war as soon as the war commenced.

CHAP. III.

DIPLOMACY OF THE GERMAN AND NORTHERN COURTS, AS RELATING TO THE WAR IN THE BALTIC.

CONTINGENCIES AS TO ALLIANCE OF THE GERMAN POWERS WITH FRANCE AND ENGLAND.— SQUADRON CAUTIONED NOT TO ATTACK THE RUSSIAN FORTS. — NO "DESPERATE SERVICE" REQUIRED OF IT. — DEMONSTRATION ITS FIRST PURPOSE. — MILITARY OPINION AGAINST ATTACKING SEBASTOPOL, CRONSTADT, OR SWEABORG. — GOVERNMENT GUIDED BY MILITARY OPINION. — RELATIVE POSITION OF GERMAN STATES. — THE GERMAN AND SWEDISH PEOPLE WITH US. — TURKISH STAND AGAINST RUSSIA. — FLEET AND ARMY DESPATCHED TO THE CRIMEA. — CRIMEA A NON-VITAL POINT OF THE RUSSIAN EMPIRE. — INCOMPETENCY OF BRITISH SQUADRON. — GERMAN COURTS ALIVE TO THIS. — DALLIANCE OF PRUSSIA WITH AUSTRIA. — PRUSSIAN INTIMIDATION OF AUSTRIA. — AUSTRIA SUMMONS RUSSIA TO EVACUATE THE PRINCIPALITIES.— RUSSIAN DIPLOMACY TURNS SUMMONS TO GOOD ACCOUNT.— PRUSSIAN TREACHERY TO THE ALLIES. — RESULT OF THE INADEQUACY OF OUR PREPARATIONS. — OUR AMBASSADORS IN GERMANY URGE THE ADMIRAL TO STRIKE A BLOW. — POLICY OF PRUSSIA THOROUGHLY RUSSIAN.— POLICY OF SWEDEN. — SWEDEN WILL NOT MOVE WITHOUT AUSTRIA. — A SLIGHT PRESSURE ON SWEDEN ONLY REQUIRED. — DANISH POLICY.— GERMAN DEMAND ON DENMARK TO JOIN AUSTRIA. — PRUSSIAN CONFEDERATION.— LORD ELLENBOROUGH'S OPINION. — SIR CHARLES NAPIER'S OPINION. — EVENTUAL FAILURE OF OUR DIPLOMACY. — MISERABLE CONDUCT OF SECOND CAMPAIGN IN THE BALTIC. — CONCLUDING REMARKS.

IN a work of this nature, the reader will naturally expect information relative to what may be termed the diplomacy of the war, so far as regards the states more immediately connected with Russia in the North. At the period of which we write, the

daily papers exerted every nerve to penetrate the
secrets of Cabinets, and arrived at no small amount
of truth, coupled with much that was erroneous, and
more that was conjectural. The Government too
communicated much that was expedient — but no
more. We will endeavour to give a synopsis of our
diplomatic position at the Northern and German
Courts as far as is necessary for the comprehension
of our narrative,— for we are not writing the
diplomatic history of the war. In so doing, we shall
go to sources beyond the possibility of error, for
which, if it be made, we must be held accountable.

Whilst war was yet imminent, it was impossible to
predict with any degree of certainty what might be
the combinations for or against us. The contingencies which might have arisen as regards Austria,
Prussia, and Sweden were endless. Whilst we were
at war with Russia, Austria might act against
Russia, in favour of her, or be neutral. Prussia
might be neutral, whilst Austria remained so.
Prussia might act with England, whilst Austria
remained neutral. Prussia might act in favour of
Russia, whilst Austria was neutral. Austria might
act against Russia, whilst Prussia was acting of-
fensively in her favour. Austria might act in
favour of Russia, whilst Prussia was acting against
her. Both Austria and Prussia combined might
act for or against Russia. In short, these complications might be interminable. Yet the course to be
pursued was clear enough, viz., how to meet the
greatest combination that could be formed against

us, or how to procure the greatest combination in our favour.

There was no existing combination against us to meet; consequently the movements of the Government were confined solely to one object, to procure combinations in our favour; viz., those of Austria, Prussia, and Sweden in the first instance, which would be followed by the petty states of Germany, and perhaps Denmark, on compulsion.

Now for the steps taken by the Government to this end. A squadron was despatched to the Baltic, and the often repeated instructions to the Admiral may be confined to three heads, which were kept constantly in view: First, to keep the Russian fleet shut up in the Baltic, in order to prevent their cruisers from slipping out to the injury of our commerce and coasts. Secondly, on no account to attack the Russian forts, or, as Sir James Graham phrases it, not " to run his head against stone walls," not " to play the enemy's game," &c.: this caution was constantly reiterated. Thirdly, to " look to Aland," as a bait for Sweden to enter into the combination desired, as well as for the aid of her gun-boats ; — this being stated in direct language, which will be afterwards adduced, it being necessary to mention it here, because it is important, before we can follow the course of the campaign, to form a clear idea of the purpose for which the squadron was sent to the Baltic.

From the above, it is sufficiently apparent that fighting the Russian forts was not the object of the

Government — however it might be the object of the
Admiral, could he have got the means he asked
for. Those means were not supplied, which is an
additional confirmation that the Government had
other objects in view. Next to keeping the Russian
fleet from doing us mischief by getting out of the
Baltic, the object of our squadron could, at this
period, have been none other than that of turning
Sweden in our favour — as was indeed directly stated
by the First Lord — and procuring the combination of
Austria and Prussia with the Allies, by means of the
demonstration made by the fleet. That this was its
object, will by and by appear — not from argument
only, but from proof positive.

Again, the words of Sir James Graham, before the
departure of the fleet, are very remarkable. He did
not apprehend that the Admiral would be called upon
to undertake any "*desperate service.*" His after instructions, from time to time, cautioned him against
undertaking any "desperate service." Not that the
Admiral would have paid much attention to these
cautions had he possessed the means of undertaking
desperate service ; but there are the Government
cautions against it, and the Government took care
not to supply him with the means of exhibiting any
inconvenient zeal. Taking all these circumstances
together, nothing can be clearer than that the first
object of the Baltic fleet, in the estimation of the
Government, was that of demonstration to procure
German and Swedish combination in favour of the
Allies, and not fighting, unless the Russian fleet
came out.

And Sir James Graham was right, both in making a demonstration for the purpose of procuring combinations in favour of the Allies, and in not wishing to expose an insufficient and newly manned squadron to a contest with granite walls.   Not that the Admiral, in the present condition of his fleet, and without troops, would have dreamed of such a contest; but still, from some undefinable belief in the Admiral's rashness, Sir James thought constant caution necessary.   It is difficult to say how Sir Charles Napier acquired this reputation for rashness, for throughout his whole previous life he never undertook an enterprise which had not ended in immediate and brilliant victory.   In place of rashness, such victory could only have been the result of just calculation, promptly arrived at, and instantly executed.

At the risk of being deemed prolix, it is necessary, before entering on German diplomacy, to pursue this subject a little further, for it is the key to all which afterwards occurred in the Baltic, and, indeed, throughout the war; and without a correct estimation of these matters, it is impossible to arrive at accurate conclusions.

Had not the conduct of Sir Charles Napier been afterwards called in question, for not attacking Sweaborg and Cronstadt with ships alone, of so great draught of water that they could with difficulty approach the one or the other, this course might not be called for.   Both Sweaborg and Cronstadt were stronger by far, as well by nature as by art, than was Sebastopol at its first investment.   At Sebastopol the fleet could get well up to the forts, and we all know what trifling impression the attack made on them. Neither Sweaborg nor Cronstadt could be attacked unless first pounded with gun and mortar-boats, and the Admiral, having neither the one nor the other, very wisely refrained from attacking them. At Sebastopol a larger army than had ever before been collected for a siege, backed the fleet, and finally rendered it subordinate, as being of no use against the forts. Sir Charles Napier had no troops at all, for the French troops suddenly, and by express order of the French Government, left him immediately after the fall of Bomarsund. Is it not then absurd to have expected Sir Charles Napier, without troops, and at the commencement of winter, to do that which a vast army, after two campaigns, and with enormous loss of life, only partially succeeded in effecting?

These remarks, though premature as regards our history, are nevertheless called for here, in order that we may afterwards place the objects of the Baltic fleet beyond question. A few words on Sebastopol, the weaker fortress, will show that an attack on Cronstadt or Sweaborg was not amongst those objects. A high military authority (whose name we are not at liberty to mention), on the 14th of·March, the day after the Admiral left England for the Baltic, wrote on this subject as follows: —

"As to attacking Sebastopol, this appears to me to be an operation of so desperate and reckless a character, that I hope no French and British Generals will be found who would attempt to carry it into execution. On the sea side, the defences are so formidable that *to attack it with ships alone would be in the highest degree rash and unjustifiable.*

As to attacking it from the land side, there can be no doubt. But on that side the place is fortified by a line of forts, which would form a completely fortified line of battle for the garrison.   These forts are bastioned, of masonry, and so strong that to reduce them could only be accomplished by a regular attack with heavy artillery ; whilst to occupy these works, the garrison cannot be supposed to be less than from 30,000 to 35,000 men.   All the sailors and marines of the enemy would be available for defence.   To force such a line of defence would of itself be extremely difficult, and *would require considerable time.*   But what in the meantime would the Russian army outside be doing ?   The whole disposable force of Russia would be diverted for its relief ; so that there is a certainty that the besieging force would be attacked by a great army.   The operation therefore would be of the most formidable kind, and the besieging army, if defeated, would also be destroyed ; *so that, of all the operations which may be attempted, this one appears to me about the most absurd and dangerous.*

"Exactly similar reasons exist *against attacking Cronstadt, Revel, Sweaborg, Riga, and Viborg,* or any strong place that can be supported from the land side, as those stated against attacking Sebastopol.   But the same reasons do not seem to me to apply to the Aland Islands, and I don't see why they should not be attacked."

Here we have a high military authority arriving at the same conclusions as did Sir James Graham, who was no doubt guided by competent authorities, military and naval.   To say, then, that Sir Charles Napier, with ships alone, and without troops, should have attacked Sweaborg or Cronstadt, is the height of folly, and is so regarded by all military and naval authorities.   To say that the squadron itself was intended to attack such forts is no less an act of folly, even had not Sir James Graham himself repudiated such intention.

We are now in a condition to comprehend what was its intention.

On the entrance of the British squadron into the Baltic, the whole Northern diplomatic question resolved itself into a small compass. The objects aimed at by the British Government were the co-operation of Prussia, Austria, and Sweden. Had this co-operation been obtained, the adherence of the petty German States would have followed as matter of course. The Baltic provinces of Russia would, in all probability, have withdrawn from their allegiance. Denmark, though thoroughly Russian, and ever eager to join her, could it have been accomplished in time, must either have joined the confederacy, or have been reduced to a nonentity; whilst Finland, though not revolutionary, as was represented in England, might reasonably have been expected to yearn towards the country from which she had so recently been separated.

These were, doubtless, great objects; but in considering them, we have only to deal with three states — Prussia, Austria, and Sweden, and with these three in the order mentioned; as the influence of Prussia was great over Austria, which again would have been followed by Sweden. Prussia was all along the stumbling-block, or rather enemy, of the Allied diplomacy; and at the period when the British press was exciting public ill-will against Austria, Prussia was in reality the power against which that ill-will ought to have been directed.

At the outset of the war, the German people were with us—the Swedes were even more so. Not that the German people had any wish to plunge heedlessly into war, but they would have been quite content that their Courts should have done so, if necessary. The Courts of Germany — with the exception of Prussia, whose diplomacy was as completely Russian as though it had emanated from St. Petersburg itself—presented no insuperable barrier to the Allied interests, but as they were controlled or influenced by Prussia. They had simply been for many years in confidential relationship with Russia, and did not know how to realise the possibility of a rupture with her. To break this barrier—slight, though venerable from age—required the success of our arms ; or what would, at the time, have been equivalent, the adoption of a naval and military course in the Baltic on such a scale as, under the ordinary circumstances and calculations of war, must have commanded success.

It was in not adopting this course that we failed from the outset throughout the whole war, and were, in the end, compelled to patch up an inconclusive peace. Our national means were abundant, had they been rightly directed ; but in place of so directing them as to attach the German powers to us, those means could not have been better directed had our object been to detach them from us—and in this we succeeded.

The Turks held their own against Russia without any assistance from us, though, perhaps, it may be conceded that a knowledge of coming assistance rendered the Russians cautious in the prosecution of the war against Turkey. Had the Allies confined themselves to securing the integrity of Turkey, and directed their main strength on the Baltic, nothing could have saved Russia; for, with adequate means, some of her fortresses were *not* impregnable, but on the contrary might, with proper appliances, have been destroyed; and this would have answered our purpose better than capturing places which, under no circumstances, could we have held during the winter. Our national ability to destroy the Russian fortresses in the Baltic will abundantly appear in the following narrative.

In place of this, we despatched an enormous fleet and army to the Crimea, a non-vital point of the Russian Empire, and from that moment Russia was safe. So long as she could amuse us at Sebastopol, and *prevent our retreat*, — which had it been attempted, must have become a second Corunna,—she had nothing to fear for her northern capital, where her power really lay; and, by securing her ships behind the thousands of guns of her Baltic fortresses,—themselves impracticable to large ships, which, when the blow ought to have been struck, had not so much as a gun-boat wherewith to approach them,— she saved her navy also. The best proof of the fears entertained by Russia for her Baltic territories, and even existence, when, in 1856, a large army was ready to second our fleet in earnest, and when that fleet was about to be rendered for the first time efficient, is, that she accepted the terms of peace offered rather than run the risk of attack where she was most vulnerable, — trusting to her diplomacy, which, as usual, has stood her in better stead than her arms could have done.

The German Courts became instantly alive to the error which had been committed. At first, they trembled for Russia, when it was determined to

carry the war into the Baltic. But perceiving the inadequacy of the fleet to the purposes of war amongst
the rocks and shoals of a sea in which, from the
magnitude of the ships and the total want of small
vessels, it could do nothing, they triumphantly pre-
dicted that Russia˙had nothing to fear from Sir C.
Napier, who would only inflict injury on his own
ships if he attempted anything against the forts of
Russia, or the fleets they sheltered.

Prussia, though professedly standing aloof, now
began to dally with Austria, and used all her influence with the young Emperor to induce him to
withdraw from the Western Powers. She had,
shortly after the entrance of our fleet into the Baltic,
signed a convention with Austria, leading the
Allied Powers to believe in her eventual sympathy,
if not adhesion. Austria, though ignorantly abused
by the English press, was showing every symptom
of a nearer approach to us, if it could be done in
concert with other German powers; and had she
persevered in this course, Prussia must have followed as a matter of necessity. A meeting of the
sovereigns of Prussia and Austria took place in
Bohemia, and had the effect of checking the honest
sympathy of the young Austrian Emperor; and
thenceforth all positive and direct interest on the
part of Austria ceased; the policy of Prussia became
thoroughly Russian, and was, no doubt, directed by
Russia herself; as no one supposes the King of
Prussia to possess the capacity to enact the masterly
though Machiavellian part which he afterwards took
in the interest of Russia.

The course adopted by Prussia, in order to check Austria, was that of intimidation. The Austrian Emperor was told that if his leaning towards the Allies — for it really existed—led him eventually into serious difficulties, as it might do, he must not count on the support of Prussia or the other German powers, but rather on their enmity. The Emperor became alarmed at the prospect of becoming isolated in the midst of enemies, and yielded to the representations of Prussia, as regarded active co-operation with the Western Powers.

The influence of Prussia on Austria was not, however, altogether decided. Austria sent a summons to St. Petersburg, demanding the evacuation of the Principalities. If this was refused, it was understood that Austria would at once march on them, but without herself declaring war. Fearing the consequences of this determination, Prussia despatched an officer to St. Petersburg, urging the Czar to negotiate.

The Czar was greatly irritated at the Austrian summons, which the masterly diplomacy of Russia, however, soon turned to good, and even decisive account. In place of a flat refusal to the Austrian demand, as Prussia had anticipated, the Cabinet of St. Petersburg, perceiving a latent advantage in the matter, resorted to negotiation; and in place of refusal, a rejoinder only was sent for the sake of delay, whilst the matter was more fully considered. The result was, it was seen by Russia that, if the Principalities were turned over to Austria, Germany would be *fully satisfied*, and every chance of an alliance between Austria and the Western Powers dissipated. This masterly diplomatic move was therefore determined on, ostensibly to meet the wishes of Austria and Prussia, but really to neutralise Austria, in which, by turning over the Principalities to her protection, Russia completely succeeded. What British diplomacy was about in the meantime, is another question.

Prussia warmly seconded the move, but still made a show of adhering to the clumsy policy of putting an end to the war by negotiation. On finding that the Baltic fleet failed to effect anything of importance against Russia beyond blockading her ports, — which was of no great consequence, as Prussia threw open her own ports to the Czar, who forthwith confined his ships of war to the protection of his fortresses,— Prussia threw off the mask, and whilst giving us fair assurance of formally adopting the "Four Points," as had been done by Austria, she repudiated her policy, perfidiously addressed a circular to the German Courts in a totally different and contradictory sense, and henceforward succeeded in nullifying our relations with Austria and the rest of Germany. It is more than probable that this was not effected by any superfluity of diplomatic tact on the part of Prussia, she rather acting the part of Russia.

Had the means employed by us in the Baltic been such as even to *promise* success, — to say nothing of being sufficient to secure it,— our relations with Germany would have been different, even with Prussia against us, as she would have been under any circumstances. But the fleet was far wide of its mark, and, demonstration apart, it was not calculated for effect otherwise than by keeping Russia on the *qui vive*, whilst we were operating where she could well afford to laugh at our efforts. Our Ambassadors saw this at the time, and were urging on Sir Charles Napier the importance of a blow in the Baltic, in order to make a wholesome impression on the German Courts. The Government, blind to this importance, or having some other undefinable policy in view, was instructing him to be careful " *not to run his ships against stone walls ;* " and neglected the means of attack which he pointed out. Had it been otherwise, Austria would have gone with us, and Sweden would as certainly have followed, whilst the minor German Powers could have no longer held aloof, even under the influence of Prussia, whose conduct, or, perhaps, obedience, was all that Russia could desire. Prussia was her bulwark, without being called upon to undertake her defence ; and as the Baltic fleet, of necessity, produced few effects to neutralise the course pursued by Prussia, the influence of Prussia upon the other German States kept alive the Russian prejudice amongst them, checked Austria in a course honestly begun, supplied her with a pretext for retracting this course, and annulled the co-operation both of Germany and Sweden with us. Our own want of foresight was our first enemy, Prussia our second and worst.

We are not, however, the apologists of Austria. Her former character is against her, and though now sincere in her wish for peace, she would, no doubt, have played the same game as have done other states in history, viz., stood near the field of battle; professing all sorts of amiabilities, but with the intention of joining the strongest. That Austria earnestly desired the maintenance of peace, there can be no doubt. If at war with the Allies she must lose her Italian provinces. If at war with Russia, she might lose her very existence as a nation. Hence her efforts to make peace were naturally very great, and no doubt were made in earnest. But from our beginning the war in the wrong place, the Crimea, and sending Sir Charles Napier with a demonstration-fleet only to the Baltic, the real seat of Russian power, whilst that demonstration was only one of unfitness of the squadron for any decisive purpose, Austria would have been insane to have made common cause with us against the Czar. As far as her own safety was concerned, it would rather appear to have been her interest to have gone with the Czar and against the Allies, and this, had the latter sustained any reverse, she no doubt would have done.

A few words must be said relative to the position of Sweden in these affairs. The feeling of the Swedish people, on the entrance of the British squadron into the Baltic, was decidedly in favour of an alliance with us against Russia, and was, indeed, almost enthusiastically so; it would not have been difficult to have raised this feeling to a pitch which would have rendered neutrality almost impossible. Sweden, however, would not act without guarantees and assurances, which, at one time, the Allied Governments seemed well enough inclined to give, though afterwards, for some undefinable reason, they declined to give them.

The turning point was, however, the course pursued by Austria. If she had moved in the direction of the Allies, Sweden would, no doubt, have followed, — but would not set the example, — preferring to wait till Austria had declared one way or the other. In the meantime, the whole force of Sweden, naval and military, was placed in a state of equipment that would have rendered it immediately applicable to offensive or defensive war, had either become necessary. The course which Austria took, under the influence of Prussia, has been detailed ; and we need not allude farther to the co-operation of Sweden than to say that it was never given, nor, after the defection of Austria, do any attempts seem to have been made to secure it; though, considering that our army and fleet were wasting their strength in the Black Sea to small purpose, the co-operation of Sweden, with her army, fleet, and superb flotilla of gun-boats, of which the Baltic fleet had not so much as one, was of the greatest importance. A slight pressure only was required, and we shall not go far wrong if we state that this was refrained from on the score of economy ! Our fleet in the Baltic was paralysed from economy, and our diplomacy there seems to have suffered from the same disease. For this economy the nation has had to pay but too dearly.

As regards Denmark. Before the Admiral had been long in the Baltic, and some time before he had reached the Gulf of Finland, the Danish Government was invited by Prussia and Austria to accede (for Holstein) to the Austro-Prussian Convention of the 20th of April. To be thus appealed to in her

German capacity, whilst her leanings were Russian in her Danish capacity, was embarrassing enough to Denmark; as it was a demand which could not be well avoided on the one hand, and on the other might have led to the abandonment of her professedly neutral policy, and to her being dragged into a war against Russia. It is plain that the secrets of the German Courts had not been confided to her. To comprehend the exact position of Denmark, it may be as well to particularise the object of the Austro-Prussian Convention, viz., that Prussia was to protect the territories of Austria, should the latter power find it necessary to her interests to interfere in the war in Turkey. To this treaty Denmark was asked to become a party for her German provinces; i. e. she was asked to act against Russia, should it become necessary. After a lengthened deliberation, the Danish Government, knowing from ocular demonstration that the Baltic fleet, in its present condition, would not be able to do Russia any serious damage, and, no doubt, feeling that the German Courts would not be long in coming to the same conclusion, and would modify their tactics accordingly, solved her *dilemma* by cutting the Gordian knot, and *refused to support Austria.*

When this convention, by which the Allies had been amused into the hope of co-operation on the part of the German powers, was going on, the Admiral was threading his way amidst the shoals and fogs of the Baltic towards Stockholm, with the intention of seeing what could be done with Sweden. The tactics of the German Courts were soon modified, for they too had acquired an accurate measurement of the capabilities of his fleet, saw that little was to be feared from it, and that the military and naval power of the Allies was being exercised *in the wrong place* —the Black Sea. After this there was no hesitation on their parts as to the course they should pursue. The very course which Prussia took is a proof of the influence which our inadequate preparations in the Baltic had on her. When the fleet with its well experienced commander was about to enter the Baltic, Prussia, with the rest of the world, felt that Russia was in danger. When she saw that the fleet was without the proper means to get at Russia in her shallow waters, in which huge ships could not float near enough to her fortresses to be of use, she viewed it in its right light, of an imposing parade of ships which no commander could use effectively, because they could not come nigh the foe. Even when they were joined by the French fleet, effectiveness was not obtained, for the French fleet, like the English, had no gun-boats which could have got at the enemy in their fastnesses, and had, moreover, the disadvantage of being composed, with one exception only, of sailing ships, which required the utmost vigilance to prevent their getting aground in such waters. Even a non-naval power like Prussia could correctly calculate the chances of such a fleet as this. The naval power of Great Britain appears to have not been competent to calculate them.

Lord Ellenborough was amongst the few statesmen who saw the error of the Government in the insufficiency of our Baltic preparations. Looking on the Baltic as the vital point of the Russian empire, and fully aware that in no other way than by attacking Russia there, with a powerful army as well as with a fleet, could we exercise any influence upon the Courts of Germany, he urged the despatch of an army where alone it would tell with effect, contenting ourselves in the East by merely providing for the safety of Turkey.

This view was moreover urged upon the Government by Sir Charles Napier himself, as soon as he had found out what was his real position in the Baltic. He too told the Government that they were fighting in the wrong place, and plainly said, that " *without an army it was by no means clear what he could do.*"

Our unsatisfactory career in the Black Sea and the Baltic, and the utter failure of our diplomacy in Germany and Sweden, incontestably prove the soundness of the views which have been here given. As was before said, if there be any error, it must arise from our own want of ability to comprehend the sources from whence these views are taken, for the sources are undeniable and beyond the possibility of error.

In the Black Sea our army gained no satisfactory victory, whilst our navy, by the admission of members of our own Government,—such admission now lying before us,—suffered a defeat at Odessa, having there made a demand upon the Russian authorities which was not acceded to, and which we failed to enforce. Had our attack been rightly directed on the Baltic instead of the Crimea, how different would have been the result ! Russia was not unassailable in the

Baltic, for some of her gigantic fortresses there were reducible; and Sir Charles Napier pointed out the means necessary to reduce them as a matter of *certainty*, but those means were not supplied to him, and but partially to his successor. It is too late to retrieve our error; but it is folly to shut our eyes to it.

CHAP. IV.

TRANSACTIONS OF THE FLEET AT KIOGE BAY.

ADMIRALTY REPROOF OF SIR CHARLES NAPIER FOR QUITTING WINGO SOUND. — ADMIRALTY COMMENDATIONS FOR THE SAME STEP. — INJUNCTIONS TO COMPLETE HIS FLEET BY PICKING UP SEAMEN IN THE BALTIC. — ADMIRALTY AUTHORITIES ON OFFICERS' WANT OF EXPERIENCE. — DANISH OPINION OF SQUADRON. — PRUSSIA ASSISTS RUSSIA IN GETTING CONTRABAND OF WAR. — ADMIRAL TOLD TO CAPTURE. — EXPECTATIONS OF SWEDISH CO-OPERATION. — ADMIRAL TOLD NOT TO EXPEND SHELLS FOR PRACTICE. — ADMIRAL PLUMRIDGE'S SQUADRON SENT ON TO EXAMINE THE ICE. — DENMARK PROHIBITS PILOTS FROM SERVING. — ADMIRALTY REFUSES TO PAY ORDINARY WAGES. — INFORMATION RESPECTING ALAND. —INSTRUCTIONS OF MINISTER-AT-WAR. — DECLARATION OF WAR. — SIR CHARLES DOES NOT SEE WHAT CAN BE DONE WITH FORCE UNDER HIS COMMAND. — DETERMINES TO PUT TO SEA. — HIS SIGNAL TO SQUADRON. — CONTRABAND OF WAR SUPPLIED TO RUSSIA BY GERMANY. — RUSSIAN ORDER TO REMOVE LIGHTHOUSES AND BEACONS. — MOVEMENTS OF RUSSIAN TROOPS. — REVEL AND ITS VICINITY. — CLIMATE OF RUSSIA.

NOTWITHSTANDING the energy displayed by the Admiral promptly to carry into effect the joint orders which he had received from the Secretary of State and the Board of Admiralty, and that by his promptness he had utterly frustrated any hope which the Russian Government might have entertained of getting cruisers into the German Ocean, — or, by the presence of her fleet off Copenhagen, of uniting Denmark with herself before we could prevent it,— Sir Charles was no less surprised than annoyed by an official reprimand, in the shape of a curt letter from the Board of Admiralty, calling his attention to their order to remain in Wingo Sound, and expressing a hope that "he had sufficient reasons for quitting it without the concurrence of the Board."

The Board had forgotten that on the 10th of March it had given him an order to "conform in all respects" to the sealed despatch from the Foreign Office; and that, in that despatch, the Secretary of State had most judiciously commanded him to take up a position which would prevent any egress of Russian ships from the Baltic or any injurious combinations of Russian ships within the Baltic; neither of which objects could be effected by remaining in Wingo Sound, as will be evident even to an unprofessional reader who will take the trouble to consult a chart of the position. The reprimand, considering the service rendered, was certainly a strange one, and can only be accounted for by the supposition that they who dictated it could not have read the order from the Secretary of State, nor even their own order commanding the Admiral to act in obedience to the Foreign office despatch; for even this, from the system in vogue at the Admiralty, is by no means beyond the bounds of probability.

As may be imagined, the Admiral was greatly annoyed at receiving such a reprimand at the very outset of the campaign — and that for implicitly obeying orders.

Accordingly, he expressed to the Board of Admiralty his surprise at their letter blaming him for quitting Wingo Sound, and referred the Board to its own orders, as well as to the Foreign Office despatch which superseded their order to remain there. He further apprised the Board, that, had he remained in Wingo Sound till the ice disappeared, and then afterwards passed the Belt, the Russians might have slipped a squadron through the Sound into the North Sea whilst his own squadron was passing the intricate channels of the Belt; and thus, the very disaster which the Government was so anxious to avoid might have happened to British commerce on the high seas, or to British interests within the Baltic.

The Admiral wrote also to the First Lord, expressing his surprise at the reprimand, at the same time pointing out the danger which would have resulted had he waited in Wingo Sound till the ice broke up, or, to use the Admiral's own words, "Had the Russians passed the Sound, what would the Government have said to me? *Superseded me — and served me right.*"

To Admiral Berkeley he complained more strongly than could have been done officially: " You sent me an order from the Secretary of State to place myself at the entrance of the Baltic, to prevent the possibility of a Russian ship getting out of the Baltic, and when I use all exertions to obey the order, you find fault with me for so doing."

The Board, however, speedily discovered its error; and, whether from compunction at the injustice committed, or from more perfectly comprehending the masterly movement which had at once deprived the Russians of the smallest chance of emerging from their own waters, to the danger of the British coast, then undefended by a single ship, the Admiralty began to load him with praises for the very step for which it had previously reprimanded him, and more especially for the able way in which the movement had been executed.

On the 1st of April the Board signified to the Admiral its approval of the new disposition he had made of his fleet. It had not, however, the candour to allude to its forgetfulness of its own previous orders when reprimanding him for making that new disposition of the fleet. A second letter from the Board of Admiralty, written on the same day, expressed the Board's approbation of the satisfactory manner in which the fleet had passed the Belt. On the 8th of April their Lordships expressed their entire approval of the Admiral's proceedings, and on the 10th the First Lord added his own individual approval by declaring his "entire satisfaction" with all the Admiral had done, even praising him highly for the very step for which the Board in its collective capacity had censured him. "I am entirely satisfied with your proceedings," wrote Sir James. "Neither Lord Clarendon nor myself anticipated your movement through the Belt, but believed you would watch in the Cattegat. *You judged, however, wisely; the time you have gained has been very precious, and the passage of the Belt in safety was a most successful exploit.*"

In the same letter Sir James reminded the Admiral

that he relied "upon his prudence in not knocking his head against stone walls prematurely, nor without the certainty of great success;" telling him, further, that "the loss consequent on attacking fortresses with ships was serious and inevitable."

The approbation of the Foreign Minister, Lord Clarendon, was prompt and unqualified. He warmly approved all the Admiral's movements, told him "he knew how difficult it would be to strike an effective blow against impregnable forts, and in shallow waters," and informed him that the Russians, deeming him capable of anything, were "fortifying St. Petersburg in an absurd manner, *as no ship could approach them.*"

Admiral Berkeley also wrote that "all the proceedings of the Admiral were highly approved of." He told him that he hoped he would not find the *Monarch's* crew so bad as he thought, though, "*if he found* 300 *able seamen on board each ship, he should be most agreeably surprised.*" "There is," said Admiral Berkeley, "a want of energy among the superior officers that must be noticed. If you have any want of energy, speak out, and you may rely on my backing you up in a way that will make the rest open their eyes." Yet afterwards Sir James Graham accused the Admiral of detracting from the professional reputation of his officers. Here we find a Lord of the Admiralty doing this before the war had begun! Were we to extract Admiral Berkeley's opinions of some by name who hold high rank in the navy, they would indeed "open their eyes,"—and the nation scarcely less so.

Notwithstanding this ample reparation for the censure which had been passed upon the Admiral, it was evident that an ill-feeling towards him existed in some quarter. The Board, though reluctantly compelled to recognise the importance of the movements for which it had so unaccountably censured him, showed an utter want of cordiality towards him, by not replying to his private letters which related to remedies for the inefficiency of the fleet. On the 8th of April, the Admiral, in very bitterness of spirit at this marked discourtesy, thus complained to Captain Milne, the Junior Naval Lord. "I have at last got a public approval of my conduct, which is preferable to reproof; but I do think the Admiralty ought to express their regret at writing to me as they did. It was most discouraging, when I was doing my best to fulfil their own orders. I never get the Board's letters I used to when I was last employed. *My private letters are not answered, and I will write no more.*" All this, be it observed, occurred ere the war had begun, whilst Sir Charles could have done nothing to interrupt that "cordial concurrence" with the Board upon which Sir James Graham had so strongly insisted—except, perhaps, the inconvenient zeal which he had manifested with regard to the efficient manning of the fleet.

Yet this inefficiency was fully and frankly admitted by Sir James Graham, from whom frequent instructions arrived to supply the deficiency of good men by picking up foreign sailors in the Baltic. The anxiety of the First Lord upon this point was excessive. He was continually inquiring whether the Admiral had been able to "*pick up any Swedes or Norwegians,* who were good sailors, and quite trustworthy." He was told to "enter them quietly." If he could not get Swedes and Norwegians, "even Danes would strengthen him, for they were hardy seamen, and brave. There was, it is true, a difficulty with their Governments, but if the men enlisted freely, and came off to the fleet, the First Lord did not see why the Admiral should be over nice, and refuse good seamen without much inquiry as to the place from whence they came."

Admiral Berkeley, moreover, instructed the Admiral to the same effect. "Have any of your ships tried for men in a Norwegian port? *It is said that you might have any number of good seamen from that country.*" On the 18th of March, the Admiral had been apprised that the *James Watt,* the *Prince Regent,* and *Majestic* would now join him; "*but men are wanting,* and it is impossible to say how long it will be before they are completed." On the 4th of April Admiral Berkeley stated, "Notwithstanding the number of landsmen entered, *we are come nearly to a dead stand-still as to seamen,* and after the *James Watt* and *Prince Regent* reach you I do not know when we shall be able to send you a further reinforcement *for want of men! Something must be done, and done speedily, or there will be a breakdown in our present ricketty system.*"

No proofs of the inefficiency of the squadron as regarded men could be more complete than these repeated injunctions to enlist foreign seamen! To the public generally—accustomed to regard the

G

British seaman as a model of perfection, as he is
when trained—such injunctions may seem strange;
but there they are, forming an incontrovertible proof
of the actual condition of the Baltic fleet; a condition
of such pressing moment as to render the Admiralty
authorities most anxious that it should be rendered
more efficient by the *enlistment of foreign seamen!*
Swedes, Norwegians, and Danes, or any of them
that could be obtained.

Nor was the First Lord less anxious about the
officers of the fleet.   He hoped that the Admiral
would "keep his captains up to the mark.   If there
was any slackness, and the Admiral reported it, he
would not hesitate to supersede."   The same injunction was dwelt upon by other Admiralty authorities
as highly necessary.   The fact was, that very few of
the captains had ever before commanded line-of-
battle ships.   The fleet had been got together,
manned, and despatched with a degree of haste
which amounted to precipitancy.   Not three weeks
had elapsed between the appointment of the Admiral
and his putting to sea.   The fault was not in the
captains, as the Admiralty authorities had assumed,
but in opportunity not having been afforded them to
acquire experience in time of peace, from a mistaken
and destructive economy, which had prevented the
formation of experimental squadrons.

That the bad state of the squadron attracted
attention, is certain.   " What is the condition of the
Russian fleet ? " asked Sir Charles of the Danish
Minister of Marine, when at Copenhagen.   " Their
condition is good.   They manœuvre well, and *sail in*

close order," was the sarcastic reply of the Danish Minister, who had no doubt watched the movements of the British fleet, and had made what he considered a hit at the Admiral. The remark was humiliating enough, but the Admiral could only reply in an evasive manner." There can be little doubt but that these shortcomings of the fleet, arising from inexperience, were conveyed by Russian agents to St. Petersburg.

This state of things was hardly calculated to make a favourable impression on the German Powers. That it did make an unfavourable impression on them is certain. Prussia was at this time undecided what course to take. No sooner had the British fleet, thus inexperienced and without a single gun or mortarboat,—the only class of vessels which could readily approach the gigantic fortresses of Russia, — come to an anchor in Kioge Bay, than the King of Prussia, as though in contempt of what he considered an idle demonstration, placed the port of Memel at the service of the Czar, and thus to a great extent neutralised the effect produced by the British fleet, which confined the Russians to their own ports, but only that their commerce, about which the Russian Government cared little, might be carried on through the ports of Prussia.

This unexpected move of the King of Prussia, who, Janus-like, thus turned a face to both the belligerent powers, appears to have taken the British Government somewhat aback. On the 16th of April, the First Lord of the Admiralty apprised Sir Charles that attempts were being made in England to get cargoes of coal shipped to Memel, with the intention of transporting them to Cronstadt. The Admiral was directed, that, if he fell in with such cargoes, he was to detain them, for that coals destined for the enemy's use would be regarded by the Admiralty Court as contraband of war, according to the laws of nations as laid down by Sir William Scott.

But unfortunately Sir William Scott had not laid down any rule by which a ship carrying coals to Memel on Russian account could be distinguished from a ship carrying coals on Prussian account. The deficiency was supplied by Sir James Graham, in a somewhat novel manner. He told the Admiral that a reasonable ground of belief that the coals were Russian, depended, in some measure, on the port of delivery, *on the character of those to whom it was consigned*, and on various minute circumstances which could not be particularised beforehand. If he had any reason to suspect that the coal was shipped on Russian account, he was to capture without hesitation, as also marine steam-engines, screw propellers, or their component parts, which must on no account reach Russia through Prussian ports.

These were truly singular instructions to a fleet of twelve sail of the line only. . With this force, taking all the First Lord's instructions collectively, the Admiral was ordered to blockade all the ports of Russia,— watch the Aland Islands,— take care that the Russian fleet, itself more than double the numbers of the British fleet, did not slip past it into the North Sea, —- and hunt up the characters of Prussian consignees,

whilst his ships were hunting for unpatriotic Newcastle colliers !

Such a jumble of orders, to means wholly inadequate to execute them, was, perhaps, never before
issued. Even had the Admiral betaken himself to
the diversion of collier hunting, the Admiralty Court,
amidst the quibbles of lawyers, could not have condemned one of his prizes. No court could have held
that a cargo of coal, consigned by a Newcastle traitor
to a characterless Prussian, was on that account law-
ful prize as contraband of war; whilst no captain,
with the fear of law before his eyes, would have
captured a ship under the " various minute circumstances," which would have told vastly more against
than for him. Had he captured a ship under such
circumstances, he would not only have lost her, but
would have had to pay the costs for his pains ; thus,
himself becoming a prize to law harpies, rather than
the contraband collier a prize to him.

The common-sense view of the matter is that
Prussia, having satisfied herself of the utter inadequacy of our Baltic fleet as against Russia, had
laughed at it, and had made common cause with the
Czar. The British Government could not help itself,
nor could the Admiral help it. That such was the
case was unmistakeable, from the advices of the Ministers and Consular Agents. If it had been wished
to stop Russian contraband of war from going through
the Prussian port of Memel, Memel itself should have
been blockaded, after conviction and warning given.
Memel was then, and throughout the whole war,
notoriously as much a Russian port, both for import

and export, as had been Cronstadt itself, before it was blockaded; and the shippers of contraband of war were too well versed in evasion, and too fully aware of the futility of English preventive measures, to run any risk of its condemnation. Had war in the Baltic been waged in earnest, Prussia ought not to have been permitted to place her ports at the service of the Czar in defiance of a nation with which she was in alliance.

It is perhaps too much to say that the war in the Baltic was not at first waged in earnest, because it is impossible to prove such an assertion, the secrets of Cabinets being too closely locked for that. What can be proved is, that, if it were in earnest, then were the ideas of statesmen as to the requirements of war somewhat of the smallest. The fleet, the offspring of necessity rather than of preparation, had no class of vessels which would float in what Lord Clarendon rightly termed the " shallow waters surrounding the enemy's fortresses," where the enemy's fleets were alone to be found, sheltered by guns more numerous than their own. The squadron was composed of little more than ships of the line, frigates of the largest class, and a few steamers, and the Admiral would have to survey every fathom of his approach to the enemy's shores, or, to use the more emphatic words of Sir James Graham, to " grope his way." Some view of the despatch of a fleet for the purposes of fortress-war—for, as the Russians had shut themselves up, there were nothing but fortresses to war with—must be taken. The solution that can be got at is, that the Government anticipated the immediate junction of the French fleet, and the eventual co-operation of Sweden with her formidable flotilla of gun-boats.   But the French fleet did not join the squadron for three months after it had sailed from the Downs ; and of the co-operation of Sweden with her flotilla there never was the least chance.   The Admiral was then placed in this unenviable position, that, scarcely had he sailed, when the nation expected news of a great victory, whereas there was no enemy whom he could get at to fight, whilst it was impossible to get the enemy to come out and fight him.   It is, moreover, clear, from the Government despatches, that he was not expected to do anything till the junction of the French fleet.   Till that arrived he was instructed only to blockade the Russian ports, to watch Aland, &c., with early intimation that when the French Admiral should join him, he must act " in entire concert and perfect understanding" with him.

Whilst at Kioge, the fleet was incessantly occupied in the exercises necessary to train the men, both at the guns and aloft; that is, as often as the weather would permit, for violent gales were constant, and ships were continually losing anchors.   Above all, firing at marks was the most essential practice, and it was diligently followed out, the captains and officers of the fleet straining every nerve to ensure progress in this most important particular.   Nevertheless the Admiral was told on the 4th of April, to " hold hard in the expenditure of shells for practice. The shells, like everything else, were *on a peace establishment*, and the Ordnance was obliged to fall back on those destined for the *advance* ships, to supply his present demands. The Ordnance was going on leisurely making so many a year to increase their stock, as if the declaration of war would wait till they were complete," &c. &c. The reader may feel inclined to doubt the credibility of such a statement; it is nevertheless given in the very words of the Admiral's instructions from Admiral Berkeley.

Now that Sir Charles had the whole Russian fleet in front of him, and that he held in his hands the keys of egress into the North Sea, his attention was especially directed to the Aland Islands, of the condition of which neither he nor the Government knew anything, nor were the Northern Neutral Governments willing to afford any information to either. The First Lord of the Admiralty complained of the doubt which still existed respecting Bomarsund as being unaccountable. The Government could obtain no information from its Ministers and Consuls who were almost on the spot, so well did Russia keep her secrets. From Stockholm, the Government had conflicting reports almost every day. Sometimes the Aland Islands were to be evacuated. Sometimes the garrison at Bomarsund had been strengthened. Sometimes this garrison consisted of 1000 men, at another it had been raised to 9000. Amidst these conflicting statements Sir James urged upon the Admiral, to make a strong *reconnaissance*, and to inform the Government of the result.

But ice was still the obstacle to further progress up the Baltic. The first step was to despatch Admiral Plumridge, with the *Leopard, Impérieuse, Tribune, Dauntless* and *Lightning*, to examine the ice, as well as the anchorage and fortifications at Hango Head, whither the Admiral first intended to proceed. Admiral Plumridge was further instructed that, if he made sure that the Russian fleet was frozen up at Sweaborg, he was to examine Revel; but he was directed to run no risk whatever.

The pilot difficulty had again arisen, and the Admiral informed the Board that the Danish government had prohibited its pilots from serving in the British fleet, though there were amongst them men well acquainted with the Gulf of Finland. This refusal was sufficiently indicative of Danish sympathy with Russia, and, negatively, of the part Denmark might have taken, had not the prompt movements of the British Admiral placed his squadron between the Danish capital and the Russian fleet.

The Admiral apprised the Board that, by high wages, Danish pilots might, nevertheless, be induced to disregard the injunctions of their Government, though with some difficulty, and that, if he were empowered to offer such wages, he might get what pilots he wanted. He represented, moreover, that these pilots, when in charge of merchant ships, earned from 25l. to 35l. per month; so that it was useless to offer them lower pay, or even that pay, unless guaranteed a pension if wounded, and a provision for their families in case of death. The Admiralty would not agree to these terms, and replied that pilots must be engaged by day pay only, but that it would give the pension demanded.

Of course, no pilots could be got on the Admiralty terms, and with the opposition of the Danish Govern-

ment. So that, for this trifling economy, the movement of the fleet was retarded, and its safety again
jeopardised, in a more difficult navigation than the
one through which it had passed. The fleet would
therefore be compelled to proceed without pilots, and
the Admiral prepared once more to " grope his way "
when his orders so to do should arrive. If he lost his
ships, the nation would blame him for the loss, whilst
the Admiralty would, by some means or other, manage to escape censure ! It was certainly a novel
thing to refuse to pay current rates for pilots in a
dangerous and — to a British fleet — unknown sea.

This pilot affair was not the only one upon which
the Danish Government manifested a want of sympathy with the British fleet during its stay in Kioge
Bay. It was a point of more importance, from the
absence of small steamers, to obtain the services of a
steamer belonging to the Danish Government. But
even this, the British Minister at Copenhagen stated,
would be a matter of careful negotiation with the
Danish Minister of Marine. The Admiral, however,
set earnestly to work to supply the wants of his fleet,
the first of which was the necessary one of water.
As the squadron had not a tank vessel, he was obliged
to turn his own steamers to this somewhat derogatory
service. But by the use of Mr. Grant's condenser, it
was able to put to sea much sooner than would otherwise have been possible.

The first definite information which the Admiral
got, relative to the Aland Isles, was, that the inhabitants mustered about 15,000 ; but of the garrison
he could learn nothing. The people were described

as hardy, bold fishermen, having a great dislike to the Russians, and anxious to become friendly to England. Suspecting this, the Russian Government had ordered an address to be read from the Aland pulpits, in which address the people were told, that if they did not fight " *Man ur Hus*," — *Anglicè*, every man and boy that could bear a musket, — they should be sent to the mines of Siberia.

No point was better ascertained than that the sympathy of the northern nations generally was with us; though their Governments held aloof as not having confidence in the policy or the power of England to effect anything sufficiently decisive to change sympathy into active co-operation.

On the declaration of war the functions of Lord Clarendon devolved upon the Duke of Newcastle, and His Grace directed the Admiral to proceed to the entrance of the Gulf of Finland " so soon as the ice broke up and he had sufficient force to undertake hostile operations." The Admiralty at the same time instructed him that he was at liberty to exercise the largest discretion in blockading such Russian ports as he could conveniently cover with the force at his disposal.

The instructions of Her Majesty's Government were very clear. The Admiral was to maintain the most friendly relations with his French Allies when they joined. Previous to this he was to establish a strict blockade of the Gulf of Finland, and to pay particular attention to the Aland Islands, ascertaining the exact strength of Bomarsund and the nature of its approaches. But his *principal object* must be to prevent the Russians breaking his line of blockade, having first clearly ascertained that there were no Russian ships in his rear, which could pass through the Sound or the Belt.

He was then to endeavour to cut off all supplies from Finland to Aland, and, having made his surveys, to report whether Bomarsund was open to attack, and, if so, what amount of military force would ensure its success. He was also to look into Revel and other fortified places in the rear of his line of blockade. Any attack upon these must be left to his own discretion. In all his operations he must regard the interests of humanity to the fullest extent they would permit, and must give positive orders to respect private property wherever it could be spared without sacrificing the objects of the war. On no account was he to attack defenceless places or open towns, but must confine his attention to the enemy's forts, batteries, and fleets.

The Admiral replied to the communication from the Board, that he had fourteen sail of the line. Whether their Lordships considered this a sufficient force he did not know, but he did not feel that he ought to stay longer in Kioge Bay than there was a chance of fine weather. He told the Board that his commencing hostilities would depend upon what he might meet. He would try to ascertain the strength of the Aland Islands, but would have to be careful that the Sweaborg fleet did not meanwhile slip out.

He farther intimated his wish to the Board that his force had been large enough to enable him to

place himself between Sweaborg and Cronstadt, so as
to prevent the junction of the two fleets; but that
at present he could not do this without running the
risk of letting the Sweaborg fleet slip out behind
him. But he assured the Board he would do all he
could to carry out the Secretary of State's orders.

It is evident, both from the Government and Admiralty instructions, that neither authority considered
the squadron adequate to the purposes of aggressive
war. And no wonder, for reasons that have been sufficiently explained. Had the Admiral waited till his
squadron was strong enough for this purpose, he
would have made but slow progress.

Whilst thus on the eve of starting for the Gulf of
Finland, the First Lord wrote to the Admiral that
he was afraid he could get no better Gulf of Finland pilots for him in England than one of those
whom he found troublesome, and sent home; at the
same time giving him the not very consolatory alternative, in a more dangerous navigation than any he
had passed, "*I suspect you must grope your way in
your own surveying vessels.*" The Admiral had "groped
his way" through the North Sea in the midst of fogs,
through the Belt in the midst of gales of wind, and
now he must "grope his way" through the shoals
of the Gulf of Finland for the rest of the campaign.
The British people, eager for decisive action, little
dreamed, at that period, that the time of the Admiral was being thus wasted, and that his ships
were endangered for want of means without which
no merchant ship would have ventured into the
Baltic.

Whilst at Kioge Bay, the *Archer*, Capt. Edmund Heathcote, joined from England. The *Archer* was despatched to Stockholm, with advices to the Hon. Mr. Grey, the British Minister at the Swedish capital. Capt. Heathcote was charged to obtain information as to the state of the ice in the Gulfs of Finland and Bothnia, and also to obtain pilots for those gulfs and the Aland Islands. Lieut. Nugent, of the Engineers, was sent by the Admiral in the *Archer* to examine any plans, charts, or other memoranda which the British Minister at Stockholm might have been able to collect. Having accomplished his mission, Capt. Heathcote was ordered to pass along the East Coast of Gottland, on his return to the squadron, keeping to the northward of Bornholm Island, and looking in at the anchorage there.

On the 5th of April, the squadron was joined by the *Boscawen*, Capt. William Glanville, and on the following day by the *Cæsar*, Capt. John Robb; the *Basilisk*, Capt. the Hon. F. Egerton; the *Desperate*, Capt. Edward D'Eyncourt; and the *Magicienne*, Capt. Thomas Fisher.

On the same day the Admiral proceeded to Copenhagen in the *Odin*, for the purpose of inducing the Danish Government to allow him the use of a water-tank for the fleet. This was refused, but with much difficulty he succeeded in procuring some water-casks from the Minister of Marine.

When at Copenhagen on this occasion, Sir Charles paid a visit to the King of Denmark at his country palace. He was civilly received by His Majesty.

On the 7th of April the *Cruizer*, Commander the

Hon. G. H. Douglas, and the *Driver*, Commander the Hon. A. A. Cochrane, arrived from England.

On the 8th of April, the Admiral addressed a letter to Lord Clarendon, in which he tells his Lordship that he feared it would be no easy matter to strike a heavy blow at Russia, but he would do his best. He at the same time expressed an opinion to his Lordship that " *if the combined armies had been sent to the Baltic instead of to Turkey, they would have been of greater use.* We might have attacked some of their strong fortresses and have alarmed the capital. At all events we should have given occupation and marching to upwards of 100,000 men. I know," said Sir Charles, " by experience, how steamers, with a small force, can keep large armies on the trot, and I should recommend your Lordship to get a floating army here as soon as possible."

The failure of the steps pursued with regard to the Russian war, should at least induce reflecting men to give credit to Sir Charles Napier for the course which he here indicated to Lord Clarendon. Had that course been pursued, there are few who will not admit that the result would have been very different.

Whilst in Kioge Bay the squadron encountered an almost constant succession of heavy gales, and it was only in the occasional lulls that the operations of coaling and watering the ships could be carried on.

The *Dauntless* now returned from the advanced division, bringing intelligence from Admiral Plumridge that he had reconnoitred Sweaborg, and had observed there seven sail of the line and a frigate. He also reported the Gulf free from ice as far as

Sweaborg, and even beyond, so that the rapid movements of the squadron through the Belt were not unnecessarily made.

Upon receiving this intelligence, the Admiral determined to put to sea without delay, confident that, should the Russians venture out to meet him, he should be able to give a good account of them, notwithstanding that his fleet was not yet up to the mark.

As a preparatory step he announced to Lord Bloomfield, the British Minister at Berlin, that the squadron was about to sail for the Gulf of Finland, and to place in a state of blockade the whole of the Russian ports in the Baltic, and in the Gulfs of Bothnia and Finland. He also addressed similar letters to Messrs. Buchanan and Grey, the British Ministers at Copenhagen and Stockholm, as well as to Colonel Hodges, the British *Chargé d'Affaires* at Hamburg.

Before quitting the transactions of the squadron at Kioge Bay, we must not lose sight of the signal made by the Admiral, notifying to his ships that war had been declared against Russia, and the more so as the propriety of this signal was for the first time called in question in the House of Commons in March, 1856, two years after it had been hoisted at Kioge.

The signal was as follows:—

" Lads, war is declared, we have a bold and numerous enemy to meet. Should they offer you battle, you know how to dispose of them. Should they remain in port, we must try and get at them. Success depends on the quickness and precision of your fire. Sharpen your cutlasses, and the day is your own !"

This signal was purely given by way of putting the fleet in good humour, and that in terms to which sailors love to listen. Yet it had another and more definite object, viz., to give the squadron a good-natured hint on some very material points, in which, from the inexperience of the men, it was most deficient. In the present condition of the fleet, no more judicious signal could have been made, and this appears to have been the opinion of the Admiralty, which, when it was communicated to them, found no fault with it, as they assuredly would have done had they deemed it inappropriate. But the naval portion of the Board well knew the temper of sailors, and the necessity of putting them in good humour.

Had the Russian fleet put to sea and offered battle to the Admiral, as was reasonably to be expected, seeing the comparatively small numbers of the British squadron, — had the Admiral boarded them, as was his intention in case he fell in with them, — and had he captured them, as our national vanity in sea affairs will not consider improbable, though from the state of the squadron it was by no means certain, — this signal would have been lauded to the skies as a noble instance of the blunt, straightforward language of a British Admiral. In place of alluding in terms of ridicule to the cutlass-sharpening portion thereof, Sir James Graham would have employed all his parliamentary eloquence to show the impulse which such pointed signals imparted to the British sailor, and would have highly eulogised the Admiral for making the signal. It was not the Admiral's fault that the Russians would not come out to meet him, but it was decidedly the fault of the Government for not supplying the Admiral with the means of getting at the Russians. Had these been at his disposal, he would have justified his signal, as, throughout his victorious career, he had justified every signal he had formerly made, and would either have driven the enemy from his shelter or destroyed him within it. None will doubt this who know his victories of old. But the Russians did not dare to venture out, and without means the Admiral found it impossible to get at them,—Sir James Graham himself, moreover, bearing witness to the impossibility. Was this a reason why the First Lord should turn into ridicule a signal which for two years he had tacitly approved? Was it not rather an indication that his own management of the Baltic campaign had been so indifferent, that it required any argument, however desperate, to defend it; and that when argument failed, he relied for defence upon his own peculiar weapon — sarcasm? — a weapon which should never be employed by a truly great man, strong in self-reliance upon his own acts.

The information of Russian movements in the interval embraced by this chapter may be summed up as follows.

It was ascertained at Paris that large supplies of articles contraband of war were being shipped from the Hanseatic Towns for Russia. M. Drouyn de l'Huys sent for the Minister of the " free towns," and reprobated these proceedings in strong terms, observing that they were a bad requital for the efforts made by France and England to preserve neutrals, as far as possible, from the calamities of war, and assuring the Minister that the greater the liberty which had been granted, the more France was determined to act with the greatest severity against those who abused the privilege allowed. Colonel Hodges was directed by the British Government to use the same language to the Governments of the Hanseatic Towns. So pertinaciously was this traffic carried on, that it would almost appear as though every port, from Ostend to Memel, was assiduously employed in the interest of Russia—the ships of Belgium, Holland, and the whole northern seabord of Germany being engaged in the traffic. A mere enumeration of the vessels so employed would occupy pages of our narrative.

The Consul at Antwerp discovered that two vessels, the property of neutrals, viz., the *Thetis* and *Pappenburgh*, were loading there with arms for Russia. A Dutch vessel, the *Jonge Dinf*, had sailed from Antwerp with twenty-seven cases of arms for the same destination. Shipments of arms and munitions of war were going on generally under the Hanseatic flag on Russian account. A number of cases of Congreve rockets had been embarked at Ostend, through the medium of the Hanseatic Consul himself, in a Hanoverian brig, which had sailed immediately.

The Consul at Riga reported the total removal of the lighthouse at Dünemunde, rendering the navigation of the Livonian Gulf impracticable, as it formed a landmark in these shallow and intricate waters. Every precaution was taken by the Russian Government to prevent this from becoming known. An ordinance was published in the *Riga Journal*, prohibiting all persons from coming within six versts of Bolderau and Dünemunde. It was considered to be the object of the Russian Government to erect a *fac simile* of the lighthouse in another place, so as to mislead ships.

The following resolutions had been come to by the Navy Board of Russia, and sanctioned by the Emperor.

All the Finland lights were ordered to be put out, except those of Narskärs and Enskärs in the Gulf of Bothnia; and these were directed to be discontinued on the appearance of the first hostile ship. The pilot stations on the coast of Finland and in the Aland Isles were to be removed; but those to the north of Aland and in the Gulf of Bothnia might remain till further notice, unless the British fleet made its appearance, when they were to be broken up : all beacons and seamarks were to be taken away; and, should the British fleet appear off Hango, the pilots were to be taken into the interior, and all seamarks removed. The Governor of Finland was charged with carrying out these instructions, and to report to the Imperial Government that all had been done according to order.

On the 14th of March, the Emperor and his four sons visited Sweaborg, and minutely inspected the fortifications during two days, assuring themselves, in the words of the informant, that "everything was in readiness to give the British fleet a hot reception."

On the 6th of April, the Admiral learned from our

Consul at Memel that large bodies of Russian troops were expected at the various country towns of the adjacent provinces; also that five Russian vessels had arrived at Memel as a neutral harbour, to be laid up awaiting events. More, under similar circumstances, were expected. The number of troops mentioned was 80,000 men. The peasants had received orders to clear the roads of snow for the passage of artillery. Some of the troops were to pass Garsden, two German miles and a half from Memel, and move on along the borders of Polangen. Forty thousand of these troops were to be stationed along the sea-coast from Polangen to Libau. It was remarked that on the call for additional recruits being made, it was not this time at the *command* but at the *request* of the Emperor.

Some interesting information respecting Revel, collected by Mr. Consul Gardner, was transmitted to the Admiral by the Board of Admiralty.

Revel has lost much of its former importance as a commercial mart from the rise of St. Petersburg, which has monopolised the supply of imports for the interior, formerly derived from Riga and Revel, when Hanseatic ports. As a compensation for the loss, attempts have been made by the Russian Government to render Revel available as a naval station, and works adapted to this purpose have been constructed at considerable expense to the Government.

The entrance to the port is marked by the small island of Dargo. The bay, when viewed from the heights, appears very capacious. A small islet, a short distance from the city, is converted into a strong covered fort. On the right is a dock, surrounded by a wharf, and strong stone ramparts.

This dock is capable of admitting vessels of considerable draft of water. It is open, and without flood-gates. There is a perceptible tide here, sometimes to the amount of six feet, but much of this is no doubt owing to the direction of the wind.

The land around the Bay of Revel is generally low, but with some commanding heights near the town and suburbs. The place is a fortress with ramparts and ditches, and is divided into the upper and lower town. The Upper Town, or *Dom*, completely commands the Lower Town forming the sea front. The ascent from the one to the other is so steep as to be dangerous for carriages; a circuitous communication has therefore to be made. The ramparts round Revel are low, but regular, according to the Vauban system of fortification.

Quitting the dock is a covered way leading to the Arsenal. This covered way is lined with guns and mortars, painted *drab colour*, which is generally used for the artillery on the ramparts and bastions.

On the left of the bay from the town, is a large castellated fort, the plan of which was furnished by the Emperor Nicholas himself, who, before his accession, was commander of the Engineers and Master-General of the Ordnance, and was specially educated for these departments, in which he was considered to have attained no ordinary proficiency. This fort, which will be again alluded to in the future *reconnaissance* of Revel, is formed entirely of granite, which abounds in the vicinity. Its front towards the bay presents three tiers of batteries, rising one over the other, like the decks of a line-of-battle ship, which seems to have furnished the idea of Russian fortresses generally.

The waters surrounding Revel are shallow, but afford excellent anchorage. The Russians consider Port Baltic preferable to Revel as a naval port, as it will admit vessels of the largest class and is seldom frozen over during winter. The Russian Government has formed the same opinion of its importance as a naval station, and has contemplated the construction of works to render it an arsenal, but these have not yet been carried out.

Hapsal is an estuary of large extent, and though now only the resort of fishing boats, must contain anchorage for vessels of large burthen. This was a place of great importance to the Teutonic Knights. The ruins of a large castle enclosing a Gothic church in a state of good preservation, and around which the modern town is built, testify that in former days it was a place of note, though the port and town are now defenceless. During the summer months it is much visited by families from St. Petersburg and elsewhere, for the purpose of sea-bathing.

The islands of Oesel and Dago in the immediate neighbourhood offer good roadsteads. Like our Cornish coasts, they have their legends of wrecking. Some time since the chief of the family of Aremsburg was sent to Siberia, where he ended his days, for decoying vessels by means of false lights, and afterwards plundering them, when their crews were either drowned, or had abandoned them.

The recollections of the former visits of the English fleets have not entirely faded. There are many who can still remember them ; and by the present generation they are regarded as unconquerable but generous foes. There are some amongst the Esthonians who would have hailed them as Liberators, but the conduct of these was narrowly watched. The majority have become Russian. The sons of most of the chief families are now in the ranks of the Russian army, and constitute not a few of its generals.

Observations made by the people of Revel show that the waters of the Baltic recede from the land to the extent of some inches per annum. Indeed, much of the land in Esthonia has been recovered from the sea, and it is the general belief on these coasts, that the Baltic will eventually be comprised within narrower limits than at present, and that hence political influence on its shores will be much altered. The seers and prophets of past ages—and the shores of the Baltic have abounded with them — appear to have based not a few of their predictions upon these phenomena, so that the predictions have rarely failed in accuracy. This is certainly a much more philosophical way of prophesying than that pursued in England, where, literally, nothing is too absurd for popular credulity. All must recollect the deluge of prophesy in England which accompanied the outbreak of the war ; and great sums were realised by the prophets, one of whom, a clergyman, is understood to have netted a tolerable fortune by his prophecies, not one of which, it need hardly be said, has come true. The Esthonian seers are at any rate far in advance of our own, and in many cases can triumphantly boast of the fulfilment of their predictions, simply because they were based on natural facts.

Some of the Baltic traditions are, however, more speculative than true. They even ascend to the Deluge ; and it is to this day a prevalent belief that the great mundane shock which caused the Deluge was chiefly felt in Finland, where the waters deposited at the same time the rich alluvial soil and the huge boulders of granite and marble which form the peculiar geological character of the country, and render the cultivation of the earth difficult. In Poland these boulders are collected into cairns, and so abundant are they, that no necessity as yet exists for quarrying stone. The magnificent monoliths which decorate St. Petersburg and form the bases of the Russian fortresses, bear ample testimony to the irresistible force of waters which deposited them amongst the morasses of the Baltic.

It is a prevalent idea in these provinces that the prescience and sagacity of the Russian Government in directing its attention to Constantinople and the Black Sea have arisen from the certain disadvantages and uncertain future attendant on the site of St. Petersburg, whose river at the first formation of the capital was deemed sufficient for all purposes, though it has now become a shallow stream, unnavigable for ships of large burthen. Any reverses sustained by Russia in the Baltic would only have directed her attention more strongly to the East, as indeed the late war itself has done already. The occupation of the East by Russia is only a question of time, which all the blood and treasure of the West will not be able to prevent, though where the East is accessible to Western power it may be temporarily checked. Convinced of this, Russia has begun to operate vigorously in places inaccessible to Western interference, and will proceed stealthily and unchecked in spite of it.

Russia, since her conquest of the Baltic provinces, has pursued towards them an enlightened course. In a future chapter we shall have occasion to allude at some length to her policy in Finland, so that it need not be mentioned here. In her German Baltic provinces she has emancipated the population from the system of serfage which rendered their former so-called liberties somewhat questionable, the liberty being for the most part that of one man to hold numbers of his fellow-men in bondage. This emancipation was decreed by the Emperor Alexander at the period when the Diet of Warsaw was closed by his orders after the Congress of Vienna.

The religion of the nobility and peasantry of Esthonia is Protestant, and its ministers are persons of the purest zeal and piety.

The changes of climate in these provinces are almost magical. The transition from winter to summer can scarcely be called such—it is immediate. From the storms and ice of winter to the verdancy of spring is but a step,—the rapidity of vegetation, till Nature stands forth in her full adornment, being no less wonderful. The *Flora* of the country abounds in richness and variety, and is all the more enjoyable from the fact that the summer may be described as a long polar day, scarcely so much as degenerating into twilight.

As it will be necessary to form some idea of the obstacles to be encountered by a fleet, in the upper waters of the Baltic, we will here insert the following " Remarks on the Climate of Russia," from the work of Germain de Lagny.

" In the Russian climate there is no transition; everything is abrupt. You emerge from one season to fall suddenly into another. The change takes place in a single day. Yesterday, there were fifty-two degrees of heat; this morning there are twenty degrees of cold and ten inches of snow. Yesterday, you sailed in a boat down the Neva; and this morning you drive over it in a sledge. I will not compromise myself by asserting that spring and autumn exist; winter begins, so to speak, in the middle of August, and terminates in the middle of May. Summer consequently lasts only during June and July, in which time, however, there are often falls of snow. In summer there is no night. It is a change from suffocating heat, during which the air is obscured by dense clouds of dust, to a penetrating humidity, which paralyses the limbs. On the average, at St. Petersburg and Moscow, the thermometer marks more than twenty degrees of cold; on the severest days the mercury frequently descends to twenty and forty, sometimes even sixty-six degrees below freezing point.

" Owing to the proximity of St. Petersburg to the Baltic Sea, the climate there is most changeable, and the difference in the temperature extreme. I have seen in the month of January rain in the morning with a complete thaw, and the streets buried beneath a thick covering of mud; while in the evening there are thirty-four degrees of cold. In 1798, the thermometer sunk to about seventy-four degrees of Fahrenheit, and during thirty-five successive days to from forty-eight to fifty degrees.

" We find from the tables of the Observatory, that on an

average, in the course of ten years, during the month of March there were nine days of clear weather, eleven days of fog, eleven days of snow, and two days of rain; that in the month of September there were only seven days of clear weather: that the month of May is sometimes exceedingly cold and inclement, and that during the summer there are frequent instances of hoar frost.

" We also learn from the same authority that in the month of December, the days are only five hours long; that in the month of November there are only three fine days, but eight days of fog and twenty days of snow; and that the month of January is pretty much the same : during neither is the day longer than three hours.

" At St. Petersburg and Moscow there are, every year, 123 days of rain, and 87 fine days; during from 190 to 200 days there is a continued frost, of 92 days of which period the snow falls to the amount of *twenty-three thousand cubic inches.* The greater portion of the time may therefore be called winter.

" The breaking up of the ice never takes place before the middle of April, and sometimes later. When the ice is once set in motion, the bridges of boats swing round on their anchors, and remain on one side or other of the river.

" The ice while undergoing the process of decomposition, invariably obeys certain fixed rules. First of all, the layer of snow which covers it melts, and is succeeded by a layer of water; this being warmed by the temperature, which becomes milder every day, eventually pierces the ice, that turns black and spongy, and becomes disaggregated, when woe betide any one who is imprudent enought to venture on it.

" Winter is a boon to the inhabitants of the towns as much as to those of the country : as soon as sledging has commenced, the markets are actually encumbered with provisions of every kind, which the peasants bring in from all quarters. Vegetables, meat, fish, game—in a word, everything is frozen. Nothing can be more grotesque to behold than the markets peopled with frozen pigs, sheep, calves, and oxen, standing on their hind legs or placed upon all fours around the tradesmen's stalls : a person would almost think that these animals were going through the exercise of the learned pig.

" When there is a deficiency of snow the towns suffer; living becomes very dear, and sometimes there is a famine; navigation as well as sledging being suspended, the provisions cannot be forwarded to their destination, or, if they can, reach the town in a damaged state, and are exorbitantly dear. Again, the earth, and the seed in it, not being protected by a layer of snow, the severe cold kills all the corn.

" The transition from one season to the other occupies only a few days. After a week, at most, of fine icy rain and thick hard sleet, the heat begins to be felt and goes on increasing every day. Vegetation progresses with prodigious rapidity; in the space of a single day, especially after a warm rain, the trees bud and are covered with green leaves: but it would be a piece of great imprudence to trust this apparently fine weather; storms frequently are formed upon the Ladoga, whence they come and break over the towns, in the shape of hail or snow.

" From the middle of February the days begin to grow longer. Towards the middle of April the ice on all the rivers commences breaking up. Towards the middle of May the sun sets between ten and eleven o'clock ; while in June and up to the middle of July it never leaves the horizon. People can read, write, and play all night, without the aid of any artificial light whatever. For twenty minutes at the most does the sun seem to disappear, but the sky remains perfectly lighted by large clouds of warm red vapour, like those produced by a large building on fire during the night: shortly afterwards the sun re-appears with increased brilliancy. The shadows caused by its rays are immense; those of the trees and public monuments are actually gigantic in their proportions.

" On one occasion, as I was returning home, at two o'clock in the morning, I had the curiosity to measure my own shadow, and found it more than 250 paces long."

CHAP. V.

THE squadron left Kioge Bay on the 12th of April,
passing to the northward of Bornholm and the eastward of Gottland. Before following it, it will be
necessary to convey some idea of the numerous surveys
necessary to be made in the as yet untried waters of
the Baltic, — an operation which had to be performed
previous to every movement of the ships throughout
their course. This operation never seems to have
been taken into account by the public or the Government, though itself a work of great magnitude,

comprising innumerable difficulties inseparable from a pioneer expedition like that of the first Baltic campaign.

On the 7th of April, Captain Sulivan, in the *Lightning*, had been despatched to survey Faro Sound, and on the 10th he reported that the inner anchorage was sufficient for the smaller class of vessels, especially for colliers, it being an object to find a convenient port for this necessary class of ships. The holding-ground was excellent, in from five to seven fathoms, and secure from all winds. Steamers drawing less than twenty-two feet might also enter, but with care, as there were only twenty-three feet of water in the channel leading to the inner harbour.

The outer anchorage, inside Bunge Island, had a depth of from twenty-four to thirty-four feet, with space for three or four large ships, but with foul ground, this being both stony and rocky. Neither did Captain Sulivan consider it would be safe to ride in a southerly gale outside the entrance, in what may be termed Faro Roads. There was, however, here from twelve to sixteen fathoms, with clean bottom ; and, with the wind off shore, this anchorage would be safe for coaling the large ships, but too exposed for them to remain if the wind was strong on shore.

The port does not afford any facilities for watering the fleet, as the supply is small, and could only be depended upon for small vessels. Heavy gales prevented Captain Sulivan from sounding with his boats ; but he found that in some places the soundings differed materially from the charts — in one instance no less than fifteen fathoms.

Captain Hall, in the *Hecla*, was despatched to the north end of Gottland, where he arrived on the 8th of April; and finding Captain Sulivan engaged in examining the anchorages, Captain Hall went on to Gottska Sando, an island to the northward of Gottland, and lying in the track of the fleet.

On landing, Captain Hall commenced digging for water, which he found everywhere at the depth of a few feet, replenishing his own vessel from this source. There was also an abundance of firewood, the island being covered with firs and the beach with driftwood. In a bay to the westward of his anchorage, on the N.E. side of the island, Captain Hall found water in the same abundance ; and as there was anchorage all round the coast, ships had only to bring up under its lee, where they would find shelter. From the information of the inhabitants, and from his own soundings, Captain Hall judged that the screw line-of-battle ships might anchor within a mile of the shore. The only dangers to be avoided were the reefs off the S.W., N.W., and E. points, extending upwards of a mile. These were distinctly visible at a considerable distance.

On the 6th of April, Captain Yelverton had been sent in the *Arrogant* to examine the island of Bornholm, where he arrived on the 7th, and surveyed the anchorage of Nexo on the east side, having been unable to reach Rönne. He reported the shelter afforded at Nexo as being good with westerly winds; but the anchorage was not to be depended on. The *Arrogant* dragged considerably, and only brought up with ninety fathoms of chain, whilst the bottom was rocky.

On the morning of the 8th, the gale moderated so that Captain Yelverton could communicate with the port, which he found well adapted for watering the fleet, as well from wells as from a lagoon near the town, though he doubted whether in the summer the latter would be wholesome, from diminution of its volume as well as from decayed vegetable matter.

Bornholm is about twenty-four miles from the Swedish coast, and about seventy miles from Zealand. It is about twenty miles in length and fourteen in breadth. It is one of the most considerable of the Danish islands, having a population of 25,000. Rönne, the capital, at the S.W. angle of the island, is well fortified.

Mr. Biddlecombe, the master of the fleet, was sent forward in the *Hecla* to examine Hango; and whilst thus engaged, several guns were fired at the ship from the Russian forts, but without effect. A minute examination was also made of the anchorage to the east of Yassuri, as well as to the westward of Hango, the *Hecla* steaming into the anchorages of Oro and Uto, Mr. Biddlecombe landing to reconnoitre the latter place. Tracings of the coast and other sketches were made by Mr. Evans, master of the *Lightning*, who accompanied Mr. Biddlecombe.

Captain Buckle, in the *Valorous*, was sent to examine a bay to the southward of Slito, and the coast as far as Gotham Head. He found good anchorage in all parts. The Swedes were constructing a strong circular earthwork, designed for twenty-four guns, of

I

which twelve were mounted *en barbette*. Two Swedish men-of-war were at Slito, which port was interdicted to the Allies. There were also ten gun-boats, and a Swedish squadron was expected from Carlscrona with reinforcements of troops.

It would be easy to multiply these surveying reports, and would only be creditable to the officers who executed the surveys under great disadvantages; but enough has been adduced to show that no reliable information had been previously obtained with regard to the comparatively unknown waters upon which the squadron had entered. Could pilots have been obtained, all this time and trouble would, to a great extent, have been saved, as would also have been the case had our ministers and consuls in the Baltic been directed to procure trustworthy information. As it was, the whole sea ahead had to be surveyed; and thus the squadron had to assume all the character of a surveying expedition before it could even approach the enemy's coasts.

On the 14th of April the squadron was rejoined by the *Archer* from Stockholm. Captain Heathcote had only been able to procure one pilot. A Swedish lieutenant came with him from Stockholm to join the fleet. On the same day the *Conflict* and *Cruiser* were sent to blockade the coast from Libau to the Gulf of Riga; and on the following day the *Archer* was despatched to cruise off Felsand, and the *Desperate* to watch Dager Ort.

Shortly afterwards, Rear-Admiral Corry, with his squadron, consisting of *Neptune, Royal George, Boscawen, Hogue, Blenheim, Ajax, Euryalus, Dragon*, and

Vulture, was left between Dager Ort and Hufvudskar, to intercept all vessels in that direction.

The Admiral himself stood on towards the Gulf of Finland with the following ships — *Duke of Welling-ton, Edinburgh, St. Jean d'Acre, Princess Royal, Cæsar, Cressy, Impérieuse, Amphion, Leopard, Magi-cienne, Gorgon,* and *Driver.*

On the 16th, Captain Foote, in the *Conflict,* cap-tured a Russian barque belonging to Riga and sent her into Memel. On the following day he captured three more prizes, and on the 18th landed at Memel to make arrangements for sending the prizes to Eng-land. On the evening of the same day Captain Foote was unfortunately drowned, together with four men, in going off to the *Conflict.* Captain Foote had been cautioned not to cross the bar with his own boat, but had neglected the warning. The *Tribune,* which had been sent on ahead to examine the ice, had also captured six prizes, with which she proceeded to England, and was afterwards sent to the Black Sea.

On the 16th it blew a gale, and on the 17th the Admiral stood towards Hango Head, with the inten-tion of running up to Sweaborg on the following day; but the wind coming direct into the Gulf, with a falling barometer, and the weather looking threat-ening, he abandoned his intention.

In the night the fleet tacked, every two hours, between the shoals of Hango Head and Dager Ort, — by no means a pleasant cruising-ground with a squa-dron not accustomed to manœuvre in such waters, and in the midst of fogs and gales. Under all circumstances, the inexperience of the fleet, now that it was on the enemy's coast, was but too apparent. To remain, therefore, at the entrance of the Gulf, in the weather at present prevailing, was dangerous, as the least inattention to, or misapprehension of, signals — in the night especially — might have been attended with fatal consequences. The squadron was without local pilots, whilst the Russians had removed all the beacons and lights, and had, moreover, locked up all their own pilots, lest the Admiral should entice any of them into his service.

The Admiral, therefore, apprised Sir James Graham that, considering the early period and the adverse circumstances in which he found himself, he should postpone entering the Gulf of Finland for a short time; and the more so as, on referring to the proceedings of the Baltic fleet in 1808, it appeared that they did not enter the Gulf till the summer was well advanced. As all the lights and beacons were removed, he did not consider that his ships were sufficiently well in hand in the event of bad weather; and added, that he should like to have the views of the Admiralty upon the subject of entering the Gulf.

The Admiral informed the First Lord that he had not been able to look at Aland, nor to obtain any Danish, Norwegian, or Swedish seamen. He again urged the necessity of some effort on the part of the Government to get pilots, remarking that it was surely worth the while of the Admiralty to engage some of the captains of steamers who had traded to St. Petersburg before the war. *Even one of these would be an acquisition; and it should be remembered that the loss of one ship of the squadron would pay for a great number of pilots.*

It was further urged upon Sir James to make an effort to supply the *Edinburgh* with top-men, as this ship was badly off for them; though the *Monarch* was even worse. The condition of the fleet was certainly improving, but another collision had taken place between two of the line-of-battle ships, though, fortunately, without much damage. " The state," continued the Admiral, " to which the navy was reduced will, I trust, *be a warning to all future Governments, never again to reduce the force so low, and to keep a squadron constantly together as a school, or disasters will happen.*"

Sir James Graham, in reply to this communication on the 1st of May, approved all the Admiral's movements and intentions, especially *that he had not gone to Sweaborg.* He told him that when the whole fleet had assembled, he would have a force sufficient to close the Gulf of Finland, and, as he hoped, to prevent the junction of the two divisions of the Russian fleet from Cronstadt with the squadron which had wintered at Sweaborg.

The First Lord instructed the Admiral that he would judge whether, in the rear of his blockading squadron, he could safely make any attack upon Aland ; that much would depend on the strength of Bomarsund. He advised him that Sweden was well-disposed, and perhaps her own interest would one day compel her to join us. This was a reason why there was no need be in a hurry about Bomarsund, which would always be open to attack, if he could prevent the passage of troops from Abo to the Aland Isles. The hope of regaining these islands would be the strongest possible inducement to Sweden to embark in the confederacy; and if Sweden led the way, Denmark must follow. Bomarsund should therefore be closely watched ; but the necessity or policy of an immediate attack on that fortress was not apparent.

" In the first instance," continued Sir James, " you must feel your way, and make good your hold in the Gulf of Finland. By this is meant, *that I by no means contemplate an attack either on Sweaborg or Cronstadt. I have a great respect for stone walls,* and have no fancy for running even screw line-of-battle ships against them. Because the public may be impatient, *you must not be rash.* Because those at a distance from danger are foolhardy, you must not risk the loss of a fleet in *an impossible enterprise.* I believe both Sweaborg and Cronstadt to be *all but impregnable from the sea, Sweaborg more especially ; and none but a very large army could co-operate by land efficiently, in the presence of such a force as Russia could readily concentrate. If you have no means except naval at your command,* you must pause long, and consider well, before you attempt any attack on the Russian squadron in their strongholds, and I am afraid they are much too cautious to come out and meet you. Had you been weaker, they might have done so. Now they will wait, and watch an opportunity, in the hope that you will seriously cripple your force by *knocking your head against their forts,* when they may take you at a serious disadvantage, and inflict a fatal blow. These considerations must not be overlooked by you. I recall them to your mind, lest, in the eager desire to achieve a great exploit and *to satisfy the wild wishes of an impatient multitude at home,* you should yield to some rash impulse, and fail in the discharge of the noblest of duties— which is the moral courage to do what you know to be right, at the risk of being accused of having done wrong. It is enough to present that view to your deliberate attention. You will reflect on it, and I am certain that your judgment will not err."

This masterly piece of writing, which has few superiors even in a literary point of view, will long remain a monument of Sir James Graham's administrative caution; but it will, at the same time, remain a monument showing how great administrative ability can afterwards swallow its own injunctions, when it may become expedient that they should be forgotten. As far as the conduct of the war goes, no instructions could be more explicit, and, as we go on, it will be seen how well they were obeyed to the letter.

In accordance with the Admiral's well-founded determination not to enter the Gulf of Finland — a determination which had thus been approved by Sir James Graham — the squadron went into Elgsnabben Roads, below Stockholm, where there was a good harbour, but little fresh water. This was of the less consequence, as twelve of the ships distilled their own water when the steam was up; indeed, when they entered the Gulf of Finland, they might have no other resource. The squadron was now employed in setting up rigging, and equalising provisions and coals. The Admiral's opinion upon the latter, as expressed to the Board of Admiralty, may be serviceable in future wars. With the exception of the *Duke of Wellington*, which was supplied with Welsh coals, the other ships had Newcastle coals, the smoke from which was so intolerable that, in coming in, the channels could scarcely be distinguished. The Admiral gave it as his opinion, that, in going into action with a fleet, or even with batteries, such a smoke would be injurious to the correct performance of evolutions, and that, therefore, it was a matter of great importance that coals making the least smoke should in future be supplied.

On arriving at Elgsnabben, it was ascertained that Admiral Plumridge's squadron was off Aland; and Captain Scott, in the *Odin*, was forthwith despatched to meet him, and to assist him in surveying the navigation of the islands.

It has been mentioned that Captain Heathcote had brought to the squadron a Swedish volunteer, who was anxious to see the operations of a British fleet. Not only was the Admiral enjoined to enter Swedish, Norwegian, and Danish seamen, how or whenever he could get them; but on his arrival at Elgsnabben, he found that the British Minister at Stockholm had been authorised by Her Majesty's Government to offer the rate and allowances of a lieutenant in the British navy to *Swedish officers* who might be willing to join it. These negociations, though diligently entered into, in obedience to the Government instructions, for the most part failed, from the uncertainty which Swedish officers felt as to their future prospects when the war was over.

It was now learned that vessels were loading at Antwerp, with arms destined for Russia, these being transmitted through Prussia. From the same source it was learned that Prussia had signed the Protocol with the other three powers at Vienna; "but," added the informant, "there was little confidence to be placed in the King of Prussia or his government."

To the request of Sir Charles to be furnished with the opinions of the Admiralty upon the subject of entering the Gulf of Finland, the Board replied, that he had better occupy such position within the Gulf as might best enable him to intercept the movements of the enemy, and to watch the principal ports on both sides; but that he must not proceed to the upper part of the Gulf till the weather admitted, and his own judgment prompted him to do so. This was satisfactory, as implying the Board's approbation of his not having entered the Gulf on his arrival, for reasons before adduced.

The chief reason why the Admiral had determined on going to Elgsnabben was, that in a few days the weather in the Gulf of Finland might become more favourable. At that early period of the year he had already gained experience of the bad weather which accompanies the breaking up of the ice. The passage across the Gulf is only seventeen or eighteen miles, and shoals innumerable exist on either side; so that it would have been rash, in thick weather, to have entered with large ships in line what to the Admiral was an unknown navigation — which was alike unknown to the captains and officers of the fleet. He therefore judged that by the time he should equalise his coal and water, the weather would clear sufficiently for him again to proceed to the Gulf.

The result proved the correctness of the opinion. Whilst at Elgsnabben, a succession of fogs and heavy gales set in, which might, had the fleet been in the Gulf, have proved perilous in the extreme; and with no friendly port to run to for shelter, the loss of some of the ships might have ensued.   As it was, he was compelled to remain at Elgsnabben for a fortnight, in place of the two, or at most three, days which he had proposed to himself to remain on his first going there.

The squadron anchored in Elsgnabben Roads on the 21st of April, nine days after leaving Kioge Bay. Admiral Berkeley's anxiety about men for the fleet, seemed now to increase far beyond ordinary anxiety. On the 9th of April he communicated to Sir C. Napier the ill-success of the Admiralty's arrangements, in the following terms:—" I hope the *St. George* will soon follow *Cumberland*, but *men — men — men are wanting.*"

On the arrival of the squadron at Elgsnabben, the Swedish people were in a state of ferment, or, to use the words of one of the British authorities, " This is a new era in Sweden, the people are all mad about the fleet."

On the 24th, the Admiral wrote to the Board that he had despatched the *Odin* up the Swedish coast to examine the harbour of Anholme, opposite the Aland Isles, and to collect information relative to the latter. He further told the Board that he had not succeeded in getting pilots, so that the fleet would still have to depend on its own resources.   When Admiral Plumridge joined, he would send him with two of the steamers in the direction of Aland, to get what information he could.   The Admiral, however, added, that if our representatives at Stockholm could get no information, it was scarcely likely that Admiral Plumridge would be able to do so.

It had been observed in some of the ships that ordinary evolutions were somewhat clumsily performed, and on inquiry it was found that they were deficient of " leading men ;" in some of the ships there were scarce any. The Admiral therefore wrote to the Admiralty, urging them to send out seamen, *if only twenty to each ship !* He further suggested that intelligent young officers might surely be found in the merchant navy who would join the fleet; and who, if not retained when the war was over, might be discharged with a proper remuneration. The Admiralty promised that such arrangements for petty officers should be made as would supersede the necessity of having recourse to the merchant service. Few, however, were made ; and even in 1855 the Admiralty had to hold out offers to the merchant service in order to get second masters.

When at Elgsnabben the Admiral paid a visit to the King of Sweden. He was very cordially received, the reception being partly friendly and partly ceremonial. It was conducted with much state, intended, no doubt, to mark a warm feeling towards Great Britain. The unusual compliment of invitation to breakfast was made ; this, no doubt, being intended to neutralise the state with which the King deemed it incumbent on him to receive the British Admiral. There was good taste and good policy in a reception of this nature, considering the difficult circumstances in which the King of Sweden was placed, and amidst which he has throughout conducted himself with an ability which marks him as an able and enlightened man.

The interview commenced by His Majesty paying Sir Charles Napier many compliments on his arrival, to which the Admiral replied, that he was proud of commanding a British fleet in one of His Majesty's harbours; adding, that he had directions to be of use to His Majesty should he wish to avail himself of his services. The King, perhaps thinking Sir Charles a somewhat off-hand diplomatist, took no notice of the offer; and after saying that the command with which Sir Charles was entrusted was a very important one, he entered into a conversation as to the change which must be effected in the art of naval warfare by the introduction of steam and shells.

Passing from this, His Majesty broached the question of the war, especially as regarded Turkey; giving it as his opinion that Turkey was only a secondary object, and that the war bore an European rather than a Turkish aspect. It was clearly the opinion of the King of Sweden that it ought to be rather an European than a Turkish question; but he must since have been miserably deceived by the peace, which has converted it into a purely Turkish question,—left the European question altogether unsettled, and Turkey little better off than before. That peace is the greatest victory Russia ever achieved. It has trained her armies, at no cost beyond their maintenance, given her fortresses the reputation of being impregnable, and bestowed upon her a warlike *prestige* of the highest character, in place of the questionable one which existed before the war. The Allies have gained little beyond the cost of the war, and England in particular absolutely nothing.

To the remark of the King on the European aspect of the war, Sir Charles Napier replied, that as regarded the Turkish question it was impossible to foresee what would happen ; that if Russia adhered to her first resolution of acting on the defensive, and contented herself with the occupation of the Principalities, it might be difficult to drive her out. On the other hand, if she crossed the Danube, Austria would probably act, and, if she crossed the Balkan, would certainly do so, and not only impede her progress, but stop it altogether ; and in that case, the Allied Powers would assuredly not be satisfied with the present *status* of Europe. Sir Charles said this, as knowing that the hope of the Allies as to the co-operation of Sweden rested mainly on the attitude assumed by Austria, but the King, evidently considering these remarks to be thrown out as a feeler, made no reply.

Sir Charles then said, that in case of the war becoming an European question, it appeared to him that the position of Sweden was such that she could take a great part in the final settlement thereof; that Russia was within four hours' steam of Stockholm, and that Sweden must always be in danger so long as Russia possessed the Aland Isles. He represented that England and France had a large fleet in the Baltic, but few troops, and those marines ; whilst, with an enemy's fleet in front, it would not be advisable to land a force sufficient to take the Aland Isles. He represented, moreover, that Sweden had a good army and a good fleet of gun-boats, and that if she came forward at once, it would hasten the settlement of the question, and greatly tend to improve her own condition.

The King said this was all very well, but neither he nor his people required conquest, even of the Aland Isles, whilst the neutrality of Sweden was secured. His position was delicate, and he would remain as he was. It was true that Russia was rather a formidable neighbour, but he did not know how an alliance with the other Powers would mend his position.

His Majesty was not to be shaken. He was anxious to impress on Sir Charles Napier that he was most friendly to Great Britain, but his position was peculiar, and he must not vacillate. He said he had spoken frankly to Sir Charles, as one gentleman to another. Beyond this, His Majesty left the Admiral to draw his own inferences.

After about an hour's conversation, His Majesty introduced the Admiral to the Queen's apartments. The Queen received him very graciously, afterwards presenting him to the Queen Dowager and to her own sons and daughters, as well as to the Crown Princess. After this ceremony, the whole Royal family, together with the Admiral and the Hon. Mr. Grey, the British *Chargé d'Affaires* at the Court of Sweden, sat down to a sumptuous breakfast, which passed away with all the ease and familiarity observed amongst private families. After breakfast the conversation was resumed pretty nearly in the same strain as before; and some time having been thus passed, the Admiral took his leave, returning to the fleet in the King's yacht, which had been placed at his disposal.

On his return to the fleet the Admiral wrote to Lord Clarendon the result of his visit to the King of Sweden, saying, that "he himself was no diplomatist."

Lord Clarendon replied that "his visit to the King of Sweden had produced an excellent effect, which was not likely to be thrown away." Lord Clarendon told the Admiral, moreover, that "the Government had watched all his proceedings with the deepest anxiety, and everybody rejoiced that he had the moral courage to resist impossibilities that could only have been attempted to satisfy the public at home." His Lordship added, that if, with the French troops which would join him at the end of the month, he could make the Aland Islands change masters, it would be a "right good deed."

Posterity will with difficulty believe that, with this unqualified praise on the part of Her Majesty's Government, the Admiral, from this judicious act of going to Elgsnabben, was afterwards accused of "being unwilling to enter the Gulf of Finland."

This is the more strange as Sir James Graham could not have found fault with him for his attempt to enlist the King of Sweden on the side of the Allies, this being one of the First Lord's highest aspirations and objects, even, as it would appear, to the neglecting to supply the fleet with gun-boats, in the hope that Sweden would supply the deficiency by hers, as Sir Charles had suggested to the King of Sweden. How important this was in the estimation of Sir James Graham, may be gathered from the following extract of a letter from him to the Admiral on the 9th of May, after Sir Charles had failed to persuade the King into the alliance: "Much depends on the final decision of Sweden. *If she will join you with her gun-boats and her army*, not only Bomarsund, but

Sweaborg will be within your power of attack. I venture to hope that at all events Bomarsund may be found assailable." Here is a plain admission on the part of Sir James Graham, that, without gun-boats and army, neither place was assailable, and also a plain admission that the Swedish gun-boats were an important *desideratum.*

Of these gun-boats, the small state of Sweden had no less than *three hundred and twenty-eight,* whilst the great naval power of England could not supply *a single one* to her fleet! Surely this was not the fault of the Admiral who had done his best to get the Swedish gun-boats! Of these vessels fifty-four carried two guns each, in some cases 84-pounders, and in no case under 32-pounders. Two were bomb-ketches, carrying one mortar each. A hundred others carried one 32-pounder each. Of the armament of the remainder nothing certain appears to be known. These vessels were distributed between Stockholm, Gottenburg, and Horten.

There is no doubt but that Sir Charles Napier had an eye to the Swedish gun-boats when he took the fleet to Elgsnabben, and the more so that he himself was deficient in this arm altogether.

If the British Government had desired to secure Swedish co-operation, it should have given the Admiral a fleet fit for all purposes. It was too palpable to Sweden that she was expected to render the British fleet efficient, and she declined to be put to any such use.

It was the interest both of France and England to have made every effort to secure the co-operation of

Sweden. She was, both as regarded her fleet and her army, in a perfect condition for immediate war; whilst even a subsidy would not have cost half the money which was expended on worthless foreign mercenaries and Turkish contingents, which were of no use whatever.

The Swedish fleet, properly so called, comprised ten ships of the line, sixteen frigates and corvettes, twenty-one brigs, sloops, and fourteen steamers, and the 328 gun-boats before spoken of, — a force vastly more fitted for war with Russia than the one under the command of Sir Charles Napier.

At Stockholm the Admiral had learned from the best sources that the Aland Islands were not evacuated; and that, instead of abandoning them, — as he had been led to believe when at Copenhagen, — it was the intention of the Russians to defend them. He learned, moreover, that the Russians had destroyed all buildings capable of being fortified by an enemy, taken the boats up the country, removed all the buoys and lighthouses, and even carried off all the coast pilots to one village in the interior. He learned also that the Russian garrison at Bomarsund consisted of 2500 men, and that the Government was about to reinforce them; whilst it was evident that it would be difficult to prevent them unless he had a fleet of gun-boats. The innumerable rocks and shoals with which the Russians were well acquainted gave them facilities which he had not, and it was too early in the year to send away the boats and marines. Nor would this have been prudent, till he knew something more of the naval force with which he might have to contend in the Gulf.

On ascertaining these particulars from sources on which he could implicitly rely, Sir Charles Napier wrote to Sir James Graham that "there would be some difficulty in getting at the Aland Islands, but should there be an intention of attacking them, it might easily be done with the assistance of Sweden, could she be brought to co-operate. Should Sweden not consent, it could be done with 8000 or 10,000 men; but this must be later in the season, as there would be a good deal of boat-work. If Sweden could be brought to assist, the Islands could easily be taken; her gun-boats, being supported by light troops, would be very efficacious amongst the Islands; but that it would not do to unman our ships till we knew what force the Russians really meant to send against us. Nor would he like to send a steam force up the Gulf to Bomarsund till he was reinforced."

Sir James Graham wrote to the Admiral on the 2nd of May, that he might shortly expect the French fleet to join him, and that "the French Admiral's instructions would be officially communicated to him, mention being made of attacking St. Petersburg, if it be within the power of man. You will observe," said Sir James, "that it is not an instruction to make the attack, but the statement of a wish that it were possible, — two very different things, — *and your duty does not extend to the impossible ; it is limited to the possible and the expedient.*"

On the 2nd of May, Sir Charles Napier informed the Admiralty that he was still at Elgsnabben, from stress of weather ; which, from its continuance, with heavy snow-storms, had prevented him from putting to sea. When lying there, the fleet had been visited by crowds, who came in steamers from all parts of the coast, and evinced the utmost enthusiasm.

Commander Arthur Cumming, of the *Gorgon*, was promoted by the Admiral in Capt. Foote's vacancy. Commander P. Cracroft joined the *Gorgon* in Capt. Cumming's place. Lieut. Anderson and Mr. Brett received promotion in consequence.

The squadron had now been joined by the *Porcupine*, Lieut. G. M. Jackson; the *Prince Regent*, Capt. Henry Smith; the *Cumberland*, Capt. G. H. Seymour; and the *Austerlitz*, French line-of-battle ship, Capt. Laurencin. It has been omitted to be stated that the *James Watt*, Capt. Geo. Elliot, joined the squadron the day before it left Kioge Bay.

More definite information now began to be received relative to the movements of the enemy's troops. The first *Corps d'Armée*, comprising 60,000 men, was stationed in Poland, together with two divisions of the corps of Grenadiers, and a corps of cavalry amounting to 6000. At Riga were stationed the reserves of the Guards. At Revel was one division of the Guards; at St. Petersburg two other divisions of the Guards. At Viborg was a division of the corps of Grenadiers; and at Helsingfors a garrison of 12,000 men were stationed, in addition to the garrison of Sweaborg.

On the 19th of April, the Admiral learned that Denmark had raised new obstructions, by stating her intention to levy a transit duty on coals trans-shipped within her harbours or waters; and he was instructed to make arrangements for coaling without their limit.

This had no doubt been done in consequence of remonstrances which Mr. Buchanan had been directed
to make to the Danish government, relative to the
facilities which she was giving in getting articles contraband of war to Russia.

On the 25th, the Admiral obtained drawings from
St. Petersburg of the " infernal machines " and other
kinds of defence which the Russians were sinking in
the channels leading to the Gulf of Finland ports,
especially at Cronstadt.   It was understood that no
merchant vessels would be allowed to leave Cronstadt
at the opening of the navigation, for fear of disturbing
those preparations, which, as the ice cleared away,
were to be increased.   He was also apprised that
there was no chance of the navigation at Cronstadt being clear before the 1st of May.   The reinforcements intended for Finland had marched from
St. Petersburg, but 6000 men destined for Aland had
not yet been sent.   It was now ascertained that there
were 2000 men at Bomarsund, and 4000 at Abo.   If
the gun-boats building at Abo could be got ready in
time, the latter force was to be sent to reinforce
Bomarsund.   This the Admiral took prompt steps to
prevent.   It was the opinion of General Bodisco that
the fortress of Bomarsund could not be approached
by large vessels, and that it could only be taken by
landing troops.

Colonel Hodges apprised the Admiral that at Hamburg there were three or four screw engines ready for
the Russian service, and that a Dutch vessel had just
taken on board at Antwerp a large quantity of arms
for Russia.

CHAP. VI.

THE weather having somewhat moderated, the squadron weighed anchor, and quitted Elgsnabben on the 5th of May, proceeding to sea under steam. Shortly after it had sailed, a sudden fog arose in the most dangerous part of the Channel, and the whole of the ships were for some time exposed to great peril. So dense was this fog that neither land nor ships could be distinguished, and that in a navigation thickly studded with rocks and shoals. The Admiral described the fog as being the thickest it was ever his lot to encounter, so much so that he thought it almost impossible the fleet could escape; and the anchorage was very bad.

K 3

The squadron was for some time in this perilous position, and the *Cæsar* and *Cressy*, as well as the flag-ship itself, had narrow escapes, as indeed had the whole of the ships, which, to use the Admiral's words, "escaped, as if by miracle." " I never, in my life," said he, when reporting the circumstance, " passed such a night ; and not before four o'clock on the following afternoon were my anxieties removed by the junction of eight ships. The rest did not make their appearance till the day after."

An occurrence here took place, which forcibly shows the way in which the operations of war were conducted at the Admiralty. On the 2nd of May their Lordships acknowledged the receipt of the Admiral's letter of April 18th, notifying the steps taken for the blockade of the Russian coasts in the Gulf of Riga. This letter was never supplied to the Queen's Advocate, so that the greatest confusion arose in the Admiralty Court, relative to the condemnation of prizes captured on that coast, the merchants contending that no formal notification of blockade had been made, and that therefore the prizes could not be condemned. The consequence was a great amount of expensive litigation, and, finally, the despatch of Dr. Deane, an Advocate of the Admiralty Court, to the fleet, to take the affidavits of the Admiral and his officers as to the fact of any blockade having been formally established. When the Queen's Advocate saw both the notification and the Admiralty acknowledgment of it, he was naturally much annoyed at the vexatious delays which had taken place, and, no doubt, on his return, expressed a pretty strong opinion on the subject, when the Board denied having received any such notification from the Admiral. Their acknowledgment of it, dated 2nd of May, now lies before us, as does their denial, dated 5th October. We notice this matter here, as, in proceeding, we shall have to remark on denials of a still more important character, though to suitors in the Admiralty Court this denial of blockade must have been sufficiently vexatious.

Sir James Graham, having been much annoyed at the reports of the squadron, which found their way into the newspapers at home, wrote to the Admiral that he had reason to believe some of the London newspapers had paid correspondents amongst the officers of his ships. It was very difficult, said the First Lord, to check the evil, and he did not see how the Admiral could control it ; but it was an evil, and a very serious one, as such officers, by their misrepresentations, as well as comments, were producing false impressions upon the public mind, and rendering the conduct of warlike operations more difficult. The First Lord, therefore, directed his attention, if possible, to correct the mischief.

The Admiral knew well enough who these newspaper correspondents were, though few amongst them occupied a position in the fleet which entitled them to form a judgment ; the less so, as, from want of experience, they were incapable of comprehending what could, or what could not, have been done. Not caring what they said of him, he did not think it worth his while to interfere in the matter. Before leaving England he himself had been applied to, to permit the presence of a newspaper correspondent on board his own ship, but had declined, as such a course would have been contrary to the injunctions of the First Lord. It would, perhaps, have been better to have acceded to the request, as the public would have been saved no small amount of misrepresentation.

Shortly before quitting Elgsnabben, the Admiral, in answer to the queries of Admiral Berkeley as to the condition of the fleet, replied that some of the ships were getting on very slowly; " they were short of leading men; were badly manned; whilst all of them were deficient in quarter-deck petty officers." He apprised Admiral Berkeley that he had communicated with the Admiralty on the subject, and urged him to make a stir in the matter, adding: " When we come to boat-work, what are we to do ? "

It has been said that the *Prince Regent* joined the squadron at Elgsnabben, and it may be useful to know the condition in which she had been sent out from England, now with the certainty of instant war before her, had the Russians ventured to come out. The Admiral thus wrote home, as regarded that condition: " The *Regent* has arrived, without midshipmen or master's assistants. Really it is dangerous to have raw ships' companies without officers. Who are to look after the men in action ? Who are to command the boats when that service begins ? How are the men to be disciplined ? Should we go into action with raw crews, who is to show an example to them ? It is all very well to send out ships to me; but should we meet with any disaster, what will the country say ? "

The truth of the remonstrance was fully admitted, and an assurance was given that the evil would be remedied as soon as the *Fox* arrived from India. He was then to have all the mates, midshipmen, and blue-jackets in her and the *Portland*, which was expected from South America; though, if the Russians intended to meet our fleet, it was scarcely to be expected that they would wait the arrival of these ships; or, if they did, that the number of mates and midshipmen which two ships could have furnished was sufficient for a squadron, some of the ships in which could not have fought their guns effectively for want of officers to distribute amongst them.

The solution of the matter is not difficult. Notwithstanding the war, the mania for economy had not yet subsided. It was the ambition of Sir James Graham *to conduct the war economically*, and hence no bounty was offered in the outset, nor afterwards, by which alone seamen could be procured. It was evidently wished to show how cheaply war could be conducted, and this was shown to demonstration, though it was at the same time shown how worthless were naval armaments when altogether inadequate to their purpose.

This condition of the navy had been forcibly portrayed by Sir C. Napier, when previously in Parliament, as likely to be injurious in case of war; and now that his forewarnings were realised, he was told by Admiral Berkeley, who had the charge of manning the fleet, to " *show it all up:* he must act up to what he said when unemployed." This referred to the Admiral's numerous writings on the same subject. He did " *show it all up*," and brought upon himself the wrath of the Admiralty for so doing.

Not only did the showing it all up incur the displeasure of the Admiralty, but, what was worse, it failed to impel them to make the fleet fit for the mission on which it had been sent. The only practical result was, that the First Lord was made a Grand Cross of the Bath for the cheap zeal which he had manifested in equipping the fleet, and Admiral Napier got a force inadequate to effect anything of importance — still less to satisfy the expectations of the public.

On the 5th of May, the Admiral got another hint that his zeal in practising his men was inconvenient. He was again told to " nurse his shells, or the Board of Ordnance would be blamed for having reduced their stock so low."

If the determination to render his fleet efficient had at all equalled the amount of official frankness which was accorded to the Admiral at the outset of the campaign, his fleet would indeed have been highly so. He was told by Admiral Berkeley that " three ships had started to join him, but that none of them would add to his *bed of roses*, when he had them to cruise in the narrow channels of the Gulf—tacking and wearing every two hours." As regarded some of his ships of the line, he had even requested that they might be sent home, and had been told that, in case of bombardment, they would do to be knocked to pieces as well as any other, and therefore he had better keep them.

Yet, with ships in this state, he was blamed for not

having at once entered the Gulf of Finland, though the Government had praised him for his negotiations with the King of Sweden; but in place of two days, as he had calculated, he had been detained in Elgsnabben Roads for ten days by fogs, and, as far as the safety of the fleet was concerned, luckily so detained. That under such circumstances any operations could have been undertaken is absurd to suppose, and Sir James Graham had expressly praised the Admiral for not attempting it.

Yet, on the 2nd of May, the Board of Admiralty called his attention to the fact that, in the years 1808-9, there were no ships of war propelled by steam employed within the Gulf of Finland. There was now a material difference in that respect, and that every consideration should induce him to occupy such positions within the Gulf as might best enable him to intercept the movements of the enemy, and to watch the principal ports on both shores. It was with this view that the surveying vessels attached to his squadron had been supplied with buoys and lights, and he must use them accordingly.

These instructions would seem to imply that the squadron was amply provided with means for the purposes indicated. The surveying vessels amounted to two only, the *Lightning* and *Alban;* and, in the weather which had prevailed, neither buoys nor lights would have been of much use, nor was there any object to be gained in entering the Gulf amidst fogs.

To these intimations the Admiral replied as follows : —

" In their Lordships' letter of the 2nd of May, commenting on a paragraph of my letter of the 19th of April, they
appear to think I have been *going too slow.* When I passed
the Belt, their Lordships thought I was *going too fast.*

" I am perfectly aware that steam makes a great difference
in naval operations; but steam has *no effect on fogs,* and has
not prevented two collisions, and very nearly a third, which
might have disabled half a dozen ships. Their Lordships
will have observed by my last letter that fogs detained me
ten days at Elgsnabben, and a fog was very nearly the cause
of the loss of the fleet. It therefore behoves me to be careful, and act with judgment in operations with this fleet.

" Their Lordships abstain from pressing me to proceed to
the upper part of the Gulf of Finland till the state of
weather and my own judgment may dictate. Their Lordships may depend I shall go to the upper part of the Gulf
when I can; but I must leave a sufficient force off Sweaborg,
where there are eight or nine sail of the line; and then I
must have force enough to take care of twenty sail of the
line, besides frigates and steamers in Cronstadt. How this
is to be done with twenty sail of the line, some of which are
perfectly unfit to go into action, I really do not know; but
all that can be done, I will do."

This reply to the Board of Admiralty was written
off Hango. As the reader is aware, a squadron had been
detached under Admiral Corry to Gottska Sando, and
other steamers were detached under Admiral Plumridge to the Gulf of Bothnia. Others had again been
despatched to the Coast of Courland, and elsewhere.
The actual force with the Admiral consisted of six
ships of the line, two blockships, two frigates, and
two paddle-steamers, viz.: the *Duke of Wellington,
Edinburgh, St. Jean d'Acre, Cæsar, Cressy, Princess
Royal, Hogue, Blenheim, Impérieuse, Magicienne,
Gorgon,* and *Dragon.* The Admiral's object in thus

reducing his squadron, was the full expectation that the disparity of his force to the numbers of the Russian fleet would induce them to come out and attack him,—an object of far greater importance than that of making idle demonstrations with his whole force within the Gulf, and in the midst of fogs. Had he done this, he could have adopted no surer means to induce the Russians to keep close under the shelter of their fortresses, instead of quitting that shelter.

The Board of Admiralty saw this, on explanation, and replied that it had no intention of commenting on his proceedings, and was unwilling to limit the exercise of his judgment. Their Lordships were satisfied that every exertion on his part had been used, and they continued to confide in his abilities and judgment. As has already been stated, the First Lord had warmly approved the Admiral's judgment in not going to Sweaborg, as had been at first intended, had the weather permitted.

In his communication with the Board, the Admiral had complained that some of his ships were unfit to go into action, for reasons with which the reader is now but too familiar. The Board expressed its surprise that, with such an intimation, he had not been more explicit in details of unfitness. The Admiral replied that he alluded more particularly to the ships which had joined after he first sailed, which ships had not fired a shot; and ships in that state he certainly considered unfit to fight. He further reminded their Lordships that the fleet was newly manned, and that, at the time he wrote, it was only two months from England, — two months not being sufficient to organise a fleet. With regard to detailed reports, he did not consider that the Reports of Inspection were sufficiently satisfactory to lay before their Lordships, and that he had waited till he could send a proper report. In the meantime the Admirals were indefatigable in the inspection of the ships, and the Captains as zealous in disciplining them.

It will have been gathered from various portions of this narrative that Bomarsund was expected to be amongst the earliest objects of attack, Sweaborg and Cronstadt being as evidently considered beyond the means of the squadron. Whilst at Stockholm the Admiral had therefore diligently employed himself in gaining all the information possible about this portion of the Russian territory.

He apprised the Admiralty that he should send Admiral Plumridge into the Gulf of Bothnia with a squadron of steamers, whilst he himself went up the Gulf of Finland. He had already despatched Capt. Scott up the Gulf of Bothnia with the *Odin*, and Captain Scott had reported ice as far as Bijorneborg on the Russian side.

Sir Charles, moreover, informed the Board that gun-boats were being built at Abo and other ports on the Gulf of Finland; but that it would be extremely difficult, if not impossible, to get at them amongst the islands, even with steamers, as the islands would be completely covered with riflemen. " If we are to operate here," continued the Admiral, " it must be with steam-vessels, boats, and troops, — the latter to occupy the islands as we go along. We want a much larger force of steam-vessels. We ought to have a force in Riga Bay, a force in the Gulf of Bothnia, and a force when I go into the Gulf of Finland. I cannot have less than four steamers from Libau to Dager Ort, as attempts will be made by neutrals to get contraband of war along that coast."

To the First Lord the Admiral wrote that he had sent two steamers into the Gulf of Bothnia to intercept some gun-boats that he heard were going there, and he should reinforce them with a strong squadron. Instead of four or five fathoms of water at Bomarsund, he had ascertained, on good authority, that there were not twenty feet; and if the Russians had submarine engines, it was just the place where they could use them with effect. If the King of Sweden would come forward, we could act against Aland, and if we had troops we could do so. He would not say we could not do so without troops, but he did not see his way yet. War here was very different from war in other places. The coast was surrounded with islands innumerable, and the British squadron had not a soul who knew anything about them. Even steamers were, to a certain degree, useless amongst these islands.

As to his strength, the Admiral told the First Lord that he had now seventeen sail of the line and three heavy frigates, which he might count as three more; so that he had nothing to fear from the Russian fleet. But the want of officers was a most serious inconvenience, and, with a sturdy enemy, would be dangerous.

It has been seen that the Admiral had all along

been urgent to be supplied with a class of steamers suitable to the navigation of the intricate coast and island channels, and had expressed an opinion that without such steamers nothing could effectively be done amongst them. In place of these, the First Lord, on the 9th of May, recommended him to *hire steamers from Sweden !*—"We have given you the largest discretion in the respect of *hiring* steamers from Sweden; and if you exercise this power within moderate limits, no arrangements can be made which will so promptly increase your steam power *against* gun-boats, and none in the long run will be *so economical.*" Excellent economy, indeed, to frustrate the very object of the costliest of wars for the sake of the expense of a few small steamers!

The Admiral did not want small steamers for his defence against gun-boats, but for the purposes of aggression, as without them the enemy could neither be got at in his shallow channels nor in his fastnesses. This, as Sir James Graham truly stated, he " had urged upon the Admiralty from the first hour of his appointment," but in vain. To be told, now that he was upon the enemy's ground, to " hire steamers from Sweden," was puerile. Sweden refused to co-operate with him in any way, much less to let him have steamers with which to act against Russia,—an act which would have been tantamount to a declaration of war on her part, going far beyond the act of the King of Prussia in placing his ports at the service of Russia. Sweden was too wary to permit anything of the kind.

Sir Charles might as well have been told to hire

his officers from Sweden, as he had formerly been told to hire his seamen. His hiring, as regarded ships, officers, and men, would then have been complete. He was not told so to hire his officers, but the British Minister had been so told, and was unable to get them. On the 15th of May, Sir Charles again addressed the Home Authorities: " I have repeatedly written about sending me officers and some leading men for *Edinburgh, Monarch,* and *Cressy.* I had better have a ship less than be in this condition. *Ajax* is of no use to me, as she cannot keep her station without steam ; *Edinburgh* got one of your short-service men the other day, fifty-seven years old, has not been to sea for seven years, and has got a pension. Much use such men as this will be."

To the unprofessional public perhaps some explanation is necessary as to this constant stress laid upon midshipmen, petty officers, leading men, &c. Petty officers and leading men are to a ship what non-commissioned officers are to a regiment. It is their office to teach, both by precept and example, and not only to teach others, but to preserve that fine order and discipline without which no ship can be efficient, any more than troops could be efficient without non-commissioned officers, who form the soul of the regiment.

With regard to midshipmen in general, of whose services the public has not an adequate idea. They are amongst the most valuable officers in action. It is their duty to superintend the men at their guns, and to keep them to their work ; to convey the orders of the superior officers, without which those orders cannot be communicated with sufficient rapidity to give prompt effect to them, — a most important point, as upon the instant execution of an order the result of an action might turn.   Ships destitute of, or not sufficiently supplied with, this class of officers in time of war, are, then, destitute of one of the most important elements of efficiency, the middy being literally the telegraph whereby the orders of the one ruling mind at the head are communicated to the men, who without such telegraph must to a great extent remain inactive, or wait for such orders till they are too late for effect.

The cause for the deficiency of this class of officers, the future admirals and captains of our navy, is not far-fetched.   Formerly, every captain of a ship had the power of appointing his own midshipmen, hence he took care to secure the full number from amongst his own friends, selecting them for their pluck and intelligence; and it was from such that our Nelsons, Howes, and other naval heroes of a past generation sprang.   In our day, the Admiralty has usurped the appointments for the sake of patronage; the youngsters are selected from interest, without regard to fitness; a smaller number than formerly are now appointed; and from this class there is but too much reason to expect that naval heroes may not spring as of old. Insignificant as it may appear, this Admiralty usurpation of appointing midshipmen is one cause of the unquestionable deterioration of our navy. Other naval nations are most careful in this respect. We care nothing about it, and shall one day reap the fruits thereof.

On the 14th of May, Capt. Key reported that, on hearing there was a Russian frigate with some gunboats in Riga Roads, he proceeded in the *Amphion* in quest of them. On arriving off Lyser Ort on the morning of the 27th of April, he fell in with the *Cruizer*, Commander the Hon. G. H. Douglass, who offered to accompany him, stating, however, that he had received certain information that the ice in the Gulf was still unbroken. Capt. Key having communicated his intentions to Capt. Cumming, of the *Conflict*, the *Amphion* and *Cruizer* got to the edge of the ice, thirty miles N.W. of Riga, where several vessels were observed blocked up in the pack, with others waiting to enter.

On standing to the westward, Capt. Key found an opening near the shore, and, getting his steam well up, pushed through the loose ice round the shore of the bay towards Riga. When within ten miles of the town several steamers were observed endeavouring to approach the blocked-up vessels, in order to extricate and tow them into the harbour. On approaching within gunshot, the steamers bore up and returned to Riga.

Observing that there were some vessels in the Roads, Capt. Key pushed through the ice alongside the Russian barque *Carolina*, and towed her out into clear water. She had been frozen up for a month. The other vessels were in a denser pack of ice, so that after endeavouring in vain to get at them, Capt. Key was obliged to give up the attempt, and anchored off the south shore.

On the following day the *Amphion* and *Cruizer*

again stood in towards Riga. The Roads were freer
from ice, but no vessels were now at anchor there.
The river was crowded with shipping. There were
three steamers, with their steam up, but no men-of-
war nor gun-boats were visible. The entrance of the
river was too shallow for the frigate, and as there
were two forts on the left bank, and one larger fort
on the right, Captain Key, very properly, did not send
in his boats. The forts fired at the British vessels,
but the fire was not returned.

The *Amphion* and *Cruizer* then skirted the south
shore of the bay, and, taking the prize in tow, passed
through the loose ice to the clear water to the northward, examining several vessels, but only capturing
one other, which was Russian. Captain Key then
stood on with his prizes to Faro, and the *Cruizer* returned to her station off Libau.

Lieut. Priest, of the *Leopard*, had been despatched
to examine the neighbourhood of Hango Head. He
reported that the western side was defended by two
forts. One, apparently new, had remarkably low
embrasures. The other was of considerable altitude,
and had guns on its summit. From the form of this
fort only three casemated guns were visible.

The eastern side of the entrance was defended by
a strongly-built stone fort, with eleven casemated
guns, and one large gun *en barbette*. More than
three miles to the eastward another stone fort was
observed, mounting four guns, *en barbette*, and eight
in casemates. On the extreme right two embrasures were observed, and it was probable several more
guns than those seen were mounted.

The French Consul at Lubeck had reported to the

Minister at Copenhagen, that, to provide against the blockade, several mercantile houses at Lubeck, Memel, and Libau, were forming themselves into a company, having for its object the neutralisation of the blockade. Goods for Russia were to be sent from Lubeck in neutral vessels to Memel, there transhipped to steamers of light draught, and conveyed to Libau. From the numerous shoals on that part of the coast, the company fully relied on being able to carry on their operations in sight of the British fleet, which had no class of vessels to prevent this, notwithstanding the emphatic warning of Sir Hamilton Seymour, of the absolute necessity of vessels of light draught of water, the neglect of which warning enabled the Russian Government to carry on its commerce through Memel without much inconvenience. When, afterwards, a statement was made in one of our police courts, that an uninterrupted Russian trade in tallow was being carried on through Memel, considerable surprise was excited in England as to how this could be effected with bulky articles of small value. The fact just narrated will, however, fully explain the matter.

The activity manifested at Memel in the interest of Russia appears to have been excessive. Lord Bloomfield, on the 1st of May, had ascertained that percussion caps were being forwarded from Memel to Russia, *under declaration of the Prussian Custom House!* His Lordship, of course, remonstrated with M. Manteuffel on this subject. At the same time H. M. Minister at Brussels discovered that an American vessel, the *Sealark*, had taken upwards of 5000 stand of arms on board, as was suspected, for Russia.

Lead continued to be shipped on Russian account from Lubeck in large quantities, in Swedish vessels. The French Government also ascertained the measures adopted by Russia to get, through Prussia, articles required for the manufacture of gunpowder ; and the Admiral was in consequence directed to cause a most vigilant watch to be kept upon all vessels destined for Prussian Pomerania, with the view of preventing any warlike stores from being introduced through Prussia into Russia. It would have been more to the purpose to have supplied him with the means of watching. We have just shown how articles of any kind were got from Memel to Libau, so that to talk of watching such a navigation without an abundance of small steamers is so much nonsense. The most strict watch, as far as the capacity of the steamers went, was kept by the *Amphion, Cruizer, Conflict*, and *Archer*, and most admirable was the vigilance displayed by the commanders of these vessels ; but they could not effect an impossibility by cruising in the inshore channels, where they could not venture, though Prussian steamers of light draught of water could move with ease. So long as contraband of war could get to the Prussian port of Memel, there was no difficulty in getting it to Russia, considering that the distance to the Russian territory was not more than some seven or eight English miles.

A most important fact was ascertained by M. St. André, the French Consul at Dantzic, viz., that Russia was generally considered to be in want, not only of powder, but of the necessary materials for making it ; and that, in consequence of the blockade, she could only be supplied through Prussia. He ascertained that these supplies were being taken to Memel, and thence across the Russian frontier, whilst some were sent by the Vistula from Dantzic to Warsaw. It is by this river that all shipments of colonial produce consumed in the interior enter Poland, so that there is little doubt as to Prussian sympathy, and even active co-operation with the Czar, who thus, though wanting the materials for powder, was always abundantly supplied with powder itself. It is simply folly to suppose that Prussia could shut her eyes to the nature of the merchandise passing her frontier into Russia in such unwonted profusion; and the more so as at this time a Russian Colonel had arrived at Dantzic on a mission which was kept a profound secret, even by the Prussian Government, though there was little doubt as to the nature of the secret.

Some idea as to the extent to which arms were shipped from the Belgian port of Antwerp alone may be gathered from the following list of vessels, as furnished from the Customs' returns obtained by the British authorities there. The arms were chiefly of Liege manufacture, so that our Belgian ally must have been pretty nearly as active as our Prussian ally.

List of vessels : —

Spiridion, Cito, Alexander, Puffenborg, Thetis, Amicitia, Earl Powis, Azoff, Margaret (the last three English), *Jeannette, Marie, Josephine, Laurent, Currstuck.* The *Spiridion* was a Greek vessel. Others were suspected.

CHAP. VII.

TRANSACTIONS OF THE SQUADRON AT HANGO.

ON the 20th of May, the squadron anchored off Hango Head in twenty fathoms, and Sir Charles reported to the Board his arrival with the following ships: *Duke of Wellington, Edinburgh, St. Jean d'Acre, Cæsar, Cressy, Princess Royal, Hogue, Blenheim, Impérieuse, Magicienne, Gorgon,* and *Dragon.* Rear Admiral Corry had been left off Dager Ort with eight sail of the line.

The object of the Admiral in entering the Gulf of Finland with so small a force, was, as has been said, in the hope of drawing the Russian fleet out; but, failing in this, he stationed a squadron of frigates between Hango Head and Sweaborg, to watch the motions of the enemy, and to communicate the same to him. The batteries at Hango Head, he reported to the Admiralty, could be destroyed if necessary, but with considerable loss of life, which their importance scarcely warranted; besides which, if he destroyed them, he had no force to hold the place, so that their capture would not do any good.

Some of the captains being, however, anxious for a brush with the enemy, asked permission of the Admiral to try the range of their guns on the batteries; and as the Master of the Fleet had reported a corner of the fortress where, in his opinion, its guns would not bear upon a ship placed under cover of an intervening island, the *Dragon* was sent under the island, and told to try the range of her guns. This was ably done by Capt. Willcox, who took up a position flanking the principal fort, Gustavsward, and found that only two of the enemy's guns could be brought to bear upon him. The *Dragon* immediately opened fire; after a few shots the fort replied, and, having got her distance, hit her several times, killing one of her men. The *Magicienne* and *Basilisk* also fired some shells, in order to try their range, as did the *Hecla*. It was with great difficulty that the Admiral was able to restrain the ardour of these vessels, and he was compelled to make several signals before he could get his orders obeyed. The authorities at home agreed with the Admiral that Hango was not worth caring about.

The squadron sent forward in the direction of Helsingfors consisted of the *Impérieuse*, *Arrogant*, *Dauntless*, *Magicienne*, and *Gorgon*. They were instructed to keep a sharp look out on the Russian fleet at Sweaborg; and Captain Watson, who commanded the detached ships, was told to place his fastest ships nearest to Sweaborg, so as well to reconnoitre it, communicating with Sir C. Napier by the *Hecla*. On the 25th, the *Dauntless* returned, and Capt. Ryder reported that the weather was too hazy for him to see into Helsingfors from Renskar; he therefore proceeded through the entrance of the channel leading to Helsingfors and obtained information that 24 gun-boats had been towed out of Sweaborg, as was supposed, for Viborg. He could get no other information about Sweaborg, but learned that there were at Cronstadt 10,000 troops, besides the seamen attached to 20 line-of-battle ships, 3 large steamers, and 16 small river-boats. The line-of-battle ships were moored in couples, head and stern, across the narrow channels under the walls of Cronstadt.

Captain Ryder also got drawings of the submarine shells distributed over the inner channel. These were reported to contain 450 lbs. of powder, to be fired by galvanic batteries, as will be hereafter described. From a Danish brig he learned the loss of the *Tiger* in the Black Sea.

After writing this, Captain Ryder made a drawing of Helsingfors, and got a view of thirteen men-of-war lying at Sweaborg, which he enumerated in the order in which they lay, but which it is not necessary to repeat here.

The *Dragon* now arrived with some prizes, which the *Magicienne* took to Dantzic and Copenhagen, being directed on her return to communicate with the squadron on the coast of Courland. The *Basilisk* was sent to cruise off Renskar lighthouse; and the *St. George*, which had joined at Hango, was despatched to join Admiral Corry off Gottska Sando.

On the 27th of May, the Admiral advised the First Lord that he was waiting to see whether the Russians would come out; that he was all ready banked up, and, if they did come out, he should lead them down to Rear Admiral Corry's squadron near Dager Ort, and then dispose of them. He was, however, afraid they would not give him the chance. He was very much inclined to have taken Hango, as he could easily have done; but, on reflection that there was little use in so doing, whilst he should have lost a good many men, and, in all probability, have got some of his ships disabled at a critical moment as regarded the Russian fleet, he had refrained.

Captain Sulivan had thus reported on the forts at Hango : — " There is good anchorage for four ships between Koppskar and Maskar Islands, from whence Gustavsward fort can be already seen. Its chief lines of defence can be shelled at 2400 yards. If necessary to place a heavy ship nearer, it might be done at 2000 yards. She would be exposed to the guns on the flank of the battery, and to as many more as could be trained to that flank; but after Gustavsward was silenced, she would be in a good position for shelling the other forts and buildings.

" Skams Holm fort appears built of earth faced with wood. Ten guns on the east front seem well hid from fire, but two guns on the south flank are only in a wooden stockade, and the barracks, &c., in the rear could be easily destroyed by shells. The other fort at the head of the bay is on old Tull Holm, but the islands are not correctly placed in the chart, so that this may be a mistake. The fort has eight guns, and would be difficult to silence with a front fire, as a rock in front forms a natural glacis nearly as high as the guns. It is, however, open to flank and rear, and, after silencing Gustavsward, the steamers might move to the westward, and look into the rear flank.

" On the west side of the same island is a battery of four heavy guns, looking down the channel round Hango Head. The same steamers could take these in flank. There is a good position for two ships on the flank of Gustavsward through the opening east of Ryson Island, at a range of from 2000 to 2500 yards. I think if this fort was silenced, and its defences destroyed, the others could be so injured — not silenced — by the flank fire of shells, as materially to assist a direct attack in front. If Skams Holm battery were silenced, those on old Tull Holm, shaken as they would be by the flank fire, would be deserted or their men cut off.

"Damans Holm fort has a new square bastion with a gun on each face; but the guns on each front could be silenced by two ships placed west and south-east. Each would be exposed to the fire of the bastion guns, which, being in a large embrasure, could soon be silenced. The parapet between the guns is so loosened by loopholes that it could not stand long a close fire.

" Gust. Ad. Faste would require to be silenced at

the same time, and a ship could be so placed as to avoid the fire of the seven guns in casemates. Those on the projecting angles *en barbette* could, I think, be silenced with grape-shot. The ships would be exposed to a raking fire from Damans Holm; it would therefore be necessary to send the ships against all three batteries at the same time. This plan supposes that Gustavsward is first attacked and silenced by shell-fire at long range."

Whilst at Hango, the Admiral thus wrote of the condition of the fleet to Sir J. Graham : —

" We are improving in gunnery. I do hope the navy will never again be so reduced, and our lists never overburdened. The French system is much better than ours. A French officer can never get out of employment ; an English officer hardly ever can get employment : how, then, is it possible that he can know his duty.

" In some instances captains have not chosen their own commanders. This is wrong. A captain will generally choose the best, and he never ought to be interfered with. Patronage is the bane of the naval profession. In the French service, in the lower ranks, one half go by seniority and one half by choice, and the choice is not so abused as with us ; whilst their rules and regulations are better attended to. One Government cannot undo with the same facility what another does. This is not a recent evil ; it has been going on for years. Look back to Lord Collingwood's letters. I think he says that if he can get one lieutenant besides the first, who knows his duty, he is content. If these things are not changed, we shall come to grief — that is inevitable. I write to you, Sir James, plainly what I think. I have no object, but the good of the service. It is, in all probability, the last time my flag will ever be up, and I think it my duty to do my best to correct existing evils."

In case the Russians decided on venturing out to meet the squadron anchored off Hango, Admiral

Corry was instructed to keep well up to Dager Ort, for the reasons which have been adduced. It is more than probable that the Russians saw through the stratagem as they kept close.

On the 21st the *Hecla*, Captain William H. Hall, arrived with a prize in tow, which prize had been obtained in a gallant manner from before the batteries at Eckness, a town situated on the banks of a river twelve miles in the interior. This exploit must have shown the Russians that they were not safe, even in their own country towns, when approachable by water.

Captain Yelverton, in the *Arrogant*, and in company with the *Hecla*, was about to anchor a little beyond Teneramine, when a strong force of the enemy's troops opened fire upon both sides of the intricate channel in which the ships were, the troops being themselves protected by extensive sand banks. A few broadsides from the ships, however, soon dispersed them, and no one was hurt in either of the steamers.

Capt. Yelverton having ascertained from a pilot that three large Russian ships were loading at Eckness, eight miles to the northward of them, determined to make a dash at them, and to give the Russian troops a further lesson at the same time. Accordingly he ordered the *Hecla*—she having the lightest draught of water — to lead the way, an operation by no means easy to perform in a narrow and intricate passage, exposed, as she was, to the first of the enemy's fire, proceeding from a strong battery, as well as from a mortar, and five field-pieces, which were handled very efficiently. Capt. Yelverton soon dismounted two of these guns, and Capt. Hall dismounted and brought off three others. The Russians fought with great bravery, returning to their guns twice in the midst of the fire, and only quitting them as the guns were destroyed by the shot and shells of the steamers.

Having fought their way to the anchorage at Eckness, the steamers discovered that two of the loaded merchantmen had been run aground; when Capt. Hall dashed at the third, she being afloat, and brought her out under the fire of a battery, which the *Arrogant's* draught of water would not allow her to approach near enough to destroy. In this operation, Captain Yelverton carefully avoided injuring the town, directing the whole fire of the ships exclusively to the batteries and troops attacking them; the latter consisting, in addition to a brigade of horse artillery, of a considerable body of cavalry and infantry, moving abreast of the *Hecla* as she advanced. In such a contest, the troops, exposed to the fire of the steamers, must have suffered fearfully; but they bore it with unflinching bravery, though they could not prevent the merchantman from being carried off by the steamers. In this gallant affair Capt. Hall got a bruise on his right leg from a spent rifle-ball. The *Arrogant* had two men killed; the *Hecla*, an officer, Lieut. Read, severely wounded, and one seaman hit by a round shot, and afterwards drowned; these, with eight others slightly wounded, being all the casualties sustained by both ships.

The Russian account of this affair at Eckness,

dated May 11th, 1854, is worthy of notice.   It states
that the British ships were repulsed with trifling loss
to the Russian troops, one officer and three men
being alone killed.   The loss sustained by the British
must have been considerable.   One sixteen oared
boat was so terribly handled by Lieut. Gunning,
that it had only two rowers left when retreating!
Fearful havoc was also made of the men in the
rigging of the *Arrogant* and *Hecla*, which ships
sustained serious damage from the well directed fire
of the coast batteries.   After this, the British ships
"had not the courage to attack the town," but dis-
creetly withdrew!   The Russian account omitted to
notice that Capt. Hall landed on "the well directed
coast battery," and, in face of the Russian troops,
who bolted to a safe distance, brought off one of the
guns to the *Hecla*.   The damage done to the ships
was, in reality, trifling, unless the hulls of both being
well studded with Minié rifle balls can be so termed.
The version given by two deserters (Fins), who had
been impressed at Eckness, was the more probable, viz.
that the fire of the ships in fighting their way up
had caused terrible slaughter amongst the Russian
troops.

Whilst at Hango, Sir James Graham despatched
another of his "cautions" not to make any "rash
experiments."   On the 20th of May, he wrote to the
Admiral as follows : — "We hear a great deal of
submarine barricades by which the North Channel in
Cronstadt is closed, and an entrance into Sweaborg
out of reach of the defences.   Would it be impossible
to remove these obstructions by diving bells and

blasting under water ? In France they have a notion
that the batteries at Cronstadt might be turned by
floating batteries heavily armed, with steam power
and light draught of water, — to be used at the outside of the South Channel in the shallow water,
beyond the range of the greater part of the defences.
But if the construction succeeded, and the batteries
were passed, I do not see how this flotilla could cope
successfully with the Russian fleet of twenty sail of
the line moored ready to receive them in the inner
harbour. If anything can be done, you will discover
the best method of doing it; but ' no *rash experiments* must be tried ' which do not hold out a reasonable prospect of success."

The plan of getting up piles by means of diving
bells, and that in the presence of the enemy who
drove them down, is an engineering idea that will no
doubt amuse the Russians when they read these
pages: such an idea may be statesmanlike, but is not
half so nautical as is the French plan of floating
batteries, the chief drawback to the latter plan being
that there were no floating batteries to experiment
with. A more feasible method was that proposed by
M. Dotizac, the French Minister at Copenhagen, which
plan was forwarded to the Admiral by Mr. Buchanan. M. Dotizac suggested that if the fleet could
not get into Cronstadt, the best plan would be to
adopt Cardinal Richelieu's idea for keeping the
English out of La Rochelle, viz., to run a dam
across the Cronstadt channel, out of range of the
batteries: if this did not bring out the Russian fleet
at once to protect the channel, it must render

Cronstadt useless as a naval station for many years to come. To this plan Sir Charles Napier replied that it would require the removal of a mountain to block up the channel, and he scarcely thought the Russian gun-boats would be idle whilst the work was being done. At any rate, he had no gun-boats to superintend such an operation.

For several days afterwards the weather again became threatening, and nothing was done beyond despatching Captain Sulivan in the *Lightning* with the *Driver* to the Aland Islands, and the *Cruizer* for the Coast of Courland. On the 2nd of June, the Admiral determined to move onwards, and the *Desperate*, *Dragon*, and *Gorgon* were sent forward to mark the shoals, Mr. Campbell's yacht *Esmeralda* assisting, and the fleet shortly afterwards following, and coming to an anchor the same evening in Baro Sound.

On the following day the Master of the Fleet, and the masters of the *Edinburgh*, *Acre*, *Hogue*, and *Blenheim* were employed in surveying the anchorage of Baro Sound. On the 5th, the same officers were despatched in the *Porcupine* to reconnoitre Helsingfors and Sweaborg.

Sir Charles had reported to the Admiralty that the Russians had seven or eight sail of the line at Sweaborg, and, as far as he could learn, about twenty sail at Cronstadt, all well secured above the batteries; their front being covered with " infernal machines," so that a passage through these would be very difficult. He further informed Sir James Graham that an American ship had been towed in and out by a steamer, as the Russians would not allow her to sail out, for fear of getting foul of them. The Admiral added : " All this may be true or not, but it is quite certain that Cronstadt is impregnable ; indeed the Gulf is lined with troops on both sides. Revel was reconnoitred the other day, and the Russians made a great show. Even here, where I am lying, they are very thick. It would be easy to drive them out of the batteries at Hango, but I could not hold them; therefore it is better to let it alone. I threw a few shells from steamers into the citadel; but it would just have been as well to throw peas against their granite walls."

This opinion coincided with that of all who knew anything on the subject, including the Admiralty itself. Just at this period, Lord Bloomfield wrote to Sir Charles from Berlin : " I can well understand all you say about the impregnable state of the coast, or rather the inutility almost of attacking their strongholds; but I still hope you will be able to make an impression somewhere. In Germany it is believed that we can do the Russians no serious injury, and that our ships will get knocked to pieces if they attack the Russian batteries."

Whilst off Dager Ort, Admiral Corry wrote to Sir Charles that his division was greatly inconvenienced by fogs ; and he expressed his opinion that if the Admiral's squadron experienced similar weather, the enemy's gun-boats might pay him a visit some night during the fogs with red-hot shot. Nothing would have been more easy ; but this evidently formed no part of the Russian plan, which was to entice an attack on their batteries, about which they cared nothing, so that the ships suffered.

On the 4th of June, Sir Charles wrote to Admiral Berkeley : —

"The French squadron has not made its appearance. I hear it is at Kiel, but I suppose does not like the fogs, which are very bad. We have had two collisions and *two misses ;* one there were neither drums nor bells going, and the pilot heard the ripple of the water : so much for look-out.

"I can see Helsingfors from the top of the lighthouse here, and I stop the whole of the trade. We see eight sail of the line, three frigates, and three steamers lying there. The Cronstadt fleet don't seem inclined to surprise us as yet.

"I am going to look at Nargen, and have written to the French Admiral, telling him my plans, and asking when I am to see him. I propose, if he agrees, to leave a force here to watch the Sweaborg squadron, and go up with the rest of the fleet to Cronstadt. But if Sweden would lend a hand, Aland is the place we ought to attack ; but it could not be done without troops and gun-boats, because we must keep our ships at hand in case the Cronstadt fleet should come and disturb us."

On the following day, the admiral wrote to Sir James Graham : "I expect Admiral Corry here every day, but when the French fleet will come I don't know. My present intention is to arrange with the French Admiral to leave a force here to watch Helsingfors, and stop the trade, and then go on to Cronstadt. Of course, if I hear that Sweden intends moving against Aland, I cannot go to Cronstadt, for I should not have force enough for the three operations. I reconnoitred Sweaborg yesterday by the Master of the Fleet. It is impossible to touch them. If the bird's eye-view that is published of Cronstadt be correct, the Emperor may sleep sound."

On the 8th of June, Sir Charles Napier received an exact report as to what was going on at Cronstadt. The reports about "infernal machines" were quite correct, these being scattered in all directions. Some of them had broke from their moorings and were floating about, the Russians carefully picking up and replacing them. It was, however, generally believed that they would prove failures, and that their connection with the electric batteries in the forts would turn out to be incomplete. It was found that they would not explode by concussion, as was expected. The Russians were making prodigious exertions to equip gun-boats. Forty of these had left for the Gulf. Seventy more would be ready within a week, and 290 would be completed by August. These gun-boats were described as drawing only two and a half feet of water, and each was armed with two guns, one 60-pounder and one 74-pounder. Each boat was manned with a crew of eighty men. With this force of gun-boats it is somewhat strange that no attempt was made on the British squadron during thick weather, as Admiral Corry had surmised. It is probable that furnaces for heating shot were not forthcoming, or had been overlooked.

On the 10th of June, the Admiral apprised Sir James Graham that he had learned further that the north passage into Cronstadt was closed by a double row of piles, with granite blocks let in between them; the whole being protected by batteries. He gave it as his opinion that these piles were immoveable by divers or diving bells, so long as they were protected by an enemy.

As to the batteries at Cronstadt being assailable by floating batteries, as had been suggested by the French Emperor, Sir Charles gave it as his opinion, that this would not lead to the capture of the place, though there could not be a doubt but that floating batteries could be built with guns that would reach the enemy's forts without themselves receiving much injury. But a great number would be required, and an attack of this nature, if continued for the whole summer, would not take Cronstadt, even if the floating batteries were forthcoming. Should this mode of attack afterwards be adopted, the enemy could fill vessels with stones and sink them in the passage; and this there was no question they would do, even were it necessary to sacrifice their whole fleet for the purpose: whilst, as Sir James Graham had justly observed, if the floating batteries succeeded against the forts, they would not be capable of contending against the Russian fleet moored in the inner harbour.

On the 6th of June, Admiral Berkeley wrote to Sir Charles: "You cannot enact impossibilities. *You cannot get at the Russian fleet, neither can you destroy Sweaborg or Cronstadt. The destruction of Hango is not, to my mind, worth the lives it would cost, or the risk and ruin to some of your best ships."*

On the 9th of June, the squadron again weighed, and proceeded up the Gulf of Finland under steam, accompanied by the French screw-ship *Austerlitz.* The same evening it was obliged, an account of fogs, to anchor off Renskar lighthouse. On this day, Sir Charles sent orders to Admiral Corry to join him as quickly as possible, and apprised him that he had sent steamers to mark the shoals, so that he might steer for them in confidence, and thus come to Baro Sound.

On the 10th of June, the *Driver* and *Lightning* returned from the Aland Isles, Captain Sulivan having made an excellent examination of the forts and various approaches to them. Bomarsund was reported by him as being very strong. He was well received by the inhabitants of the islands, who told him that the forts, at present, were garrisoned by about 2500 men. The fortifications consisted of solid granite, with two tiers of guns, and were supported by three round towers. As regarded the channel, Capt. Sulivan did not think there would be water enough for large ships ; whilst, if so, there was not room enough before the fortress for more than two or three ships, which would be inadequate to reduce it. He, however, reported that a land force could be used to great advantage, if supported by ships, which for this purpose would find a secure harbour.

In accordance with this report, the Admiral wrote to Sir James Graham on the 12th, that he had anticipated him in the survey of Bomarsund, and told him that, if 10,000 troops could be spared, the fortress might be reduced, though a strong garrison would be required to hold it when taken. He suggested to Sir James, that no time should be lost, as the Emperor might send his fleet to endeavour to save Bomarsund.

The Admiral further observed that, as Admiral Corry had joined him, the whole fleet would be collected in the Gulf. He reported to the First Lord, that "the Emperor might have saved himself much trouble, as Sweaborg was so well fortified by rocks and shoals."

As to Cronstadt, if it were as strong as represented, it would be impossible to touch it. All he could do would be to offer the Russians battle, and if they did not accept it, to return and see what he could do along shore. More large ships would be unnecessary, as the Russians would not come out to fight a large force, though they might come out to fight a small one ; and unless the First Lord intended to send out troops to make an attack upon Aland, the Admiral saw no use for more ships.

To this communication Sir James replied on the 20th of June that he was "well pleased with all the Admiral's operations," and especially with the concentration of all his forces within the Gulf of Finland. The squadron would now be strong enough to prevent the escape of the Russian fleet in Sweaborg when he proceeded with the rest of the combined fleet to Cronstadt. "But this," said the First Lord,—

" I am afraid you will find unassailable. If the Russian fleet will not come out to meet you, and you find that you cannot reach them,—after having well reconnoitred the works, and having ascertained what is possible and impossible to do,— your return to the more open sea below Helsingfors would appear to be a judicious measure, every necessary precaution being taken to prevent the reunion of the Russian force, now divided at Cronstadt and Helsingfors.

" I do not see any great advantage in the capture of Bomarsund, with a serious loss both of ships and men, if Sweden stands aloof from the contest and adheres to her neutrality. If she will take a part, with the aid of her troops and gun-boats, the capture of the Aland Isles is an easy operation ; and the principal benefit will fall to her share, for she alone can hold those islands in defiance of Russia during a Baltic winter.

" I am well aware of all the difficulties of your position, and of the *impossibility* of triumphing over an enemy who will not fight you on fair terms ; *but you will discipline our fleet, and make our officers and men fit for any service.* It is a disgrace to Russia that she dares not show a ship in her own waters, and that she is driven to seek for safety under the shelter of her fortresses. It would be madness to play her game, and *to rush headlong on her granite walls,* risking our naval superiority, with all the fatal consequences of defeat, in an unequal contest with wood against stone, which in the long run cannot succeed.

" I had reliance on your prudence, which was doubted. Your brilliant courage was proved long ago ; you will now show to the world that you possess a combination of those great virtues which are necessary to make a *consummate Commander-in-Chief.*"

It had been discovered that the Minié rifles sent out to the fleet were in the case of some ships without ammunition ! and this circumstance having reached the authorities at home, the Admiral was asked to ascertain the truth of the report, which was found to have been well grounded.

On the 21st of May, the *Penelope,* Capt. Caffin, arrived from England, bringing out some twenty mates and midshipmen, who were very acceptable, though they scarcely amounted to one for each ship of the squadron. Still the Admiralty had no doubt done its best to collect even this insignificant number. The *Penelope* also brought out some petty officers and seamen.

The Admiral was at the same time apprised that some old steamers would shortly join him, viz., *Cuckoo*, *Otter*, *Zephyr*, *Pigmy*, &c. "If he could make a bonfire of them, to the annoyance and detriment of the enemy, it would be the best service he could get out of such craft." If the ships were of this character, their commanders were not. One of these, Lieut. Hunt, had been formerly with the Admiral in his attack on Sidon, where he had highly distinguished himself by his bravery, and had, in consequence, received his promotion to the rank of lieutenant.

Before the squadron quitted Hango, Commodore Seymour was promoted to the rank of Rear Admiral. On the sailing of the squadron, the *Penelope* was left to watch Hango, and to send any ships arriving there on to Baro Sound. Before quitting, Sir Charles Napier apprised Admiral Parseval that he would find a steamer at Hango, and for his guidance buoys had been laid down on the reefs.

We have frequently had occasion to mention the energy displayed in Lubeck in favour of Russia. An additional movement was there set on foot, to which, as it is of the first consequence to the conduct of maritime warfare as regards neutral powers, we shall allude at some length.

A plan, favoured by the Senate of Lubeck, was put in operation: first, of making fictitious sales of Russian vessels to Lubeck citizens, and thus enabling them to escape capture; secondly, of making these fictitious transfers of Russian vessels whilst lying in the ports of other countries, and then sailing with Lubeck papers and under the Lubeck flag, the papers being transmitted to them authenticated by the Lubeck authorities; thirdly, of making such fictitious transfers of Russian vessels in foreign ports under the Lubeck flag, but with papers signed by the Lubeck consul.

In the first case, it was the opinion of her Majesty's Government that the transfer was legal, and that no capture could be made. In the latter cases, it might be made, but subject, as has been before said, to the quibbles of the Admiralty Court. An order to the Admiral and his captains to capture under such circumstances, was tantamount to an order to ruin themselves by law costs, the object of the lawyers of the Admiralty Court not being the condemnation of prizes to the use of the captors so much as the individual gain arising from disputing the prizes.

The opinion of the lawyers whom the Crown consulted differed from the Crown itself. In the first of the above cases, no capture could be made; in the second, the ships would not be duly documented; and in the third, it would be a "suspicious," i. e. doubtful case. This very opinion showed that the lawyers consulted were themselves ignorant on the subject; for, as the consuls of Lubeck in foreign ports had no power given to them to grant new papers to a ship under such circumstances, the third case never could have arisen at all, as was pointed out afterwards by our consul at Lubeck. Amidst all this discrepancy and ignorance on the subject, the Admiral and his officers were urged to capture vessels, which could either not have been condemned, or would have become the subject of endless litigation. As the object of the British fleet was not privateering, no such captures were made. In a future war, the best way of preventing the mischief — which by the treaty of Paris may now be carried on with perfect impunity — would be to lay hands on the Hanse Towns themselves at the outset.

The evil was, however, serious. The British consul at Lubeck forwarded a list of the names of thirteen Russian vessels which had been so transferred to Lubeck citizens, some from the Russian ports of Revel and Viborg.

Col. Hodges transmitted from Hamburg a still more formidable list of Russian vessels which had been similarly transferred to different persons at Hamburg, Bremen, Kiel, and Altona. This list comprised *nineteen* vessels transferred to Hamburghers, *six* to Bremen merchants, *one* to a Kiel merchant, and *thirteen* to merchants of Altona. These, with the Lubeck vessels, made a total of *fifty-two* Russian ships transferred for Russian purposes to our trusty neutral friends.

Similar transfers of Russian vessels to Swedish merchants were made with perfect impunity, Lubeck being still the port for shipping articles to Russia. The plan was to change the name of the Russian vessel, when it was remeasured by the Lubeck Custom House authorities; and the original Russian certificate was exchanged for another given by the Lubeck authorities ; this again being backed by the Swedish consul. Thus furnished, the vessels loaded at Lubeck, and sailed for Haparanda, a Swedish port in the upper part of the Gulf of Bothnia, from whence cargoes were easily transferred to Russia.

It may be useful, in case of future wars, to record what were the views of Lubeck on the legality of these fictitious transfers, viz., that when such transfers of Russian vessels lying in Russian ports were made to Lubeck citizens, they were not fictitious, but must be regarded as legal, provided the vessel so trans-ferred proceed direct from the port where the alleged transfer was made to Lubeck, for the purpose of being duly registered.

The Swedish vessels alluded to above as clearing for Haparanda, did not in reality go there, but to the Russo-Finnish ports of Christianstadt or Jacobstadt ; Haparanda being merely the pretence, if boarded by the British blockading squadron, when they were, of course, safe from capture. The only way to put a stop to this trade would have been to station a small steamer at the mouth of the river Tornea ; but there was no small steamer to station : nor could such vessels be prevented from entering the ports on the west coast of Finland, without numerous small steamers, of which there were none, so that the trade may be said to have been uninterrupted.

To the credit of the Danish Government, be it said, it refused to grant certificates under such circumstances, and addressed a circular to this effect to the authorities at the various Danish ports.

On the 23rd of May, Capt. Heathcote in the

Archer detained a Dutch vessel deeply laden with wheat, coming out of the Gulf of Riga. Several other vessels bound for Riga were warned off by Capt. Heathcote, though, as it would appear, with more forbearance than was necessary, as the masters admitted they were liable to seizure, but stated that they had been induced by large offers for freight to run the risk of the blockade. On the 26th, Capt. Heathcote seized a Norwegian vessel laden with grain, and a Dutch one laden with timber, sending them to Faro Sound. A strict blockade was now established at Libau and Windau.

CHAP. VIII.

RECONNAISSANCE OF SWEABORG. —JUNCTION OF THE FRENCH FLEET
AT BARO SOUND.

SQUADRON ANCHORS OFF SWEABORG. — SURVEY OF THE CHANNELS. — MR.
BIDDLECOMBE'S REPORT ON HELSINGFORS AND SWEABORG. — PREPOS-
TEROUS EXPECTATIONS OF THE ADMIRALTY. — ARRIVAL OF THE FRENCH
FLEET AT BARO SOUND. — LISTS OF THE COMBINED SQUADRON. — NO
SUPREME COMMANDER. — EVILS OF DIVIDED COMMAND. — EXAMINA-
TION OF PLANS AND CHARTS OF SWEABORG. — COMPLIMENT PAID TO
CAPTAIN LAURENCIN. — SIR C. NAPIER'S STATEMENT OF OPERATIONS. —
SATISFACTION OF THE GOVERNMENT. — ANALYSIS OF ADMIRAL CHADS'
REPORT ON THE FORTIFICATIONS OF SWEABORG. — SWEABORG BE-
LIEVED TO BE IMPREGNABLE. — SWEDISH ACCOUNT OF SWEABORG. —
EXAMINATION OF PASSAGES INTO THE GULF OF RIGA. — ADMIRAL
SENDS TO STOCKHOLM FOR VOLUNTEERS, AND TRANSMITS TO SIR JAMES
GRAHAM, A SECOND TIME, THE PLAN OF A GUN-VESSEL. — BLOCKADE ON
THE COAST OF COURLAND. — INADEQUACY OF THE BLOCKADE ORDERS.
— REMARK OF THE CZAR ON THE SAFE ARRIVAL OF HIS GUN-BOATS AT
SWEABORG.

On the 12th of June the squadron anchored off Sweaborg, as near as it was prudent for the fleet to approach with safety, from the anchorage being new,
and — except from charts obtained from Sweden,
which charts had yet to be tested — indeed unknown. Despite his cautions "against granite walls,"
and "*especially Sweaborg*," to use the words of Sir
James Graham, the Admiral lost no time in making
himself acquainted with all which pertained to the
place.

On the day of his arrival, the *Impérieuse* and *Basilisk* were at once sent in to see what they could make
of the enemy's squadron; and they observed seven or

eight sail of the line, one frigate, and some smaller vessels at anchor inside; but these showed no intention of coming out to molest them.

The next object was to survey the channels, and more especially Miolo Roads, which constituted the outer roadstead of Sweaborg. There was not a pilot on board any of the ships who knew anything of the anchorages within the Gulf, much less of the channels leading to Sweaborg; this being ascertained by the Master of the fleet, Mr. Biddlecombe, having communicated with the whole of the pilots. The survey had to be made by the Masters themselves.

The Master of the fleet and Mr. Moriarty, the Master of the *Duke of Wellington*, were therefore sent in the *Bulldog*, accompanied by the *Driver* and *Basilisk*, to survey the passage into Miolo Roads and the eastern channel leading to Sweaborg, which survey was completed in a masterly manner and without molestation from the enemy.

The following is Mr. Biddlecombe's report: —

HELSINGFORS AND SVEABORG.

Renskär lighthouse in Barö Sund, being well seen nearly 20 miles distant, affords a good object for proceeding eastward towards Sveaborg, which, with the cathedral dome at Helsingfors, are readily seen 15 miles, and enable you to determine your position sufficiently in coasting; and when the island of Nargën is seen, its lighthouse is another good object. Otherwise there would be much difficulty, as the sameness of the coast defies your determining any point positively when some distance seaward, which is necessary from the numerous shoals extending off the shores.

Stora Miölö Island, about 50 feet high, is well defined at its western part, where it is covered with trees, with a look-out house on its southern extremity. At its eastern part it is low and barren. There are a few huts called a farm on its northern side, sheltered by trees.

Torra Miölö is also wooded, and its east and west sides are well defined.

Grohara Beacon, 50 feet high, is a remarkable object. On the Admiralty chart, No. 2224, copied from the Swedish survey, and also No. 2246, from the Russian survey, it is placed on the *wrong islet*.

Its position on the Swedish chart should be on the S.W. part of Stor Enskar; and in the Russian on the S. part of Grohara Island, instead of the island N.E. of it, as described; as proved by my angles.

Outer Gräskärs are rocks about 3 feet above water, well fixed in the Russian chart.

Liubim or Arrans Ground, and New Ground. The few hours we had did not enable us to determine their positions; but, in the Baltic Directions, page 98., the Grohara Beacon is described as a mark to be used in line with Sveaborg castle, N. by E. ½ E. to clear them. I have already described the Grohara Beacon as being on Stor Enskar of the Swedish chart, and therefore it cannot be in that bearing when in line with Sveaborg castle; consequently great caution is necessary.

West Tokan Islet by the Russian survey is well placed. It is bare and knob-like, about 20 feet high. This islet, with the west part of Stora Miölö, the cathedral of Helsingfors, and the Grohara Beacon (on Stor Enskar, Swedish chart), enables you to determine your position well when passing up the channel to Sveaborg, and also enables you to take up an anchorage to await pilots, if you do not know the channel.

We anchored in 32 fathoms, mud; the cathedral of Helsingfors N. 2° 30′ W., extreme west part of Stora Miölö 12° 30′ E., and West Tokan N. 38° E., where, it may be well to observe, that although we had mud, there were very different soundings, such as sand and gravel, in the neighbourhood.

N

CHANNEL TO SVEABORG.

The channel used by the Russians appears difficult, except when it is buoyed, as it is by them in the season; that being, however, impracticable, I proposed to try a channel to pass eastward of Stora Miölö, and entered on the line south of that island: the soundings confirmed my opinion that a proper channel could be obtained, which was afterwards proved to be the case.

The cathedral of Helsingfors N $\frac{1}{3}$ W., Grohara Beacon N. by W. $\frac{1}{2}$ W., and the west part of Stora Miölö, N. $\frac{3}{4}$ E. is a good position to make for, when you will see the Outer Gräskär rocks. Then steer eastward, keeping the island of Stora Miölö open on your port bow until the west part of that island bears N. $\frac{1}{4}$ W., when it will be in line with the hollow of the land at Kungs Sound, as described in the sketch; keeping that bearing or steer up with it till the Grohara Beacon comes in one with the easternmost of the Svartbodan rocks bearings N. W. by W. $\frac{1}{2}$ W., where there is a good muddy anchorage of one mile in extent; then steer for the centre of Stora Miölö Island until Helsingfors cathedral comes in one with the west part of that island bearing N.N.W. $\frac{1}{2}$ W., from which position you should steer to the N.E., keeping *fully* half a mile from the island. There is a shoal described in the chart of $3\frac{1}{2}$ fathoms; we passed just outside it in $6\frac{1}{2}$ fathoms. When the north part of the islet Miölö Knekt comes open of the N.E. point of Stora Miölö, haul up to the northward, and on to the anchorage inside Stora Miölö; *the bottom is loose sand and gravel, consequently not good holding ground*, but closer to Stora Miölö the bottom may be better, where vessels would be well sheltered.

The points of Bak Holmen and Kungs Holmen are low, which enabled us from the paddle-box boat of the steamer *Bulldog* to see, between those islands, the main deck ports of the enemy's ships.

The only fortifications in view from our extreme position were 6 guns at the signal station, on the S.W. part of Bak Holmen.

The reader will be able to judge from this masterly survey by Mr. Biddlecombe, whether it would be possible to take a fleet in the winter into Miolo Roads, without pilots, beacons, and buoys, in the midst of heavy gales, and with *"holding ground of sand and gravel!"* Yet it will be hereafter shown that Sir Charles Napier was expected by the Board of Admiralty to choose a "fine day at the end of October" —when fine days there were none—and take his fleet up to Sweaborg to attack the Russian fortifications. When Admiral Dundas afterwards bombarded the place with his mortar vessels, he said that "from rocks under water and awash, there was hardly room to lay a gun-boat," much less a line-of-battle ship; and though it had been well surveyed by Captain Sulivan, *the Merlin had got on shore on a rock that had been missed.*

Let us suppose a Russian fleet off the Isle of Wight, as a British fleet was off Sweaborg; that all the buoys and marks were removed, as at Sweaborg; and that no pilots were to be had. What should we have thought, had the Russian Government urged their Admiral to run his fleet into Portsmouth Harbour! though this would have been an easier feat than to have run the British fleet into Sweaborg? What, then, must the British nation think of the Board of Admiralty goading on Sir Charles Napier to run thus madly on Sweaborg, after all along cautioning him "not to run his head against stone walls?" Surely they must have been thought incapable of comprehending what ships could do, or of deliberately sacrificing the fleet to satisfy popular clamour. Yet these very men still direct the movements of British fleets; and though throughout the

campaign in the Baltic they highly eulogised the
prudence and ability of Sir Charles Napier, some
amongst them have since, individually and personally, been actively engaged in the endeavour to
ruin his reputation, which they themselves had so
materially enhanced. But more of this in its place.

It will have been seen that Mr. Biddlecombe had
not, in this survey, gone further than Miolo Roads,
and could, therefore, give no opinion on a nearer
approach. It was arranged, on his return to the
Duke of Wellington, that, early on the following morning, he should return and place buoys for the fleet at
the muddy anchorage above described. Whilst preparing to do so, the fleet was signalled to weigh, and
he was directed to shape its course for Baro Sound.

The cause of this sudden alteration of purpose for
the moment was as follows: Captain Sulivan, in
the *Lightning*, had arrived in the middle watch, and
reported the arrival of the French fleet off Baro
Sound, which had been thoroughly surveyed before.
It was therefore necessary, no less as a point of national etiquette than of safety, that the British squadron should suspend its operations, and join its allies,
the services of Mr. Biddlecombe being especially required to pilot both fleets to the anchorage in Baro
Sound, notwithstanding the intention of the Admiral
to go on with the survey of the Sweaborg channels.

At 10 A.M., Admiral Parseval saluted the British
squadron, which hoisted French colours and returned
the salute. Commodore Seymour, with Mr. Biddlecombe, went on board the French Admiral to place
the British steamers at his disposal to tow the French
sailing ships to the anchorage, with which they were

unacquainted. These services being accepted, the combined squadron stood into Baro Sound, where they came to an anchor shortly after mid-day.

The Allied fleet now consisted of the following ships : —

FRENCH SQUADRON.

Sailing Ships of the Line.—L'INFLEXIBLE (Flag of Vice Admiral Parseval), HERCULE, JEMMAPPES, TRIDENT, LE TAGE, DUGUESCLIN (Flag of Rear Admiral Penaud), DUPERRÉ, and the screw ship of the line AUSTERLITZ.

Sailing Frigates.—SÉMILLANTE, ANDROMAQUE, VENGEANCE, POURSUIVANTE, VIRGINIE, and ZÉNOBIE.

Steam Frigate.—DARIEN.

Steamers. — PHLEGETHON, SOUFFLEUR, MILAN, LUCIFER.

Total, 19 vessels.

BRITISH SQUADRON.

Screw Steamers of the Line.—DUKE OF WELLINGTON, ST. JEAN D'ACRE, PRINCESS ROYAL, ROYAL GEORGE, JAMES WATT, NILE, CÆSAR, MAJESTIC, CRESSY, EDINBURGH, BLENHEIM, HOGUE, and AJAX.

Sailing Ships.—NEPTUNE (Flag of Rear Admiral Corry), ST. GEORGE, PRINCE REGENT, MONARCH, BOSCAWEN, and CUMBERLAND.

Paddle Steamers.—PENELOPE, MAGICIENNE, BASILISK, DRIVER, PORCUPINE, PIGMY.

Surveying Vessels. ALBAN, LIGHTNING.

Hospital Ship.—BELLEISLE.

Total, 27 ships.

Total combined fleet, 47 ships.

When the French Admiral joined, Sir Charles Napier ceased to have sole command, except of his own squadron. Sir James Graham had before instructed him that the supreme command was vested in neither Admiral, but that each would be independent of the other, though acting in concert. Sir James had hence pointed out to Sir Charles the necessity of cordiality, both as regarded opinion and action.

It will be better, perhaps, to give the precise instructions of the First Lord on this point, as written to the Admiral on the 28th of May. " The French fleet will have joined you in large force, and I hope that the most friendly and confidential relations will have been established between you and the French Admiral. The conjoint service of the Allied fleet cannot be conducted on any other footing. The supreme command not being vested in either of you, mutual confidence and forbearance must be the rule, and the general plan of operations must be the result of previous concert and deliberation."

The evil attending instructions of this nature, whereby divided command was enjoined for an object which required undivided purpose, as emanating from one mind, has been but too often exemplified during the late war, and indeed in all wars, whenever it has taken place. After the battle of the Alma, it is now pretty generally understood that the reason why Sebastopol was not at once entered, was, that the generals in command could not agree upon the point, when one general gave way to another, whereby a protracted siege was entailed upon the Allied army—

a circumstance which afterwards even tended to lessen cordiality of operation. Much more was this divided command undesirable as regarded the operations of fleets. This was no fault of the Admirals themselves, who were bound by their instructions. But as experience of the evils of divided command existed, it should have been taken into consideration by the Allied Governments, which ought to have provided, that either Sir Charles Napier or Admiral Parseval should have assumed the supreme command. Sir Charles Napier, had this course been pursued, would willingly have acted as second in command to Admiral Parseval, and no doubt Admiral Parseval would not have considered it derogatory to his professional reputation to have acted as second in command to Sir Charles Napier, had the Allied Governments so provided. The experience and the opinions of both Admirals would have been equally available, and their object would have remained the same, though the operations to be undertaken and the mode of conducting those operations might have been different. The instances where divided command has succeeded in its common object are indeed few ; and the reasons why it ever has been, and must ever be so, are not difficult to estimate. The Duke of Wellington, when once asked to go to Canada to co-operate with the Admiral there, replied, in his usual pithy manner, "I will go, provided the Admiral be placed under my orders, or myself under the Admiral's orders, but not otherwise." The Duke did not go to Canada. In the Baltic we had two commanders-in-chief and a general all independent of each other, and therefore without that strict unity of opinion which is indispensable to oneness of purpose.

Considering the relations of the Allied forces during the whole war, the most natural, and even efficient, division of command, would have been that the military force should have been under the direction of the French authorities, whilst the naval force should have been under the English Admiral; an unity of purpose would thus have been secured, whilst the *amour-propre* of both nations would have been satisfied.

In obedience to their instructions, the French and British Admirals lost no time in examining the plans of Sweaborg which had been furnished by the British Government. Others had been obtained from different sources in Sweden, where the Admiral had made the best use of his opportunities, whilst at Elgsnabben, having there procured information far more correct than that which had been furnished by the Government at home. He had obtained charts giving better, but still imperfect, information on this point. He had also procured plans of the fortress, whilst at Elgsnabben, together with other particulars, detailed at great length, and implicitly to be relied on. In addition to this, the in-shore squadron had been indefatigable in surveying the approaches, even to within gun shot of the enemy. The Miolo Roads had been accurately surveyed, as had also the eastern passage to Sweaborg, as far as it could be undertaken without coming under the fire of the fortress. In short, every necessary information had been obtained both from extraneous sources, and afterwards from careful examination on the spot.

After the most mature consideration of the very complete information which had thus been obtained, both Admirals decided that, *without gun- and mortar-vessels*, and without laying down beacons up to the fortifications, which would have been a long process, and could only have been effected under cover of gun- and mortar-boats, an attack on Sweaborg was perfectly impracticable.   Indeed, when Russia wrested Sweaborg from Sweden, the fortress in its then condition had resisted all attacks from the Russian army and navy combined, and was at length only captured by bribing the commander.

It has been said that the French line-of-battle ship *Austerlitz* had for some time preceded the French fleet, and had been under the orders of Sir Charles Napier.   When giving her up to the French Admiral, Sir Charles Napier paid a well-merited compliment to her commander, Captain Laurencin, on the manner in which his ship had been conducted.   So satisfied was the British Admiral of her efficiency, that on forming line of battle, with the hope that the Russians would have accepted, he had appointed Captain Laurencin to lead the fleet on one tack ; and he informed Admiral Parseval that, had opportunity offered, he was quite satisfied that Captain Laurencin would have sustained the honour of the French flag and justified the Admiral's choice.

On the 20th of June, the Admiral wrote fully to Sir James Graham with regard to what had been done by the fleet, and what was capable of being done.

Neither matter can be better related than in the Admiral's own words:—

" I have now before me the Duke of Newcastle's instructions, and all your letters. I have carefully studied them, and think I have accomplished them.

" You say, ' a complete blockade of the Gulf of Finland ' must be my first operation, as well as the occupation of an anchorage within the Gulf, where I can command a supply of water. That is done. You then wish me to look at Aland, and see what can be done there. That is accomplished also, and I send you the plans by this mail.

" I have also sounded up to Sweaborg, and can take the fleet up to Miolo Roads; but as for going into Sweaborg, it is quite impossible. The entrance into the harbour, I understand from several Captains of colliers, and from the pilot of the *Majestic,* is not much wider than the length of this ship ; and across the passage a three-decker is placed, ready to be sunk. Besides this, all the beacons are removed, and the smoke alone, without guns, would defend the harbour. *The only way to take Sweaborg would be by a large military force occupying the islands, and throwing shells into it. I send you Admiral Chads' report on the subject.*

" I now come to our future operations. We have three courses to follow. The first, is to lie here all summer, and be content with the blockade of the Gulf of Finland. That won't please the people of England.

" The second, is to go to Cronstadt, offer battle to the Russian fleet,—which they won't accept,—or attempt the harbour. I look on the latter to be impossible. The channel is narrow, very shallow, and the batteries would destroy you if you succeeded in getting into the channel, as only one ship can enter at a time. This information I have on reliable authority.

" The third, is to attempt the Aland Isles. To do this, as we have no troops, it would be necessary for the whole fleet to proceed to the anchorage pointed out in Captain Sulivan's chart,—leaving vessels in the entrance of the Gulf only, to watch the Helsingfors squadron,—land all the marines and the French troops, which would amount to 5000 men,—land a great number of heavy guns, and lay siege to Bomarsund, attacking at the same time in front, if found practicable,—if not, landing 10,000 seamen, and making soldiers of them. I lean to this, and shall propose it to the French Admiral. If we succeed, it will be a great *coup*. If we fail, we cannot have much loss; and if the Russian fleet come out to raise the siege, we shall be sure of taking them.

"Whether you would like this plan in England I cannot tell. If it is not decided on—which I do not expect—we shall probably go up to Cronstadt, and that will give the Government time to send us a few troops if possible : if not, either to sanction or forbid the operation.

" I have no vessels to blockade with higher up the Gulf. I have stationed six from Libau to Odensholm, and across to Hango ; four steamers in the Gulf of Bothnia, which is not half enough, as the whole trade will be carried on from Sweden. It takes one to do the duty between this and Dantzic, two frigates and a steamer across from Helsingfors to Revel, and I must always keep three with the sailing fleet, besides the surveying vessels. The French are going to send two frigates off Revel, at my request, but the Admiral will not part with any steamer from his fleet.

" Since writing thus far, I have been on board the French Admiral. He has some doubts about the policy of attacking Bomarsund, as well as the propriety of doing it without troops. He thinks it better to go to Cronstadt first, as it would be of little use going to Bomarsund unless we attacked it. I have fallen into his views, and decided to go to Cronstadt.

" I shall leave Admiral Corry off here with his squadron, two French line-of-battle ships, two frigates, and the *Ajax*, and will go to Cronstadt with the screws, six French ships, and one or two frigates.

" I shall come back as soon as possible, and hope to find some troops here, or that Sweden has consented to assist ; for if we do not attack the Aland Islands I don't see what else we can do."

The Admiral further explained to Sir James Graham that it was his wish that Admiral Parseval should leave the French fleet to guard Sweaborg, but that he did not consent to the proposition, because he thought it was but right that the French force should accompany the British squadron to Cronstadt.

To the preceding communication from the Admiral, Sir James Graham replied, on the 27th of June, that he was glad he was going to Cronstadt, to see with his own eyes what it might be possible to do there. " Whatever man can do," said Sir James, " I am certain will be done by you ; and if you are restrained by a sense of duty *from embarking in any desperate enterprise,* on your return to Baro Sound you shall receive full instructions from me respecting an attack on the Aland Islands." Sir James Graham highly approved of Sir Charles having acquiesced in the opinions of Admiral Parseval, at the same time giving him cogent reasons why he should continue so to do.

Admiral Berkeley, with all the frankness which distinguished his communications, wrote to the Admiral on the same day : " *You are giving the Government satisfaction, and the Board, by your general proceedings.* We all feel—no one more than myself—that *nothing can be done against such places as Helsingfors and Cronstadt ;* and I have the most full reliance that, had anything been possible, you would have attempted it. *They won't come out, and you can't get in. A strict blockade is all that can be expected. At Sebastopol, nothing can be done by ships.*"

The following is an analysis of Admiral Chads' report on the fortifications, dated 14th of June, 1854:—

1st. The fortifications of Sweaborg are built of granite blocks, and are formed on several small islands and rocks united by two bridges. The fortifications are of large extent, mounting 2000 guns of the largest calibre, and altogether are of enormous strength.

2nd. These fortifications are surrounded by deep water channels, and command the entrance to the harbour, which is only two or three hundred yards wide. The Russian ships lie, for mutual support, in a line close up to the forts at the entrance.

3rd. From the position and strength of these fortifications, they must be considered as unassailable but at immense sacrifice of life and loss of ships; and even then an attack would be of very doubtful success, as all attacks on them must be made by ships.

4th. As no attack can therefore be made on these forts with a fair hope of capture, it remains to be considered how the enemy's ships lying there can be destroyed, as well as the arsenal, and other buildings within the forts.

5th. I should propose a combined land and sea force posted on the island of Sandhamm, to be supported by the fleet lying outside of the island, with their boats ready, and a steam flotilla within, to guard the various passages against annoyance from the enemy's gun-boats. This force should consist of 6000 troops, and 3000 or 4000 seamen and marines.

6th. The nearest part of Sandhamm lies upwards

of 2500 yards from the fortifications, consequently too distant for any serious interruption to works thrown up upon it. From this point, guns ranging 5000 yards will cover every part of the harbour, and the enemy's fleet would not be secure, but might be destroyed.

7th. I should propose that forty guns of large calibre, such as are now being constructed, should be prepared, and placed in battery on Sandhamm, with a supply of 250 or 300 rounds of ammunition per gun, which is probably as much as the guns would stand with safety. Similar guns might also be placed on board the steamers, to increase the annoyance to the forts.

In addition to this report by Admiral Chads, Mr. Biddlecombe, the Master of the Fleet, had made a minute survey of Miolo Roads, and the channel leading to Sweaborg, which report had been forwarded home, and had been printed by order of the Admiralty.

It will distinctly have been seen that, in the opinion of Admiral Chads, Sweaborg could not have been taken by any available means; but that, with forty Lancaster guns, the ships, arsenal, &c., might be destroyed. At this time there was not one Lancaster gun on board the fleet, though *one* was afterwards brought out by the *Vulture* and put on board the *Edinburgh*. It is then clear that the " guns of large calibre " were not supplied to the fleet, which therefore could not be in a condition to destroy the Russian shipping, &c., according to the plan of Admiral Chads, even if the Admirals had agreed that Sweaborg was assailable. It was this want of means which made the Admirals agree that an attack on Sweaborg was perfectly impracticable. Even on the 27th of June, Sir James Graham wrote that only "*eight* Lancaster guns were ready, and *very few of the shells;* the experiments are still in progress, and are not complete." We must request the reader to bear these matters in mind.

Independently of the plans of attacking Sweaborg above alluded to, the Admiral had procured from a Swedish source an account of the fortress, which of itself supplied more accurate information than any which he had the means of acquiring. The information alluded to is so complete in itself that we subjoin it, as being no less masterly than complete:—

" SWEABORG is built upon five islands, or rocks, in the Gulf of Finland. Three of these rocks—Western Swarto, Little East Swarto, and Great East Swarto—lie in sight of the town of Helsingfors, from 2000 to 2600 yards distant. From this side they protect Vargo, which is separated only by a narrow sound—partly filled up—from Vargskarsholme, situated at the entrance of the harbour. Langoren is a sixth separate island, which is also fortified, and on the western side of the small entrance generally used by merchant ships.

" On all these islands a mass of fortifications is built, chiefly of granite ; these are as solid as the rocks on which they stand. The surrounding water forms natural ditches to the forts; but still ditches are here and there excavated out of the rocks. The works are partly regular, broken with bastions, and partly irregular, but form together a fort of the first order. Vargo is the most important point of the fortress. It is surrounded by casemated fortifications, broken into six bastioned fronts with *tenaille* works here and there between them ; and has a very strong interior work crossing the fortifications, and forming two bastioned fronts. In the centre of them again is a keep of several tiers, including a courtyard, in which Ehrensward's tomb is situated. On the south side, towards Vargskarsholme, is a ravelin and a covered way, with a glacis running along the beach. Towards the sound, between Vargo and Great Eastern Swarto, are the docks, protected by walls of masonry of bastioned form, with a bridge leading over to the latter island. The fortification contains large stores and magazines, most of them bombproof; and roomy barracks for the garrison, some of which are not bombproof.

" Gustafs-sward is a fort on Vargskarsholme, which, with a triple line of batteries, commands the large entrance, said to be only fit for large ships. The fortifications close to this entrance consist of a casemated strandwork in *tenaille* form, within which is another work, with open terre-pleins, and an inner defence of bastion-formed masonry. Within this is a casemated bastioned front with batteries *en barbette;* and within this again is a very narrow triangular work with bastioned fronts—here and there studded with casemates and open terre-pleins. The large fort called the ' King's Gate ' opens here towards the entrance to the harbour.

" Great Eastern Swarto has, towards the harbour and its entrance, bastioned lines with open batteries. On the north side is the rope-yard, protected by single walls, with embrasures and caponniers flanking them. To protect the passage to Vargo a hornwork and one crownwork are built—the crownwork consisting of barracks forming two bastioned fronts. The wings of the hornwork are also barracks adapted to defence.

" Little Eastern Swarto is surrounded by bastions and *tenaille* lines, the former with casemates and open terre-pleins. Immediately behind the curtain of the front, situated towards the western entrance, is the arsenal. On this island is the dockyard belonging to the fort.

" Western Swarto has, towards the sea, two bastioned fronts, with guns *en barbette*, containing barracks, bakehouse, magazines, and hospitals.

" LANGOREN.—The fortifications here consist, towards the
sea, of a large bastion closed in the gorge by an intrenchment, with a casemated bastion on each side.   Towards the
harbour there is only a strandwork, with inner defence from
the intrenchment.   The walls of this intrenchment are—as
the walls generally are—twenty-eight feet high, but those of
the large bastions and the strandwork are only fourteen
feet.

" Opposite Gustafs-sward, and on the other side of the
entrance, is an island called Skanslandt.   Here the point
nearest the entrance is cut off by a covered way, behind
which is a *flèche* of brickwork.   This fortification seems
to be intended for the protection of troops retreating from
Skanslandt.

" From a view wholly tactical, Sweaborg can only be considered as a sea fortress, without any other influence on the
defence of the country than the protection it can afford the
fleet which is indispensably necessary for the protection of
the extensive coast of Finland; as well as a *dépôt* during
war for materials necessary for the defence of the country.
Still its situation on isolated rocks and islands makes the
communication with the mainland very difficult; and an
army which has got a firm stand in Helsingfors and its
neighbourhood, and which is supported by a fleet, is able to
cut off the communication altogether.

" The distance between the fort and the town is, nevertheless, not greater than that the town may be totally
destroyed by fire from the fort; as well as it may be very
much annoyed from batteries on commanding heights in the
neighbourhood of the town.   The Russians, during the war
in 1808, constructed batteries on the Skatudden and Ulricasborg—the extremities of the town on the east and west—
which caused great damage in the fort, by setting part of it
on fire.

" I now come to the force of the garrison and ordnance.

" Although it may be impossible at present to ascertain
the actual condition of either the one or the other, it seems
probable that the garrison is not now less than it was during

the war in 1808, when it consisted of between 7000 and 8000 men, or, more accurately, of 200 officers and 7386 non-commissioned officers and privates, 720 of whom were sailors. The ordnance, which at the capitulation was delivered up to the Russians, consisted of 50 brass and 1975 iron guns of different calibre, part of which were mortars.

" It is difficult to point out the weak points of the place, as the fortifications in general are pretty equal in strength as relates to their site. The Langoren and Western Swarto seem the most accessible points. Vargo is weakest on the north-western side, where the fortifications partly consist of single walls, inclosing the dockyard and a powder magazine, which, when those walls are breached, may, by direct fire, be reached and destroyed. But before trying an assault, it is necessary to have for several days incessantly cannonaded and shelled the fort, to effect every possible destruction, and tire out the garrison, and then attack several different points simultaneously.

" Besides Ulricasborg and the southernmost point of this peninsula, both of which are said to command the fort, there are to the east and west of it several islands and rocks from which it may be possible to attack the fort, and at the same time be properly protected from its fire.

" The splinters from the granite in the walls of the fort will make the defence very dangerous to the garrison. As no sally from the fort can be made, it may suffer extremely from a close blockade, together with shelling from the islands around, as well as from the points inshore already mentioned; and the shells may be expected to cause a great destruction on many of the buildings that have not bomb-proof roofs.

" The way of proceeding to carry Ulricasborg is very difficult to determine, as it depends altogether on how the defence of this part of the country is arranged and prepared. Yet, it seems that this point can be taken by disembarking troops; the landing of which can be effected without much danger from the fire of the fort, so long as the attack by sea is superior, *i.e.*, so long as it can keep the Russian fleet at bay.

The occupation of this point would also force the enemy out of Helsingfors, because the town could be entirely destroyed from this point in a few hours. Ulricasborg, as well as Sandwicken — the harbour in the rear of the town — must have at present only field fortifications, having only been commenced building this spring, and is said to consist of two batteries on Ulricasborg, two on the heights to the north of Sandwicken, and two more on the island in the middle of the bay at Sandwicken.

" The large entrance of the harbour is about 400 feet broad; that between Langoren and Wester Swarto about 1000 feet. The distances between the different islands are from 200 to 300 feet.

" Vargo and Gustafs-sward have a great many casemated and loopholed defences. The other works have their guns mostly *en barbette,* with covered defences here and there. Vargo is the very centre of the fortress, from which all the surrounding fortifications are commanded. Gustafs-sward is chiefly meant for commanding the entrance. Both the fortifications are, for their destined purpose, most formidable, but lose their importance in proportion as their inner defences get damaged from bombardment. An assault vigorously and simultaneously enterprised against Langoren, Wester Swarto, and Little Easter Swarto, would have, after such a bombardment, great chance of success. The fortifications on these islands might, by very little labour, be transformed into breach and *ricochet* batteries, the fire from which would soon complete the destruction of the other part of the fortress."

Besides these plans, many others of the most reliable character were obtained, for which it is impossible to find space in this work. Enough has, however, been adduced to show that in place of Sweaborg not having been sufficiently reconnoitred, as was alleged, a larger amount of knowledge as regarded the fortress had been obtained, both by inspection and otherwise, than had perhaps ever before been obtained of any enemy's fortress. We may safely challenge the whole naval literature of England to show such a mass of information, on the first appearance of a fleet before any fortress, as is alone contained in this chapter.

Captain Cumming, in the *Conflict*, was now despatched to join Captain Key in the *Amphion*, the station of which ship was extended to Dager Ort, in consequence of Admiral Corry's squadron having left to join the Admiral in Baro Sound. Captain Willcox, in the *Dragon*, was directed to proceed to Wormso and examine the passages in that direction, leading into the Gulf of Riga. He was also to endeavour to open a communication with Dago and Wormso, for the purpose of procuring cattle, if possible.

The crews of several of the ships not having been completed with seamen from England, the *Porcupine* was despatched to Stockholm to enter for the fleet any able-bodied seamen, Swedes or Norwegians, who might volunteer. The orders of Sir James Graham to enter foreign seamen as the squadron went along could not be carried out, as none could be obtained, partly owing to the vigilance of the Swedish and Danish governments, and partly to the unsatisfactory terms which could alone be offered. Now that the fleet was going to Cronstadt the matter became serious. Not that the Admiral had any idea of attacking Cronstadt, as he had before told the Admiralty authorities; but if the Russians now intended to fight at all, it would be before Cronstadt that they would meet the Allies; and therefore it became necessary to make every effort to strengthen the ships' companies.

On the 20th of June, Sir C. Napier the second time transmitted to Sir James Graham a plan for a gun-vessel, or rather raft, which had been submitted to him. The advantage was that, being solid, it could not be sunk, and hence it bore some resemblance to the plan of the Emperor Napoleon for indestructible floating batteries. The Admiral, however, told Sir James that it would be difficult to manage. There can be no question as to the utility of such batteries, as was afterwards proved at Kinburn, where one of the Emperor's floating batteries made great havoc, without being itself injured. We shall, however, have to return to this subject farther on, so will not pursue it here, except to remark that, in face of the facts scattered through our narrative hitherto, it is difficult to conceive how Sir James Graham could have afterwards told Parliament, that, had Government been apprised in time that such means were wanted, they could easily have been supplied.

On the 14th of June Capt. Key made a report of his blockade on the Coast of Courland. Since his previous visit to Riga the *Amphion, Conflict,* and *Archer* had again been in, and had examined the anchorage at Pernau and Riga. Nothing was visible at the former place, and Riga was much in the same state as on Capt. Key's previous visit. The ships were not, however, fired at from the forts.

Since Capt. Key was first entrusted with the duty of blockading the coast of Courland two ships had been cruising off the entrance of the Gulf of Riga, in a passage limited *by the shoals* to a breadth of three

miles. If the reader will refer back to the efforts
made at Memel to get vessels of light draught through
the shoals, he will see how impossible it was for
Capt. Key, with his class of ships, to have prevented
such traffic.   This could only have been done by
small steamers, of which the fleet had none adapted
to this purpose.   Two other ships passing between
Windau and Memel laboured under the same disadvantage.   The orders to the cruisers were, that if
any doubt existed as to the knowledge of the blockade,
vessels were to be released, and under these orders
no less than 154 vessels had been warned off since the
establishment of the blockade, instead of being captured.   Of course, those which had taken in cargoes
at Riga, in defiance of the public intimation of
blockade, could not plead the excuse, as could those
coming from distant ports, and were detained and
sent to England.

So little were the blockade orders deemed adequate
to the purpose, and so many chances were there of
escape, that on the 20th of June the Admiralty gave
notice to Sir Charles Napier that a British Steam Navigation Company was being organised to run between
Dunkirk and Memel, with a view of evading the blockade. Indeed, so many were the opportunities of carrying on a trade with Russia, through the medium of
Prussia, that the traffic may be said to have been
scarcely interrupted.   It was only when vessels,
tempted by high rates of freight, ran the risk of
sailing direct from Russian ports, that they were
captured ; those conveying goods to Russia being in
little danger, as an excuse, coming within the above

orders, could readily be found, as, if detected, they could make for a Prussian port, instead of going direct to a Russian port. Danish vessels appeared to be the most daring. On the 21st of June, Capt. Heathcote, in the *Archer*, captured three, which were boldly coming out of the Gulf of Riga.

In the same way Lubeck ships came from Russia to Copenhagen. Vice Consul Blackwell reported several to Mr. Buchanan, as having arrived at Copenhagen from Nordland, according to the "Travemunde list," but in reality from Christianstad, in Finland, with full cargoes of pitch, tar and planks. These had evaded Admiral Plumridge's squadron, no doubt by skulking amongst the islands; and it was very probably a knowledge of such practices, which he could not prevent for want of small steamers, that induced Admiral Plumridge to destroy all the Finnish naval stores within reach, as will be narrated in the next chapter.

Singular to say, on the 19th of June the Board of Admiralty transmitted to Sir Charles Napier a somewhat hard rap on its own knuckles for not supplying the class of steamers so requisite amongst the shoals and islands which line the whole Finnish coast; as amidst these the Russian gun-boats were passing and repassing, without the least danger of molestation, because the fleet had no class of vessels which could get at them. The Admiralty communication from a reliable source, stated the Czar to have remarked: "I have received, by courier, the gratification of knowing that the twenty-four armed gun-boats, which

I sent to Sweaborg, have arrived, *sous le nez de cette fameuse flotte anglaise.*" The communication was, no doubt, intended as a hint for the Admiral; but the hint rather suited themselves, as they must have known that ships of the line were not quite adapted to follow gun-boats amongst the rocks and shoals of the inner channels on the shores of Finland — these offering an easy transit for the enemy's gun-boats beyond the reach of molestation.

CHAP. IX.

PROCEEDINGS OF ADMIRAL PLUMRIDGE'S SQUADRON IN THE GULF OF BOTHNIA, AND OF DETACHED SHIPS ELSEWHERE.

BEFORE following the combined fleet to Cronstadt, it will be necessary to allude to the transactions of Admiral Plumridge's squadron, which, since the 5th of May, had been cruising in the Gulf of Bothnia. He had been despatched to examine the Aland Islands, but not being able to procure pilots, he considered the hazard too great. He therefore proceeded up the Gulf of Bothnia, encountering great difficulty from floes and fields of ice, in which his squadron was en- tangled up to the 30th of May. The same circum- stance had prevented him from communicating with the Commander-in-Chief, who began to feel great uneasiness at his long absence without report, and the more so, as he could gain no intelligence of his movements from the British authorities in Sweden.

Captain Buckle, in the *Valorous*, was ordered by Admiral Plumridge to make an attempt to procure pilots at Grizelhamm, but did not succeed; arriving, moreover, at the conclusion that pilots were not permitted by the Swedish Government to serve in our ships of war. He heard that there were not more than 1000 troops at Bomarsund, but could gain no information about the Russian gun-boats there. The inhabitants of Aland, he was told, were well disposed towards the British, and had refused to take up arms against us. This was all he could learn at Grizelhamm, where the Swedish officer in command was very anxious to know whether his post-boat would be intercepted, to which Captain Buckle replied that it would not, unless it contained military despatches to or from the Russian Government.

Captain Buckle then proceeded in the direction of Wardo Island and Bomarsund, capturing, on his way, a Russian bark bound from St. Ubes to Abo. At the Island of Saggo, where the bark had taken refuge, he found the village deserted, but made the master of the bark write a letter, stating that the English would not molest the inhabitants, or touch their property, but would pay for anything they had to dispose of. This letter having been left, and a Russian revenue cutter burned, Captain Buckle steered towards Bomarsund.

From the master of the bark, Captain Buckle learned that the Russians had 500 troops at Marsund, and 1500 at ports among the islands, but principally at Bomarsund. Some, he said, were stationed where he was captured, and their watchfires on the hills supported the assertion.

On approaching Bomarsund, Captain Buckle found the channels very intricate, and far from corresponding with any of the charts. Having no pilot, he proceeded cautiously, keeping the lead constantly going. He then observed the two casemated batteries at Bomarsund, which he described as having double loopholes below and embrasures on the summit. Nearing these, he observed the mastheads of several vessels over the land. Standing cautiously towards them, — the ship, however, touching the ground, as it had done at Saggo, — he anchored, in company with the *Vulture*, about a mile from the vessels. On sending in the ship's boats, they were found to be deserted, and consisted of six schooners and a brigantine, two of the schooners being fitted for gunboats. These schooners and the brigantine were brought out, and the schooners burned. As the brigantine apparently belonged to the people of the place, Captain Buckle left her untouched, as he considered it advisable to gain their good will.

From the discrepancy between the soundings and the charts, and from having no pilot, Captain Buckle did not deem it advisable to proceed further amongst such intricate channels, and left without molestation, though so near Bomarsund; only a few people of the village being seen at a distance. The innumerable rocks and islands were so intricate that Captain Buckle considered it unsafe to proceed farther south than

Wardo without a pilot, nor could he find the track by which he had entered; but fortunately the water was smooth, so that the ship could be steered by the eye as well as the lead.

Admiral Plumridge issued a notice to the inhabitants of the coasts, stating that he would not molest or injure private persons or their property, but the property and defences of the Russian Government alone. So long as the inhabitants continued peaceably within their houses they would be protected, but should they render assistance to the Russian troops, they would be treated as enemies.

This notice was issued by the Admiral when off Uleaborg, and preparatory to an attack on the ships and warlike stores there and in the vicinity. Contemplating the attack, Admiral Plumridge further requested that women and children should be sent out of the place.

This being done, Lieut. Priest, senior Lieut. of the *Leopard*, was sent on the 1st of June with the boats into Brakestead Harbour; where, after clearing the ice, in which the squadron had been blocked up for twenty-four hours, he inflicted the following damage:—

Ten large vessels,—one barque, one brig, three schooners and five sloops,—burned and totally destroyed.

Three detached stores of shipbuilding timber, and two detached storehouses, containing some thousand barrels of pitch, tar, and oil, totally destroyed.

The total damage being fourteen vessels, 25,000 barrels of pitch, &c., a vast quantity of materials for shipbuilding, and three building-yards, with their workshops, &c.

The inhabitants immediately yielded, and great care was taken not to damage the private houses. Lieut. Priest also spared two large stores, containing flour, which he had reason to believe was private property.

The boats employed were those of the *Leopard*, under Lieuts. Priest and Hammet; of the *Vulture*, under Lieut. Wise; and of the *Odin*, under Lieuts. Mould and Carrington. The force engaged was fourteen boats, twenty-five officers, and 279 seamen and marines, under the command of Lieuts. Thelwall and Lewis.

On the 4th of June, Capt. Giffard, of the *Leopard*, reported further destruction at the town of Uleaborg, as follows :—

Twenty vessels destroyed by Lieut. Priest's division of boats,

Three by Lieut. Graham's,

Five by Lieut. Lloyd's,

Three by Lieut. Young's;

Total, thirty-one vessels.

Besides these, 50,000 barrels of pitch and tar, 6000 square yards of rough pitch, a vast quantity of timber and shipbuilding materials, a large number of storehouses, workshops, forges, &c., with their contents, and several building-yards were totally destroyed, the estimated damage being 300,000*l*.

In this second destruction, the boats of the *Valorous* took part, under Lieut. Dent: Lieut. Fellowes and the marine officers Davis and Lewis were added to those who had been engaged at Brakestead.

Taking possession of the town of Uleaborg, Lieut. Graham examined the buildings, but none appeared to belong to the Russian Government, except the Cossack barracks in the heart of the town ; and as the destruction of these by fire would have involved the burning of a large number of private houses, if not of the whole town, containing several thousand inhabitants, he judged it better to spare them.

On the island of Ulkonargaick, Lieut. Graham destroyed several other vessels, amongst which was a barque of 600 tons, lying at anchor. At Killon Kraseli, Lieut. Lloyd performed a similar service.

On the 9th of June Lieut. Priest was again despatched to the Tornea river and town. The garrison went away at the approach of the boats. Having taken possession of the town, Lieut. Priest found that the storehouses had been cleared out, and their contents conveyed across the barrier into the Swedish territory. The public buildings and barracks had been destroyed by the inhabitants, and the boats returned to the squadron. On the same day, Lieut. Lloyd went up the Kemi river, where he destroyed a quantity of shipbuilding timber, sparing at the request of the inhabitants all that was not fit for shipbuilding.

On the 14th of June, Admiral Plumridge reported that he had despatched Capt. Glasse with the *Vulture*, to Old Carleby, on a similar errand of destruction, with instructions to bring off a small screw steamer said to be there. Capt. Glasse was afterwards to rejoin the squadron at Hallgrund Beacon.

Capt. Glasse reached Old Carleby on the 6th, but

from bad weather had to put to sea again, returning
on the following day and anchoring off Trullön
Island, the *Odin* being in company.

The boats of the *Vulture* and *Odin* were at once
sent in under the command of Lieut. Wise. Having
anchored the boats in line abreast, with their guns
pointing towards the beach, Lieut. Wise landed with
a flag of truce, for the purpose of communicating with
some persons seen on shore. The flag was duly received, and Lieut. Wise was met by the Burgomaster,
of whom he demanded the surrender of the property
of the Russian Government, in which case private
property would be respected. Not getting a satisfactory answer, and communication with the Governor
being refused, he re-embarked and directed Lieut. Carrington to proceed ahead to sound ; ordering the other
boats to weigh and form in two lines abreast. Before
the order could be executed, the Russians opened fire
on the right with field-pieces and musketry, which
was promptly returned from the boats.

The enemy were in great force, and their position
well chosen, besides being completely concealed by
wood and houses, from behind which they poured a
destructive fire, under which Lieut. Wise recalled the
boats.

He could not, however, effect this. The paddlebox
boat of the *Vulture* was destroyed by the enemy's
fire, and a severe loss of officers and men took place.
Lieut. Carrington with eleven men, in the *Odin's*
cutter, were struck down by the first fire, by which the
proximity of the enemy was first ascertained. In fact
the boats were completely taken by surprise, as an

enemy's force does not seem to have been ever dreamed of; though with two Captains present in the ships, neither of whom was with the boats, it might be thought that this fact should have been ascertained before the boats were sent in, or that one of the Captains should have accompanied the expedition in person, so as to add his judgment to the gallantry of officers of less experience.

The fact was, the Russians had a large force of regular troops present, and these well placed in ambuscade, whilst the attacking force was insignificant in comparison to the enemy it had to encounter. The wonder is that the whole expedition was not destroyed or captured. On the following day Lieut. Wise was sent with a flag of truce for the purpose of ascertaining the condition of the wounded and captured. The flag was not acknowledged! But Lieut. Wise reported on his return that a regiment of regular troops was drawn up during the time the boat remained off the beach; whilst, from the different uniforms, another regiment was engaged in throwing up earthworks with embrasures.

To encounter these two regiments, with artillery, there had unwittingly been sent 21 officers and 231 men, amongst whom sad havoc had been made. In the boats which escaped, three officers had been killed, Lieutenant Carrington and Messrs. Montague and Athorpe, and two wounded, Lieutenant Lewis and Mr. Magrath. Mr. Morphy, a midshipman of the *Vulture*, had died ashore in the hands of the Russians, making six officers, or nearly a third of the whole. Three men were killed, and fifteen wounded

returned to the ships; whilst of those captured by the
Russians nine died, and all but three were wounded.
The number of captives was twenty-eight, according
to the list of Captain Glasse; so that this ill-starred
expedition had cost six officers and forty men, without effecting anything. Nor was this destruction of
property worth going after. Very little, with the
exception of a few barrels of pitch found at Brakestead, was the property of the Russian Government.
It was the private property of shipbuilders and
others, and no small portion was English property!
upon which money had been advanced, as is customary in the English market. Apart from this, the
materials destroyed were the property of the Fins, who
had not offended us, and with whom it was politic to
maintain a good understanding, this great object
being frustrated by a wanton destruction, which gave
great pain to the Admiral Commanding-in-Chief,
and which barely comes within the pale of civilised
warfare.

A fortnight after this disaster, a gallant, though
extraordinary affair, was projected and carried out
by Captain W. H. Hall of the *Hecla*, assisted by
Captain C. M. Buckle in the *Valorous*, and Captain
F. Scott in the *Odin*.

Captain Hall had been despatched by Sir C. Napier,
with instructions to Admiral Plumridge to join the
fleet at Baro Sound, in order to procure provisions
for his squadron in the Gulf of Bothnia. On his departure, Admiral Plumridge left the squadron under
the charge of Captain Hall till his return, at the

P

same time sending instructions to the captains of the squadron to obey the orders of Captain Hall as their senior officer, in accordance with the instructions by the Commander-in-Chief, that, during the absence of Admiral Plumridge, Captain Hall would watch the enemy in the Gulf of Bothnia.

The orders of Admiral Plumridge were, that Captain Hall should proceed, in the first instance, in the *Hecla*, off Lagskaren lighthouse, which, to a distance of ten miles round, he was to consider the rendezvous of the *Valorous*, *Vulture*, and *Odin*, till Admiral Plumridge's return from Baro Sound, and where he was to leave one vessel with information where he was to be found. These orders were given on the 19th of June.

On the 21st, Captain Hall wrote to Admiral Plumridge that he had been fortunate enough to lay hold of a pilot for the southern part of the Aland Islands, and that taking advantage of this, he had gone up as far as Flaka in Rôd Bay, where he had cut out a Russian brigantine. On his return to the rendezvous, he found there the *Valorous* and *Odin*, which ships he had taken in to reconnoitre as far as Ango Sund.

On the 22nd Captain Hall reported to Admiral Plumridge that he had attacked Bomarsund! The French and English Governments had deemed it expedient to send out an army for this purpose, commanded by one of the ablest generals of France. To the surprise of every one, Captain Hall thought his three steamers sufficient for the purpose, and to work he went, with a spirit which appears somewhat to have exceeded his respect for the orders given to him by Admiral Plumridge, who, had he judged it prudent to attack Bomarsund with his whole squadron, would have made the attack had he been ordered so to do.

The details will be better given in Captain Hall's own words:—

"Adverting to my letter of yesterday, wherein I mentioned having cut out a merchant brig at Flaka and procuring pilots, I have the honour to inform you, that on my return to the rendezvous off Lagskar lighthouse, I found there H. M. ships *Valorous* and *Odin*, and proceeded with them to reconnoitre the Russian fortifications at Bomarsund.

"I thought it right to put on board both vessels a Finland pilot; and having arranged with Captains Buckle and Scott my plan of operations, and ordered them to be prepared against red-hot shot, rifle shot, and the likelihood of getting on shore, &c., I proceeded through the archipelago of the Aland Islands,—the channel being only from one to two cable lengths wide, but with not less than five fathoms water, *Hecla* leading the way in close order.

"At 4. 30 P. M. entered the narrow channel of Ango Sund, firing on the woods as we passed to prevent surprise from riflemen, and, on opening the strong casemated fortifications of Bomarsund, I made the preconcerted signal (white ensign at the main) to engage forts, and opened fire from the *Hecla*'s 10-inch guns with shot and shell, which was followed by the other ships.

"The enemy did not for some time return our fire, evidently wishing to draw us within range, which, however, I carefully avoided, finding that our shot and shell reached the fort. At 5. 35 the largest battery, a casemated battery of two tiers, mounting between 70 and 80 guns, opened on the squadron, and a masked battery of 6 guns, from the southern part of the bay, much nearer to us, opened a smart flanking fire with shot, shell, and rockets, and a body of riflemen from the same quarter kept up a continuous fire.

"I directed a heavy fire to be kept up from the ships to silence the 6-gun battery and the riflemen, which were accompanied by a body of Horse Artillery, all of which were finally driven from their position apparently with great loss.

"At 8. 50, from the numerous shoals and the danger of getting on shore whilst manœuvring and firing at the different batteries, signalised to the squadron to anchor with springs on their cables, to enable them to bring their broadsides to bear on the forts in a part of the bay least exposed to the enemy's fire, continuing the action without intermission.

"At 10 observed that the shell of the squadron had set fire to the public storehouses and buildings in the rear of the fort, and part of the fortress. At this time, nearly every shot and shell fired by the squadron appeared to take effect. The action was continued with great spirit until after midnight, when I made the signal to discontinue the engagement, the squadron *having expended nearly all their shot and shell* for the large guns, and the fire from the enemy having slackened to only an occasional shot.

"At 12. 58 weighed and proceeded with squadron in company through the same channel by which we had entered to Rôd Bay, where we anchored at 4 A. M. this day, having left the extensive military government storehouses in rear of the fort and part of the forts still in flames, and the fire increasing.

"I cannot speak too highly of the assistance afforded me by Capts. Buckle and Scott throughout the whole of the engagement, and of the admirable manner in which both ships were manœuvred in such narrow waters. Capts. Buckle and Scott speak in the highest terms of their senior lieutenants, W. Mould, and Jos. Edye, as well as the whole of their officers, seamen, and marines. I have also great pleasure in being able to speak in the highest terms of the conduct of Lieut. Battiscombe, Mr. E. Tucker, Master of the *Hecla*, as well as the rest of the officers, seamen and marines, and Mr. Lucas, Mate; and with regard to Mr. Lucas, I have the

pleasure to report a remarkable instance of coolness and presence of mind in action,—he having taken up and thrown overboard a live shell thrown on board the *Hecla* by the enemy,
while the fusee was burning. I have also to mention that
Capt. Thomas Lyons, who is on board as a volunteer,
from his knowledge of the language rendered most efficient
service.

" I beg to enclose a list of casualties during the action,
which I am delighted to say is slight: only five men were
wounded. The ships were hulled repeatedly by the enemy's
fire, and the spars and rigging also suffered, and the boats
of the *Hecla* were rendered, for the time, unserviceable. I
beg also to enclose a rough tracing of the squadron's track
from the sea to Bomarsund, also an outline of the position of
the ships in the bay, and a rough sketch of the principal
forts, &c.

"For further details I beg to refer you to Capt. Scott of
the *Odin*, who is the bearer of this despatch.

"I have, &c.,

"W. H. HALL, Captain."

It is not necessary to comment upon this action,
further than to say, that the "broadsides" of the
squadron which thus, at a range out of harm's way,
silenced 70 or 80 guns of the sea front of Bomarsund,
—amounted only to two guns on a side of each ship,
or six in all; and that, when Bomarsund was afterwards captured from the rear, both the sea front of
the fortress and the guns were found in excellent
preservation. Of the damage done to the ships, some
notice must be taken, as in the returns the carpenters
testify that "the above damages can be made good on
board." The injury to the boats, as given by the
survey, was " two shot-holes in 1st cutter."

One matter is, however, very important, as bearing on the whole Baltic fleet, viz., that in an action of only eight hours' duration, Capt. Hall's ships expended nearly *all their shot and shell.* There can, therefore, be no question that the squadron was incapable, at this rate, of sustaining an action of more than eight hours' duration; and not Admiral Plumridge's squadron only, *but the whole fleet was in the same condition!* whilst no reserve had been provided, as was the case in the following campaign.

On the 23rd of June, Capt. Hall addressed another despatch to Admiral Plumridge as follows:—

" With reference to my letter of yesterday, wherein I gave you an account of a successful bombardment made by the small squadron you did me the honour to place under my command, I beg further to state that my conviction is, that if that success was taken advantage of immediately, the result would be the capitulation of the Island of Aland, and that without any great loss of men, from the effectual way in which their masked batteries were silenced, their large bodies of riflemen and horse artillery dispersed, and the destruction from the shell of all their military storehouses, &c., being in a blaze; and I have no doubt that the forts must have suffered greatly from the same cause, if we may judge from the awfully grand appearance of the flames when the squadron left.

" I have, &c.,

" W. H. HALL, Captain.

" Rear-Admiral Plumridge, &c."

It is perhaps needless to add that Rear-Admiral Plumridge did not act on Capt. Hall's recommendation to " take advantage immediately of his successful bombardment:" nor does it seem to have occurred to Capt. Hall that Admiral Plumridge could not have done so, had he been so inclined; for all the shot and shell of his squadron had been fired away, for no other purpose than to show that guns of long range can fire with impunity at a fortress mounting guns of shorter range; though the demonstration of this self-apparent problem was hardly worth the powder and shell expended on it ; and the less so, as Admiral Plumridge's squadron could get no more till it had been sent out from England.

We will not give the comments of the Admiralty authorities upon this occurrence, for though Sir James Graham praised the skill of Capt. Hall in Parliament, he wrote very strongly to Sir Charles Napier on the subject, and Admiral Berkeley still more so. The action was, however, a godsend to the Government at the moment; as, provided something is done, the public is not over particular in inquiring how or where, or whether by order or not, though this is of the first importance in the conduct of a fleet. Had Admiral Plumridge's squadron been placed in circumstances requiring their shot and shell, the want of these would have proved a very serious affair; and had the Russians been aware of the fact given in Capt. Hall's despatch, they would no doubt have brought the matter to a test ; as at Abo, within a few miles of Capt. Hall, they had a squadron of steamers and gun-boats far superior to his own in point of numbers, and well supplied with munitions of war of all kinds.

What injury this distant bombardment had done to

the forts will be estimated when we come to consider Admiral Chads' firing at the same sea-front of Bomarsund, at ranges of 1060 and 480 yards, in August following. Capt. Hall's bombardment, like that of Admiral Chads, was an experimental trial of range, not so much for the amount of damage inflicted, as for ascertaining how far his guns would tell. The experiments of Admiral Chads showed that, even at 1060 yards, shell fired against a fort was inferior to shot: Capt. Hall's shell, then, at long range, must have been absolutely thrown away beyond the burning of a few outbuildings, and how little store the Russians set by these is apparent from the fact, that, when Bomarsund was attacked in earnest, the Russians themselves set fire to every combustible building in the place, before a shot was fired on either side.

Altogether, it was an untoward affair, for the Commander-in-Chief was getting repeated injunctions from home to be sparing of shot and shell for practice, the Board of Ordnance having only a limited supply; a lamentable proof of our unprepared condition for war, though actually engaged in it. Even Admiral Plumridge himself had no orders to attack Bomarsund when his squadron was collected, much less would he have made the attempt with three ships only. To the officers and crews of the steamers under the orders of Capt. Hall, every praise is due for having so ably seconded him. The bravery of the gallant youth Lucas was above all praise; for, by his presence of mind in throwing the burning shell overboard, he no doubt saved many lives in addition to his own.

Viewing the act in this light, the Royal Humane Society voted him his medal, a novel instance of such an award to an officer engaged in destroying human life. Mr. Lucas was elevated to the rank of lieutenant for his bravery, the Commander-in-Chief warmly congratulating him on his promotion.

The mischief which might be expected to result from this attack in Bomarsund was that the Russians would throw in reinforcements and otherwise strengthen their position; thus causing additional trouble and loss of life when the Allied Admirals should consider the time to be arrived for attacking the fortress in earnest, as soon as the French army should have joined them.

On the 21st of May, Capt. Wilcox of the *Dragon*, who had been despatched on a reconnoitring expedition in the direction of Sweaborg, ran into Revel and cut out two beautiful brigs, in the presence of the enemy's fortress. Capt. Wilcox was shortly afterwards recalled by Capt. Sulivan in the *Lightning*, and arrived at Hango in time to try her guns on the forts there.

We will here mention a daring exploit performed by Capt. Key of the *Amphion*, which led to the surrender of the town of Libau and the shipping in that port. Capt. Key had arrived off the town on the 16th of May, in company with the *Conflict*, commanded by Capt. Cummings. Capt. Key having ascertained that the town was defended by only 500 or 600 Russian troops, and that several Russian merchantmen were lying dismantled in the port, determined on capturing them. Accordingly, by careful sounding, he succeeded in anchoring both ships within gunshot of the town ; and, having done so, he despatched Capt. Cummings on shore with a flag of truce to the Governor, commanding him to surrender the merchant ships in the harbour within three hours, or he would attack the town.

The Chief Magistrate, in the absence of a civil or military Governor, at first refused compliance with the demand, but said that he would give a final answer within the time specified. While on shore Capt. Cummings had discovered that there was a considerable body of Russian troops in the town; but, nothing daunted by this, at the expiration of the time specified he again landed, to learn the Chief Magistrate's answer. An offer had been made to spare the town on the surrender of the vessels, in which case not a shot would be fired, whilst the men who brought off the vessels should be again landed under a flag of truce. In case of non-compliance Capt. Key had requested the Governor to send the women and children out of the town, and to remove the invalids to a conspicuous building, which should be respected in case assault was necessary.

The reply of the Chief Magistrate was ready by the time appointed, and contained a prompt compliance with the demand for the surrender of the ships; his worship saying that the town, being in a defenceless state, had no power to resist the demand, and that therefore the peaceable inhabitants could only submit. The demand that the ships should be sent out was, however, too much for the worthy functionary, who replied that they could not be delivered within the time prescribed, as most of them were un-rigged, but Capt. Key could inspect them, and bring them off in his own way.

This experiment was somewhat hazardous, as the ships lay up a creek a mile and a half long, and no more than fifty yards broad, whilst there was no lack of troops to assault the boats. Adopting, however, every precaution, Captain Key took the boats of both ships, and, with Captain Cummings, entered the river, the troops keeping out of sight. No obstruction whatever was offered, and the ships were taken possession of by Captain Cummings and Lieutenants Wodehouse and Hore. A steamer was amongst the prizes, and Captain Key got up her steam, intending to use her as a refuge in case of attack. Eight merchant ships, all new and well found, were brought off, notwithstanding that some of these had been scuttled, and were aground.

This affair was the more extraordinary, as from the large number of Russian troops in the town they could have successfully attacked the men in the boats, whilst the latter were pulling up the creek. The townspeople stated that the reason for this surrender of their ships was, that, had a contest with the British force taken place, they expected another visit from a large force, and thought the first evil the least. The Russian Government pretended that the capture of the ships by Captain Key was unfair, but such assertion was, of course, untenable.

Up to this period the squadron had captured a goodly number of prizes, viz.: the *Tribune*, six prizes; the *Alban*, three; the *James Watt*, one; the *Gorgon*, one; the *Impérieuse*, one; the *Magicienne*, one; the *Euryalus*, one; the *Amphion*, two; the *Vulture*, one; the *Bulldog*, two; the *Amphion*, with *Conflict*, eight; the *Dragon*, two; the *Archer*, nine; the *Cruizer*, two; the *Conflict*, seven; the *Arrogant* and *Hecla*, one; and the *Valorous*, one.   Total, 49 prizes.

CHAP. X.

THE RECONNAISSANCE OF CRONSTADT.

FLEET SAILS FOR CRONSTADT. — ANCHORS OFF SESKAR. — CHASE OF A RUSSIAN STEAMER BY THE " BULLDOG." — TERROR OF THE PEOPLE IN THE VESSELS BOARDED BY THE ENGLISH.—ASPECT OF THE SHORES OF THE GULF. — ARRIVAL AT CRONSTADT, AND DECLARATION OF THE BLOCKADE. — DISAPPOINTMENT OF THE TARS ON FINDING THE RUSSIAN FLEET UNAPPROACHABLE. — COMPLETENESS OF THE RECONNAISSANCE. — POSITIONS OF THE ENEMY'S SHIPS. —THE ADMIRAL'S REPORT TO SIR JAMES GRAHAM. — BEST PLAN OF ATTACK. — INFORMAL REPORTS TO THE ADMIRALTY NOT TO BE RECOGNISED.—THE MEANS OF ATTACK INSUFFICIENT.—INSTRUCTIONS FROM THE ADMIRALTY RESPECTING THE BLOCKADE.—CLASS OF WAR STORES AND VESSELS DEFICIENT. —" AN ACT OF MADNESS."—IMPRUDENCE OF MAKING AN UNSUCCESSFUL ATTACK. — LOSSES IN THE REDUCTION OF THE SOUTH SIDE ONLY OF SEBASTOPOL. — COMPARISION OF THE MEANS USED FOR THE TWO EXPEDITIONS TO CRONSTADT AND SEBASTOPOL. — COMPLIMENTARY LETTERS FROM ADMIRAL BERKELEY AND LORD BLOOMFIELD. — OPINION OF CAPTAIN MILNE. — SIR R. PEEL'S UNJUST ATTACK ON SIR CHARLES NAPIER REFUTED. — ADMIRAL BERKELEY DEFENDS SIR CHARLES. — LORD PALMERSTON'S ESTIMATE OF THE ADMIRAL'S SERVICES.—ADDITIONAL MEASURES OF THE ENEMY FOR DEFENCE.—FORCES AT HELSINGFORS, SWEABORG, AND RIGA.—CHOLERA IN THE ALLIED FLEETS. — EXPECTATIONS AND CONSTERNATION OF THE RUSSIANS. — ADMIRAL PLUMRIDGE IN THE GULF OF BOTHNIA. — RUSSIAN VESSELS DESTROYED.

ON the 22nd of June, the combined fleet weighed anchor, and proceeded towards Cronstadt, leaving Admiral Corry with nine sail of the line, one frigate, and five or six steamers, to guard the Russian squadron at Sweaborg. To this force, at the request of Sir Charles Napier, two French frigates were added by Admiral Parseval.

The British squadron proceeded under steam, the French sailing ships being taken in tow by British and French steamers. The fleet consisted of twelve English ships of the line, and six French, with nine steamers, which were afterwards joined by the *Arrogant* and *Gorgon*.

On the 23rd, the Admiral sent two steamers to examine the anchorage on the east side of Hogland, intending to anchor there; but Admiral Parseval giving it as his opinion that Seskar would be a better rendezvous, Sir Charles assented to this arrangement.

On the 24th, the Allied Fleet stood towards Seskar, and anchored off Nerva Beacon at two A.M , on account of sudden fog. This was necessary, as the ships were compelled to steer from rock to rock; whilst on the first appearance of fog a signal for the fleet to anchor instantly had to be made from the Flag-ship.

At five A.M., the weather having cleared, the fleet again weighed; and as all the beacons had been removed, steamers were sent ahead to mark the shoals, which were thus cleared in safety; and at ten A.M. the fleet anchored at Seskar, where it was found that the enemy had destroyed the lighthouse. On going ashore, the town was found to be deserted by the inhabitants.

A Russian steamer having been observed engaged in watching the movements of the fleet, the *Bulldog* was despatched in chase of her, but without effect, as the Russian instantly put about, and proceeded again towards Cronstadt.

In proceeding up the Gulf, chase had to be given

to vessels which may not improperly be termed floating villages, for they were crowded with poor terror-
stricken creatures, flying from the ruthless English!
A shot was always fired across their bows previous to
boarding them; and the frightened women were
usually found stowed away in some hiding-hole half-
dead with terror. They were scarcely able to believe
their good luck, when, after being kindly treated, they
were set free, and allowed to pursue their own course
unmolested. To assure the women, their captors for
the time being fired off their muskets, to show them
that there was no intention of harming any one; but
this rough way of assuring them had only the effect
of frightening them worse.

The Gulf now narrowed, as the fleet approached its
great *cul-de-sac*. The land on either side was covered
with rich woods of pine-trees, especially on the
Finnish shore, which is the higher of the two shores;
amongst these woods were open spaces, revealing snug
hamlets and cultivated fields sloping down to the
waters of the Gulf.

Whilst off Seskar, the Admiral wrote to Sir James
Graham, telling him that he had not seen the French
Admiral since leaving, so that he did not know what
the arrangements would be as regarded Cronstadt;
but, continued the Admiral, "I presume we shall
offer battle to the Russians and go back, if they do
not come out; and on my return I hope to hear what
your intentions are about the Aland Islands. I shall
survey Aspo Roads, and, if the anchorage is good,
shall go there, and see if there is anything to be done;
but the whole coast is a labyrinth, and not a fit place

to knock a fleet about without danger, as we are forced to survey every place we go to, and make beacons of our steamers. I shall be glad if the French squadron will take the south coast on their return."

To Admiral Berkeley the Admiral wrote: "We came here very well, for the weather was fine. The Gulf is not fit to be navigated with a fleet, and we steer from rock to rock. This morning a fog came on; the signal was made to anchor instantly, which was well done. The fog cleared away, and we weighed. I am sorry to say the cholera has broken out in this ship."

On the 26th, the combined fleet again moved onward, sending the *Impérieuse* and *Arrogant* ahead to look for " infernal machines." At eight A.M., the *Impérieuse* descried the Russian fleet at anchor, and telegraphed the same to the Admiral. Shortly afterwards the *Desperate* telegraphed that the enemy's fleet consisted of thirty sail, anchored in three columns. At ten o'clock, the Admiral himself had observed them, and at noon he went on board Admiral Parseval's ship, when a joint declaration of the blockade of St. Petersburg and Cronstadt was made by both Admirals. After this, the combined fleet wore in succession, stood down the Gulf, and at two P.M. came to an anchor eight miles from Tolboukin lighthouse. The *Arrogant*, *Desperate*, *Impérieuse*, *Magicienne*, *Bulldog*, and *Lightning* were the same afternoon despatched to reconnoitre Cronstadt.

On approaching Cronstadt, a rumour prevailed throughout the fleet that the Russians, not expecting it to come so high up, had anchored outside the forts, and the tars exulted in the prospect of catching them, the more so that not a breath of wind prevailed to carry them inside the protection of their batteries; but this expectation was doomed to disappointment. The ships ahead looking out for "infernal machines," found, as the mist cleared away, that the Russian fleet was safely ensconced within the harbour, and under the guns of the huge forts, which alone presented their fronts, as if in mockery of a force which could not get near them.   There was no doubt the usual amount of swearing at an enemy who would not come out to be killed, but beyond this ebullition, the ships had nothing for it but to come quietly to an anchor. On the approach of the squadron, there was, however, evidently a great stir amongst the Russian fleet; the steamers got up steam, and all seemed on the alert to meet an attack, should the Allied fleet come within reach, of which there was little danger, as the large ships-of-the-line could not have been floated in, and there were no other vessels with which an attack could even have been attempted.

On the 27th, three steamers were sent in, and the *Driver* was despatched to reconnoitre.   A Russian steamer, with an admiral's flag at the fore, was observed coming out of Cronstadt, and the *Penelope* with the *Desperate* instantly started in chase.   The Russian, however, on seeing their intention, put back, and returned under cover of the fortress.   A close reconnoissance of the shores of the island was made by the steamers.

The reconnoissance was very complete, and drew forth a warm eulogium from the Admiralty.   The report made by Captain Sulivan in company with the French steamer *Phlegeton*, will show the nature of the examination made.

Captain Sulivan anchored at about 3000 yards from Fort Risbank,—a Russian steamer running under the fortress as he approached. Having remained here sufficiently long to examine everything carefully, the *Lightning* proceeded to the north side of Cronstadt, but as it was blowing strong, had to anchor somewhat further off on that side than was intended.

Captain Sulivan found seventeen sail-of-the-line, of which three three-deckers were moored outside the basin, in the channel, between Fort Cronslott and the south extreme of the Man-of-war Harbour. Two other three-deckers were moored with their heads to each other across the channel, abreast of Fort Menschikoff, their broadsides commanding the channel. Three more were moored above these, with their broadsides bearing on the opening between the two last named. Three more were stationed a little above the gates.

On the west side of the Man-of-war Harbour, five other ships-of-the-line were placed, and four more off the south corner of the same harbour. All these had their broadsides bearing on the channel, through which only one of the combined fleet could pass at a time, so that the ships of the Allies, had they attempted to enter, would have singly received the broadsides of these ships in addition to the fire from nearly 1000 guns of the forts. Six of the enemy's ships were afterwards moved and moored in line along the wall between Fort Menschikoff and the open gate of the middle harbour.

The total force observed by Captain Sulivan was twenty-two ships of the line, five frigates, four corvettes, seven paddle-steamers, and twenty-five gunboats, the rest being out of sight behind the defences. These, together with the guns of the fortress, the strongest in the world, were opposed to the Allied fleet, consisting of eighteen ships of the line and eleven steamers; but without gun- or mortar-boats of any description.

On the 28th, the fleet was much surprised by the approach of the *Hecla*, with the signal flying, "*Bomarsund has been successfully bombarded.*" All thought the days of magic were returned; till, on the *Hecla* coming to an anchor, it was found that the bombardment amounted to Captain Hall's having fired at the forts nearly all the shot and shell of Admiral Plumridge's squadron, as described in the previous chapter, and then leaving the place.

On the 30th, the Allied Admirals made a personal reconnoissance of the fortress, the British Admiral going in the *Driver*, and the French Admiral in one of his own steamers. On their return Sir Charles reported to Sir James Graham as follows:—

"The French Admiral and myself have had a close reconnoissance of Cronstadt, and I send you the drawings made by Lieutenants Nugent and Cowell, which are very correct, and quite agree with the plans sent me by the Admiralty.

"You will see by these that any attack on Cronstadt by ships is entirely out of the question. On going in to the south, the batteries are most formidable — all constructed of solid masonry. They are three or four deckers, of stone instead of wood, and ships going in would be raked by them the moment they came under fire, and would be sunk before they reached the enemy's ships, which are placed with their broadsides also bearing on the passage. The channel is narrow, and we had, in running in, quarterless five, four miles from the ships, hardly enough for the *Duke of Wellington,* and I conclude there would be less higher up, whilst it is most probable that there is only room for one ship, so that the chances are they would be sunk one after the other ; or, if the smoke from the guns and funnels was dense, that they would miss the channel and go ashore. All attack from the southward is, therefore, out of the question. It does not appear to me necessary to lay down infernal machines, as, by all accounts, the Russians have done.

" In addition to the drawings, I send you a chart with the distances set off in circles, to show the possibility of an attack by *gun-boats,* throwing shells 5000 yards, provided the enemy let you alone.

" No. 1., where the anchor is marked, would be the position of our gun-boats, 3000 yards distant ; where they would seldom be hit, and would throw their shells amongst the ships, and into the Arsenal.

" No. 2. would be 5000 yards from the centre of the shipping, but too close to the south shore, which the Russians would fortify.

" No. 3. would be 3000 yards from Fort Alexander, which might be annoyed by steamers.

" No. 4. would be 3000 yards from Risbank Fort, which must be seriously pounded during the attack. You will see by the soundings, the steamers could give no support to the gun-boats.

" No. 5. shows where the enemy would place their gun-boats to take ours in flank. They would be supported by their steamers, which could also pass to the eastward of Risbank, and attack our steamers attacking that fort. The fleet would be anchored outside. Our boats would support our gun-boats and steamers, and theirs would do the same.

" This attack is *practicable.* It would be attended with great difficulty, and success would depend upon who would bring the greatest number of gun-boats, and ships' boats into action ; whose guns went furthest ; who fired best, and who had the greatest quantity of ammunition.

" I now turn to the north side of Cronstadt. That is certainly the weakest point. A landing might be made on the island of any number of men, and the town might be besieged. But you must expect the Russians will always outnumber you, and if you fail, your army would be lost, whilst if you succeed, it would probably be starved during the long winter. I presume, therefore, that will not be thought of. It may, however, be bombarded.

" No. 1. shows a space of 2600 yards in a line parallel to the walls of the fort, where you could place *fifty gun-boats* 3000 yards distant. They could throw their shells into the Arsenal, but could not reach the shipping outside the Moles; but we must calculate, that if they set fire to the town and Arsenal, there would be great confusion; the boats would then advance, and ultimately reach the shipping. The enemy, however, would not be idle.

" No. 2. shows the probable position of the enemy's gunboats, supported by the steamers.

" No. 3. shows the position of their blockships and frigates which would support the steamers.

" Our fleet would be in good anchorage to the north of the island, and both parties would employ the boats of the fleet.

" Besides shells, we must be supplied with a great number of rockets of the largest size.

" I have drawn up this statement with great care, and I think you may depend upon it. I took Admiral Chads in with me, and he quite agrees with me. I have thought it better to *send this and all the drawings to you privately.* The engineer officers deserve credit for the drawings, and the assistance they have given me. I send Captain Sulivan's report to the Admiralty, and you may rely upon it.

" P.S. The best plan of attacking Cronstadt would be by beginning with St. Petersburgh. You might land an army either to the north or south, and march on it; but it must be an army that the Russians could not meet, and you must not have a reverse, or it would become a campaign as disastrous as Buonaparte's."

It will have been observed, and it will be essential

to bear the matter in mind, that the more important documents of the war were written to Sir James Graham in his capacity of First Lord, and not direct to the Board of Admiralty itself; as Sir Charles Napier says, " I have thought it better to send this and all the drawings to you privately." The reason is plain. Had they been sent to the Admiralty direct, the plans of attack would necessarily have been open to the perusal of a great number of persons; so that secresy would have been impossible. Government clerks must not shrink from this, for it is no new thing to find public documents transcribed and given to the newspapers. It is not long since a circumstance of this nature gave rise to serious discussions; and, in the case of a plan of attack to be executed a year afterwards, the caution observed was highly to be commended, as being the only one adapted to ensure secresy.

But we must extend these remarks a little further. These plans of attack were of course laid by the First Lord before the Board collectively. This plan of attack on Cronstadt was so laid before the Board; but a more important plan of attack, which had in like manner been sent privately to the First Lord, *never was laid before them !* viz., the Admiral's plan of attacking Sweaborg. In a future chapter this plan of attack will be given, together with the reasons why it was withheld. The Admiralty said it had never been received, and that they were not aware of it. It is, no doubt, correct. But when Sir Charles Napier said that it had been sent privately to Sir James Graham, as had been the plan of attacking Cronstadt, and for the same reasons, the Board said it would not recognise *informal documents ; i. e.,* documents not sent direct to itself. The caution of the Admiral to ensure secresy, was thus, when expedient, termed *informality,* though of the greatest importance, and with the full approbation of the Board of Admiralty itself.

To the Board of Admiralty, Sir Charles, on the 1st of July, wrote as follows : —

" I have to request you will inform their Lordships that the combined fleets arrived at Cronstadt on the 26th ultimo, after anchoring one night at Seskar.

" I have, in conjunction with the French Admiral, well reconnoitred Cronstadt, and I find, on inspection, that it agrees so much with the different plans sent by the Admiralty, that I have nothing to add except that the difficulties of approach are great, and the batteries are so very strong that any attack upon Cronstadt *with our means,* appears to me perfectly impossible, and I believe the only way to attack Cronstadt is by a large army landing on the coast, and beginning with St. Petersburgh.   I enclose Captain Sulivan's report.   I sent him in several times, and think his is the most correct report of any I have had, and it agrees pretty nearly with our own observations."

The reader will observe the expression, " *with our means.*" With the means indicated, the Admiral, in his Report to Sir J. Graham, had shown that what could be done towards destroying Cronstadt was to render it untenable in the following campaign, for the means could not have been supplied in the present year. But those means were not even supplied to Admiral Dundas in the following campaign in sufficient abundance to induce him to attack the fortress, which *then,* as now, remained unscathed for want of means, not from the fault of the Admirals, but from the fault of the Admiralty itself; the country being urgent that means should be supplied. On the 11th of July, the Board of Admiralty replied, that having given their best attention to the "able and well-executed survey" that the Admiral and his officers had made of the fortifications and approaches to Cronstadt, it "had full confidence in his judgment, and placed complete reliance in his Report." He had "offered the enemy battle at the mouth of his *impregnable fortifications*, of which opportunity he was not inclined to avail himself." It would now be for the Admiral to seek for other points where "he might be more vulnerable, and to cause him all the annoyance possible upon his own shores and in his own waters."

The Admiral was further instructed, that the great object in view, since the enemy "dared not meet him in fair fight, was to render his fleet useless by confining it to its moorings within the fortified harbours."

The Board of Admiralty then instructed Sir C. Napier, that a number of ships with French troops on board, were about to join him. It is not necessary to enumerate these here, as their movements will, in their place, form part of this history.

The Admiral was, however, instructed that, whatever might be the operations which he and his French colleague might deem it right to undertake, he must never lose sight of the great responsibility which rested on himself; his *primary object* being the close blockade of the enemy's fleet and of the Gulf of Finland. He was reminded that the enemy's fleet consisted of twenty-eight sail of the line, besides steamers and frigates, and that he must always keep together a sufficient force to hold this fleet in check, and where-

ever the bulk of his fleet might be, his duty as Commander-in-Chief was to be with it, and the paramount
duty of this command must not be delegated to any
other officer. The distribution of the French troops
when they arrived must be made as he and the French
Admiral deemed most advisable. The Board had
confidence that both he and his French colleague
would carry on the service with the best feeling of
unanimity, and it was equally confident that when
their plans were digested, they would succeed, to the
honour and credit of the Admiral and of all employed
under him, as well as to the discomfiture of the
enemy.

It may be remarked that this despatch of the Board
of Admiralty bears the signature of Admiral Dundas,
the successor of Sir C. Napier in the command of the
Baltic fleet. It is thus evident that Admiral Dundas
was satisfied that nothing could be effected against
Cronstadt, or that the Admiralty was not in a position to furnish him with the means necessary. Yet
in the following campaign, with additional means,
he did not think himself warranted in attacking
Cronstadt — a fact which ought to be pretty decisive on the matter — and the more so, as whilst
Admiral Dundas was in office it was in his power to
urge the supply of means to any extent ; whilst the
public, so far from grudging the expenses, was
earnestly impressing upon the Government to spare
no expense.

The question, then, with the Allied Admirals was,
— could the inadequate force under their command
effect anything decisive under such circumstances ?
They decided that it *could not,* and the Board of

Admiralty fully endorsed the wisdom of their decision. And, be it observed, the inadequateness of
the force did not consist in the want of ships or men
(for now there was no want of either), but in the want
of a class of vessels and other means connected with
them, such as mortars, rockets, &c., by which alone
the fortress could have been assailed or even got at.
There were *none* of these appliances whatever with
the fleet; so that none could be used. Could the
Allied fleet have got up to the fortress, as was the
case at the bombardments of Copenhagen, Algiers,
and other approachable fortresses, still the experiment
would have been hazardous, and, at best, only partially
successful; but even had this been practicable, the
attack must have failed for want of means to follow
it up. There were only a few hours' supply of shell
on board the ships, and when this was expended the
attack must have ceased, when the ships would have
been at the mercy of the Russian fleet with an abundant supply. But the fleet could not, from its draft
of water, have got at the fortress; and therefore both
Admirals decided, that, as it could not approach, and
that, as it was destitute *altogether* of gun- and mortar-
boats, it would be folly to attempt an attack, as the
mischief which could be inflicted was not equivalent
to the loss which would be sustained by the fleet;
whilst, if their limited force got crippled, were unable
to return, or got on shore, they would have fallen an
easy prey to the enemy. It was therefore agreed
between the Admirals to postpone an attack till the
following campaign, when gun- and mortar-vessels
might be supplied. Had they made the attack without these, even had this been practicable, — which

it was not, for the reasons alleged, — it would have been " *playing the Russian game*," against which Sir James Graham had so emphatically cautioned Sir Charles Napier, telling him that to do so would be " *an act of madness*." As has just been seen, the Board of Admiralty was precisely of the same opinion.

But the Allied Admirals carried their reasons further. They saw — and ought to have received credit for their foresight — that, as any attack without means could only have been followed by a retreat, if possible, with some of their ships disabled, this retreat would have been claimed — and rightly — by the Russians as a victory, as it would have been beyond question ; so that to have attacked Cronstadt, under the circumstances, would have been not so much to inflict some trifling mischief on the place, in order to satisfy popular clamour, as to have made the attack with their eyes open, and with a positive certainty of defeat. None but an idiot would have attempted such an attack — and none but a *charlatan* would urge it, or blame the Allied Admirals for refraining from it.

But the evil would not have stopped here. The necessary cessation from attack, had it been made, would have been bruited all over Europe, and especially over German Europe, with its Russian sympathies, as a victory of the first order gained by the Russians over the Allied fleets ; and thus the very object for which they had been sent to the Baltic — if object they had, — viz. to produce a wholesome impression on the German powers, so as to influence their alliance, would not only have been defeated, but might have been turned against us ; for it is a question whether Austria and Prussia, and perhaps Sweden, would not, after such a check, have joined Russia, who would have known how to turn the circumstance to good account.

Argument on such a subject is almost idle, the whole matter being self-evident. There are no two military or naval opinions that Cronstadt was at least of double the strength of Sebastopol; in short, that it is the strongest fortification in existence. Yet Sebastopol was only partially captured with the largest army and fleet of modern times. To have attempted Cronstadt then with a fleet alone, and that *without the ordinary means of warfare*, would have been an act of folly which could only have recoiled on the Allied Admirals.

We have said that Sebastopol was considered inferior in strength to Cronstadt. It will be interesting to see what it cost our French allies to reduce the south side of the place only. Our own Government has never ventured to lay our costs in human life and national treasure before the public. The following summary of Marshal Vaillant, in his Report to the Emperor Napoleon, should place the idea of capturing Cronstadt without means in a light so ridiculous as to render the detractors of Sir Charles Napier ashamed of recurring to it.

France sent to Sebastopol 309,268 troops and 41,974 horses. Of these 70,000 men died and were missing. Let us put our own loss at 50,000 men; and the result is, that to capture the south side of Sebastopol cost the Allies the loss of 120,000 lives, whilst that of the enemy who defended it could not have been under double the number, and has been computed at more than four times the number.

The French guns, howitzers, and mortars employed were 641, besides 603 contributed by the marine, and 140 Turkish guns. This was siege artillery alone; the field artillery raised this amount to 1700 pieces of cannon. We have no means of ascertaining what was the amount of our artillery; but set it down at one half the French, and we have a total of 2500 pieces of artillery. Had not peace been concluded, France was prepared to send 400 mortars of large calibre, and she did send and use 2,000,000 shot and shell, with 10,000,000 lbs. of gunpowder. Sir Charles Napier had not a mortar in his fleet, nor a mortar-boat to carry one, if he had it. A survey of his ammunition gave 12,000 shells; yet with these he and his French colleague were expected to reduce a place stronger than Sebastopol! The comparison is so absurd, that we feel ashamed to pursue it, and are surprised that the maligners of Sir Charles Napier should in the face of such facts carry their enmity further.

Here, then, are two distinct plans of attack, equally elaborate with those which the Admiral sent home relative to an attack on Sweaborg. But, like the attack on Sweaborg, *gun-boats* and mortar-boats formed the condition on which alone the attack could be made.

On the 11th of July, Sir James Graham acknowledged the receipt of the Admiral's Report and of Captain Sulivan's plans. We have already seen what was the opinion of the Admiralty upon these, and will now detail the opinion of Sir James Graham in his own words.

" Your Report, together with Captain Sulivan's plan, is a clear and very able exposition of the strength of the Arsenal, and of the extreme difficulty and uncertainty of an attack, even if sustained by a large force of gun-boats and of troops, which are not at present at your disposal. I had anticipated your return to the westward, after an offer of battle which I felt certain the enemy would decline, and it now remains for you to blockade the Gulf of Finland, to keep the fleets at Cronstadt and Helsingfors disunited, and to await the arrival of the French troops, when you and the French Admiral and General must deliberate on the operations to be undertaken by the combined forces.

" Bomarsund will clearly be within your reach. Sweaborg, if it were possible, would be a noble prize ; but on no account be led into any desperate attempt, and above all things avoid the least risk of the Russian fleet slipping out of the Gulf of Finland when your back is turned, and be slow to land your marines — without whom your line of battle is disabled. These Russians, though shy, are crafty, and if they can catch you at a disadvantage they will be down upon you."

On the same day Admiral Berkeley, who had then succeeded the late Admiral Parker, as senior naval Lord of the Admiralty, thus wrote to Sir Charles Napier : —

" Your survey of Cronstadt, and your judgment and *discretion*—I don't mean to play on that word—are highly approved. You have had a difficult part to play, every tomfool expecting you to eat Cronstadt and the Emperor to boot. I believe the Government are perfectly satisfied with your proceedings, and I can only say that you deserve every credit for the manner in which you have handled your fleet in such waters. The world—the public—don't know what

it is to command an *inexperienced* fleet—I may say officers
and men, on such a service, in such a sea—much more trying
to the nerves than any general action."

This expression of Admiral Berkeley's sentiments
is highly honourable to him, and the more so, as his
own experience at sea has been but small; nevertheless his complimentary letter to the Admiral shows
a candid and observing mind, which, though not
greatly experienced itself, could accurately appreciate
the difficulties which the Admiral had to contend
with.

To this complimentary letter the Admiral replied
on the 18th of July :—

"I am glad you all approve of my proceedings. It is hard
that hitherto it has not been in my power to do anything
with this powerful fleet, but attacking either Cronstadt or
Sweaborg would have been certain destruction.

"You may well say, commanding an inexperienced fleet
is more trying to the nerves than a general action. It has
knocked Corry up; but I have stood it tolerably well, and
hope to do so to the end of it."

Lord Bloomfield, on receiving the result of the
Admiral's reconnoissance at Cronstadt, wrote in
a manner equally frank with that of Admiral
Berkeley :—

"I am glad to know your opinion of Cronstadt. I have
always thought it impregnable. Without a land force, under
no circumstances could it be taken, and the fleet and dockyard
destroyed; without heavy loss ? I fear that the gun-boats
which are being built for you will be ill calculated to your
work, and that they will draw by far too much water to
render their services available."

Captain Milne, Junior Lord of the Admiralty, thus wrote to the Admiral:—

" The entrance and forts of Cronstadt are evidently too strong for you to make any attempt. The only thing which appears to me worthy of consideration is, an attempt to burn the town, &c., by means of rockets from the north side of the island; but it would require *a large number of small vessels* of light draft of water. It is rather disheartening to go away from before the enemy's fort, *but it is sound discretion so to do.*"

In the estimation of naval men, this opinion of Captain Milne would alone be decisive in the matter, even unaccompanied by the opinions of the other Lords. To have attacked Cronstadt, in Captain Milne's opinion, would have required *a large number of small vessels*, none of which the combined fleets had; and, unluckily, this department did not fall under the orders of Captain Milne, who, with these correct views, would not have lost any time in supplying them. The acumen of Captain Milne thus points out what the inexperience of his more influential colleagues withheld. Throughout the whole naval service there are no two opinions on this point, nor is there any difference of opinion on the extreme folly of attempting any attack on Cronstadt with the insufficient means at the command of the Allied Admirals.

Such were some of the warm expressions of approval which the Admiral received of not making any attempt on Cronstadt without the means of effecting even temporary mischief to any extent worthy the British navy. It is most derogatory to the Board of Admiralty that, after the lapse of more than two years, Sir Charles Napier should have been selected by a civil Lord of the Admiralty, and his colleague, a naval Lord, as an object of attack for the very transactions for which he had been so highly praised.

On the 21st of October, 1856, one of the Lords of the Admiralty (Sir Robert Peel, son of the great statesman of that name), delivered himself, at a public dinner in the Shire-hall of Stafford, of the following ungenerous and unjust attack on Sir Charles Napier : —

"I have visited the fortress of Cronstadt, and there was but one opinion from the Grand Duke Constantine down to the youngest Russian middy on board the *Vladimir*, that had the energy of the commander equalled the pluck of the British navy, that fortress, at the present moment, would be crumbled in the dust. If the man who had commanded the fleet at Copenhagen had commanded the Baltic fleet, or if a man who possessed the spirit and capacity of a Nelson had commanded that fleet, I have not the slightest doubt that, as the fortress of Copenhagen had yielded, so would Cronstadt have fallen."

That a Lord of the Admiralty should have given expression to such opinions, in defiance of the opinions of his colleagues, is a pretty clear proof that Administrative Reform has not yet reached that department of the Government. That he should have done so at all, with the knowledge that the means not supplied to Sir Charles Napier were, to some extent, supplied to his successor in the command of the Baltic fleet, and that, notwithstanding Cronstadt is not "crumbled in the dust," is an equally clear proof that the speaker must have been ignorant of

R

the most prominent events of the war. That he should impute blame to *the* Commander of the Baltic fleet, is proof positive that he did not know there were two Commanders of the Baltic fleets, viz., Admiral Parseval and Admiral Napier, and that the latter was imperatively commanded by Sir James Graham to act in the most perfect cordiality with his ally. If Sir Robert Peel knew this, he has had the bad taste to impute " want of energy and spirit " to Admiral Parseval no less than to Sir Charles Napier, — a proceeding by no means in accordance with what might be expected at the hands of a Lord of the Admiralty acting in alliance with France.

Not that Admiral Parseval, in all probability, would attach more importance to the opinions of Sir Robert Peel on naval matters than did Sir Charles Napier. Put the antecedents of the three together, and the value of Sir Robert Peel's opinion becomes infinitesimally small; so much so that the reader may possibly inquire why the opinions of Sir Robert Peel are brought forward in a work professing to be a consistent narrative of the war in the Baltic. The answer is plain; viz., that Sir Robert Peel is a fair sample of those non-ministerial Government officials who have for two years been pretty actively engaged in periodically reminding the public of the deficiencies of Sir Charles Napier in those matters for which Ministers themselves had so highly praised him, that it would be extremely inconvenient for the superiors themselves to eat their own laudations of the Admiral's skill, prudence, and courage. It was much more expedient to delegate the task to others, whose blind zeal prevented them from seeing the uses to which they had been put.

The father of Sir Robert Peel — beyond question one of the greatest statesmen of his day — said of Sir Charles Napier, that, by his brilliant courage, " he had changed a dynasty in two minutes." After such an eulogium, the opinion of his son is of little importance, except as he was a member of the Government. The praise of the father will, in the estimation of history, rise superior to the post-prandial speeches of the son.

Sir Robert Peel, in a subsequent speech at Tamworth, justified the opinions he had advanced, by stating that he was borne out in them by " the highest authority in the realm." Who this " highest authority in the realm " was, Sir Robert Peel does not state, leaving the public to infer that it was no less a personage than Her Majesty herself. All that can be done in such a case is to adduce the opinions of the highest naval authorities of the realm.

" After two days' inspection from the lighthouse, and full views of the forts and ships, the former are too substantial for the fire of ships to make any impression. They are large masses of granite. With respect to an attack on the ships where they are, *it is not to be entertained.*"— (*Admiral Chads to Admiral Berkeley, as quoted by the latter in the House of Commons, in reply to Lord Dudley Stuart.*)

" As to the statement that Cronstadt might successfully be bombarded by twenty vessels, he begged to read to the House an extract from a letter written by the gallant Admiral in command of the Baltic fleet. He had served with the gallant Admiral. He knew his determination, and he was sure he would leave nothing undone on his part to enable him to get at the enemy. Before the noble Lord again *talked of knocking down Cronstadt,* let him ponder on the passage he (Admiral Berkeley) was about to read. Admiral Napier said : —

" ' It has not been in my power to do anything with this powerful fleet, for attacking either Cronstadt or Sweaborg would have been certain destruction.' This was not all. Admiral Chads — than whom no man possessed a greater amount of scientific knowledge — wrote also in these terms" (*vide supra*). — (*Admiral Berkeley, in the House of Commons, on same occasion.*)

" These letters (from Admirals Chads and Napier) showed that, situated as Sir C. Napier then was, an attack either on Cronstadt or Sweaborg would risk the destruction of the British and French fleets." — (*Admiral Berkeley, on same occasion.*)

" We *all feel* — no one more than myself — that nothing can be done against such places as Sweaborg and Cronstadt, and I have the most full reliance that had anything been feasible you would have attempted it. *They won't come out, and you can't get in.* A strict blockade is all that can be expected. At Sebastopol, nothing can be done by ships."— (*Admiral Berkeley to Sir C. Napier, June* 27*th,* 1854.)

" We have not one ship to supply casualties, either for you or for the Black Sea." — (*Admiral Berkeley to Sir C. Napier, July* 4*th,* 1854.)

" I don't believe that more could have been done in the Baltic." — (*Admiral Berkeley to Sir C. Napier, July* 31*st,* 1854.)

" I told Sir James Graham, and I repeat it to you, that I think all your arrangements, under the circumstances, quite satisfactory." — (*Admiral Berkeley to Sir C. Napier, August* 8*th,* 1854.)

" Suppose you could have destroyed the sea front of the batteries at Cronstadt, could you have got at the fleet? Could you have landed? Could you have done anything beyond knocking down those defences? *Was that to be done with the means at your disposal?* Questions like these *must* disarm clamour." — (*Admiral Berkeley to Sir C. Napier, October* 22*nd,* 1854.)

" If anybody attempts to bully and find fault, I shall not be backward in taking up the cudgels; but John Bull is beginning to return to reason. Sebastopol proves a much tougher job than he contemplated, and his eyes begin to open—he sees that it is easier to talk than do."—(*Admiral Berkeley to Sir C. Napier, November 5th,* 1854.)

" *You were quite right in not making an attack on Sweaborg or Cronstadt,* and I am not aware that any individual in the Admiralty disagrees with me in that opinion." — (*Admiral Berkeley to Sir C. Napier, December 25th,* 1854, *after the Admiral had returned from the Baltic.*)

We must here notice, that although Sir R. Peel quoted the Grand Duke as his authority, His Highness wrote to Sir C. Napier that he had never spoken to Sir R. Peel but once in his life, and Cronstadt was not even mentioned by either.

Before the Sebastopol Committee Sir J. Graham held that private letters on public service were always to be considered public letters; and Sir James Graham is no doubt right; the public business both of fleets and armies being chiefly carried on by private letters from the home authorities. But, without taking Sir James Graham as our guide, we have here followed the example of Admiral Berkeley himself, who in debate makes use of the private letters of Admirals whenever it suits his purpose; and there can be no question of Admiral Berkeley's right to do so, as they all relate to public service, and are therefore official.

But in the debate of 1856, Admiral Berkeley accused Sir Charles Napier of having used *his private letters!* The gallant Admiral must have forgotten that he had made use of Sir Charles Napier's private letters, as well as those of Admirals Chads and Seymour, in the House of Commons. Is it, then, to be said, — when Admiral Berkeley's letters on the public business of the nation most completely exonerate Sir Charles Napier from all the accusations that have been brought against him, and *especially from Admiral Berkeley's own subsequent accusations*, — that Sir Charles Napier is to be restrained from using Admiral Berkeley's opinions on public matters, when these are amongst his best means of defending his own reputation ? The Admiral is not to be struck with his arms folded.

" He (Admiral Berkeley) had repeatedly assured Sir C. Napier, that if fault should be found with his conduct in that House or elsewhere, *because he had not attacked Sweaborg or Cronstadt*, he (Admiral Berkeley) would stand up in his defence. Could it be supposed possible, then, *that he would have consented to cast any censure on the gallant officer ?* He denied having done so, and he denied also that the Board of Admiralty had ever censured Sir C. Napier in any way with respect to his conduct and his management of the fleet before Cronstadt and Sweaborg."—(*Admiral Berkeley on Mr. Malins' motion in the House of Commons in* 1855.)

" I have had the pleasure and honour of a long acquaintance with the gallant Admiral, Sir C. Napier. I am proud to say, that I think the courage, the gallantry, the professional skill and ability of my gallant friend stand as highly now as they ever did. It has been my fortune on a former occasion to profit, in the official capacity in which I was acting, by the invaluable services of Sir C. Napier. He rendered the most important service to the country on that occasion by the able and distinguished manner in which he performed his duty ; and it is only due to him, in my opinion, to say, that nothing has occurred in the course of the last year which *in the slightest degree* diminishes the high character which he has attained in the service of his country. (*Cheers.*)

Sir C. Napier rendered important service in the command of
the Baltic fleet. (*Hear, hear.*) He showed the greatest
skill in conducting that fleet through the most intricate and
dangerous navigation.   He brought back a magnificent fleet
without any injury, under circumstances in which a man of
less skill and less judgment might have sustained serious and
great disasters; and he secured the country against all those
evils which might have arisen if the Baltic fleet of Russia
had been permitted, either wholly or in part, to quit its ports
and scour the sea. (*Cheers.*)   I think the character of Sir
C. Napier *stands as high as it ever did, and that my honourable and gallant friend will rank for ever amongst the most
distinguished ornaments of the naval profession.*" — (*Lord
Palmerston on Mr. Malins' motion in the House of Commons,*
1855.)

Were it worth while, it would be easy to multiply
these extracts from almost every man of eminence in
the Government.   The above, however, are sufficient
to meet the subsequent assertions of Admiral Berkeley and Sir Robert Peel; and as Lord Palmerston is
the "highest authority" in the Government of which
Sir Robert Peel is a member, the above extract of
Lord Palmerston's opinion with regard to Sir Charles
Napier will form a fitting text for Sir Robert Peel
when he next has occasion to " dine out;" whilst
some others, hereafter to be adduced, would be still
more appropriate.

We have now seen Sir Charles Napier's Report on
Cronstadt as well as that of Captain Sulivan, and the
opinions of Admirals Chads and Berkeley, those of
the latter as expressed to Sir Charles Napier and in
Parliament.   Yet Admiral Berkeley stated in Parliament in 1856, that it was Sir Charles Napier's fault
that Cronstadt was not attacked in 1854!   Perhaps

Admiral Berkeley can explain how, two years afterwards, he was induced to change his opinion, though, as will be seen in another place, Lord Palmerston has never changed his opinion! How was it, too, that when in 1855 Admiral Dundas appeared off Cronstadt, he had only *three* gun-boats supplied to him, which were afterwards increased to *fifteen*, to meet the *two hundred* gun-boats of Russia under the walls of Cronstadt? We have heard a very awkward story of the Russian gun-boats having at Cronstadt sent us a challenge to meet them, which challenge had to be refused for want of means, even in 1855. We have no document to prove this assertion, but have good reason to rely on the correctness of our information.

It has been said that in the second year of the Baltic war, the Russians had constructed a new *barrage* at Cronstadt; but this was not complete, for Admiral Dundas was inside of it, and had he been supplied with gun- and mortar-boats, he could certainly have attacked the north of Cronstadt, as could the Allied fleets in 1854, had they been supplied with them. A sufficient force of gun- and mortar-boats was not completed till 1856, when they were of no use, for had they appeared off Cronstadt they would have found *another barrage* constructed, which, together with the additional batteries that had been erected, would have rendered *any attack impossible.* From the low state to which the navy had fallen in consequence of a false economy, it may be admitted that there was some excuse for a proper force not being supplied in 1854, though it was most undignified to attempt to throw the blame on the Admiral. There was, however, no excuse why a proper force *should not have been supplied in* 1855, so as to have enabled Admiral Dundas to attack Cronstadt. In 1856 it was useless.

Whilst the Admiral was at Cronstadt, Admiral Corry had been indefatigable in obtaining information as to the strength of the Russian position at Sweaborg. He ascertained that infernal machines were placed in the channel at the entrance of the harbour, across which chains were stretched in both passages. There were 2000 troops at Helsingfors, and 8000 at Sweaborg, besides some 20,000 or 30,000 in the neighbourhood, so that on the arrival of the French troops they would be no match for the large Russian army in and around one of the strongest fortifications in Europe.

The naval force at Sweaborg has been before enumerated. In addition to this it was ascertained that the Russians had twenty-one steamers in the Neva, along the shores of which river they were actively engaged in erecting masked batteries; this, as no ships of war could enter the Neva, being a proof that they expected, sooner or later, to encounter a military force sent against the capital itself. They had also in the Neva a considerable flotilla of gun-boats, as well as at Riga. Indeed, gun-boats appear to have abounded every where except in the British fleet, where they were indispensable. Even the Russian Government appears to have imagined that we had a formidable flotilla of gun-boats at hand, for such preparations were made in St. Petersburg itself as are usually made in towns about to be exposed to a bombardment. The Russians could not understand why a fleet which could not get at them should have been alone sent, and regarded the fleet as only a precursor to a more efficient flotilla near at hand. The inhabitants of St. Petersburg must have felt greatly relieved when they saw the Allied fleet sail away, morally defeated from the want of means which could have alone secured victory.

When lying before Cronstadt, the combined fleet was severely attacked by cholera, having lost upwards of 100 men, with a large number sick. As it was agreed by both Admirals that nothing could be done with the means at their command, and as it was desirable to remove as quickly as possible down the Gulf, on account of the health of the fleet, they decided on retracing their steps. After leaving the pestiferous waters of Cronstadt the health of the men speedily improved.

Before arriving at Cronstadt the Admiral received intelligence that the Russians had stationed large bodies of troops at Strelna, Peterhoff, and Orienbaum. On Cronstadt itself were as many troops as the island could accommodate, or to use the words of the writer, "as it would hold." Every means was taken to keep up the communication with the main land, the water between the island and the main being a mass of gunboats and other boats.

Amongst other defensive measures adopted at St. Petersburg, was the erection of an image of St. Nicholas on one of the bridges. In all the churches, candles were kept burning day and night, in front of the patron saints of Russia, and the people were called upon to make frequent offerings, being told that "what they offered in the war, would be given to

God and the Church, against which the debased Christian powers had conspired."

Reports from England — though totally false ones — had reached St. Petersburg, that Sir Charles Napier was receiving *a great quantity of small vessels*, drawing little water, which would be able to get close in under the land. The consternation at St. Petersburg was hence excessive. As has been before said, all kinds of preparations were made in case of bombardment of the metropolis itself. Trials were made in the presence of the Emperor and his sons to ascertain how far the works could defend themselves against such vessels when close in, and the result of the trial was not considered satisfactory, as the fortifications were not deemed sufficient to act with success against this dangerous mode of attack. The Russians must have been not a little rejoiced to find that the Allied fleets were altogether destitute of the class of vessels, the report of which had caused such serious apprehensions, though those very apprehensions of themselves form a severe comment upon the British Admiralty, which had neglected to supply the only class of vessels which could have proved serviceable. The Russian Admiralty evidently believed such an error impossible.

The subject of the defences of Cronstadt and other places, is, however, too important to be summarily dismissed, so that these will form the subject of the next chapter.

We will here glance at the movements of Admiral Plumridge in the Gulf of Bothnia. Admiral Plumridge quitted Baro Sound on the same day that the Allied fleets went up the Gulf of Finland to Cronstadt. He was accompanied by the French frigate *Andromaque*, Capt. Guillaume, and the English steamer *Cuckoo*. On the 23rd he fell in with the *Odin*, and despatched her and the *Andromaque* to lat. 64° 45′ long. 23° 20′ E. to blockade the northern division of the Aland Islands. The next day he was joined by the French frigate *Virginie*, Capt. De Rivieres, off Lagskaren, and on the following day despatched her with the *Valorous* to blockade the southern division of the Gulf, assigning them the position of 61° 40′ N. long. 19° 30′ E.

On the 26th, leaving the *Cuckoo* at the rendezvous at Lagskaren, with instructions for the *Poursuivante* or any other ships which might arrive, Admiral Plumridge proceeded to the northward to make himself acquainted with the passages leading to Bomarsund; but thick weather coming on, he was compelled to stand to the southward till it cleared, when he resumed his voyage towards Bomarsund, and had got as far as Baklandet Beacon, when hearing heavy guns firing, he proceeded in the direction of the sound. The guns had been fired by the *Cuckoo* whilst in chase of a Russian ship, which she captured.

On the 28th Admiral Plumridge reached the entrance to Bomarsund, the navigation being so intricate, that it required the greatest circumspection to conduct a ship of the *Leopard's* draught of water from coming in contact with rocks; nor did all the skill of her commander, Capt. Giffard, prevent her from grounding. On the 29th thick weather again compelled the *Leopard* to remain at anchor, as any attempt to go onward in such a navigation must have caused the loss of the ship.

It was not until the 2nd of July that Admiral Plumridge could move onward with safety. On proceeding he fell in with several Russian vessels bound to Aland, which vessels were not aware of his proximity. As their cargoes consisted of salt and other articles of no great value, and as it was inconsistent with the service he was upon to encumber himself with prizes of this description, he took out the crews and sunk the vessels.

On the 3rd he communicated with the French frigate *Poursuivante*, Capt. De Barre, and directed her to cruise to the southward of Lagskaren. On the same evening he anchored at Huddiksvall. On the 4th the *Leopard* anchored at Orengrund, where she found the *Hecla* with despatches from the Commander-in-Chief, and ammunition and stores for the *Odin* and *Valorous*, with which the *Hecla* was sent on to the northward. Leaving Orengrund on the 7th, the *Leopard* returned to Lagskaren. The further examination of the Aland Isles by Admiral Plumridge will be given in the order of time in which it took place.

CHAP. XI.

CRONSTADT AND ITS DEFENCES.

FOUNDATION OF ST. PETERSBURG.—THE ISLAND AND DEFENCES OF CRON-
STADT.—THEIR STATE ON THE ACCESSION OF NICHOLAS.—WORKS EXE-
CUTED DURING HIS REIGN.—FORT PETER THE GREAT.—FORT ALEXANDER.
— FORT RISBANK.— FORT MENSCHIKOFF.—FORT CRONSLOTT. — FORTIFI-
CATIONS OF THE " ENCIENTE."—THE MOLE.—IMPREGNABILITY OF CRON-
STADT.—SIR ROBERT PEEL AND THE ADMIRALS.—PROJECT OF PETER
THE GREAT REALISED. — NAVAL ESTABLISHMENT OF ST. PETERSBURG
SECURED FROM ATTACK — COST OF THE CRONSTADT DEFENCES.—CAP-
TAIN WASHINGTON'S REPORT ON CRONSTADT.— REMARKS ON HIS GOSSIP-
ING CONFABULATIONS WITH THE GRAND DUKE CONSTANTINE.—POSITION
AND CAPABILITIES OF THE GRAND DUKE.—ANALYSIS OF SIR W. WISEMAN'S
REPORT. — UNPOPULARITY OF THE NAVAL SERVICE IN RUSSIA. — THE
RUSSIAN STEAM-FLEET. — THE DOCKYARD OF CRONSTADT. — NAVAL
SCHOOLS.—SUBMARINE MINING.—M. NOBELL'S INVENTION.—SUBMARINE
ENGINES OF DESTRUCTION.— BOOMS AND STAKES. — KNOWLEDGE POS-
SESSED BY THE ALLIES OF THE VARIOUS SUBMARINE DEVICES OF THE
RUSSIANS.

Now that the Russian war is concluded, an account
of the progress and condition of this celebrated
fortress, from reliable information acquired during
the campaign, will be no less interesting to the reader
than useful in a naval point of view.

St. Petersburg was founded by Peter the Great,
in 1703, on a number of flat and marshy islets in the
Neva, near its junction with the Gulf of Finland.
At the period when the capital was founded, the
principal arm of the Neva had a depth of water
sufficient for large vessels, but the alluvial deposits

since formed at the mouth of the river, have reduced the depth of water, so that large vessels can no longer enter it.

As this deposit was rapidly going on during the reign of Peter the Great, he deemed it imprudent to form a naval establishment of any magnitude at St. Petersburg itself, and therefore chose the island of Cronstadt as the nucleus of his future maritime empire. He, nevertheless, retained its administration at his new capital, where he also constructed dockyards for the purposes of ship-building, to which building-yards others have been since added, and are solely used for the construction of ships of war, which are floated down to Cronstadt on " *camels*," and there finished, armed, and equipped.

The island of Cronstadt lies about fourteen miles from the western point of Vassili Ostrof, one of the islets of St. Petersburg. Its length from north-west to south-east is about eight miles, and its greatest breadth about three miles. The town occupies the eastern extremity of the island. The western side, which fronts the island, is protected by a fortified *enceinte*. The great roadstead is to the south and east of the *enceinte* of the port, and is the only one in which ships of war and large merchantmen can anchor. The roadstead is much exposed to south-west winds, which are very frequent and boisterous. The little road lies to the eastward of the town, and is more sheltered, but is only accessible to small vessels.

The breadth of the Gulf opposite to the west of

the island is about thirteen miles. The water is sufficiently fresh to be drinkable, only becoming salt several leagues further down. That portion of the Gulf, then, between Cronstadt and St. Petersburg can only be considered as an enlargement of the Neva.

There were originally two passages round the island — one to the north and the other to the south. The former passage was rarely frequented by vessels, from the number of shoals which render its navigation dangerous. Nevertheless, to prevent its offering, in time of war, facilities to an enemy in turning the defences of Cronstadt, and in order to prevent the necessity of fortifying the island to the northward, the Russian Government has obstructed the passage on that side by sinking *caissons*, laden with stone, so that all vessels of any draught of water are compelled to enter the south channel, whether their destination be Cronstadt or St. Petersburg.

This south channel, on leaving the western part of the island, has, generally speaking, a sufficient depth of water; but as it advances eastward, the passage narrows, and on arriving at the port, a sand spit, running from Orienbaum, contracts the channel, near the *enceinte* of the port, to about 300 yards in width, so that only one ship can pass at a time, and this one commanded by the guns of the fortress.

Peter the Great and his successors caused the erection of works, in that day, sufficient for the protection of this channel, and also other works to prevent the disembarkation of troops on the island; at the same time rendering the town secure from any assault which could be attempted from the land side. The following is an enumeration of the works as they existed at the accession of the Emperor Nicholas.

On the north side there were a succession of wooden batteries, thrown up on the shoals in advance of the shore. Intrenchments were also thrown up at the point of the island, supported by a bastioned redoubt, called on the old plans "Fort Alexander." These works were built by Peter the Great during his wars with the Swedes, and were designed to prevent any disembarkation of the Swedish troops which might attempt to destroy the new establishments in course of construction at Cronstadt. Since the obstruction of the north passage, these works have either been abandoned or destroyed as useless.

To protect the rising town on the land side, a deep ditch, full of water, was dug from one shore to the other. This ditch was supported by a wooden citadel which was destroyed when the masonry *enceinte* was begun. The ditch, however, remains.

The means of defence were principally accumulated on the South side. At 3000 yards from the west of the salient angle of the port, and commanding the spot where the channel begins to narrow, is Fort Constantine. To the south of this, on a shoal which extends to the island, is Fort Risbank, designed to cross its fire with Fort Constantine. These forts were originally of wood, and consisted of two tiers of guns.

Between Fort Constantine and the island was the

s

Citadel Battery, also of wood: this battery crossed its fire with that of Risbank. The Citadel Battery has since been replaced by Fort Peter the Great, constructed on the same site.

Lastly, near the salient angle of the port, and at about 300 yards from the Orienbaum spit, where the channel has its *minimum* width, Peter the Great constructed Fort Cronslott, partly of wood and partly of granite. The western face of this fort rakes the channel, whilst its northern face flanks it at a short range. In support of this fort are the guns of the western face of the *enceinte* of the commercial harbour and of the little bastion which flanks its south range.

Supposing these obstacles overcome by an enemy's fleet, it would then have to pass, in single file and at short range, the vast battery which forms the *enceinte* of the port, and also that on the long western face of the Man-of-war Harbour. This defence was long considered amply sufficient to repel any attack; but as the works, being chiefly constructed of wood, were of a transitory character, it was determined to reconstruct them with more durable materials.

This brings us to the works executed in the reign of the Emperor Nicholas.

The first work undertaken was the construction of Fort Peter the Great, on the site of the Citadel Battery. This fort is of granite, its front being a tower casemated, with two lines of fire, the rest of the fort forming an open battery. The whole mounted eighty-five guns.

Fort Constantine being found in a very ruinous state, it was determined to construct another in its place, which was called Fort Alexander. The site of this fort was selected nearer to the channel and to Fort Risbank; and was to cross its fire with the latter. Fort Alexander occupied eight or nine years in construction, and was finished in 1846. It consists of a semi-cylindrical battery of four tiers, mounting 128 shell-guns. The lower tier contains thirty-two 112-pounders, the middle tier thirty-two 98-pounders, the upper tier thirty-two 74-pounders, and the roof thirty-two 48-pounders, *en barbette;* the whole forming, perhaps, the strongest fort in existence, before which no ship could long stand.

The guns in Fort Alexander are similar to the *canon obusier,* and are on the non-recoil principle. The fort is built of immense blocks of red granite, some fifteen or sixteen feet long, by eight or ten thick. There are also extensive barracks within the fort. On the construction of this fort, Fort Constantine was abandoned.

Fort Alexander is circular in plan, terminated by shoulders of smaller radius. The space between the shoulders is occupied by an arched building, one story high, serving as a barrack for 150 men. On the south side, and for half its distance, the fort is casemated in three tiers, each casemate being available for two guns. The shoulders have but two tiers, each with six guns in three casemates. The platforms extending above the casemates are similarly disposed for artillery, and are armed with the same number of guns. There are also some small howitzers.

s 2

The munitions are deposited in two square towers, one on each side of the central casemates. Remarkably elegant iron staircases communicate with the casemates and upper batteries. All the facings are of superb Finnish granite, but the arches in the heart of the work are of brick. The whole rests on piles, which have to bear an enormous pressure, calculated by the Russian engineers to be twelve pounds to the square inch. The depth of water on the shoal on which the fort is built is eighteen feet, very large piles being used for the foundation. The whole has been constructed with great care and under the most minute inspection.

About 1400 yards from Fort Alexander is Fort Risbank, the works of which were commenced in 1848, and it was in a very complete condition at the period of Sir C. Napier's reconnoissance. Like the rest, Fort Risbank consists of several tiers of guns, being adapted for 220, of which 190 were mounted. From the positions of Fort Risbank and Fort Alexander, a hostile vessel could not pass between them without being within close range of one or the other, and under fire of both at the same time.

The part of the fort which fronts the passage is so designed as to gain a large field of fire, and has three tiers casemated, and one *en barbette.* A raking battery below the ground tier was designed to meet a hostile vessel with Congreve rockets! a new and powerful auxiliary against a fleet. Seven staircases communicate with the tiers of casemates, and are disposed in towers projecting into the interior courts.

On the bastion of the body of the Merchants'

Harbour, and near the western salient, is Fort Menschikoff. This fort is designed to rake vessels which may have succeeded in passing the batteries before spoken of. It mounts forty-eight heavy guns, all twelve-inch 110-pounders, except the end guns, which are eight-inch carronades.

Fort Menschikoff rakes the channel throughout its whole length. It is partly surrounded by a ditch, the object being to leave open the foot of the battery, which is constructed with magnificent blocks of Finnish granite. The bastion, in the interior of which Fort Menschikoff has been raised, is of old construction. The *terre-plein* is of made ground, piles fifty feet long being driven upon the whole site. The pressure upon these is so great, that the right face of the bastion and the *caissons* which form its base have moved forward several inches. The Russians have stopped this movement by sinking other *caissons* at the foot of the *revêtement,* an operation easily performed during the winter by filling the *caissons* on the ice, which is afterwards broken, and the *caissons* submerged gradually. The masonry of the fort itself has not at all given way, the intervals between the piles beneath the fort being filled with concrete.

Fort Cronslott, though amongst the oldest of the forts, is built of granite, and is therefore in a good state of preservation, though at the period of the war it had undergone considerable improvement, being assimilated to Fort Risbank, and calculated to mount 250 guns of large calibre, eighty of which were mounted. Fort Cronslott consisted of a triple tier of guns, which, from its western face, add their fire to that of Fort Menschikoff. This face is calcu-lated for sixty-six guns.

We now come to the fortifications of the *enceinte* of the body of the place. Notwithstanding that a dis-embarcation is little to be feared on an island whose shores generally are only approachable by boats, and in the vicinity of which there is no safe anchorage, the Emperor Nicholas determined that the town should be secure from a *coup de main;* with this idea he caused an *enceinte* to be raised round it, extending from the N. W. angle of the Merchant Harbour to the landing place.

On the land side the *enceinte* presents a salient, flanked by two large casemated towers, each being pierced with twenty-two embrasures. These towers are supported by loop-holed barracks. Between the barracks is an *escarpe* about fifteen feet high, sur-mounted by an earthen parapet. In front of the old ditch which originally protected the approaches to the town, and which is about thirty-five yards in width, is traced a covered way. Redoubts are thrown up on the eastern angles, and are separated from the *terre-plein* of the covered way by ditches full of water, which do not communicate with the principal ditch. It is the opinion of all engineers that this place could not be taken by assault.

On the north and east of the town is a wall, about fifteen feet high, loop-holed for musketry. Inside and below its crest is a *banquette* carried by masonry arches, under each of which are three loop-holes. This wall is flanked at intervals by little towers; and baĉked against the *enceinte* are barracks, where are quartered the infantry and artillery, designed for the defence of the town.

In addition to the works enumerated, the Mole mounted 140 guns. These together with those of the ships of war, numbering more than 3000 guns, could be presented to the passage of an invading squadron, which would thus be opposed to an immense development of fire. If we consider that the whole of this formidable armament is designed to play upon a very small space, and that in three batteries alone, viz. Forts Peter, Menschikoff, and Cronslott, more than 200 heavy guns would effectively enfilade such vessels as might have run the gauntlet of the three advanced works, there is no other rational conclusion than that the channel to Cronstadt cannot be forced by any fleet, be it ever so numerous.

This is the opinion of one of the most able of French officers, to whom a reconnoissance of Cronstadt had been entrusted sometime before the war, and from whose able report nearly the whole of the preceding particulars are gathered; a report which forms a marked contrast with the reports of some of those whom the British Government had despatched on the same errand.

With the fortifications of Cronstadt, then, those of Sebastopol will not even bear comparison. Yet when Sir Charles Napier and Admiral Parseval were before this, the strongest fortification in the world, with *only eighteen sail of the line*,— the Russian fleet, in addition to the fortifications, numbering the same, with a swarm of gun-boats, — they were expected to attack, and are now accused by members of Her Majesty's Government of not having had the "energy and spirit" to attack Cronstadt! * The Russians, moreover, — both ships and forts, — were amply supplied with every material of war. The British fleet had not so much as a single mortar on board any of the ships, not one rocket in the whole squadron, and not even a sufficient supply of shell for an action of a few hours' duration, supposing all the ships to be engaged. Before the war, Sir Hamilton Seymour had told the Government that the Russians had 180 gun-boats; and *not one gun or mortar-boat* had been supplied to the Admiral to meet them. The Russian *matériel* of war had been supplied regardless of expense. The equipment of the British fleet had been supplied with a view to nothing but economy!

Yet with these singularly disproportionate forces, and with ships alone, the Allied Admirals were expected, according both to Sir Robert Peel and Admiral Berkeley, since the war, to attack a fortress stronger than Sebastopol, which, after two campaigns, with a fleet efficiently equipped, and backed by a vast army, was only partially taken. The Admirals, with a fleet of eighteen sail of the line only, and no troops, were expected to do what a quarter of a million men, troops and sailors, had not been able fully to accomplish ; and because Sir Charles Napier did not insanely present his few ships as targets to the

---

* Sir Robert Peel, a Lord of the Admiralty, in the presence of the Earls of Lichfield and Harrowby, at a public dinner at Stafford, on the 21st of October, 1856, made this assertion, as regarded Sir Charles Napier.

Russian forts, — even though he had but one voice in the matter, — he has ever since been hunted down by Government officials, who, if he had so lost his ships, would to a certainty have tried him by a court-martial, and perhaps shot him, even though his rashness had been exercised to save an incompetent Government.   To have pursued such a course towards Sir Charles Napier was the deepest insult which could be offered to Admiral Parseval, who was united with him, but who relied upon such information as that we have been detailing as the result of the investigations of French officers, and not upon the superficial verbosity which was supplied to the British Government.

To return to our analysis of this masterly French report.

Cronstadt itself can never be carried from the land side but by a regular siege.   On one side the form of the island shoals, on the other the total absence of anchorage near the shore, renders the disembarkation of troops and the necessary materials for a siege almost impracticable.   The Emperor Nicholas had realised the project of his ancestor, Peter the Great, and had effectually secured the advanced guard of his capital from attack, and had there formed a naval establishment in security from any foe.   This establishment, in addition to the forts, comprises dockyards, docks, careening ships, a naval hospital, vast marine barracks, schools, &c., which are all on a scale combining grandeur with excellence.

The expense must have been enormous, and the sacrifice made by the Russian Government during the reign of the Emperor Nicholas for the defence and improvement of Cronstadt may safely be taken as a measure of its importance. Fort Alexander cost 32 million francs. The steamboat establishment is valued at 20 millions. The value of the remaining works is not known, but, estimating them by the ratio of their magnitude to the two just named, their cost cannot be less than 200 million francs, expended within twenty-five years.

We will now subjoin some extracts from Captain Washington's report on Cronstadt made in October, 1853.

Captain Washington says : —

" The approach to Cronstadt from seaward is very imposing. Fully 300 guns, chiefly of the largest calibre, on either side and in front, command the channel. During the time I was in Russia, I went four different times to Cronstadt, and had ample opportunities of seeing everything. Through the kindness of Mr. Simpson, the British Consul, ——, a Captain in the Russian navy, obtained permission of the Governor of Cronstadt to see the dockyard, and I found a barge in attendance to take me on board any ship I wished, a carriage to drive me round the town and dockyard. Accordingly, we set off, and — with the exception of an excellent lunch at the Consul's — spent from ten o'clock till five in visiting the place. I observed seven docks for repairing line-of-battle ships; in two of them a line-of-battle ship and a frigate were having a screw-propeller fitted to them. Here is a magnificent ropery, a stand of arms for 30,000 men, mast and boat-houses, rigging lofts, and all the naval requisites of a dockyard. Within the last year a steam factory has been added, the exact counterpart of that at Woolwich!

" We then went round the *Port Militaire*, in which were twenty-two line-of-battle ships. Of these nine were rigged, seven were advance ships, and six had only their lower masts in. I went on board the *Empress Alexandra* and the steam frigate *Olaf*. After rowing round the War Harbour, we pulled to the Merchants' Harbour. On our way we passed close to the new Menschikoff battery, when my conductor said, 'Would you like to see our new fort?' Of course I replied, 'If such a thing be permitted.' 'By all means; anything you like.' We landed accordingly, and walked all over it. It is a fine specimen of granite masonry, — casemated, but well open in the gorge for ventilation, — in four tiers with forty-four guns, chiefly 120-pounders. All the guns point directly down the channel; and, if well served, *this fort alone ought to sink any vessel that approached by day; and the nights in summer are very short.*

" My second visit was under still more favourable circumstances. The Grand Duke Constantine had appointed an interview with me at his palace at Paulusky, on the subject of life-boats. I proceeded there by rail at ten o'clock in the morning, but at a station about half-way was met by an *aide-de-camp* of the Prince, to say that a new frigate had arrived the night before from Archangel, and he was obliged to go to Cronstadt to see her, and would be glad if I would accompany him. Of course I was but too happy to do so: in a few minutes the Grand Duke reached the station, invited me into his carriage: we travelled together to St. Petersburg, where the Imperial yacht lay waiting with her steam up alongside the quay, at once embarked, and steamed for Cronstadt. The party consisted of the Grand Duke, his A.D.C. Prince Galitzin, young Count Louis Heydon, son of the Admiral who commanded the Russian Squadron at Navarino in 1827; Admiral Moffatt (of Scottish extraction), recently promoted for breaking the enemy's line in the sham fight off Hochland in July last; Colonel de Bock (?), *Ingénieur Constructeur en chef*, and myself. On arrival at Cronstadt, we went directly to the new frigate — *Salchan*, I think, is the name — built at Archangel for a screw-propeller, it was said on the lines of the *Impérieuse*. The Grand Duke was received by the men 'at divisions.' He walked round and closely inspected the men, speaking to many of them, calling them by name, they having sailed with him in the *Ingermannland*, when in England in 1847. H. I. H. afterwards went all over the ship, examining every part most minutely, even to the opening for the propeller shaft, in which he went to the extreme after end. He then inspected the lines of the ship, all the drawings of which were laid on the cabin table, examining them critically, pointing out that he thought one of the after lines a little too hollow, and that altogether he feared the ends of the ship were too fine to bear the weight. After spending more than an hour on board, we left the ship. This frigate is built of larch, apparently well finished in all parts; she has a bridge on deck immediately over the wheel, with an additional steering-wheel upon it, connected with the lower wheel by a flat linked chain and cogs, for steering in a river or amongst islands; an invention of the captain of the ship, I was told, and I think might be worth copying if we have it not in our own navy.

"On our way to the yacht in the boat, we passed some of the steamships lying in the roadstead, when the conversation happened to turn on pivot-guns, and the Prince said that he much approved of two pivot-guns abaft. I said that I thought they might make the vessel labour, and would be difficult to work clear of each other. 'I will show you in a moment that nothing can be more easy,' said he, and immediately ordered the boat to be steered alongside the *Diana* steam frigate, ran up the side, called out to man the after guns, and, in a few minutes from being housed, the guns were pointed out on each side, first shifted to the other pivots, again fired, and brought back to be housed for sea. Whether the *Diana* is a screw-ship or not, I do not know, but this manœuvre was executed rapidly, thoroughly, and without noise or confusion. We afterwards landed at the dockyard, again walked over it, saw the library for the officers and men containing 36,000 volumes, and the school for the seamen, with their barracks; then embarked again in the yacht, and returned to St. Petersburg, dining on board *en route*, and landed at six o'clock, having passed seven hours in almost continual conversation, H. I. H. speaking English as well as myself. Indeed, so did the whole party, and the conversation at the dinner table was generally in English.

The yacht was built by Mare at Blackwall, engines by George Rennie, and is a very fast and nice vessel: the chief engineer an Englishman; crew ninety in number, sailor-like looking young men. The Grand Duke pointed out to me the yacht having been built in England; he was determined to acknowledge it, and had emblazoned on the paddle boxes the arms of Russia and England united.

" There was great frankness and sailor-like manner in the Prince. The first thing on going on board was to put on a pea-jacket over his undress Admiral's uniform, and he told all the officers to do so likewise. In seven hours' conversation, it may be supposed many points were touched upon. When the Prince found that I had witnessed the naval review at Portsmouth, he was most anxious to hear every detail: he knew by name every ship that had been present, and asked an infinity of questions referring to the subject again and again in the course of the day. His knowledge of the British navy is wonderful; he knew the H. P. of the *Duke of Wellington*, the *Agamemnon*, and whether they had new or old engines, spoke of the above-named ships and the *Impérieuse* with great admiration, said he knew their lines by heart, as he had a drawing of them always in his room; and when I mentioned that I had seen the *Agamemnon* steam nearly eleven knots, making scarcely a ripple on the water, he said he should have expected it, yet thought the *Impérieuse* would prove the faster ship. The Prince said frankly, ' We are determined to have a match for your *Duke of Wellington ;* the order is given to build her, and she shall be called " *Ivan the Terrible.*" The Prince asked after many officers he had known in England, and especially ' your excellent Admiral, Sir W. Parker.' On landing at St. Petersburg, the Prince shook me heartily by the hand, and said, ' I trust that England and Russia will always be good friends.'

" I have to apologise for this *apparent gossip ;* but under the present political circumstances I have thought that even this gossip of the Lord High Admiral of the Russian Fleet *was admissible in a Report,* especially as it denotes so friendly a feeling towards this country. Doubtless the being so civilly treated by an Imperial Grand Duke has thrown a certain amount of dust in my eyes, and may have blinded me to some defects; but I can conscientiously declare that I never remember meeting a more accomplished or better informed young man of twenty-five years of age, nor apparently a more amiable person or a more intelligent officer."

We do not think this "apparent gossip" is exactly the thing in a report, the first object of which ought to have been an examination of the strength and resources of Russia, instead of the Grand Duke's yacht. For this reason we shall not give the remainder of the report, the reminiscences of the Grand Duke comprising *four pages* out of *seven pages* devoted to Cronstadt, the rest being a mere enumeration of the Russian Navy as taken from Russian reports, combined with a description of their armaments, which was a matter of the least possible importance. It might have been very important to play Boswell to the Grand Duke Constantine, but this was hardly what Capt. Washington was sent to Russia for. The Grand Duke, when in England, appears to have made good use of his opportunities; and the opportunities of Capt. Washington, according to his own account, were as good as were those of his Imperial Highness when in England. The forts were what he should have looked after, in place of reporting, "I should pursue this report to a wearisome length, did I enter into any details as to the Russian forts!" If Capt. Washington, with his opportunities, had made an examination of the north side of Cronstadt, he would have done good service; and though this might not have been so amusing as were his confabulations with the Grand Duke, it would have been vastly more to the purposes of the Allied Fleet when at Cronstadt. Whether Sir Charles Napier did right or not, in not attacking Cronstadt, Admiral Parseval assuredly did not do wrong in following the report of his own officer instead of Capt. Washington's report. Both are before the reader, who can draw his own comparisons.

The Grand Duke Constantine is all, and more than all, that Capt. Washington describes him to be. That is, he is, in his own person, an efficient Board of Admiralty. He is actively engaged in raising, and will raise, a steam fleet that may one day put an inefficient British Board of Admiralty to its wits' ends. When the next struggle between England and Russia takes place, — and, judging from appearances, it may not be far distant, — a few more fleets equipped like that of Sir Charles Napier may lead to another Sinope. Fifty years ago, Spain had a navy nearly equal to our own in numbers, and was equally confident in its efficacy. Where is the navy of Spain now?

Commander Sir W. Wiseman, of the *Excellent*, had also been despatched to Russia for the purpose of procuring information, and had made an admirable report to the Government of the naval and military condition of Cronstadt. As the forts have been already described, with some of Sir W. Wiseman's remarks incorporated, we shall not again allude to them. The following is an analysis of the remainder of Sir W. Wiseman's report : —

" Everything about the forts was in first rate order, with all the stores at the guns. So satisfied were the Russians with their perfect condition, that they rightly deemed them impregnable ; and the people related a story that when the Emperor inspected the fleet in the winter of 1853, the section of a line-of-battle ship was erected on the ice, on which the fire of the fort guns having been concentrated, they knocked her to pieces with a single discharge.

" Though, with a commendable degree of pride, the Russian Government was ready enough to show its forts just before the war, it would give no facilities for inspecting the fleet housed in for the winter at Cronstadt. It was, however, gathered, that their ships were built of fir, coppered, and copper fastened as far as the water-line; above which they were iron fastened. Their decks were low, and their ports small and close together : their lower deck guns were also carried very low, which, in the smooth waters of the Baltic, is perhaps no great defect. Formerly, they constructed their ships at Archangel, of red pine ; but this had been discontinued.

" The Russian fleet was nominally commanded by a Grand Admiral, the Grand Duke Constantine (now really its commander). There was also a Minister of Marine, Prince Menschikoff; but in reality the Emperor Nicholas was the head; and had a telegraph in his room at the Winter Palace, by which he conveyed orders to Cronstadt, without reference to the High

Admiral or the Minister. In July, he generally inspected the fleet, when at anchor at Cronstadt.

The naval service is not popular amongst the Russian officers. They have little or no employment, being shut up in the ice seven months of the year; and, having no enemies to contend with, are without opportunities of distinguishing themselves in their profession. Their promotion is, consequently, very slow, and forms a marked contrast to that of the army, which, from constant active service, is very rapid. The naval service, moreover, held a secondary place in the estimation of the late Emperor; who, when inspecting the fleet, if he saw any number of fine " sea soldiers,"—as the Russians term sailors, —had them marched off to the army. The result is, that the Russians will not join the navy, if they can get into the army, which monopolises all the youth of family and interest, whilst second-rate men officer the navy.

The Russian steam fleet was not numerous, consisting of five large steamers only, but with a considerable number carrying light guns. The *Kamtschatka*, built at great expense in America, was their largest ship, being of 2300 tons burden, and 600-horse power. Her armament consisted of two 8-inch guns, placed fore and aft, two brass 24-pounder broadside guns, and sixteen 24-pounders on her main deck. All her engineers were Russian.

The *Terrible* steam sloop was of 1000 tons, armed with two 10-inch guns and four 36-pounders. Her engines are of 200 horse power. The Russian Government is now very anxious to organise an effective

T

steam force, and a commission has been appointed to superintend the building and equipment of steam fleets.

Attached to the fleet at Cronstadt were eighty large gun-boats, each carrying an iron 36-pounder aft, and a brass 24-pounder forward. They appear chiefly intended for the defence of Cronstadt.

Their dockyard would seem to be well organised. It covers a large space, and is surrounded by a canal, upon which all their storehouses open, so that stores can always be received without going through the yard. This must greatly facilitate the equipment of a large fleet.

At one end of the dockyard they were building a magnificent steam factory, on the plan of the one at Woolwich, but double its size. Close to this factory are two new granite docks, one for a line-of-battle ship and the other for a frigate. Near this is another dock, begun by Peter the Great, capable of holding five or six large ships ; but, as all are in the same dock, one cannot be taken out without floating the whole.

The Government builds its ships of war by contract, and all the extensive repairs are done in the same way. They say the saving is immense. There are about 3000 men employed in the dockyard, for whom, as well as their wives and families, barracks are provided. Every " sea soldier's " wife is allowed a ration, and each of his children half a ration, no matter how many. There are also barracks for the 30,000 " sea soldiers," who are equipped in great coats, boots, and chakos.

.There is a small arsenal at Cronstadt, containing 30,000 stand of arms; but the principal arsenal is at St. Petersburg, and this has a cannon-foundry attached to it.

It will be interesting to notice two other establishments at Cronstadt, in connection with the dockyard, viz. two admirable institutions serving as nurseries for a future navy.

These are schools, the superior one for the sons of officers in the navy. This consists of about 400 boys, who are educated as pilots (corresponding to our Masters in the navy). These boys are carefully instructed during the winter months in the scientific branches of their profession; whilst, during the summer, the elder boys are at sea, either in men-of-war or merchant ships, learning to become pilots for the Baltic and Gulf of Finland. At the age of seventeen they leave the institution, and every year twenty-five are received into the navy, whilst the remainder become mates and masters of merchantmen.

The other school is for the sons of the "sea soldiers," or common sailors. Of these, there are upwards of 600, who, during the winter months, are taught reading, writing, and navigation, also to rig, splice, &c. In the summer the elder boys go to sea for practice in a small craft, and at the age of eighteen they are sent into the men-of-war, where, after a certain time, they become petty officers; so that, in course of time, the whole of the petty officers of the fleet will be taken from this school. Better materials for a future navy it is impossible to conceive. If this system be kept up,—and Russians do not do things by halves,—and our system keeps deteriorating, as of late years it has lamentably done, a very few years may see the Russians with a steam navy which even our national vanity will do well not to despise. The *physique* of Russian sailors is quite equal to that of English sailors, whilst their bravery is not a whit less. Should war arise they will meet then on fair terms, whilst steam is every day lessening the superiority of naval manœuvre ; and war will become, as Sir Charles Napier observed at Cronstadt, merely " a question of who has most guns and can fire fastest." To preserve our own naval superiority will require infinitely more vigour than we displayed in the late war.

As Russian submarine mines, and various other devices for destroying an enemy's vessel, have made considerable noise in the world, it will be necessary to allude to the subject more particularly than has been hitherto done.

Some ten years previous to the late war, the Russian Government had made some successful experiments with submarine mines. These were the invention of M. Nobell, a Swedish engineer, who had taken out a patent, which he sold to the Russians for 80,000 roubles, at the same time establishing a factory in St. Petersburg, which factory was in existence at the time of the war.

The construction of M. Nobell's mines has been carefully kept secret since his connection with Russia ; but as his experiments previous to that period are known, the general arrangement of his invention is probably as follows : —

Iron or wooden cases are plunged down in a narrow passage or channel, at about a ship's width from each other. Inside these cases, when filled with gunpowder, are glass pipes, containing sulphuric acid, surrounded by a compound of chlorate of potass, sugar, and sulphur, which explodes when the glass pipes containing the acid are broken ; and this again explodes the gunpowder. To ensure the breakage of the glass pipes, long arms or levers extend horizontally from the cases. To these are fastened a thick metallic wire or piston-rod, running through a stuffing-box on the top of the case, and communicating with the glass pipe containing the acid. By any pressure upon the levers, as of a ship's bottom in passing, the glass is broken, and the powder explodes.

These cases were frequently picked up, and were found to answer admirably. By examining one too closely, Rear Admiral Seymour lost his eye, through incautiously moving the lever. The charge of powder in those picked up was found to be only about eight pounds ; but with larger charges of powder there can be no question but that this machine would prove very destructive ; whilst if in contact with it, as in the shallow channels of the Russian ports it must be, the destruction of the ship may be reasonably expected to ensue. From the small charge of powder used, those ships which came in contact with these machines escaped with an abrasion of their copper and the destruction of their crockery ; though in one case, still severer damage was sustained.

The way of obviating the effect of these machines

is to send flat-bottomed boats into the channels with very long ropes to which drags are attached. These coming in contact with the levers, of course explode the machines. In the war these were so thickly planted that the Russian vessels themselves would not venture amongst them, which may, in one point of view, account for their keeping so closely in port; for of the efficacy of the " infernal machine," if heavily charged with powder, there can be no question, *i. e.*, in a shallow channel, where every vessel that passes must touch a lever and explode the machine. Great numbers, however, did not explode; but the reason of this was plain. Every machine was provided with a " safety-cap," which it was the duty of those who laid them down to remove before sinking them. The Russian sailors, evidently believing the machines to possess extensive powers of mischief beforehand, wisely took the precaution to sink them with the safety-cap still remaining on them ! when of course they were harmless ; and in this condition numbers were picked up.

In an experiment made with one of these at Riga, with a heavy charge of powder, the vessel which was exposed to it was completely cut in two.

Another plan, which has never been thoroughly fathomed, was to defend Cronstadt by something considered to be of the nature of the late Captain Warner's submarine shell. Whatever it might be, the experiment had been tried and was found favourable ; and there are reasons to believe that the plan consisted of a line of explosive machines connected by a cased wire, and this again connected with an electric battery, by which the whole line drawn across the channel could be simultaneously exploded.

A third plan was disclosed by a workman in the employ of the Russian Government, who showed the one on which he was at work. It consisted of an outer case or shell of iron, an inner one of wood, and an interior one of copper. The last was charged with 450 pounds of gunpowder. A wire went through the three cases, and extended to a galvanic battery in the fort. The infernal machine was suspended from a buoy at about three feet below the surface of the water. On a ship coming sufficiently near, as determined by the look-out in the fort, the battery was fired. An experiment tried on an old vessel was perfectly satisfactory. Nor could any ship in the narrow channels of Cronstadt avoid coming sufficiently close, so that it must receive the full force of the charge.

To these cylinders, thus charged, two tubes with wires were attached, to complete the galvanic circuit. Some of the machines floated on a level with the water, or barely beneath it. In the month of March about fifty or sixty of these mines were ready at Cronstadt, and were placed in the channels, as well as in the direction of Peterhoff.

In the month of April, 525 of these machines were completed, and eleven per day were turned out at the Leuchtenberg works, but with a marked improvement in their construction. A lever and piston was attached, as in the infernal machines first named, and this being struck by a vessel in contact with the machine, completed the circuit of the wires, which were attached to galvanic batteries, kept constantly charged in the forts. The nature of the mechanism by which this was effected is unknown, but there is no difficulty in devising such mechanism.

Drawings of these machines were supplied by Russian workmen, who even asserted that some were made with an electric battery connected with the machine, or rather contained within it, this being renewed as its power became expended. These machines were placed in the water between the forts.

In the month of April 1854, an American, named Smith, left New York for St. Petersburg with a Russian officer, some English and Irish workmen, and a French diver in his company. The name of the officer was Grunwald, and the whole particulars are detailed in the *New York Herald* of April 7th, 1854. Smith's plan, however, appears to have been nothing more than the old American torpedo experiment, which was a failure, and is by far inferior to the Russian modes, every one of which is practicable in their own peculiar shallow waters, though of little value elsewhere. Smith's object appears to have been to get up a company, stipulating for so much for every vessel destroyed. Nothing seems to have come of it, the Russians being better versed in such matters than the Americans.

The Russians had also another very formidable submarine engine of destruction, invented by a French gentleman in 1839 when director of a scientific establishment in St. Petersburg. He termed the machine the "*Fulminifère*," a name sufficiently indicative of its nature. It was about the size of a soldier's knapsack, and contained its own electric apparatus always ready to work. It was intended to be used on the ground or in the air, as well as under water, by means of conducting wires; and when afterwards submitted to the French Government, as certain to be used against the ships, if they came near enough to the forts, Commissioners were appointed to examine it, and reported most highly of it, as being "as quick as thought in action, with no doubt as to exploding a submarine mine the instant any vessel approached it."

The channels leading to Sweaborg and Cronstadt were also well defended by ordinary booms. One class of booms, which were known to be thickly scattered in the channels, was not, however, of ordinary construction. It consisted of two huge spars bolted together, and anchored in such a way that it floated eight feet beneath the surface of the water, where it would form a formidable impediment to a ship coming in contact with it, inflicting serious injury on her bottom.

The stakes with which the channels were thickly studded were still more formidable. A huge trough was formed, in which thick beams or stakes shod with iron were placed at an angle of about thirty degrees, supported by and built into the base, by strong uprights. A ship going at an ordinary rate of speed and encountering these stakes in from twenty-four to twenty-eight feet of water, must infallibly have had some of them through her bottom, when they would have acted as efficiently as a shot would have done.

The whole of these particulars were known to the Admirals of the Allied Fleets long before they reached Cronstadt, for the Russians did not succeed in preserving their secrets in this respect. In those channels where these contrivances were known to abound no ships ventured, and the Russians themselves took good care to steer clear of their own devices, which, as will have been seen, are not to be classed as "wonderful inventions," but were in every case simple though scientific in conception, and perfectly practicable in execution, provided the ships went near them, and this, if they entered the channels at all, could not by any possibility be avoided. In deeper waters than those of the Russian forts, the whole would scarcely be worth a thought; but the shallow waters of Russia are her greatest protection.

When, however, these devices are superadded to the fire of the strongest fortifications in the world, it is no wonder that the Allied Fleets, without the ordinary means of warfare, should not venture into such channels, or that their respective Governments should praise them highly for their caution, as has been seen. In the following year Admiral Dundas with more than double the force of the first fleet, took equal care to steer clear of Cronstadt, and was still more highly praised for so doing than had been Sir C. Napier.

CHAP. XII.

RETURN OF THE FLEETS TO BARO SOUND.

As nothing could be effected before Cronstadt, for want of gun- and mortar-vessels, and as it was not desirable to alarm the Russians by useless demonstrations, that could only have resulted in showing them their weak points, which would have thus been strengthened before means could be supplied in the following campaign, the Admirals were anxious to get away, in order to prepare for an attack on Bomarsund, as had previously been determined. Indeed, since the summer was now far advanced, no time was to be lost in this operation, as in case of a protracted siege, the capture of the place might not be effected before bad weather had set in; whilst, by the Government at home, it was deemed highly desirable that Bomarsund should be taken, in order that something might be done to satisfy the public, this being now the chief aim, as it was pretty clear that Sweden would have nothing to do with it when taken.

Whilst at Cronstadt the Admiral had learned that Russia had sent a squadron of small steamers from Svensk Sund to Sweaborg. Svensk Sund is near Viborg, a port at the north extremity of Biorko Sound; he therefore despatched the *Impérieuse, Arrogant, Desperate, Bull-dog, Magicienne,* and *Lightning* under the orders of Captain Watson, to reconnoitre Biorko Sound and the channel leading to Viborg. Captain Watson found a spacious anchorage nearly land-locked and not fortified,—but no gun-boats, which confirmed the information previously given. The fact was, that there was an inshore channel leading from Viborg to Sweaborg, within which none of the vessels of the combined squadron could have penetrated from their great draught of water, so that gun-boats could move about as they pleased. Had the fleet been provided with vessels of light draft, this would not have happened.

The Allied Fleets left the anchorage before Tolbouken on the 2nd of July, and stood to the westward, some of the French ships being taken in tow as before. It was the wish of the Admiral to have instituted as thorough a search as his means would permit of the numerous harbours and lurking places on both sides of the Gulf; and with this view he expressed a wish to Admiral Parseval, that in returning, he should take the south shore of the Gulf, whilst he himself inspected the northern shore. But, on re-consideration, it was deemed by both Admirals desirable that the fleet should make the best of its way to Baro Sound, in order to prepare for an attack on Bomarsund; so that no reconnoissance was made.

The combined fleet anchored at Seskar on the same day as it left Cronstadt. Whilst at Seskar, chase was given to a Russian steamer inshore, evidently bound from Sweaborg to Cronstadt, but from her speed and knowledge of the channels she escaped. Some schooners carrying wood to St. Petersburg were intercepted, and targets were at once made of them, in order to try what the practice of the ships might be as against gun-boats, should they be fallen in with. Admiral Chads, who before the war was in command of the *Excellent*, gunnery ship at Portsmouth, was ordered to fire at them; the result of the experiment proved that it was a difficult matter to hit vessels of this class, from large ships, the shot ricocheting over them. Had the Russians themselves previously instituted such an experiment, their gun-boats might have inflicted no small damage on our ships, without receiving much injury in return.

On landing at the town of Seskar, the inhabitants had all fled, locking up their houses, and leaving their church in its ordinary condition, even to the prayer books, &c., ready for use. This was evidently done in reliance that nothing would be injured ; and the reliance was well placed, as nothing belonging to the inhabitants was touched.

The combined fleet again weighed anchor on the 5th of July, the French squadron in tow of French and English steamers. On this day, the fleet was joined by another French war steamer.

On the 6th, the combined fleet stood in for Admiral Corry's squadron off Helsingfors; and at 7.45, the Admiral repaired on board the *Duke of Wellington*. It has been said that Admiral Corry was left at Baro Sound, in order to watch Helsingfors during the absence of the combined fleet at Cronstadt. Fearful lest any Russian vessels might escape him, he had taken his squadron to Helsingfors, where he so disposed it as to prevent any chance of escape, leaving, however, some ships in Baro Sound, in order to prevent the Russians from conveying stores and guns to the ports in the Gulf of Bothnia, as well as to prevent an extensive squadron of gun-boats from proceeding to Sweaborg from Abo and other places, where they had been built with the intention of arming them at Sweaborg.

The position which Admiral Corry had occupied throughout was one demanding increasing care and vigilance, as well as subjecting his squadron to no small amount of exertion. When cruising off Dager Ort, he had been exposed to constant fogs, which, though they might induce the Russians to keep within shelter of their ports, entailed on him increased difficulty in seeing that they did not slip past him. Admiral Corry's squadron consisted for the most part of sailing vessels, and in the strong gales and fogs, which had been incessant, it required no small amount of care and judgment to keep ships in safety without steam, in a navigation where, from the constant sudden shoaling of the water, the lead was not to be relied on, as under ordinary circumstances.

Whilst at Baro Sound, Admiral Corry learned that thirteen English prisoners had been brought from Gamla Carleby to Helsingfors. These formed part of the *Vulture's* crew, which had been captured there. Others of the captured crew had been taken elsewhere, it being no doubt a part of the Russian policy to parade them as widely as possible, as evidence of the victories which the Russian Government every now and then put forth as having been gained over the British fleet! As those to whom these victories were announced had no other means of ascertaining the truth respecting them, Russia must, in the estimation of her own subjects in the interior, have been highly successful. The puzzle was that the British, after being so often beaten off, would not go away, and the Russian Government, no doubt feeling the ridicule of this, afterwards began to diminish the number of its victories. The Russians refused to exchange prisoners, on the ground that combatants and noncombatants were not to be placed in the same scale.

The British squadron again anchored in Baro Sound, the French following. The *Duguesclin* unfortunately got ashore, notwithstanding all the precautions taken. The launches and pinnaces of the fleet went to her assistance, lightening her of every-thing removable ; but she was not got off till after a lapse of eighteen hours. On the 7th, the *Duguesclin* returned to Baro Sound, in tow of the *Phlégéton*.

The Admiral had been apprised by Sir James Gra-ham that, on his return to Baro Sound, he should have full instructions as to an attack on Aland, but that it was necessary first to communicate with the French Government. As these instructions had not arrived, the fleet had no alternative but to wait till they should be received, though much time was being wasted.

The interval was diligently employed in exercising the boats in such evolutions as would shortly become necessary. Every day the squadron manned and armed boats, which exercised in divisions ; the French squadron doing the same. The marines were sent on shore under Col. Graham, and the seamen were provided with scaling ladders, with which they prac-tised upon the lighthouse at Renskar. Sham fights were also organised, and every possible kind of in-struction given which might afterwards be useful at Bomarsund.

On the 10th of July the Admiral wrote to Lord Bloomfield the result of his examination of Cronstadt as follows : — " I have been to Cronstadt: it is im-pregnable. I never in my life saw such a force of guns. There are more by one half than is necessary ; nevertheless they drew their ships into the inner basin, for greater security." The Czar had refused to allow an exchange of prisoners ; and Sir Charles told Lord Bloomfield that, if he persisted in this, he would make prisoners of all his fishermen, who had hitherto been released, and it would be as well if the Russian Minister at Berlin were told this.

Lord Bloomfield replied that "he was glad the fleet was away from the pestiferous waters of Cron-stadt, as they had heard in Berlin that the cholera was raging very badly there. His Lordship trusted that the Admiral's plan of destroying the town, docks, and fleet from the back of the Island would be carried out *next year*, when he would be better sup-plied with gun-boats and troops.

On the 2nd of July, Sir James Graham wrote to the Admiral as follows :—

" The Cabinet has taken into consideration the statement contained in your private letter to me of the 20th ult., from Baro Sound. You were then on the point of starting for Cronstadt, intending to offer battle to the Russian fleet, but without much hope of the challenge being accepted ; and under a strong impression that the entrance into the harbour would be found inaccessible, and if so, your return to Baro Sound is expected.

" We have collected also from the various reports that, with 10,000 men, Bomarsund and the Aland Isles may be taken ; *and being of opinion that the presence of the Allied fleet in the Baltic must be marked by some result*, we determined to propose to the Emperor of the French to send there forth, with 6000 soldiers; and these in addition to your marines and to the troops now on board the French line-of-battle ships, will raise the effectual military force at your disposal to 10,000 men.

" The two Governments have arranged their measures in consequence, and on the 14th of this month 6000 French soldiers, with ten guns, fifty horses and *caissons*, will be embarked on board British ships of war and transports, for conveyance either to Baro Sound or Faro, as may be thought most expedient: I incline to the latter place, an attack on Bomarsund being the first object, unless indeed you agree with the Emperor that Langhorn is assailable, in which case Baro Sound must be the rendezvous, and Sweaborg the object at which we must aim.

"I am disposed to begin with Bomarsund, but you and the French Admiral must decide; your success there may be reduced to certainty, and it will be the first hard blow in the battle. Moreover, while Sweden is hesitating, France and England will have gained a possession without her aid, which she might have won for herself, and which to her is of inestimable value. She must become our suitor when we hold Aland, and we shall be enabled to command her future assistance on our own terms.

" I wish you would have Abo closely examined and watched; and, with our views on Bomarsund, it is of great importance that no reinforcements should pass from Finland to the Aland Islands. It will be known that troops are about to be sent to you, and you must endeavour to mask your real object of attack, and point rather to Revel and Riga than to Bomarsund and Langhorn.

" I send my son out in the *Dauntless* to join the *St. Jean d'Acre*. Perhaps you will allow him to wait on you, and to make your acquaintance; and *I am glad that in his early life he should have the honour and advantage of serving in a fleet under your command.*"

On receiving this letter, Sir Charles Napier sent two additional steamers to Admiral Plumridge in the Gulf of Bothnia, with instructions to prevent succours being thrown into the Fort of Bomarsund, as 6000 French troops were coming out to attack it. Admiral Plumridge was directed to watch all the passages, but not to create suspicion. He was also instructed that everything else must be given up, to prevent troops and provisions being thrown into the fortress, and that he must, especially, gain every information he could about the north passage.

On the 4th of July, Sir J. Graham instructed the Admiral to send at once one of his own surveying vessels, to help the line-of-battle ships conveying the troops through the Belt. Two would be better than one, and if Sir Charles could send an officer who " *knows your own way of threading dangers, which has been so successful, it would be of great service.*"

In accordance with these instructions, the Admiral despatched the *Bulldog* on this service, her commander, Captain W. K. Hall, having had considerable experience there since the Belt was first passed. Captain Hall had also previously piloted the French fleet through the Belt.

The First Lord apprised the Admiral that Colonel Jones, of the Royal Engineers, would also be sent, with the rank of Brigadier-General, to aid him in communicating with the French military authorities; and that he would bring with him two officers on his staff, and eighty sappers and miners, with two subalterns to command them. Colonel Jones was to be ready to serve in different ships, and in concert with the Admiral, as the exigencies of the service might require.

Sir James hoped that this military expedition would sail on the 16th of July from the Downs, so as to join the fleet by the 1st of August. The British ships of war which conveyed them were ordered to be sent back to England as soon as they had been cleared of the troops. The details of arrangement would be forwarded whilst the expedition was on its way, so that the Admiral and his French colleague could make all necessary preparations before they arrived.

On the 10th of July, the Admiral wrote to Sir James Graham, acknowledging his advice that 6000 French troops were coming, and detailing his pre-parations to meet them. He told Sir James that the French Admiral and himself agreed that attacking Langhorn would not advance us at Sweaborg; whilst Hango was useless, now that the fleets had possession of Baro Sound. As soon as Bomarsund was taken, he would turn his attention to Abo. The Admiral added, in reply to Sir James Graham's cautions, " I shall take care to be on my guard against the Russians from Cronstadt. If they come down, so much the better."

On the 11th of July, Sir James Graham wrote to the Admiral as follows : —

" Your report, together with Capt. Sulivan's plan, is a clear and very able exposition of the strength of the arsenal at Cronstadt, and of the extreme difficulty and uncertainty of an attack, even if sustained by a large force of gun-boats and of troops, which are not at present at your disposal. I had anticipated your return to the westward, after an offer of battle, which I felt certain the enemy would decline ; and it now remains for you to blockade the Gulf of Finland, to keep the fleets at Cronstadt and at Helsingfors disunited, and to await the arrival of the French troops, when you and the French Admiral and General must deliberate on the operations to be undertaken by the combined forces.

" Bomarsund will clearly be within your reach. Sweaborg, if it were possible, would be a noble prize. But on no account be led into *any desperate attempt;* and above all things avoid the least risk of the Russian fleet slipping out of the Gulf of Finland when your back is turned. These Russians, though shy, are crafty, and if they can catch you at a disadvantage, they will be down upon you.

" Capt. Scobell has put the enclosed memorandum into my hands. I told him that the use of fireships *had not been over-looked by you from the first hour of your appointment to your present command.*

" I am afraid we shall not be able to send the whole of the French troops to the Baltic on Friday next, as I had hoped a day or two ago. The transports are not quite ready, but I still am confident that the whole number will be assembled at Faro by the 6th of August.

" Sweden will not move unless Austria go to war with Russia; and Austria still hesitates and hangs back. With *50,000 Swedes and 200 Swedish gun-boats, you might still do something great and decisive before the end of September.*"

This letter shows the first symptom of a break-down in the Admiralty plans. The First Lord tells Captain Scobell that Sir Charles had never ceased to ask for small vessels from the first hour of his appointment; — but none were sent! " Sweden will not move;" "*but with* 50,000 *Swedish troops and* 200 *Swedish gun-boats* " the Admiral might still do something great and decisive. The story of the fox and the grapes is then no fable. It is here seriously embodied in the instructions of the First Lord of the Admiralty. It was no new discovery that Sweden would not move. The Admiral had told the Government the same thing months before, and that from a very reliable authority, viz., the assurance of the Swedish Government itself. How much better would it have been for the British Government to have bestirred itself, and to have supplied means whereby the fleet could have done without the assistance of Sweden!

It is, however, quite clear, from the above letter, that without the "50,000 Swedes and 200 Swedish gun-boats," the allied fleets were not expected by the First Lord to do anything "great and decisive." It was in the hope of getting Swedish troops and gun-boats that the fleet had been sent to sea *without gun-boats!* But when this fact, that we could not get Swedish co-operation, had become apparent, on the Admiral's visit to Sweden in May, it should have been looked in the face, and not have been delayed till the nation had become clamorous, and the Admiral was without means to satisfy its demands. It was now necessary to attack Bomarsund by way of satisfying popular clamour, though Sweden would not accept it. Had the fleet been properly equipped, Bomarsund might have been a secondary object, as had before been said by Sir James Graham. Now its destruction had become a serious point.

Another part of this despatch must not escape notice, viz., that in which Sir J. Graham quotes the Admiral's opinion as to the "extreme difficulty of attacking Cronstadt — *even with gun-boats.*" The Admiral never said anything of the kind. On the contrary, his report on Cronstadt was written to show — and did show — that, with a proper supply of gun-boats, Cronstadt *might be successfully attacked* by several different methods, and with the ordinary chances of war, as against a powerful enemy. It is amusing to see how cleverly the Admiral is linked into this gun-boat excuse, though he had stated in his Cronstadt report the exact contrary! He did not conceal the difficulty of attacking Cronstadt, but he showed how, with proper means, it could be destroyed — but not taken. It was then unworthy of Sir James Graham to twist the Admiral's report into accordance with the shortcomings of the Government, at the same time that he gave him every credit for the great ability displayed in the report.

Shortly before this, Denmark as well as Sweden had represented the dissatisfaction she felt with the proceedings of Admiral Plumridge in the Gulf of Bothnia. The remonstrance was made to Mr. Buchanan, the British Minister at Copenhagen. To this Mr. Buchanan replied in a way which called forth the approbation of the British Government and prevented further interference.

Before leaving Baro Sound, Sir Charles Napier replied at great length to a communication which he had received from Sir James Graham, dated 4th of July, and enclosing a report from Capt. Washington, then employed in the Hydrographer's office, where he afterwards succeeded Sir Francis Beaufort as Hydrographer.

Capt. Washington's report was to the effect that, by means of dredging-machines, and in presence of the enemy, the Admiral should dredge his way into the passages to Sweaborg, which the Russians had blocked up with heavy stones and rubbish of every description.

As the project of Captain Washington is, perhaps, one of the most extraordinary ever broached, and as much was afterwards made of it, it will be interesting to the naval profession, in present and future times, to enter into full details on the subject.

Captain Washington's report is dated June 25th, 1854, and is addressed to Sir James Graham, who had first written to him on the feasibility of effecting a passage into Helsingfors by *dredging* (!) some of the *blocked-up channels*, and also upon the means of getting through the submarine piling on the North side of Cronstadt.

To this communication from Sir J. Graham Capt. Washington replied as follows : —

" On examining the plan of Helsingfors, it will be seen that there is an anchorage called Miolo Roads, spacious enough to contain the whole Baltic fleet, lying about two miles to the east-ward of the principal entrance to the port, but without the range of the guns of the fortress of Sweaborg. I would suppose the fleet, or a strong squadron of the fleet, to have taken up this anchorage, where they would have a full view of the harbour and its approaches, and where they could lie leisurely and deliberate upon their plans, and that the question of effecting an entrance should be under consideration.

" It will be seen, on inspecting the plan, that, besides the main channel into the harbour, which lies immediately under the guns of Sweaborg, there are three other passages, one on each side of King's Holmen, and a third to the westward of Sweaborg by Langhorn.

" Although this last-named channel is not the more immediate object in view in this letter, it may be mentioned that, supposing our charts to be correct, there is depth of water enough for the largest ships to enter by this passage. Had it not been a practicable channel, I do not think the island of Langhorn, which, strictly speaking, is not one of the Sweaborg group, would have been so strongly fortified.

" That the channel is not blocked up artificially is not a

sufficient argument against its being practicable, as the passage is much deeper, and, including both sides of Langhorn, four times in width more than any of the blocked-up channels, and therefore it would have been much more difficult to fill up.

" To enter by this passage, the fleet would approach from the south-west, and would be exposed to some of the guns on the west side of Sweaborg; also to stand end on for some time to Langhorn, mounting twenty-four guns on its south end; it is also probable that some guns may have been recently mounted on the point of Helsingfors near the baths. The distance from the spot of first coming under the fire of Sweaborg to getting out of it again inside the harbour, would be about three miles, and would occupy about half an hour of time. In the event of taking this channel, the fleet would require to be led by a surveying vessel to pilot the ships.

" To return to the more immediate object of this letter, viz., the channels to the east and west of King's Holmen.

" The grand advantage of the eastern of these two channels is, that it lies 2800 yards from the centre of the fortress of Sweaborg, and therefore may be considered out of damaging gunshot from that fort. Both the channels *have been partially blocked up with stones;* but the whole breadth of the obstacle to be removed in either channels from a depth five fathoms on the outside to five fathoms on the inside, is less then half a cable or 100 yards. To open a passage, then, through this barrier of twenty yards average width, 100 yards in length, and five fathoms in depth, would render it necessary to dredge away 10,000 cubic yards, or 15,000 tons of soil, besides removing the stones, which seem small in amount.

" Now an efficient steam dredge such as that in Portsmouth harbour, with a plentiful supply of punts to carry away the stuff, can move 200 tons an hour, or say 4000 tons in the twenty-four hours, working by relays of men night and day. Two steam dredges would then accomplish the work in two days. With regard to the stones, it depends much upon the nature of the work how they are to be removed. If of loose rubble, there would be no difficulty ; if of rough masonry, they might prove more troublesome. Probably, the simplest mode in both cases would be, as suggested by Mr. Brunel, to dredge a trench immediately on the outer edge of the barrier and close up to its face, sufficiently wide and deep to hold the portion it would be necessary to remove, say 400 tons, and then attack it by small charges of powder at its base, and, no doubt, it would soon topple over and fall into the trench.

" It remains to be considered whether the dredges could be tolerably protected from the fire of the enemy during the short time required for the operation. Much must depend on the temporary batteries the Russians may have erected on the islands called Bak Holmen, King's Holmen, and Sandhamm. In September last there were no guns on either. It is understood that lately some earthworks have been thrown up on Bak Holmen, on its south-west and south sides; but it is not probable they could be of a nature to fire over King's Holmen so as to damage the dredge working in the east channel, which is the one I recommend.

" During the operations it would be necessary to occupy the small island of King's Holmen on the west and Sandhamm on the east. These are rocky islands of a moderate height, say from thirty to fifty feet in the highest parts, and Sandhamm is thickly covered with dwarf-pine. Earthworks thrown upon these islands, and some heavy guns planted, would keep in check the Russian ships inside, which of course would attempt to stop the work. Our ships, too, might approach close to the outside of the passage, and so cover the dredges. As an additional precaution, and to protect the machinery, it would not be difficult, *by means of three layers of buffalo hides,* and short junks of cable two thicknesses crossed diagonally, to render the dredges shot-proof.

" It need hardly be pointed out that while these works were going on it would be prudent to make a feint at more points than one. Steamers might proceed up the channel north of Sandhamm, towards Hasnas Sound, and so attract attention in that quarter. Some portion of the fleet might make a demonstration by the Langhorn passage, or by distant shelling keep the enemy on the *qui vive ;* indeed the guns landed on Sandhamm might *create so much smoke,* that the operations of the dredge should not be seen or suspected. Some other modes of *raising a smoke* might also be devised.

" I am disposed to think that we *might turn fogs to good account* in our approaches to these forts and channels. A small steamer going slowly in the smooth water of these land-locked seas, is so entirely under command that she can be stopped almost instantly ; and with a platform suspended under the bowsprit, which is the proper position for a leadsman on such occasions, a steamer judiciously conducted might find her way almost anywhere in a fog, especially if there has been a good view of the land on a fine day previously.

" To return to the dredging. Supposing a practicable channel dredged wide enough for a single ship to pass at a time, two small steamers must precede the squadron, and take up a position, one on either of the two shoals inside. That done, the steam squadron has only *to dash at the enemy's fleet,* as there is ample depth of water, and lay the ships along-side. The guns of Sweaborg would be neutralised, as by firing they would be as likely to strike a friend as a foe.

" The materials necessary to dredge the passage would be four steam dredges of 25-horse power each ; forty punts or hopper barges, of twenty tons each ; and four divers to place charges of powder, &c.

" Respectfully submitting the above suggestions for the consideration of officers of more experience than myself,

" I have the honour, &c.,

" JOHN WASHINGTON.

" To the Right Hon. Sir James Graham,

" &c. &c."

The reader will no doubt have observed the way in which the movements of the fleet were directed by Sir James Graham and his coadjutors at Whitehall, whilst the Admiral himself, with " the largest discretion" given to him, was reined in at every step he took. Half of his instructions from the First Lord were made up of cautions against "rashness," "desperate attempts," "stone walls," &c., whilst not a few contained notable hints about "diving-bells to pull up the enemy's piles, holding islands during the winter, and breaking trenches of water in the ice to keep off the Russians, &c." In the above report, the Admiral is initiated into the mystery of dredging, taught the use of buffalo hides, put up to the dodge of making a smoke to blind the enemy, instructed in the utility of making feints, and finally told how and where to place a leadsman! If the document itself were not now before our naval readers, they might reasonably think that fiction had been resorted to by way of giving pungency to our narrative. Before such Cabinet guidance, blocked-up channels and masses of stone twenty yards wide, 100 yards long, and thirty feet deep, were to vanish like the smoke under cover of which they were to be blown away. Yet all these suggestions appear to have been made on the strength of Admiralty Charts by no means correct; though why this was now done is somewhat strange, as, before the war, Capt. Washington had been sent by the Government to inspect the Russian channels, and ought to have personally known all about them.

No slight portion of the Admiral's time must have been wasted in replying to such schemes; for these coming direct from the First Lord, he could not avoid so doing. On the 18th of July he thus commented on Capt. Washington's plan of taking Sweaborg : —

" MY DEAR SIR JAMES,

" I had no time to make my observations on Captain Washington's papers by last mail. I beg now to give you my opinion.

" 1st. As Brunel stipulated that the workmen are not to be disturbed by shot or shell, I shall say nothing about dredging. It is an engineer's question, and no doubt could be accomplished.

" 2nd. Capt. Washington is correct about Miolo Roads. It *has* been examined, and there is nothing to hinder a fleet lying there in security during the summer.

" 3rd. In looking at the plans you will see that Langhorn lies N.W., 500 yards distant from Wester Swarto. To approach it from Miolo Roads, you would have to pass to the southward of Abraham's Holm, and steer for Rantan, leaving several shoals on your port hand, which would be buoyed: but the large ships could not pass through the channels; *you would be exposed to the raking fire of the whole of the sea-face of Sweaborg,* when you came abreast of Langhorn, alongside of which there is only room for one ship, which certainly could not reduce it, and therefore would not anchor. The whole fleet would therefore have to pass through a most intricate channel before they arrived at Helsingfors, which I I take not to be strong, but which would still require pounding to keep it quiet.

" When at anchor the Admiral would have to consider whether he would run the gauntlet *back again*, outside Sweaborg, or go in, after taking breath and repairing damages. The chances are that he would find Sweaborg as strong as the plans show it, and return to Miolo Roads, *leaving* probably some of his ships behind, either going or coming. As the fleet is to be led by a surveying ship, *Capt. Washington should command her.* So much for Langhorn.

" The Eastern passage, by my plan, is 2200 yards from the nearest fort, not 2800, as remarked by Capt. Washington. This passage is blocked up, and he proposes, by means of two steam dredges, to remove 15,000 tons of stones and rubbish in *two days*. This he calls a 'short time' to be under the fire of the temporary batteries erected on the islands of Bak Holmen and Sandhamm, but which he considers *not likely to damage the dredges*. However, in the next paragraph, he finds it necessary to occupy the islands of King's Holmen on the west and Sandhamm on the east, where some heavy guns are to be placed to keep the Russians in check. Our ships are to anchor and cover the dredges, who are also to be protected against shot and shell by means of 'layers of bullock's hides, and short junks of cables,' which he thinks would render the dredges shot-proof, but which I think would do no such thing.

"A feint is then to be made by steamers at Hasnas Sound, where *there is only two fathoms water*, and part of the fleet is to make a demonstration by the Langhorn passage, which I have already shown is almost impassable. Finally, the dredges are to be covered ' *by smoke*,' and he is also to bring the fog to his assistance, which, however, may not appear the day he wants it. The passage being opened, the steam squadron is then to 'dash at the enemy's fleet' and bring them out; and during that time the guns of Sweaborg —said to be upwards of 2000—are to be doing nothing! The garrison, I suppose, consists of between 20,000 and 30,000 men, and all are to be idle, and allow us to land at King's Holmen and Sandhamm.

"He will require, moreover, 40 punts and 4 divers, to place powder for blowing up the stones; but he has forgotten to say that an army large enough to contend against the force which the Emperor of Russia could send against him, and which would probably be 100,000 men, would be necessary to support his operations.

"As to his opening the north passage at Cronstadt, the only observation I have to make upon the subject is, that I have no doubt it is quite practicable, provided the Russians *will let you alone ;* but as that is not likely, his plan is *waste paper.*

"I have shown you the possibility of an attack on Cronstadt, both from north and south, and the difficulties in the way. The Admiralty can judge whether its success is probable or not."

But the plans given by Sir Charles to the Board implied fighting, for which the Board was not prepared. The plans sent by Sir James Graham implied correspondence only; and as the Admiral would not be likely to adopt them in preference to his own judgment on the spot, they were no doubt put forth to show the public that all sorts of plans were sent to him, which he had not the skill or energy to adopt! — and this was the use actually made of them afterwards; whilst it is abundantly evident that they were sent to him with the above view, when it should become necessary to cover the shortcomings of the First Lord, as having supplied all sorts of suggestions in place of means to carry out the legitimate operations of the fleet. What the Admiral wanted was means, not advice how to use them. The advice he got in profusion, but none of the means asked for were ever supplied during the campaign.

It is an act of justice to Capt. Washington to say that in the above report he had only put the crotchets of Sir James Graham into ship-shape. Capt. Washington in his report is careful to point out that the report is made " in accordance with the suggestions of Sir James Graham ; " Capt. Washington himself not being over-satisfied with the nature of the task which had been allotted to him, in place of old and experienced Admirals who would have laughed at the whole affair. Sir James then, and not Capt. Washington, must stand sponsor to the plan proposed in place of the judgment of the Admiral, who was on the spot, and had only asked for means, at the same time pointing out how he could use them with success. Had the Admiral and his French colleague agreed in adopting Capt. Washington's report, the means for the operation were no more forthcoming than were gun and mortar-boats; nor could the four steam dredges, forty barges, &c., have been supplied from England till the season was too far advanced to make use of them.

We will now give Sir Charles Napier's plan of attacking Sweaborg contained in the same despatch, *provided the means asked for were supplied.* The Admiral's plan will go down to posterity side by side with that of Capt. Washington, and posterity will judge of their relative merit.

" The only successful manner of attacking Sweaborg that I can see, after the most mature deliberation, assisted by Admiral Chads, who is a practical man, and knows more about gunnery than any man in the service, is *by fitting out a great number of gun-boats,* carrying one gun each, with a long range, and placing them west of Sweaborg, and south of Helsingfors. Every shell fired from these would tell somewhere, and perhaps not five per cent. from the enemy would take effect. Back these gun-boats by the fleet, to relieve the men, and in the course of the summer Sweaborg would be reduced to ashes, and Helsingfors also, if it was thought proper; and I don't see why we are to be mealy-mouthed in time of war. The ships, you will see, could not be destroyed, because they could move out of the way.

" I was at the siege of Martinique many years ago. We could not batter Fort Bourbon, as it lay higher than the ground around it; but fifty mortars, in three weeks, plunging their shells into it, made it surrender: and whether

mortars are placed on shore or in gun-boats is quite immaterial; indeed the latter have the advantage, for when their
shells begin to tell, and our blood begins to warm, the ships
would move up to the batteries, and close quarters would
finish what the mortar-boats began.

"I sent you home, I think, copies of all the plans I have,
and if you will lay them before the Engineer and Artillery
officers, I will be bound for it they will agree with me, that
this is the only way to destroy Sweaborg, *without an army
superior to the Emperor of Russia's*, which we are not likely
to bring into the field. It is too late this year; *but be all
prepared next*, now we know the anchorage, and begin early.

"I forgot to say that the islands within range may all be
put in requisition for thirteen-inch mortars. The expense
would be very great, no doubt; but if we are to bring
the war to a conclusion, expense must not be thought
about."

The preceding extracts, which only form a portion of the Admiral's letter, are sufficiently elaborate
as to the practicability of attacking Sweaborg *with
proper means*, and that with a loss of only 5 *per cent.*
on our side, as compared with the loss of the enemy.
Yet afterwards, when it was desirable to throw the
odium of not having attacked Sweaborg upon the
Admiral, in order to avert that odium from those who
by not supplying him with the means asked for, had
alone incurred it, the Board of Admiralty, on the
10th of November, "were not aware that any such
report had been received!"

As this was the most important plan of attack
sent by the Admiral during the whole campaign, it
must not be summarily dismissed. Important as it
was, *it was never laid before the Admiralty by Sir
James Graham*, the Board being in ignorance of it

x

almost up to the end of the campaign. The reason why Sir James Graham did not lay it before the Board, must be evident to any one above the capacity of a child. The same despatch which contained Sir Charles Napier's plan of attack on Sweaborg, contained also his comments on the Graham-Washington plan of dredging, so that both must have been known to the Board at the same time. Capt. Washington had taken good care in his report to throw the paternity of the dredging plan upon Sir James Graham, from whom it had emanated, and Sir James Graham was averse to encountering the criticism of the naval portion of the Board. Hence the most important plan of attack during the whole campaign was laid aside to cover Sir James Graham's engineering project of dredging his way into an enemy's fortress in place of supplying means to the fleet to fight its way in. Had Sir Charles Napier written his comment on the dredging plan and his plan of attacking Sweaborg on two separate sheets of paper, Sir James Graham would quietly have pocketed the first and laid the last before the Board, when means might have been supplied, and Sweaborg might have been attacked. Russia clearly owes the safety of Sweaborg to the modesty of Sir James Graham, or rather, perhaps, to that weakness, peculiar to statesmen, of wishing to be thought capable of directing any department of the public service, without possessing even the first elements of knowledge with regard to it. It has been said of a far more able statesman than Sir James Graham, in time of peace, " that he would have undertaken the command of the channel fleet." Sir James had undertaken the command of the Baltic fleet in time of war, but his plan was dredging — not fighting.

The suppression of the plans of the Admiral for attacking Sweaborg, forms a black page in our narrative. It is quite probable, for a reason now plain to the reader, that the Admiralty never had seen these documents, which constituted the most important plans sent home by the Admiral. Nevertheless it is extremely improbable that plans of such great importance to the campaign should have been altogether overlooked or laid aside; hence there is another reasonable inference, viz., that they had been kept back for the purpose of *not following them out.*

It was a *cheap war* in which the nation was engaged, and the Admiral had spoken of the *great expense* which would attend the carrying out of his plans. Sir James had told the Admiral to " hire his means from Sweden, as nothing *would be so economical!* " The Admiral demanded gun-boats, 13-inch mortars, of which he had not one, and Admiral Chads wanted forty Lancaster guns, this being the meaning of " guns of large calibre." The expense of these would have been very great, had they been provided in sufficient numbers to be of use. Hence the plans were altogether ignored.

But we must go farther than this. In March, 1856, when assailing the Admiral in Parliament, Sir James Graham denied, in effect, that any such plans had been sent home, for he stated that had such plans been sent home in time, the Government could have supplied the means asked for; though even in the following year, 1855, they could not be supplied to Admiral Dundas in sufficient quantities to be of use, and he had to leave his work at Sweaborg unfinished for want of them. How far then the Government could have supplied means in the summer of 1854, may safely be left to the judgment of the reader; and the more so, as at that time they had no gunboats whatever; being in treaty with Prussia for *two gun-boats* only, which Sir Charles Napier never saw, then or afterwards.

The specious sophistry used by Sir James Graham in thus throwing the blame on Sir Charles Napier, after having stated in his letters that from the very first the Admiral had never ceased to ask for small vessels, was a daring manœuvre. The House was ignorant of dates, even if it were disposed to follow the reasoning of the ex-First Lord; who therefore boldly asserted that if *in May*, 1854, Sir Charles had asked for the class of vessels he wanted, they could have been supplied to him. Sir James Graham well knew that in May, 1854, the Admiral had not been near Sweaborg, but was at Elgsnabben and Hango! and therefore could not, of his own knowledge, have known anything about Sweaborg. Yet this sophistry passed muster with the House, as did other sophistry just as reliable.

But it was surely an idle argument that if Sir Charles Napier had asked for means in time, he could have had them. The Government ought rather to have supplied him with means without asking for. Sending a fleet to war without means, is a novelty even in Admiralty administration. But Sir James

Graham, as has been seen, testified that the Admiral never ceased to ask for means "*from the first hour of his appointment.*" Is it not then nonsense to say that, if he had asked for means in time, he could have had them? Yet this was the statement of Sir James Graham when attacking him in the House of Commons nearly two years afterwards. Sir James Graham must have a bad memory, and instead of proving his case, he only proved that the Government, to save itself, was endeavouring to throw the Admiral overboard by statements not founded in fact, hoping that the public had forgotten the few facts they were in possession of, and knowing that they were in ignorance of others. The whole facts hitherto are now supplied, and the public can draw its own inferences, which, like all public inferences, will be the right ones.

This unworthy subterfuge of imputing to the Admiral the not having asked for means in time, will be best met by again recurring to an extract from a despatch of Sir H. Seymour, the British Ambassador at St. Petersburg, dated February 4th, 1854, before the appointment of Sir C. Napier to the command of the fleet. " The Russian fleet is stated to be twenty-seven sail of the line, twenty frigates, ten steam-frigates, and 180 gun-boats. Eighty of these gun-boats will be manned by Fins, about fifty in each. *Steamers drawing little water will be required for clearing the Gulf of these gun-boats*, and their crews should be armed with Minié rifles." Here, before war had broken out, we have the British Ambassador at St. Petersburg pointing out to the Government the

precise nature of the armament required to attack
Russia; but even thus forewarned by their own Ambassador, the best judge of the enemy's force, the
Government, then and afterwards, neglected to provide any means of the kind. Even "*from the first
hour of his appointment*," as Sir James Graham himself testifies, the Admiral had asked for the means
which Sir H Seymour had so judiciously pointed out;
but had asked in vain, for at no period of his campaign in the Baltic were those means supplied to him.
Nevertheless, by the terror of his name alone, coupled by the belief of the enemy in his resources, he
"cleared the Gulf of gun-boats," for no gun-boats
ventured to make their appearance; though, had the
Russians been aware of the inadequacy of his means,
they must indeed have been destitute of courage
not to have attempted to turn their large flotilla of
gun-boats to account.

The public is now in possession of the facts of the
case, divested of the gloss of Sir James Graham's
eloquence. When *want of means* had failed, as it
always must fail, it was deemed desirable to make
Sir Charles Napier the scape-goat. Like Byng, he
was marked out as a sacrifice to incompetence, but
unlike Byng, he could not conveniently be shot. The
next best thing was to attempt to destroy his hard-
earned reputation. Whether this course was successful or not, let posterity determine.

CHAP. XIII.

ON the 18th of July, the French and English squadrons again weighed anchor and stood to sea, leaving the *Impérieuse* and *Dragon* at anchor in Baro Sound. The British squadron consisted of the *Duke of Wellington, Royal George, St. Jean d'Acre, Princess Royal, James Watt, Nile, Cæsar, Cressy, Edinburgh, Blenheim, Hogue,* and *Ajax,* screw-ships. The *Neptune, St. George, Prince Regent, Monarch,* and *Cumberland,* sailing ships; and the *Arrogant, Penelope, Magicienne, Dauntless, Amphion, Basilisk, Lightning, Alban,* and *Pigmy,* steamers; together with the *Belleisle,* hospital ship.

The French squadron consisted of *L'Inflexible,*

Austerlitz, Le Tage, Hercule, Jemmappes, Breslau, Duguesclin, Duperré, Trident, and six steamers.

The fleet formed order of sailing in three columns, and the *rendezvous* was appointed at Ledsund. The paddle-steamers were despatched to look out in advance, but shortly afterwards were recalled to tow the sailing ships.

In the evening, the fleet was joined by the French steamer *Milan,* bringing advices from Stockholm. From these the Admiral learned that any assistance to us from Sweden was out of the question, she evidently waiting to see the course which Austria would pursue. As Austria had sent an *ultimatum* to St. Petersburg, the result must soon be known. There was, in fact, no hope of Sweden joining the alliance, as the Admiral had ascertained when at Stockholm, soon after his entrance into the Baltic.

Sweden, however, was at this period putting herself in order for any course which her interests or inclination might dictate. Her army was placed in such a state of equipment that a large instalment could have taken the field in three weeks, had an order to that effect been given ; whilst her whole force of 60,000 men would only have required a preparation of six weeks. Her gun-boats could also have been got ready in three weeks, so that she was in a position either for war or to preserve her neutrality.

On the 19th of July, the *Driver,* which had been cruising off Hango, rejoined the fleet, and the *Magicienne* was sent in her place to join Captain Watson's squadron, which was watching the movements of the enemy during the absence of the Admiral. In the evening, the ships anchored to the N.E. of Bogskaren Beacon. The *Lightning, Alban, Driver,* and *Basilisk* were sent forward to buoy the passage to Ledsund.

On the 20th, the *Lightning* returned, with intelligence that the surveying vessels had discovered a practicable passage, and that the other ships were engaged in buoying it.

Early on the 21st, Sir Charles apprised Admiral Parseval that Captain Sulivan had discovered an excellent passage round Lagskaren Lighthouse, a short distance from Ledsund, and also a safe entrance to the Aland Islands; it was, therefore, his intention to get under weigh at once, Captain Sulivan leading in the *Lightning.* He requested Admiral Parseval to follow, and to send the *Austerlitz,* with Commodore Martin's ships, to the Gulf of Finland, which request was complied with.

Sir Charles Napier wished Admiral Parseval to undertake the charge of watching the Sweaborg squadron; but as the troops expected at Bomarsund were all French, the Admiral declined; nor was he willing to leave any of his squadron in the Gulf of Finland, except the *Austerlitz,* which was placed under Admiral Martin's orders.

Rear-Admiral Corry here shifted his flag into the *Dauntless,* and sailed for England, ill health having compelled the gallant Admiral to request permission of the First Lord to withdraw from the arduous duties which devolved on him as second in command of the fleet.

Sir Charles wrote to Admiral Corry regretting the cause which deprived him of his services, and expressing the highest satisfaction with the support which he had received from him in carrying out the difficult service in which the fleet had been employed.

Commodore Martin, of the *Nile*, was placed in the command of Admiral Corry's squadron, with which he was ordered to proceed to the Gulf of Finland, to watch the Sweaborg fleet, and to maintain the blockade which had been established. The Gulf squadron consisted of the *Nile, Royal George, Cæsar, Cressy, Neptune, St. George, Prince Regent, Monarch,* and *Austerlitz*. Commodore Martin was further directed to send ships up the Gulf of Finland, to observe the motions of the Russian fleet at Cronstadt, to give the Admiral notice if they should attempt to move, and, in case of necessity, to fall back on the main body of the fleet at Ledsund.

The Admiral now sent orders to Commodore Grey, who commanded the division of ships of war and transports bringing the French troops from Calais, to join him at Ledsund, calling off Lagskaren. These orders were despatched to Faro Sound and Copenhagen, at one of which places the division would, in all probability, be found.

At 11.20 A.M., on the 21st of July, the fleet weighed under sail and steam, the *Lightning* going ahead to sound. The French fleet also got under weigh, and followed. In running through this passage, the soundings were very irregular, and indeed alarming; sometimes with one cast of the lead from eighteen fathoms to eight, no notice of which appeared on the charts.

In the course of the afternoon, Admiral Plumridge

joined with his squadron, consisting of the *Leopard*, *Valorous, Hecla, Locust*, and *Cuckoo*. The *Hecla* was despatched to point out the passage to the French squadron.

At 9 P.M., the fleet anchored in succession in Ledsund, the *Duke of Wellington* leading. The *Valorous, Locust*, and *Zephyr*, which had been despatched under the orders of Admiral Plumridge to watch the passages between the Aland Islands and the mainland, rejoined the fleet.

The Admiral had naturally been desirous, now that it had been determined that Bomarsund should be attacked, to procure pilots who should be competent to navigate large ships amongst the dangerous passages of the Aland Isles, and with this view had written to Stockholm, urging the necessity of using every means to procure them. None were, however, to be obtained. Information was now gained that the Russians were actively engaged in building gunboats and other vessels in the vicinity.

On the 22nd, Admiral Chads was ordered to proceed to Bomarsund, with the *Edinburgh, Hogue, Blenheim, Ajax, Lightning, Amphion*, and *Alban*, to commence an investment of the place. At the same time Admiral Plumridge was sent to the northward of Bomarsund, with his steam squadron, to intercept any succours which might reach the forts in that direction.

On the arrival of Admiral Chads before the forts, every precaution was taken by him to prevent reinforcements being thrown in from Abo, where a large force had been assembled for that purpose, had not the movements of the Allied fleet been too rapid to permit of such reinforcements. There was also a considerable body of troops at Hango. Admiral Plumridge was indefatigable in his endeavours to find a passage to the northward of Bomarsund, where ships might be placed to extend the line of blockade. A passage was so found, but the *Leopard* got ashore in the attempt, and remained for nine hours in that position. As this passage extended to Abo, the *Hecla* and *Odin* were placed so as to prevent troops from being sent to Bomarsund from Abo ; and all chance of reinforcement was thus cut off.

The *Valorous*, whilst proceeding to join Admiral Plumridge, went on a rock not laid down in the charts. She was got off in about two hours, but not before she had received considerable injury. Fortunately she was going under easy steam, or the consequences must have been more serious. As it was, she knocked away part of her forefoot, and started the ends of some of her planks. Scarcely had she been got off, when, on again proceeding at the cautious rate of $3\frac{1}{2}$ knots, she got on a reef near the village of Dagerby, where, with much difficulty, she was got off, having been four days on the reef. It was afterwards said of the Admiral that he had a *mania* about rocks and shoals. Four accidents coming altogether, and with every care taken, was not likely to lessen that *mania*.

In the night, armed boats from the ships at Bomarsund were sent in under the batteries to sound and reconnoitre. The masters also were employed in surveying Lumpar Bay, and in sounding for a passage outside Michelso, so as to command the whole circumnavigation of the island. In this they were successful, a practicable passage for steamers being found, as well as a landing-place for the troops. During these operations the enemy showed themselves but little, and were busily employed in clearing away for the coming action, and in burning all their own buildings which were combustible.

At noon, on the 22nd, the French squadron joined the Admiral, accompanied by the *Arrogant, Penelope,* and *Hecla.* Shortly afterwards the *Gorgon* arrived with the *Tyne* in tow, laden with provisions from England. The *Kangaroo* and the *City of Norwich,* steam-transports, arriving at the same time, were sent on to join Commodore Martin's squadron in the Gulf of Finland. On the same evening the French ship *Duperré* took the ground, but the launches and barges of both fleets having been sent to her assistance with anchors and cables, she was speedily got afloat again.

On the 23rd the *Phlegeton* took the *Duperré* in tow, and proceeded through the Sound to Bomarsund, the *Hecla* leading. The *Alban* was also sent to the same place, and the *Zephyr* in coming down from Bomarsund got on shore, where she remained eight hours. On this day four French frigates arrived, and one was despatched to join Commodore Martin's squadron.

On the 24th the Admiral received advices from Sir James Graham, in which the First Lord told him that "events had occurred very much as they both anticipated." Five thousand French troops had sailed from Calais Roads in four English line-of-battle ships under the orders of Commodore Grey. The Admiral was told by Sir James that his arrangements for expediting their arrival at Faro, were " excellent, and were all that he could have desired."

The First Lord apprised the Admiral that on the following day the *Prince*, a large iron steamer, with two war steamers in attendance, would leave Calais with a second division of 4000 French troops, and two French line-of-battle ships, artillery, engineers, and all the materials necessary for a siege, would leave Calais about the same time.

Sir James told the Admiral that his block-ships, screw-frigates, some of his steamers, and a portion of the French squadron would be strong enough to invest Bomarsund, as there was no naval force except gun-boats opposed to him ; and that, after detaching these, he and the French Admiral would have twenty sail of the line at the neck of the Gulf of Finland to keep the Russian fleet sealed up.

It was not to be expected that the French Admiral would abide by these instructions ; nor did the British Admiral approve of them, for many reasons. He had not only provided for the safety of the Gulf of Finland, but by sending Commodore Martin with nine ships of the line only, had repeated his former stratagem in order to entice them out by the smallness of the force. The Admiral was desirous that the Russians *should* come out, as Commodore Martin

could have apprised him of the movement in time to
intercept them; or, failing in this, he would have
had them shut up in Sweaborg, so that the fleet
would only have had to watch them in one place
instead of in two; but the Russians deemed even
Commodore Martin's force too strong for them, and
remained in port.

The First Lord called the attention of the Admiral
to a suggestion by Colonel Hodges, that the islands
of Oesel and Dago should be seized and held during
the winter. Sir James further suggested whether,
assuming one or both to be taken, a " grave question "
would not arise as to the power of holding them
during winter when the ice afforded a passage to an
army and artillery; unless, indeed, *by constant blasting*, a trench of open water might not be kept in front
of the points of land occupied in force.

It was, indeed, " a grave question," when a Russian
army could have operated just as well on ice as on
shore; the suggestion of holding the position by
" blasting a trench of open water," was the reverse
of grave, as it necessarily supposed that a Russian
army on the other side of the trench would look
quietly on whilst our marine sappers and miners
were daily engaged in keeping their ice trench open !
To keep open a trench round an island of considerable extent, in face of the numerous Russian army
stationed at Revel and Riga, would have been a
feat unparalleled in naval warfare. Let us imagine
that during the depth of winter the sea round the
Isle of Wight was frozen to a thickness of some six

or eight feet, and that a trench of open water was to be kept round the island. It will easily be understood that if such a trench were opened in the ice at Ryde, it would be frozen up again long before the naval sappers got to the Motherbank. We may hence have some idea of the feasibility of keeping open the trench round the island of Dago, so as to prevent the Russian army at Riga from marching over the ice straight upon our post, and capturing it, as a body of Russian cavalry had once captured a Swedish squadron which had suffered itself to become frozen up in their waters. To this notable suggestion the Admiral merely replied that, " taking Oesel or Dago was out of the question, as we must certainly be driven out of it during the winter."

Shortly before the Admiral went to Bomarsund, he received orders from the Admiralty that if the point selected by the Allied Admirals for attack were within the Gulf of Finland, the four English line-of-battle ships conveying troops, might be taken to Baro Sound, but they must be sent home again without delay. If Bomarsund was selected for attack, they must not be taken with troops on board into the inner anchorage, as the dangers of the navigation were too great for ships of that size and draught of water. The utmost that could be allowed would be to convey the troops to the outer roadstead, where they must be transhipped into smaller vessels, and the ships, as well as the war steamers which accompanied them, must proceed at once to England.

On the 24th, the Admiral advised Sir James Graham that the fleet was at anchor in Ledsund, and that he had pushed up four block-ships and a number of steamers to establish a strict blockade.   The French General had not arrived, nor had the first division of troops, but all necessary arrangements were made for their reception when they did arrive, which the Admiral trusted would be very soon, as no time was to be lost.   He was already anxious about the weather, which towards the middle of August began to be unsettled, and the difficulties of weather in these seas were beyond his control.

As for preventing the junction of the Cronstadt and Sweaborg fleets, if they wished it, this, said the Admiral to the First Lord, was utterly impossible, without remaining off there with the whole fleet, and leaving the French Admiral and General to themselves at Bomarsund, which Sir James could never have contemplated.   Commodore Martin had two steam frigates and three paddle steamers in advance of him, and he would give timely notice should the Russians break ground.   " This," continued the Admiral, " is the best disposition I could make, and I hope all will go right."

On this day Sir Charles received information from the Board of Admiralty that large reinforcements of troops had been sent by the Russian Government to Finland.   This was the case; but as measures had been adopted to secure every approach to Bomarsund, their advent was of little importance.   Had not these precautions been taken, there is no doubt but that the fortress would have received a considerable accession of force.

The Admiral wrote to the Board of Admiralty, in

reply to his instructions how to act, as it might be determined whether Sweaborg or Bomarsund should be attacked, that "an attack on Sweaborg was entirely out of the question." The mention of an attack on Sweaborg with 9,000 troops was extraordinary on the part of the Admiralty, which had previously informed him that there were 40,000 troops at Sweaborg and in its vicinity. This information the Admiral knew to be correct; and to have attacked 40,000 troops with 9,000 would have been an act, the bare attempt at which would have shown his unfitness to command. Even Sir James Graham had just told him, that to attack Sweaborg *at all*, would " require 50,000 Swedes and 200 Swedish gun-boats."

But Sir Charles had literally nothing to do with this, beyond giving his opinion on the subject. The troops which were coming were French troops, and the General who commanded them was the authority to determine what should be done with them, or how he could best co-operate with the two Admirals, who were no arbiters of the disposal of a military force, as, no doubt, General Baraguay D'Hilliers would have told them, had they attempted to dispose at their pleasure of the military force under his command.

Sir Charles therefore wrote to the Board that Bomarsund was more likely to be attacked, and he had ordered the line-of-battle ships bringing the French troops to meet him at Ledsund. If the French General agreed to attack Bomarsund, the troops would immediately be moved into steamers, and the place would be invested. The steamers-of-war which accompanied the line-of-battle ships must also come on to Ledsund, the closest blockade of the islands being of the utmost importance, whilst the Admiral had not a single steamer to spare; besides which, he had to keep up a constant communication with Commodore Martin, in the event of the Russian fleet putting to sea, which, though not probable, was yet possible.

The Admiral further informed their Lordships that Sir James Graham's memorandum — the observance of which their order had enforced — must, no doubt, have been based on the certainty of success; but he must provide for the want of success also. Success might be desired, but could not be commanded; and he did not conceal from their Lordships that there were many difficulties in the way, as a view of the chart would show.

Captain Washington, in his memorandum, had stated that three steamers could blockade Bomarsund. "But," said the Admiral, "three times that number would not do it effectively."

There is something very absurd in the idea of blockading this mass of islands with three steamers, and with a large force of Russian troops at Abo watching an opportunity to throw themselves into the fortress, by means of some of the numerous channels amongst the islands, every one of which had its own separate passage, each requiring the most vigilant watching. There are literally hundreds of islets forming the group, the channels between which were known to the Russians; so that to speak of blockading the approaches to Bomarsund by three steamers, was only showing want of knowledge of the locality which was at least singular in an officer who had been specially deputed by the Government to inspect it.

On the 25th the ships were engaged in getting their provisions from the *Tyne* and other vessels. The *Desperate* was despatched to Commodore Martin's squadron in the Gulf of Finland, and the French ship of the line *Trident* proceeded to Bomarsund in tow of a steamer.

On the 26th the Admiral went to Bomarsund in the *Driver*, with the *Alban* in company. He was accompanied by the French Admiral in the *Darien*. On the 27th, the Admirals were followed by Rear-Admiral Penaud in the French steamer *L'Aigle*. During the absence of Sir Charles the British squadron was diligently exercised in such evolutions as would shortly have to be put in practice. The fleet had now arrived, in this respect, at a satisfactory degree of proficiency.

In a letter to one of the Lords of the Admiralty, Sir Charles declared himself satisfied with the progress made by the fleet. " We are all getting on very well. The fleet is respectable. Not quite so smart as we used to be in St. Vincent's squadron, because we have been obliged to give more attention to gunnery; but still they are very well, and everything is done by the watch. I believe the men are very happy and contented."

Shortly before the Admiral's departure for Bomarsund, he was apprised by Sir James Graham that General Baraguay D'Hilliers would proceed in the Emperor's yacht to Stockholm, with a view of inducing Sweden to lay aside her neutrality, but that

Austria was the great obstacle; and it was much to be feared, from the hesitation of Austria, that Sweden would be disinclined to listen to him, and that " the moment for decisive action would pass away." From this expression it is sufficiently clear, that in case of the representations of General Baraguay D'Hilliers failing to produce an effect on the Swedish Government; or, if successful, nothing further than the destruction of Bomarsund was expected by the English Government, unless the aid expected from Sweden was instantly given.

The Admiral had anticipated that nothing could be done with Sweden, — or, rather, he was quite satisfied of it, from his own personal knowledge of the intentions of Sweden. He had intimated to the Government that, from the late period of the year in which the French troops had been sent, nothing more than an attack on Bomarsund could be effected. On this account he considered the military force sent as being more than was required. On the 18th of July, he had thus written to Admiral Berkeley from Baro Sound : — " I have received Gen. Baraguay D'Hilliers' letter which you sent me, and I am sorry that so many troops are coming. Five thousand would have been quite enough to do more than we want to do ; and to do more than this would require a large army. If we take Bomarsund, — which I cannot doubt, — I don't know what we are to do with them afterwards ; for, unless Sweden comes forward to garrison it, I suppose we shall not leave a garrison there."

On the 28th the Admiral communicated to Admiral

Parseval the instructions he had received from England relative to Bomarsund, and measures were determined on in accordance with the joint instructions of the two Admirals, the opinions of both being unanimous as to the course to be pursued.

On the 30th of July, the squadron of line-of-battle ships, conveying the French troops, arrived at Ledsund, under the orders of Commodore the Hon. F. Grey, in the *Hannibal*. The squadron consisted besides of the *Algiers*, Captain Charles Talbot ; *Royal William*, Captain John Kingcome ; *St. Vincent*, Captain George Mansel ; *Gladiator*, Captain George N. Broke ; *Sphinx*, Captain William J. C. Clifford ; and *Stromboli*, Captain Robert Hall. The number of troops on board was 5000. The squadron left Calais on the 16th of July.

On the 30th of July, Sir Charles wrote to the Admiralty that he had recalled the blockading squadron from the Gulf of Bothnia, and had established a complete blockade of the Aland Isles, though nothing but a superior force of gun-boats could enter Bomarsund. He considered that the highest credit was due to Admiral Plumridge for the way in which he had placed his squadron; most of which had been on shore two or three times, notwithstanding that every precaution had been taken.

The Admiral then detailed his arrangements for the landing of troops, and trusted their Lordships would be satisfied with them. He had acted according to the best of his ability, but their Lordships were aware of the difficulties he had to contend with.

The Gulf of Finland was well guarded by Commodore Martin, and the Admiral had taken steps to act, should the Russian fleet attempt to disturb the operations going on.

On the 31st of July, General Baraguay D'Hilliers arrived from Stockholm in the Imperial yacht, *La Reine Hortense*, and was received with the honours due to his rank.   In the course of the day he visited Sir Charles Napier on board the *Duke of Wellington*, the crew of which manned yards, and saluted him with fifteen guns on his departure.

We will here resume the operations of Admiral Plumridge amongst the Aland Isles.

On the 8th of July, the *Leopard* proceeded to Arholme, meeting with many small Swedish vessels, and amongst them the Royal Swedish mail-boat from Griselhamm to the Russian port of Eckero.   In fact, the communication with Russia, from Admiralty indulgence, was in a great measure uninterrupted. On the 16th of May, the Board had requested Sir C. Napier's opinion as to the desirableness of the Swedish mail-steamer being allowed to run between Sweden and Russia with letters.   The Admiral had replied that if the Government permitted such communications, it might enable us to obtain information from Abo ; but at the same time the steamer would carry information to Russia.   It was a matter upon which the Admiralty themselves were the best judges.

When Admiral Plumridge fell in with the mail-steamer, she had regular mails on board for Abo, Viborg, Sweaborg, and St. Petersburg.   He therefore warned her off, and in a written notice told her commander that if she was again fallen in with, she would be captured.

On the 10th, the *Leopard* proceeded to Lat 61° 40', and communicated with the *Valorous* and the French frigate *Virginie*, which had been waiting in that quarter. Farther to the northward, Admiral Plumridge fell in with the *Andromaque*, and afterwards with the *Odin* at Ratan.

Quitting Ratan for the southward, he found the *Hecla*, and Captain Hall reported that, on the 7th, he had destroyed the Russian Telegraph-station and Government House on Karsaren Island, carrying off the signal-balls and documents connected with the Telegraph. The Russians in charge deserted the place on the approach of the *Hecla's* boats. In this operation the ship got aground.

On the 9th, the *Hecla* and *Odin* reconnoitred Gamla Carleby, and found that two additional forts had been built since the affair of the 7th of June. The men were at their guns, in readiness to meet any attack. The *Hecla* was ordered to proceed to Lagskaren, and in conjunction with the *Poursuivante* to do all in their power to intercept supplies to Bomarsund, and to stop Russian communications with the Aland Islands.

Admiral Plumridge then proceeded to Orengrund, where he anchored on the 14th. Off Svartken he learned from the *Poursuivante* that three small steamers had passed to the northward on the 12th. He was here joined by the *Hecla* and *Zephyr*.

On the 17th, the *Leopard* left Orengrund with the *Hecla*, to examine the northern approaches to Bomarsund. Dense fogs compelled him to anchor off Orskar ; and on the 18th, the *Leopard* struck on a sunken rock, but was backed off, and anchored to examine the position of the rock. The ships then proceeded towards the northern part of the Aland Islands, and anchored off Saggo. The boats were sent ahead to examine the passage between the islands, the *Hecla* following them, but all were compelled to return for want of sufficient depth of water.

On the 20th, Mr. Swain, master of the *Leopard*, who had been sent to examine Captain Sulivan's track, reported a passage with five fathoms clear ; and the *Hecla* was directed to follow Mr. Swain's soundings, and come out to the southward, whilst the *Leopard* went outside to Lagskaren. On the 21st, Admiral Plumridge assigned to the *Valorous*, *Zephyr*, and *Locust* the positions they were to occupy in the *cordon* to be established round the Aland Islands. There were altogether seven stations assigned to the different vessels, the stations being marked by their latitudes and longitudes. The instructions were, to keep these stations as closely as circumstances would permit, with due regard to shoals ; especially to keep in the latitudes assigned, even if compelled to move farther to the westward ; the object being that the vessels should be no farther apart than that constant and certain communication might be kept up, so as to report to each other everything seen. They were in the meantime directed to take soundings in their neighbourhood, and to prepare accurate charts of the same.

The steamers were, however, too few to establish perfectly a *cordon* of such magnitude, and the Russians broke through them, notwithstanding their vigilance. On the 10th of August, Lieutenant Day, commanding the *Locust*, observed a vessel under sail coming from the eastward to seaward of the islands. On being observed, she made instantly for the shoal water and rocks, where the *Locust* could not follow her. Whilst endeavouring to find another passage for this purpose, two more vessels, full of troops, made their appearance from behind a small island, which had masked them, and ran for a creek in the mainland, the *Locust* giving chase. They hoisted Russian colours; and, steaming slowly and cautiously, the *Locust* opened fire on them with shell at 2000 yards distance. On this, the Russian vessels were run on shore, and the troops, jumping out, got into a wood, the *Locust* firing shell into the wood to drive them out, which was done, the men carrying their wounded with them; but they finally made their escape up the creek, and the *Locust* could not follow them from her draught of water, though she steamed within 700 yards of the shore, which was as near as she could approach with safety. A cutter, well manned and armed, was despatched, under cover of the ship's guns, in charge of Mr. Campbell, acting-mate, to bring off the enemy's boats, which he did; but it was unsafe to send boats farther, where the cover afforded by the wood was so thick, and the troops joined the garrison without further molestation.

Just on the eve of attack, this was very vexatious;

but the want of small vessels on our part gave the enemy, who was well acquainted with every creek and shoal, a manifest advantage in movements which we could not follow.

CHAP. XIV.

BEFORE entering on the details of the siege of Bomarsund, it will be necessary to allude to the surveys and other measures which the Admiral had made to render his knowledge of the locality as complete as possible, preparatory to an attack on the place. This is the more necessary, as some of the captains of the large ships had complained that their vessels were not allowed to come up to Bomarsund, and that they thereby lost the opportunity of distinguishing themselves in the siege.

The reason why the large ships were not brought up to the fortress was the evident one that they might be wanted to meet the Russian fleet, should an attempt be made by the enemy to raise the siege. They were therefore kept in readiness at Ledsund, should Admiral Martin have had occasion to fall back on them whilst the Russian fleet approached. It was the hope of the Admiral that the Russians would do so, and this was why he had left Admiral Martin with so small a force, taking care, however, that the main body of the fleet was within easy reach. This precaution of keeping the large ships at Ledsund was the more necessary as Admiral Parseval decided on taking the greater part of his ships to Bomarsund, being unwilling that the French squadron should be separated from the French troops; this arrangement rendered it imperative on Sir Charles to keep his large ships in readiness for any attempt on the part of the Russians. He had been strictly enjoined by Sir James Graham not to leave the Gulf at all, and when Sir James found that the bulk of the fleet was at Ledsund, he expressed his fears lest the Russians might succeed in getting out.

The block-ships, or that class of the British ships-of-the-line which drew least water, were taken to Bomarsund, and with the French ships were more than enough for the work to be done. It would then have been useless to have taken up the large ships.

An accurate idea of the nature of the navigation of the channels in the vicinity of Bomarsund will be gathered from Captain Sulivan's report on his survey of the place, of which report the following is an analysis.

" We followed the track marked in the chart round the Scarf rocks, and to the eastward of Biorkor Island. We found dangerous rocks, with as little as two fathoms on one of them, right in the track. Between Orskar and Osterhara Islands we shoaled to five fathoms, and without a further examination of that passage I could not recommend it for large ships.

" Immediately inside of Morkor Island there is excellent anchorage for a fleet, and apparently no danger of any kind. The small rocks or islets marked in the chart between Biorkor and Valo we could see nothing of, all appearing clear as far as Kongso, after passing which the depth becomes less and very irregular. With care we were able to find a channel, with not less than four and a half fathoms, till we anchored off Brando Island.

" We then entered a channel to the eastward of Jarso Island, but found islands and rocks not marked in the chart, and had to proceed very cautiously to keep a depth of four fathoms. The open space in the chart to the N.E. of Gotholmar was so studded with islets and rocks that we had to join the west side of the sound again, by passing between Gotholmar and Jarso in four fathoms. I went on to the northward, hoping to find a passage round the north end of Busso, and so into Lumpar Bay, on either side of Kalfholme, but the passage between Busso and Ballero is so intricate, that after the *Driver* touching in fourteen feet in mid-channel, I was obliged to anchor her outside, and the *Lightning* was only able to proceed to the anchorage marked in the chart.

" I then proceeded with the boats of the steamers into Lumpar Bay, round Kalfholme, and though the passage is commanded by the wooded shores on both sides, to my surprise no attempt was made to oppose us. We reached a good position on the west side of Michelso, about 3000 yards from the fort, from whence we had a good view of the position; and as the passages into the bay were evidently unoccupied by the enemy, I thought it best to bring the vessels in through Ango passage, if possible, so as to ascertain how far it was fit for large ships.

" At the entrance of Ango passage we, with some difficulty, found a very narrow channel. Farther on, we found a clear and deep channel through the passage, fit for the largest ships. It was, however, very narrow, and in some places commanded by wooded rocks on either side, so that it might easily be defended. Inside the passage there is a bank with four and a half fathoms, but with that exception the bay opposite Bomarsund has good anchorage for a fleet in from five to fourteen fathoms mud."

We have not space to follow Captain Sulivan further in his explorations of the Aland Archipelago, nor to give the many interesting particulars with which his report abounds; but will now proceed to his description of the fortress itself.

" The defences of Bomarsund will be best described by Lieutenant (now Major) Nugent, of the Royal Engineers, to whose drawings I beg to refer you. .

" The large fort has only guns in the two tiers of casemates. The top is covered by an iron roof, to protect it from the weather. The casemates appear small, and do not give a large angle for training the guns — probably thirty of which might be brought to bear on one ship. One advantage in such casemates is, that few shot would enter. The eastern portion has no guns, but is probably used as dwellings.

" The towers are all of similar construction — two tiers of casemates, with an iron roof above. If the number of guns stated is correct, they can all be mounted on one side, as there are many more casemates.

" On the slope of the hill, behind No. 1. tower, an extensive new building is going on, which is evidently intended for a new and very heavy fort, from its position commanding the bay, and flanking the approach to the large fort. It will, if completed, materially add to the difficulty of attacking the place by sea.

" The tower on Presto Island is on the extreme low point which forms the channel. It is apparently formed with four casemates in most of the sides. About ten guns can be brought to bear on one point, and the same number, or rather more, from the northern tower on the opposite point of the passage. This tower is circular. Other works are being commenced, which will make the defences most complete.

" With regard to attacking the forts by ships, it is quite impossible to make any serious impression on any of the forts by shelling at long range, as there are no guns on the roofs, and besides being bomb-proof, a depth of sand has been recently added to the large fort. For a more direct attack by large ships, about six or seven could be placed at a range of about 1400 yards. They would be opposed to the fire of about sixty guns in the large fort, and at the range of from 2000 to 2300 yards to the fire of the guns in the towers, which it would be almost useless to return. As at 1400 yards the fire of the ships would do very little damage to the masonry of the fort, I think it would be totally useless to place ships at that distance from it, unless for the purpose of covering the approach of three or four heavy ships, to take up a position within the smaller bay at a range of 500 or 600 yards, which would be the only means by which the large fort could be silenced; but these ships would probably suffer so severely from the cross fire of the three towers, in addition to the direct fire of from fifty to sixty guns in the large fort, that their success would be doubtful. The attention of the two northern towers might probably be occupied by ships on that side, but the guns in the western tower would, from its position, do serious injury.

" On the whole, therefore, I am of opinion that an attack by ships would be attended with a loss and risk too great to warrant the attempt, unless aided by a sufficient land force to assist, by first carrying the tower by assault, or by regular approaches; or by carrying on direct approaches against the large fort from Presto Island."

The reader will probably smile when he contrasts this able report by Captain Sulivan with the " successful bombardment" of Bomarsund by Captain Hall, with three steamers only.

The general name " Aland " is given to several hundred islets lying near the entrance of the Gulf of

Bothnia. At the commencement of the campaign of 1808, the Russians held these islands ; but the Swedes, on the breaking up of the ice, attacked the southern part, when the inhabitants rising, *en masse*, over-powered the Russians. The remainder of their force was blockaded by the Swedes in Kemmlinge, the island nearest to the mainland, and surrendered after a resistance of eight days.

The Russians afterwards determined to effect their re-conquest, and an expedition of 40,000 men was prepared in Finland for the purpose. A truce which was then existing was declared at an end, and 30 battalions, 4 squadrons, and 200 Cossacks, with 20 guns, were landed at Kemmlinge. As no provisions could be got in Aland—the Swedes having conveyed the inhabitants away—a month's provisions were also landed. Sweden was well enough inclined to defend the islands, but as the forces in the archipelago were not sufficient for this purpose, the Swedish General Dobeln had to retire. The islands were thus recaptured, and Russia was confirmed in their possession by the Treaty of Fredericshamm. In the same year (1808), the Gulf of Bothnia was frozen over, and the Russians formed the daring project of crossing on the ice to Sweden, and attacking Stockholm.

The Aland group lies about twenty-five miles from the coast of Sweden, and fifteen from Finland. It is called by the Fins " Avennammaa," and consists of eighty inhabited and 200 uninhabited islets, the largest being about eighteen miles long by fourteen broad. This archipelago encloses a perfect labyrinth of channels, studded by islets and rocks innumerable, and so fringed with reefs and banks as to make the navigation often impossible—always hazardous. It will be quite evident that such ships as the *Duke of Wellington* are unsuitable to such navigation, in which alone a small class of steamers could move with safety.

As the Aland group forms the two passages which lead from the Gulf of Bothnia to the Baltic, constituting an advanced post, pushed out from Finland against Sweden, and commanding the entrances to the Gulfs of Finland and Riga, its importance has always been duly estimated by Russia. The Emperor Nicholas, no doubt with a view to further designs on Sweden, ordered, as has been said, the erection of works of a formidable character on the eastern point of the largest island of the group, so as to command the *Bomar Sund*, which separates Aland from Presto Island; hence the name of the fortress.

The fortress itself formed the segment of a circle, having a chord of about a quarter of a mile in length, and presenting to the roadstead a casemated battery of 120 guns in two tiers. The system of defence was made complete by a series of works commencing on the heights behind, and continued across the water by a chain of small islands to the island of Presto, which forms the other side of the channel. The fort to the north was called Fort Nottich, and that to the south, the Tzee Fort.

It should, perhaps, be stated, that the distance of Lagskaren, the most advanced of the Aland Islands, is only sixteen miles from the island of Soderam, the nearest spot of Swedish territory. This will give some idea of the depressed condition in which Sweden must have been in 1809, when such a frontier could have been prescribed to her by Russia. The demand for such a frontier is a convincing proof that the ulterior object of Russia, and that at no distant date, was the possession of Sweden itself. The gigantic fortresses found by the Allies at Bomarsund, either complete or in progress, can leave no doubt that had it not been for the war, the fate of Sweden must soon have been sealed.

The inhabitants of the Aland Islands amount to about six thousand in number, chiefly gaining their livelihood as fishermen, and by carrying wood and other articles between Finland and Stockholm. The boats used in this traffic are of a very primitive description, and are so constructed as to carry wood and live fish at the same time. As these boats are not adapted to encounter bad weather, the islanders only sail with a fair wind, so that they cannot be accounted either a hardy or expert race of seamen. The inhabitants are Swedes, in language and extraction, and, in addition to their fisheries, possess a few cattle and sheep. Cultivation is at a very low ebb, there being little arable land; but forests, chiefly of lime and birch, are numerous. Most of the islands stand at a considerable elevation above the sea, and are intersected by granite peaks. There are no rivers, but lakes in the valleys are frequent. The islands are divided into eight parishes, which have as many churches, besides chapels-of-ease in extra parochial districts. The religion is Protestant.

As regards the maritime operations to be undertaken at Bomarsund, the *Times* newspaper of August 16th, 1854, made some very judicious remarks, which will be rendered still clearer by the preceding extracts from the report of Captain Sulivan.

" It is clear that in the shallow waters and difficult passes of that inland sea our three-deckers can hardly ever be brought sufficiently near to the enemy's works to bear upon them with effect. The block-ships and heavy frigates are alone able to go into harbours of this description, and it was not without reason that, on the occasion of the Baltic expeditions of 1800 and 1807, *all the ships selected for that service were second or third rates.* The use of such ships as the *Duke of Wellington,* the *St. Jean d'Acre,* and the *Neptune,* in the Baltic, is to keep the Russian fleet in check ; and the manner in which these huge vessels have been handled by our masters and pilots is such as to call forth the highest eulogiums from the Russians themselves. But Admiral Napier has very wisely abstained from measuring the broadsides of any of his ships *against the batteries of a granite fortress ;* and in spite of all that has been said on the subject, the result of the experiments made in this war is decidedly favourable to land fortifications against marine artillery."

At the period of the war the defences of Bomarsund were being enlarged on a grand scale, so that in a few years they would have rivalled those of Sweaborg or Cronstadt. The island does not contain a town, and one of the chief reasons for this, appears to be the extreme rigour of the climate. The Emperor had, however, resolved to build on the island a military town adapted to the climate, the plan of which town had been approved by a recent ukase. The place was to be situated within the line of the forts, and was to have some analogy to Sebastopol, but on a larger scale.

The adaptation of this formidable enterprise to the climate deserves more than passing notice. Old men were living in Aland who well remembered having seen in 1809 a corps of Russian cavalry of 15,000 men coming from Finland, and crossing the Gulf of Bothnia to Aland on the ice. But though the Finnish division of the Gulf freezes every year, the Swedish side is seldom entirely covered with ice. This circumstance was favourable to Russia, as during six months' winter she was in direct communication with her possessions in Aland. The rigour of the climate is, however, unfavourable to health; one third of the troops at Bomarsund had to be renewed yearly, and of late the mortality amongst the soldiers had risen so greatly that the Russian government had ordered the construction of a hospital nearly as large as the fortress itself. The climate is, notwithstanding, warm in summer.

The drawback to this plan of a military town would have been the barrenness of the country, but this the energy of the Russian government would, had she not been checked, have devised some means of neutralising. As it was, the Russian troops chiefly drew their provisions from St. Petersburg, for the islands could not even feed their inhabitants, much less did they offer resources for an army or a fleet. The inhabitants pay some attention to the breeding of cattle, but these are of diminutive size, and by no means abundant. Game would be plentiful but for the droves of wolves which every year cross over on the ice from Russia. In the lakes and streams of the larger islands, fish is said to be in some abundance, and the sea furnishes sufficient even for a small export: but beyond this, the Aland Archipelago furnishes no resources which would be available for troops. To hold such a locality, then, in winter, would be out of the question.

It will not be out of place here to adduce a few reliable particulars relative to the Fins themselves, especially as a belief was generally entertained in England that Finland would join enthusiastically in a rising against Russia, and thus embrace an opportunity of being reannexed to Sweden.

This, though at one time the opinion of the British Government, was a mistake. Finland might have desired to be independent, and to have again formed a portion of Sweden, on the same terms as Norway, but even this is doubtful. The Emperor of Russia had neglected no opportunity of conciliating the Finnish people. Favours had been bestowed upon them which were unusual in other parts of Russia, and to be a Fin was a sure road to promotion in every branch of the Russian service. Hence, those best acquainted with the subject agreed that the feeling of Finland towards Sweden was more a matter of tradition than an actual fact which, on an emergency, might be counted on.

Since the junction of Finland to Russia, the commercial classes especially have enjoyed so many privileges in comparison to those granted to other provinces of Russia, whilst the laws relating to conscription have never been put in force amongst them, that they were quite content with their present rulers.

Notwithstanding this, there existed a party in

Finland amongst the commercial classes which would willingly have seen their country independent, but there was reason to believe that the blockade which had been established by Sir Charles Napier, had, by annihilating their trade, completely altered this feeling. It was true, that had the war continued, this loss of commerce in the summer would have been compensated in the winter, when all kinds of foreign produce would have been imported over the ice into Russia, viâ Finland; but even this advantage does not appear to have been taken into account by the Fins, as inducing them to wish for reannexation to Sweden, the effect being rather to draw them closer to Russia.

The people of Sweden would have liked to see Finland again joined to their country, and were loud in their prognostications that such would be the case; but the more reflecting amongst the Swedes saw that they were better without Finland, as at present Sweden had the Baltic and the Gulf of Bothnia between her and Russia; whereas, if she regained Finland, it would expose her to constant annoyance from Russia, and to every kind of pertinacious intrigue, until Russia had regained Finland. There was also an opinion that England, when her purpose was served, would leave Sweden in the lurch at some future day to fight out her own battles with Russia single-handed. Indeed, the King of Sweden, when telling Sir Charles Napier that Sweden did not want Aland, spoke the opinion of the more far-seeing amongst his people.

Had England and France guaranteed Sweden in the undisturbed possession of Finland, this feeling might have been modified. It was clearly the interest of England and France to have offered such guarantees, even if they required the assistance of Sweden in any way; but in the event of such guarantees being given, Sweden might have materially assisted in wresting Finland from Russia; whilst the popular enthusiasm of the Swedes in favour of the Allied Powers, would in that case have forced the Swedish Government into an offensive position towards Russia.

Had this, however, been done, it would have been no easy matter to have seized on Finland, a country which, from its natural strong positions, might have more easily been defended than taken. The Fins would have felt towards the invading forces much as the Spaniards did towards our troops in the Peninsula. It certainly would not have been easy to convince them that it would better their condition to have their country turned into a cock-pit.

When Aland was taken it should have been restored to Sweden, but with the strictest guarantees on the part of France and England against molestation by Russia. Sweden could not of herself have held Aland but at an enormous pecuniary sacrifice in maintaining a strong garrison at Bomarsund, especially during the winter, when the sea between Aland and the main land is so covered with ice that an army might operate upon it as well as on shore. That Aland should so be offered to Sweden, was the ostensible object of its capture. It was so offered to her, but the adequate guarantees were declined, and Sweden very sensibly refused to accept the offer.

It is now nearly forty years since Finland was

"annexed" — that being the political phrase — to Russia; when, without provocation, it was wrested from Sweden upon pretexts as frivolous as those since advanced in extenuation of the occupation of the two principalities belonging to the Ottoman Empire.

Taken by surprise, in the depth of a severe winter, and hence unable to receive any succour from Sweden, the Finlanders, nevertheless, valiantly defended their territory, till at length, overpowered by masses of the enemy's troops, they were compelled to yield.

At first the yoke of Russia appears to have been oppressive, and the Finlanders, remembering the mild sway of Sweden, repeatedly sent deputations to the Swedish Government to know if they might hope to be again united to the Swedish crown. One of these was sent to the late King of Sweden, but his majesty, closely watched by Russia, could only return the following laconic answer : " *Messieurs, l'espoir fait la vie de l'homme ;*" a reply which is still cherished by some, though laughed at by the majority.

The Grand Duchy of Finland, as it was formerly called, is one of the gems of the Russian crown. It produces abundance of corn for consumption and exportation, as well as cattle of every description. It possesses, moreover, immense forests yielding the finest timber, of which a considerable quantity reaches Great Britain for naval purposes, for which it is highly appreciated.

The country being intersected by lakes and rivers, produces abundance of fish, especially salmon, of a superior quality, which is exported either dried or pickled. Immense quantities of tar and pitch are exported to every part of Europe, and form a source of great wealth to the inhabitants.

In most of the ports are excellent ship-building yards, of which those destroyed by Admiral Plumridge's squadron in the Gulf of Bothnia may serve as specimens. The science of naval architecture is carried to a degree of perfection which will bear comparison with the state of ship-building in England. The Fins are indefatigable in producing the finest models from other countries, and their aim is, if not to improve upon them, at least to equal them. They can build ships of any size, but from the small draught of water in their shallow channels, they rarely build those of the largest class. The ships are sent to London to be coppered, and are afterwards to be found in every quarter of the globe. It will hence be seen that to a power like Russia, aiming every year more and more at naval excellence, the possession of Finland is invaluable; and the cordial co-operation of its artisans no less so. These, as has been said, have been secured by conciliations unknown in other parts of the Russian Empire.

The Finnish seamen are equally good with their ships, and from them Russia draws her best supply for manning her navy in the Baltic as well as in the Black Sea. Her seamen in the latter waters were generally admitted to be of a superior class, and these have been now transferred to her Baltic fleet; rendering it much more formidable than before the war. They are sober, steady, and active, possessing all the good qualities of the English seaman, and they perform their duties with cheerfulness, and an interest in their profession which can alone make good seamen. Hence their services are deemed desirable in British merchant ships wherever they can be obtained.

The principal towns of Finland are Abo, the former capital, and Helsingfors, the intended capital. Close to this latter town is the fortress of Sweaborg, for the most part the work of the Northern Vauban, Count Ehrensword. It was commenced soon after the disastrous wars of Charles XII., and even then required 15,000 troops to man the fortifications.

Considered formerly as the key to Sweden, the greatest attention was paid to this fortress by the Swedish monarchs. During successive contests it resisted all attempts on the part of Russia; and it was only in the course of the war, in 1809 and 1810, that the Swedish Commandant, a traitor to his country, allowing himself to be seduced by the promise of Russian gold, — like his Hungarian imitator, Georgy, — surrendered this stronghold to the enemy. It is satisfactory to know that the traitor never got his gold, but lived in poverty and contempt amongst those who first seduced and then ridiculed him.

The fall of Sweaborg, thus treacherously surrendered, caused at the time the greatest dismay in Sweden, as well as in Finland. The name of the traitor was everywhere execrated. The act had enabled Russia, when peace was not long after concluded, to dictate her own hard terms to Sweden. Since then the Russians have added greatly to the original strength of the fortress. It is now the key to Russia, as it formerly was to Swedish Finland. By the possession of this fortress, the road to St. Petersburg by an army is open, two other towns only intervening, viz., Frederickshamm and Viborg—the former already a considerable fortress.

In addition to these two capitals, Finland possesses other towns more or less dependent on ship-building and timber. These are Uleaborg, Gamla Carleby, Nya Carleby, Jacobstad, Wasa, Bijorneborg, Christenstad, Borgo, and Lovisa, all carrying on a considerable commerce to various parts of the world.

From what has been advanced in this chapter, from sources both novel and authentic, it will appear that had war been waged in earnest against Russia, Finland should have been the first object of attack, as its possession, even partly, would have been a death-blow to the naval power of Russia in the Baltic. Whatever may have been the indulgences of Russia to the Fins, they were not altogether weaned from Sweden; and, as has been said, a strong party might have been found eager for national independence. The presence of an army, together with the British fleet, would have given embodiment to these aspirations. Instead of this, we wasted the lives and strength of our army in the Crimea to no conceivable purpose, and certainly to no definite result. To England a more humiliating mistake was never made. In place of severing from Russia her best province, and thus threatening her capital with a hostile occupation, despite her impregnable forts at Cronstadt, we literally did nothing in the Baltic even so much as to alarm her. Even when we had taken the outpost of Aland, about which she cared little, except as it served to menace Sweden, the latter power refused to accept her own back again, being confident that in the end she would have to pay dearly for it to Russia; and having no confidence in our ability or inclination to protect her, even in this acquisition.

With our fleet in the Baltic, Russia, seeing the mistake we had made, treated Sweden contemptuously, even to declaring that she would not respect her neutrality. Had we gone to work the right way, instead of sending an undisciplined and worse equipped fleet to do nothing throughout the war, the hopes of Sir James Graham that Sweden would join us, might have been fulfilled. She might have sent her well-equipped army and her powerful naval armaments to co-operate with any army we might have sent, and with the British fleet, so that the conquest of Finland might have been the consequence, despite all the efforts of Russia to prevent it. The naval power of Russia would have vanished from the Baltic, in place of being, as it now is, not only safe, but most materially strengthened. When the day of contest again comes — as come it must, some day or other — Russia will not a second time decline a naval contest.

To Russia the loss of Finland would have been irretrievable. She knew this, and made every effort to detach, by an early hostile demonstration, the northern Courts from their adopted system of neutrality, and to get their concurrence in her contemplated operations. Sweden and Norway resolutely refused to deviate from their fixed plan, the anger of Russia notwithstanding; but they were paralysed by the political blunder we had committed of wasting our strength and resources in the Crimea. Sweden, however, made the most strenuous preparations for battle either by sea or land, should it become necessary in her own defence, taking every precaution to prevent Stockholm from being pounced upon by a *coup-de-main* from Aland at the outset, as well as to prevent Russia from seizing Gothland — a much-coveted prize, which, if we may judge from the continued preparations of Sweden, may not yet be lost sight of by Russia when opportunity serves. That Sweden did not accept the Aland Isles, lying within a short distance of her own capital, shows that she had little faith in the measures we had adopted, or in the policy we should afterwards pursue.

As the conquest of Finland forms, perhaps, the most complete sample of Russian progress, it may be interesting, in an historical point of view, to make a few further remarks on the subject.

Russia rarely conquers any country by force of arms, but has an adroit way of reasoning potentates out of their possessions, by what Burke sarcastically termed "a royal syllogism." England has, of late years, been somewhat addicted to the same kind of diplomatic reasoning, but more clumsily. We have recently told the King of Oude that, as he was not competent to manage the affairs of his country, it had become necessary that we should relieve him of the trouble by taking it from him. When, in 1808, a Russian army entered Swedish Finland, its commander, Count Bouxhoevden, went a more logical way to work. There was no provocation, so this was left out of the argument, and the Count merely issued a proclamation, in which he told his "*good friends*" the Fins to stay quietly at home and not oppose his designs, which were all for peace. In return for this forbearance, he promised to "respect the Finnish laws and religion." A similar document was recently addressed by Prince Gortschakoff to the inhabitants of Wallachia and Moldavia. The annexative diplomacy of Russia is stereotyped. She always pursues the same objects by the same means; and this, perhaps, is the reason why the shifty diplomacy of other countries cannot compete with her.

The Russian commander at once invested Tavastheus, a large inland town defended by Count Klingspoor. The Swedish Government had instructed their General not to endanger the Finland army against a superior force; so that General Klingspoor retired, leaving Tavastheus in possession of the Russians.

A division had been despatched by Count Bouxhoevden to invest Helsingfors, so as to isolate Sweaborg. Another detachment was placed on the ice, to occupy the space between Helsingfors and Sweaborg. The Helsingfors garrison retired over the ice to the fortress; and, in so doing, were attacked by the Russians, who took a number of guns and prisoners. The Russians now invested Sweaborg with a *cordon* of light troops, under General Raviasky.

Sweaborg was defended by Admiral Count Cronstedt, whose garrison exceeded the number of the besiegers. He was well supplied with guns and ammunition, whilst the Russians had only forty-six pieces of cannon, including mortars. Admiral Cronstedt attacked both the besieging army and the relinquished city, causing great loss to both; whereupon the Russian commander sent in a flag of truce, representing that as most of the inhabitants of Helsingfors had friends or relatives in the garrison, the latter would feel the injury inflicted on them. Admiral Cronstedt at first refused to listen to this argument, but at length was cajoled into so doing, and agreed that the works fronting Helsingfors should be regarded as neutral ground, and that no further bombardment of the city should take place; whereupon the Russians were enabled to establish their magazines, hospitals, and parks of artillery at Helsingfors without molestation.

The Russians now established batteries on the heights, from whence they fired into the fortress, setting the buildings on fire several times. The Swedish garrison was now kept in alarm day and night, and became restless and despondent, whilst their commander was evidently unfit for the defence of a fortress. From this time the Russians worked more on the *morale* than the *matériel* of their opponents, and upon none more than Admiral Cronstedt himself in personal communications. He even permitted intercourse between his own officers and the Russian officers, the latter politely supplying the garrison with newspapers and gazettes, sending, however, only those which spoke gloomily of Sweden and triumphantly of Russia. A disposition to treat was thus induced, and this ended in an armistice, extending from the 5th of May to the 3rd of June, at which period, if succours did not arrive from Sweden, the fortress was to be given up. As a security, the islands of Langhorn, Wester Swarto, and Oster Lilla Swarto were delivered into the hands of the Russians. The succours did not arrive, and on the 3rd of May Sweaborg, with a garrison far more numerous than their assailants, was given up to Russia, whose priests sang a *Te Deum* on the occasion; and, in place of reward to the Swedish Admiral, as had been promised, they treated him with the contempt he so richly merited.

CHAP. XV.

THE SIEGE OF BOMARSUND.

ON the 19th of July, the Duke of Newcastle had written to the Admiral that they were all " watching his proceedings with the greatest anxiety, but, he might be assured, in entire confidence." On the 1st of August, the Admiral replied to his Grace that Bomarsund was very strong towards the sea — that it was "a large two-decker of granite," of which the number of the garrison could not be ascertained. The navigation was very intricate; almost all the steamers had been frequently on shore, and one had her bows stove in. This rendered the service an arduous one, but he was very glad his Grace was satisfied with what had been done. It would be necessary to make quick work at Bomarsund, for the climate was very changeable, and despatch was imperative. The Admiral was sorry to hear that more troops were coming, as the fleet must begin to think of leaving this latitude in the middle of September, certainly not after the 1st of October, as from the nature of the climate it would then be useless.

On the same day, Sir Charles apprised Commodore Martin that he had been made an admiral, and that on the arrival of Captain Munday, he should take on himself to order him to hoist his flag.

Sir Charles had written to Sir James Graham that he would endeavour to comply as well as he could with all his instructions, public and private, but that all could not be complied with. He had been ordered to move the French troops into steamers at Faro, but this was impossible, as the Gulf of Finland had to be watched to prevent the junction of the Russian fleets at Sweaborg. He therefore had decided to order the troops to come on to Ledsund. He had suggested to the French Admiral to leave a mixed force of French and English ships off the Gulf, but he did not think it necessary, nor did he like to separate his ships.

A few words must be said relative to Sir James Graham's plan of moving the French troops into steamers at Faro. This anchorage is some 200 miles from the seat of operations, and had Sir Charles Napier complied with his instructions, he would have had to detach his steamers from the blockade of the Aland Islands, giving the Russians every chance to throw in reinforcements, or to execute any other movement they thought proper. An order so extraordinary could only have emanated from geographical ignorance of the localities of the war, to say nothing of the time unnecessarily wasted in transhipping troops, siege materials, baggage, &c., from one set of vessels to another, the same process having to be gone over again a day or two afterwards on their arrival at Bomarsund, and this at a time when, from the delay which had taken place in forwarding the troops, every hour was of consequence in case of an ordinarily protracted siege, before the conclusion of which, bad weather might reasonably be expected to set in.

There were then three courses to follow. First, to remain with his fleet at Baro Sound; second, to accompany the French Admiral to Ledsund with the fleet; third, to separate the British squadron. The second had at one time been decided on, but on reflection, Sir Charles thought that the First Lord would be alarmed at leaving the Sweaborg squadron unwatched, and, having got the *Austerlitz* from the French, he had left eight line-of-battle ships at Nargen, with two frigates and three steamers. These precautions could not prevent a junction of the Russian fleets were they so inclined, but they could watch Sweaborg, and communicate with him if any movement took place. The fleet could join

Admiral Martin at the shortest notice, and were also prepared to send boats to support the steamers in case of an attack from the Russian gun-boats, which was probable. It was not improbable the Russian fleet would make some movement; and if they did, the allied fleets, with the exception of the block-ships, would join Admiral Martin, while the English ships at Ledsund could be with him in a few hours. As for sending steamers to meet the French troops at Faro, it was out of the question. The Admiral had not sufficient steamers to prevent succours being thrown into Bomarsund, and he had hence ordered Commodore Grey to bring up his squadron from Faro.

The Admiral, moreover, told the First Lord that the troops ought to have been up before the season was far advanced, and we must be quick. As for any ulterior operation, it was out of the question. Sweaborg was not to be taken with a handful of men. We should have begun in June instead of the beginning of August, for, in the middle of September, it would be time to be pointing south. These seas were "not to be played with by fleets of large ships."

On the 1st of August, Sir James Graham replied, that with due regard to circumstances all the Admiral's movements had been judicious, whilst he praised his "foresight and good arrangement" with regard to the French troops. He had sent the Admiral *one* of Lancaster's guns, and "a short supply of his conical shells." "I am aware," concluded Sir James, "that Bomarsund presents difficulties; but I feel assured you will overcome them; and it is of great consequence, that while Sweden is hesitating, you should take Aland. The next movement must be well considered, but the fall of Bomarsund will be no bad beginning."

On the same day, General Baraguay D'Hilliers proceeded in *La Reine Hortense*, in company with Admiral Parseval, to reconnoitre Bomarsund, in which reconnoissance, they were joined by Sir Charles Napier and General Jones in the *Lightning*. After minutely inspecting the fortifications, the allied commanders returned in the evening to the fleet at Ledsund. On the 2nd of August, the *Termagant*, Captain the Hon. Keith Stewart, arrived in company with a transport laden with troops.

On the 3rd of August, no more French troops had made their appearance, and everything was, in consequence, at a stand still.

The desire of the Admiral to commence operations was very great. He had heard of their being at Kiel, though why they went there does not appear. "This," wrote the Admiral to Sir James, "is most serious; the summer is passing away, and every hour is precious. The French General will not land and occupy a position, till the *matériel* arrives. Getting up breaching guns will be heavy work : the sailors can do it, but it will require time. Ships can do nothing against granite walls, and the anchorage is covered by the three towers, which will knock them to pieces. If they took up a position, there they must remain, for retiring is out of the question ; there is not room to turn. If the Russians can hold out till the weather gets bad, we shall be in a mess.

All that can be done I will do, but this delay kills me."

In fact, not only the season, but the war itself, was becoming critical. The Russians, as the Admiral knew, were devising means to raise the siege; and he received intelligence from one of our ministers at a German court, that 300 gun-boats had been got ready, with which the Russians hoped to cause great annoyance to the fleet, which had but a few steamers to meet them, or rather none at all which could be spared from the necessary operations in the Aland Isles. It was then necessary that the attack on Bomarsund should be short and decisive, so as to give the Russians no time to do anything before the fleet was prepared to give attention to them.

On receiving this intelligence, the Admiral wrote to Admiral Martin, that he had better go back to Baro Sound, in preference to removing to Nargen, as he would stop anything coming to Bomarsund, and it would be safer, though he would leave this to his own judgment.

Admiral Parseval having decided that the French marines, amounting to 2000 men, should be sent to the north of the fort, as well as the English marines, Sir Charles requested of General Baraguay D'Hilliers that the whole might be placed under the orders of General Jones, which request was complied with. He further apprised General Baraguay D'Hilliers that Admiral Plumridge would be ordered to meet them, and superintend their landing.

On the 5th the Admiral expressed his fears to

Admiral Parseval that the force at Ledsund was being reduced too low, should the Russian fleet attempt to disturb that of the Allies. Admiral Parseval replied that, situated as he was, he was compelled to detach his squadron, but that he hoped the troops would soon be here.

The French squadron indeed arrived soon afterwards. It consisted of the ships of the line *Tilsit* and *St. Louis*, the frigates *Cleopatra* and *Sirene*, and the steamers *Asmodée*, *Cocyte*, *Laborieux*, and *Goëland*. These vessels, together with the transports, brought the remainder of the troops, now amounting to 10,000, the heavy guns, and other materials for the siege. The *Vulture* also arrived with the *one* Lancaster gun, which was placed on board the *Edinburgh*. On the 6th, Admiral Martin wrote to Sir Charles, that nothing more had taken place at Cronstadt, nor with the westerly wind that had prevailed could the Russians do anything. He had sent Capt. Watson to reconnoitre Cronstadt, and should send another vessel to look round to the eastward. He took care to keep up his chain of communication to Sweaborg.

Mr. Biddlecombe, the master of the fleet, was despatched to reconnoitre Bomarsund. He did so within 600 yards of the great fort, and placed buoys on the extremity of a shoal extending from the west shore. Whilst so doing, he was fired upon from the fort, as well as from the Island of Presto, a shell bursting alongside his boat, and piercing it in two places. One or two of his men were hit by musketry, but no damage occurred worth noticing.

The undermentioned masters were also employed, under Mr. Biddlecombe's directions, in sounding the approaches to the fortress: — Mr. H. A. Moriarty, *Duke of Wellington;* Mr. H. G. Raynes, *St. Jean d'Acre;* Mr. R. C. Allen, *Hogue;* Mr. J. S. Hall, *Cumberland;* and Mr. G. H. Blakey, *Edinburgh.*

The French troops were moved on board the steamers at one o'clock on the 7th, and by four the operation was complete. At seven o'clock in the evening they were all at anchor off the west tower of Bomarsund.

The landing was effected on the 8th at daylight, and that most admirably, without so much as a wet foot. The British marines, and a body of French marines under the command of Col. Graham, aided by Brigade-Major Elliot, disembarked simultaneously on the north side of the island. The Russians had unaccountably overlooked this important position, for which no defence had been prepared, and no opposition was made, though every one had anticipated a hard struggle.

The force first landed consisted of ninety men of the Sappers and Miners and a battalion of the Marines from the British squadron. These had been conducted by Capt. Sulivan through an intricate navigation to the northward of Bomarsund to join Admiral Plumridge. The advance guard was composed of one hundred marines, twenty sappers and miners commanded by Capt. King, assisted by Capts. Hambley and Clarell, and Lieut. Nugent. The main body under Col. Graham, consisted of 400 marines, 70 sappers and miners, and four field pieces. Two thousand French marines under Brigadier-General Jones brought up the rear.

On landing, the advanced guard threw itself into a wood, but without encountering any of the enemy. They marched on slowly and steadily, detaching reconnoitring parties on all sides. On the line of march they fell in with two masked batteries in course of construction to command the main road, and at length encamped on a small plain at the foot of a rocky ledge.

Simultaneously with these, the French troops landed in two places to the southward of Bomarsund. Admiral Chads took charge of landing four battalions of the 51st, and Capt. Penaud landed the Chasseurs, both operations being conducted with great ability.

The forts were now invested. The troops had been landed in excellent order, and were enabled leisurely to take up positions where they might act with most effect. On the march up nothing occurred worthy of notice.

Whilst this was going on, Capt. Key with the *Amphion*, and Capt. Desbois with the *Phlegeton*, were ordered to attack a seven-gun battery on Transvig point, in advance of the great fort. This shot told fearfully on the Russians, who with great difficulty could return their fire, the precision of which, as Sir Charles reported to the Admiralty, " was wonderful." In forty minutes the battery was knocked about the ears of the enemy, who beat a precipitate retreat. Armed boats were then sent to take possession of the battery, the guns of which were spiked.

The whole force now commenced erecting batteries

preparatory to commencing a systematic attack on the advanced tower. The French skirmishers soon found their way to the village of Finby, and the main body bivouacked on the surrounding heights; the English force at the same time constructing sand batteries on the summit of a hill commanding the eastern fort, or, as it was called, Fort Nottich. The English battery was planned by Gen. Jones, assisted by Brigade-Major Ord, Capt. Ring, and Lieuts. Nugent, Cowell, and Wrottesley. Too much praise cannot be given to these officers for the masterly way in which the work was carried on, at night, under a heavy fire from the enemy; and the spirit shown by the seamen and marines employed in the details, may be estimated when it is stated that they had to fill no less than 5000 sand bags, each of which had to be carried separately, on the shoulders of the men, up a precipitous rocky mountain. Fascines, gabions, shot, and ammunition had to be similarly conveyed, and were all brought up with the alacrity which is characteristic of the naval service.

The fleet was anchored below in Lumpar Bay. Sir Charles Napier shifted his flag on board the *Bulldog*, and went up with the troops. When the landing was completed, he pushed the *Bulldog* and *Stromboli* up a creek where he could get a full view of all that was going on.

The landing of the troops had been effected with the greatest cordiality between the two nations, each vying with the other in energy. The Admirals and Generals commanding were unanimous in opinion as in action, and when reporting the proceedings to the

Admiralty, Sir Charles warmly eulogised Admiral Plumridge and General Jones who had conducted the landing to the north, as well as Admiral Chads and Capt. Penaud, who had directed it on the south. He paid an equally warm tribute to Rear-Admiral Seymour for the assistance received from him.

The next operation was the landing of guns to complete the batteries, and this devolved on Admiral Chads. The distance they had to be dragged from the landing place to the battery was four miles and a half, over what Admiral Chads termed " execrable ground, the greater portion of which was steep rocky hills and ploughed fields."

The disembarkation of the guns took place on the morning of the 10th, each ship having previously prepared two sledges, after a pattern made by Capt. Ramsay of the *Hogue*. Upon these sledges were placed the guns with their carriages and gear, and 150 men were attached to each sledge, under their respective senior lieutenants, the whole being under the command of Capt. Hewlett, of the *Edinburgh*.

The operation was commenced at five o'clock in the morning, and by ten o'clock, the first batch of guns was in the English camp. The exertions of the seamen and officers caused no small astonishment in the French encampment, the French loudly cheering the blue-jackets in passing; and, in some of the more difficult ascents, voluntarily seizing on the drag ropes, and lending a hand with a will not second to that of the seamen themselves.

On arriving in camp, the men were much exhausted by the great amount of fatigue they had undergone, and the majority lay down on the ground to rest, whilst others prepared their dinners. Their rest was of short duration, for an order arrived to embark immediately, the *Penelope* having got on shore under the guns of the great fort, and the services of the men were required on board their respective ships, in case their aid should become necessary.

Fatigued as were the men, the order was received with loud cheers, and forgetting both their previous exertions and their dinners, they, disdaining the comparatively safe way they had come, took a short cut within range of the fire of the fort, from which they happily escaped, and reached their boats in three quarters of an hour.

The *Penelope*, in passing the large fort, had got on shore, and at no long range, about 1900 yards, from the enemy's guns. They soon got her range, and began unmercifully to ply her with red hot shot and shells. One of the shots passed through the ship's side, and took off the head of a gallant young French officer, who had come to her assistance. Another red hot shot passed through a midshipman's chest in the steerage, was coolly picked up on a shovel, and being placed on three cold shot, allowed to expend its heat harmlessly. Three men of the English squadron were also killed. The *Hecla*, which had been sent to the assistance of the *Penelope*, was considerably damaged, and had three men wounded. The *Valorous* and *Lightning* went to the assistance of the *Penelope*; and whilst so doing, the ships at anchor occasionally fired shells, at long range, at the Russian fortress.   Finding the ship immovable, the guns were thrown overboard, when she floated; but not without considerable damage to her hull.   Had it not been for the prompt assistance rendered by the ships of both squadrons, she must have shared the fate of the *Tiger*.   Her guns were all afterwards recovered.

The grounding of the *Penelope* arose from no fault of Captain Caffin, who commanded her; but from the danger of the navigation to which all the ships were alike exposed.   She was proceeding at the time through the Presto Channel at very slow speed, and had become a mark for the great fort before she grounded, though without being hit.   She had been directed by the Admiral to take up a position abreast of the eleventh embrasure of the enemy's fort; and in so doing, took the ground in three fathoms.   It was remarked that, whilst she lay in this perilous position, the enemy's shell thrown against her produced little or no effect; but the red-hot shot frequently struck her.   It should be mentioned that the *Gladiator* and *Pigmy*, which were at the other end of the passage, immediately came to her assistance, and the French Admiral sent boats from the *Duperré* and *Trident*.   As soon as the Admiral discovered her position, he sent Admiral Plumridge with orders to get her off; and he spoke most highly of the coolness and exertions of Captains Caffin, Hall, and Broke, as well as of Lieut. Hunt of the *Pigmy*, under very trying circumstances. Capt. L. Stewart also volunteered his services, and went in his boat to render aid to the *Penelope*.

On the 11th, more guns were landed in the same manner; but this time with 200 men from each ship to the sledges, as the men on the previous day had been too hard worked. These guns were in camp by half past ten in the morning. The bands of the ships attended the working parties; so that this extraordinary march resembled a triumph, as it in fact was, over difficulties which had been considered almost insurmountable, though now effected with such rapidity. The spirits of the men, when on their march, were not unfrequently excited by a dropping shot from the enemy. The zeal and perseverance displayed, was such as British seamen can alone show; and the Admiral, when complimenting Admiral Chads, his officers, and men on their work, bore testimony that, " in the course of his service, he had seen guns moved in difficult places, but never on such roads, and to such a distance, as in the present instance; the cheerfulness and exertions of the men were wonderful."

The French, having brought with them an immense amount of ordnance stores, did not accept the portion of ships' guns destined for their use. Their siege artillery and *matériel* were got up with great celerity, as they had no less than 80 artillery horses on board the transports, with some 500 engineers.

The Russians now burned everything that was inflammable in the neighbourhood of the forts, evidently preparing for a resolute defence. Three deserters from the enemy's garrison reported the arrival of an *Aide-de-Camp* from the Czar, and also that fifty gun-boats, with reinforcements were expected. The difficulty was how to keep them out, for the steamers were not half sufficient to guard the various channels amongst the islands.

General Jones, by advancing beyond his outposts, was able to reconnoitre the ground in front; and got under cover within 800 yards of Fort Tzee, where he had also a good view of the North Tower. He considered the locality favourable here for the erection of breaching batteries; and when General Baraguay D'Hilliers and General Niel, afterwards reconnoitred the ground, they decided on placing their own batteries against Fort Tzee, leaving the other tower to the English. It was the Admiral's wish that the Presto tower should also be at first invested; but this was overruled by his colleagues.

Whilst the men were gallantly exerting themselves, an incident occurred which, coupled with many others, shows that the Commissariat department of the Admiralty was not much more successfully conducted than was that of the army in the Crimea; with the exception that, as the ships were their own food conveyers, there was no want of food. The preceding almost superhuman exertions of the men had to *be made barefoot*. In the *Edinburgh* alone, Admiral Chads had nearly a month before made a demand for shoes for his men, to replace others sent back to England as being useless from their small size. The Admiralty had sent out instead of these, ninety-eight pairs of shoes only, of which eighty-five pairs were too small for issue, thus giving thirteen pairs of shoes to the whole crew of one of the flagships; the rest, of course, were barefoot! " The same complaint," said the Admiral, when reporting to the Board that Admiral Chads had complained to him, " *is made by every ship in the fleet:* when it gets cold, it will be most serious. *Even now, the men are on shore shoeless.* I fear something is wrong in the conduct of those who supply them ; otherwise, such a general complaint would not have occurred."

On the 12th, both parties were at work with their batteries, in which the guns were now placed, the French having brought up a brass field battery, and four 8-inch mortars, and the English, six 32-pounders, three only of which were placed in the English battery before Fort Nottich, the other three being destined for the French battery before Fort Tzee, but were not accepted, as the French considered their own artillery sufficient. The English batteries were placed in charge of Capt. Ramsay of the *Hogue,* and Commander Preedy, of the *Duke of Wellington,* assisted by Lieutenants Somerset, Cudlip, Burgess, Singer, and Mr. Croke, mate of the *Duke of Wellington.*

On the evening of the 12th, the whole of the batteries were ready for the attack, notwithstanding the almost continuous fire of the enemy during their formation ; but the operations had been carried on in a manner at once so scientific and safe, that one man only in the English battery had been wounded, though the French had a few casualties.

At 4 o'clock on the morning of the 13th, the French battery of four 16-pounders and four mortars opened a splendid fire on the Western Tower, or Fort Tzee. General Jones's battery, in charge of Capt. Ramsay, was directed by the French General to withhold its fire till the following day. The French had made a regular zigzag approach to the fort, the chasseurs were thrown forward almost to its walls, and kept up a deadly fire from behind every tree and ledge of rock which flanked the embrasures. The light artillery worked most effectively, starring and disfiguring the walls of the fort; but the French mortar firing even surpassed this, every bomb plunging with terrific force upon the iron roof of the fortress, and sending its fragments flying in all directions, each shock being followed by a loud cheer from the French encampment on the opposite side. The roof soon became a complete wreck, but the walls were not breached, though the stones were much broken, and many were knocked away from the embrasures. Notwithstanding this and the yet more galling fire from the Chasseurs, the garrison stood their ground manfully and worked their guns without cessation, maintaining a steady fire upon their opponents till the evening.

The storm of bullets from artillery and Minié rifles at length appeared too much for the enemy. A flag of truce was shown from one of the windows of the roof, and General Baraguay D'Hilliers, with a few troops marched up to the fort. The garrison asked for a four hours' cessation of hostilities, as the event showed, with an intention of procuring reinforcements or ammunition from the main fort. The General offered one hour, at the end of which, if the fort was not surrendered, the fire would be resumed. This not suiting the purpose of the Russians, they peremptorily ordered the parleying party away, advising them to go quickly, as they were about to recommence firing. The French troops, therefore, returned to camp, and the firing was recommenced on both sides.

The French firing now became superb; shell after shell plunging on the roof of the fort, and where the iron covering was gone, sending the rafters flying through the air. Another flag of truce was held out, and another party of French troops again advanced. Still there was something dubious about the conduct of the garrison, and the French were not admitted, but drew their pickets closer, and cut off all communication with the fort. The French troops were also thrown all round the hills for the night, so as to prevent supplies being thrown into the fort, and to prevent fugitives leaving.

At daybreak on the 14th, the French commenced by firing three guns, none of which were replied to by the fort. A body of the Chasseurs now volunteered to march up, and did so, entering without opposition. On approaching the room in which the Commandant was, the latter made a dash at the leading chasseur, who received the infuriated officer on the point of his bayonet, and was about to discharge his rifle, when the Russian officer offered him his sword, which was taken by the French officer in command, and given to the chasseur.

No farther opposition was offered. There were only a few troops found in the fort, and those few, according to Russian custom, had been made drunk before recommencing the fight, which, even under that stimulus they had refused to do. In short, there had been the day before a mutiny amongst the garrison, this accounting for the vacillation which had been made with regard to the flags of truce.

The troops found in the fort were immediately marched to the French camp, those who were wounded being left in charge of their own surgeon. The front of the fort was well battered, though no complete breach had been effected; but from the state of the walls, they could not much longer have held out. The interior of the fort was a good deal shattered, several shells having entered the embrasures, and burst in the galleries.

The Russians had about fifty killed, and these had been put in casks with lime, and then headed down, causing a putrid stench throughout the place. The fort was well supplied with provisions, and there was reason to suppose that during the parley they had got powder. Reinforcements were expected during the night, but the vigilance of the French had prevented this, and the garrison refused again to fight. This peculiarity of the Russians was afterwards apparent in the Crimea, the dead in every encounter showing that fresh troops had been brought to the attack.

It was the intention of the French to have turned Fort Tzee against the great fortress, but as soon as the great fortress found that it had surrendered, the garrison began to fire upon it, and succeeded in setting it on fire. For some time this made little progress, but at length the fire caught some of the powder in the lower basement, when the whole blew up with a tremendous explosion, filling the air with smoke, dead bodies, the bodies of the wounded, and salt fish, with which the place was well stocked. The whole now became a smouldering heap, in which guns in all positions could be here and there distinguished.

Whilst this was going on, the other forts kept up an incessant fire on the English camp with grape, round shot, shells, and other iron missiles, even to iron bars. Yet only one man, a marine belonging to the *Duke of Wellington*, was killed as he lay asleep in his tent. The effect of the shot was much diminished by the softness of the ground, into which it plunged harmlessly, and the shells, for the most part, went over. It seemed a miracle that no further injury was done.

Now came the English turn. General Jones's battery, commanded by Captain Ramsay of the *Hogue*, and manned by seamen and marines, had perforce been quiet spectators of the preceding scene. On the morning of the 15th, at eight A.M., Captain Ramsay's battery opened on Fort Nottich, at a distance of about 750 yards. The guns, thirty-two-pounders, told on the fort with far greater effect than had the light artillery of the French against Fort Tzee, and the Russians returned the fire with a vigour which deserves honourable mention ; gun after gun flashed from the embrasures, skimming over the British sand-bags, or as harmlessly burying themselves within. So admirably had the battery been constructed, that the men could not be touched. On the other hand, the granite splinters of the enemy's fort, flew in showers round the heads of the gunners. At an early period of the day, a splinter struck a brave young officer, Lieut. Wrottesley, on the hip, inflicting a mortal wound, from which he only survived a few hours. This was almost the only casualty worth mentioning. Captain Ramsay was, however, slightly wounded.

The 32-pounders soon made an impression. The English had no mortars to send the roof flying through the air, but it soon became evident that it would not be the work of a day to reduce the fort. Every shot told with full effect, leaving its mark; the next dislodged a fragment, then followed a block of granite, then the whole wall was visibly shaken, and after two or three hours' bombardment a gap had been formed, which a few more salutes increased to a regular breach, obliterating two embrasures in the enemy's upper tier, and opening to view the casemates and inner court. The fort, being circular, could only bring four of its guns to bear upon the English battery. Two of these had been silenced, and a third speedily followed, but the fourth could not so easily be got at.

The fire from Capt. Ramsay's battery now began to bring down the wall in large masses, and the ruins contributed to shelter the one invincible gun. Its embrasure had become a breach, into which the brave Russians rushed at each fresh blow from the English battery, and deliberately shovelled away the lime and stones from their wonderful gun. So thickly did the ruin accumulate around it, that there was not time to clear away the *débris*, and the gun was fired from within the heap, so as to blow away the accumulating mass. For some time yet the gun gave shot for shot, but at half-past five in the afternoon, down came the side of the fort, and the noble gun was deeply buried within the ruins. Loud now rose the British cheers, not so much for their success, as for the bravery which had been opposed to it. To resist farther was impossible, and the brave defenders of the fort hung out a flag of truce.

A hundred British marines, commanded by Major Ord, at once marched to the fort, and to them the garrison surrendered amidst the eulogies of their captors, for that the fight of the vanquished had been a gallant one the evidence was abundant, the shattered walls bearing honourable testimony to the obstinate and even desperate valour of the defenders. As the night fell, 300 marines were sent from the camp under Colonel Graham, and marched the brave garrison prisoners of war to the British camp, where they were received with all the respect their bravery had so well won. The great fortress fired shells on the British line of march, but without damage, and a volley of Minié balls was fired at the rearguard of sappers and miners, who remained behind to clear the fort.

There were 120 prisoners taken, including three officers, their numbers having been sadly diminished by the deadly fire to which they had been subjected. The delight of the seamen was excessive at the gratitude evinced by the Russians for the kind attentions shown them, and certainly everything was done to make them as happy as possible under their defeat. They were at once embarked on board the ships of war, the British officers warmly shaking hands with them on their departure, but only again to be welcomed rather as brave friends than as enemies.

When on their way to the camp, the Russian prisoners were shown the battery which had destroyed their fort. Their surprise may be conceived at only seeing three guns, and those uninjured. From the regularity and rapidity of the seamen's firing, they thought we must have had at least thirty in battery. On asking how many we had killed and wounded, and on being told that the casualties consisted of one officer killed and a few men slightly wounded, they could not conceal their disbelief in the statement, as they had made up their minds that like themselves we must have suffered severely.

It has been said by military authorities that Bomarsund was a military siege. If by this is meant that the navy had not its full share in it, a greater mistake cannot be made. It will be necessary to watch this point very closely as we proceed. Up to this period of the siege, we have the British navy bringing up its own guns, and knocking down Fort Nottich, whilst the French military force captured Fort Tzee, without effecting a breach, the garrison having surrendered. This at least was an equal share; and if to this we add, that had it not been for the energy of the British navy in getting up the guns, and the vigilance of Admiral Plumridge in checking reinforcements, though with far too few steamers to execute this duty thoroughly, the preparations would not have been made in time to prevent a protracted siege; and this, as the bad weather of the Baltic was at hand, might have led to very serious results. The Russians had 10,000 men at Abo, who were placed there for the express purpose of reinforcing the garrison, but such had been the rapidity of the movements of the allied admirals, that, with the trifling exception just mentioned, all hope of reinforcement was gone. So far then, the allied navy had at least its full share of the work.

Both batteries had been admirably constructed, and as admirably fought, General Jones speaking in high terms of the conduct of the seamen and marine artillery, especially of the precision of their fire. It was owing to this excellent construction of Capt. Ramsay's battery, that so little loss was sustained. The death of Lieut. Wrottesley was caused by a round shot entering an embrasure, and knocking away a piece of iron from a gun-carriage, a large fragment of the iron lodging in the body of the unfortunate officer, causing death within twenty minutes after he had been sent to the *Belleisle.*

During the capture of the Eastern Tower by Capt. Ramsay's battery, General Baraguay D'Hilliers was employed in establishing his breaching batteries against the great fortress. Whilst thus engaged, the ships of the allied fleet directed a well sustained fire against the great fort with their shell-guns, and severely damaged it. The ships engaged were the *Edinburgh, Ajax, Arrogant, Amphion, Valorous,*

Driver, Bulldog, Hecla, Trident, Duperré, Asmodée, Phlegeton, and *Darien.* Of course, the principal object of this attack by the ships was to draw the attention of the enemy from the operations of General Baraguay D'Hilliers.

A very galling operation to the enemy's garrison, was undertaken by Capt. the Hon. F. T. Pelham of the *Blenheim,* who with extraordinary labour got the 10-inch pivot-gun of his ship, weighing five tons, into his boat, and with his seamen alone, landed and placed it in the battery out of which the *Amphion* and *Phlegeton* had driven the enemy on the first day. Having got his gun thus far, Capt. Pelham and his blue jackets turned to with shovels and pickaxes, and reversed the battery, thus turning one of the Russian works against themselves. The gun did great execution, and when the fort was afterwards taken, unmistakeable proofs of its destructive effect were evident. This judicious manœuvre appeared greatly to irritate the enemy, who turned their attention to Capt. Pelham, greatly to the advantage of the French whilst engaged in forming their breaching batteries. The position of Capt. Pelham was one of great danger; but so well had he constructed his battery, that the men were well covered, and sustained no loss whatever, though the damage they inflicted on the Russians was very great.

When narrating these events to the Board of Admiralty, Sir Charles Napier concluded as follows:

" The General's breaching batteries will be ready by to-morrow, and they shall be well supported by the ships of the line of both nations and the steamers.

The narrowness of the ground on which the General has established his breaching batteries, very much circumscribes the space. The greatest caution will be necessary to prevent firing on his troops ; and the little space in the anchorage before Bomarsund, and the intricacy of the navigation, will prevent ships approaching the main fortress so near as could be wished, but when the batteries are established, acting in the rear of the fort, and supported by the shell guns in front, it cannot hold out more than a few hours. I have just put off to the last moment the departure of the mail, but I shall send an extra courier the moment the fort surrenders.

" The western tower was fired either by accident or design. I do not know which, and blew up at eleven A. M. yesterday.

" I am sorry to add, that Lieut. Cowell, R.E., Aide-de-camp to Brigadier-General Jones, was unfortunately wounded in the leg by the accidental discharge of his pistol. He is now on board the *Belleisle*, doing well, but the loss of his services is much to be regretted."

On the following day Capt. Pelham's battery was still at work, the enemy directing a heavy fire upon it. " It is wonderful," said the Admiral in his next despatch, " how he and his men escaped." Capt. Pelham was assisted by Lieut. F. A. Close, Mr. John J. Ball, master, and Mr. Wildman, acting mate of the *Blenheim*.

Seeing the attack thus directed against Capt. Pelham, as afterwards against four French mortars, which had now begun to play on the fort, the Admiral ordered the *Edinburgh, Ajax, Arrogant, Amphion, Valorous, Sphinx,* and *Driver,* all which ships were within long range, to open on the fort with their 10-inch guns, giving them a shot or shell every five minutes. The French breaching batteries did not open at all, not being ready, the fire being alone maintained by Capt. Pelham's 10-inch gun, the French mortars, and the shot and shell of the ships. This was, however, enough for the enemy, who, without waiting for the breaching batteries, held out a white flag. Sir Charles Napier at once despatched Capt. Hall of the *Bulldog* on shore, where he was shortly afterwards joined by Admiral Parseval's Aide-de-camp, and two of General Baraguay D'Hilliers' staff. The troops in the garrison then agreed to lay down their arms.

For military men, then, to assume that the siege of Bomarsund was a military operation is not correct. With the exception of capturing the western tower,— the marines and seamen capturing the eastern one, — the troops had literally nothing to do with it, unless it be contended that Capt. Pelham acted as a soldier. His 10-inch gun was the only breaching battery directed against the great fort, the embrasures of which bore good testimony to the efficacy of his fire. Capt. Ramsay and his seamen had captured the eastern tower, and the surrender of the place was caused by the fire of the French and English ships and the four French mortars, though these were secondary in importance to the fire of the ships and ship's guns on shore.

After the surrender of the place the Admiral

landed, and was joined by the French Admiral and the Commander-in-chief of the army. The garrison then marched out, were embarked in steamers, and were taken to Ledsund for transmission to England as prisoners of war. The number sent to England was 2255. Five died on board the *Belleisle*, and seventeen were exchanged on recovering from their wounds.

The Admiral in concluding his despatch on the occasion, begged to " congratulate their Lordships on the fall of this important fortress, which will be followed by the surrender of the Garden of Islands : and with so small a loss. I am happy to say that the greatest cordiality has subsisted between the French General and Admiral and myself, as well as between the soldiers and sailors of the two nations.

" I send this despatch by my Flag Lieutenant, John de Courcy Agnew, whom I beg to recommend to their Lordships for promotion."

On the 23rd of August the Board of Admiralty replied by expressing their satisfaction at receiving the intelligence of the fall of Bomarsund. They " cordially approved of the orders you issued, and of the judicious arrangement you made on the occasion ; and they desire you will convey to Rear-Admirals Plumridge and Chads, and to the whole of the officers and men employed on this service, their Lordships' entire approbation of their conduct."

On the 22nd of August Sir James Graham wrote to the Admiral from Portsmouth as follows : —

" I congratulate you sincerely on the success of your operations against Bomarsund, and I highly commend your prudence and wisdom in effecting the capture of this stronghold of the enemy without the loss of a ship or of many lives.

" You have judged well in every respect, both in detaining the line-of-battle ships and steamers until Bomarsund had fallen, and then in sending them home laden with prisoners.

" We can decide nothing as to the disposal of Bomarsund until we have ascertained the wishes and intentions of the French Government. If the Swedes refuse to accept it, and if the French are unwilling to garrison it during the winter, it must be blown up and levelled with the ground."

On the same day Admiral Berkeley, the senior naval Lord, congratulated Sir Charles as follows : —

" Your work, and the work of your fellow-labourers, has been done admirably. Some of the newspapers are not satisfied because you have not had a sufficient number killed and wounded, whilst the whole Government are pleased beyond measure at your trifling loss, and may well praise your skill and DISCRETION in having succeeded in striking the FIRST blow at so small a sacrifice.

" John Bull, never content, expects more than is possible. I trust you will not be goaded on, or beaten out of your own determinations. I have every confidence that you will attempt all that is feasible, and that you will succeed in all you attempt."

Captain Milne, the junior Lord of the Admiralty, added his congratulations to the Admiral, saying, " It is a most satisfactory result, and one which will

be considered as such by the English public, who
are anxious for some great event. *I hope the allied
forces will be equally successful at Sebastopol.*"

From one of the greatest of living naval heroes —
a man who, without Nelson's opportunities of fighting
great battles, can boast of even more numerous and
brilliant achievements than could Nelson himself —
Sir Charles received warm eulogy, coupled with
anxiety for his position ; viz., from the Earl of Dundonald, the living representative of the naval heroes
of other days — a commander whose deeds have
carried daring almost to the verge of romance.   We
will not extract the eulogy, for Sir Charles Napier
stands in no need of testimonials ; but Lord Dundonald's opinion of his position speaks at once the
sailor and the friend : — "Those only who are
acquainted with the difficulties you have had to
surmount, and the nature of the obstacles assigned
you to encounter, can appreciate the perseverance and
the moral courage requisite to overcome the one and
surmount the other. My anxiety lest your zeal
should induce you to yield your judgment to the
notions of the uninitiated is now quite relieved, and
the noble fleet you command is safe from the consequences of red-hot shot and other incendiary missiles.
Believe me that I sympathise with you, but do not
envy the exalted position in which you have been
placed, knowing that my remaining energies are
incapable of effecting objects which you have already
accomplished."

Lord Palmerston wrote to the Admiral : "Many
thanks for your letter, and many more for the taking

of Bomarsund, which has proved to be a most important achievement, and the more honourable to you because accomplished with so little loss. We trust both to your enterprise to do what is possible, and to your prudence not to attempt that which would be too difficult. We must, however, clip the Czar's wings before we have done with him."

All this was very satisfactory, and apparently as cordial as satisfactory. The allied forces in the Baltic had struck the *first* blow at Russia. The destruction of the dockyard at Sweaborg afterwards was scarcely an effective blow; for, after the peace, Russia, by a public proclamation, declared the departure of the fleet from before Sweaborg as a victory on her part, and this proclamation was unnoticed by our Government.

The Admiral had intended to have brought Admiral Plumridge's squadron through the Presto Channel, so as to have shelled the south side of Bomarsund; but General Baraguay D'Hilliers had so disposed his breaching batteries that Admiral Plumridge could not take the station without endangering the French troops; he therefore very wisely took up a position so that he had the Presto Tower and Bomarsund in a line, and severely damaged the former, as was subsequently found on examination. Admiral Plumridge had observed that the fire of the Presto Tower was harassing Captain Ramsay's battery, and moved the *Leopard*, *Hecla*, and the French steamer *Cocyte* against it, in such a way, that the shot and shell which went over Presto should fall into the fort. These vessels got, to use Admiral Plumridge's expression, " into a delightfully sequestered position, screened from observation by the trees on the neck of land to the eastward of the tower." The first intimation the enemy had of the proximity of the ships were three simultaneous broadsides, delivered with the greatest steadiness and precision. Admiral Plumridge paid a warm tribute to Lieutenant De Buisson, the commander of the *Cocyte*, as well as to Captains Giffard and Hall.

Having spoken of the breaching batteries of the French General being so placed as to stand in the way of the effective fire of the ships, it is necessary to say a few words more on this subject. The reader is aware that these breaching batteries were not called into play. Admirals Parseval and Napier both wrote to General Baraguay D'Hilliers, asking him to change the positions of his batteries, so as to allow the allied squadrons to take up the positions intended. The reply of General Baraguay D'Hilliers to Sir Charles Napier was as follows:

" ADMIRAL,

" Our first duty is to ensure the success of the expedition concerted between our two Governments.

" My first desire is to call on the navy to lend me its co-operation. The position of the breaching batteries is imperiously commanded by the ground, and every delay at this critical moment of the operations of the siege would be compromising my troops.

" You will therefore see it is natural, that resisting the inclination to be agreeable to you, and in order to fulfil my duty towards my country, I should main-

tain the dispositions determined on with the Generals
of the Engineers and Artillery.

"I believe, however, Admiral, that, notwithstanding the position of the breaching battery, which cannot be modified, the fleet reassembled will still be able
to lend us its support! which has already been so useful, and closing in, give a greater effect to the fire of
its artillery, and contribute to make a breach at the
same time as ourselves.

"I have the honour, &c.,

"Baraguay D'Hilliers."

It does not appear to have struck the French
General that his troops might have supported the
Allied Admirals.

During Admiral Plumridge's attack on the Presto
Tower, a gallant exploit was performed by Commander Warren, who was on a visit to his brother,
Captain Warren, of the *Cressy*. Commander Warren went on board the *Leopard*, and told Admiral
Plumridge that he should go on the island of Presto
and see what the enemy were about. Admiral Plumridge requested him to give him any information he
might obtain of the movements of the marines, or
the direction of our firing, should it interfere with
the party landed. To the astonishment of the Admiral, Commander Warren *swam off*, with the shot
and shell thickly splashing in the water round him!
and ascertained all that Admiral Plumridge wanted
to know, viz., that his fire did not in any way interfere
with the marines. Such an instance of gallantry and

zeal did the highest honour to Commander Warren, as he held no command on board the fleet, his service being purely voluntary.

We have nowhere mentioned the loss sustained by the British fleet in the siege. It was so insignificant, that we can give the whole in a very small compass.

KILLED.—The Hon. C. Wrottesley, Henry Collins, *Duke of Wellington;* and two seamen on board the *Penelope.*

DANGEROUSLY WOUNDED.—Thomas Bangham, *Blenheim.*

SEVERELY WOUNDED.—W. Mitchell, *Blenheim;* O. Carrol, *Termagant;* J. Hancock, *Belleisle.*

SLIGHTLY WOUNDED.—Mr. J. Neil, Assist.-Engineer, A. P. Brown, W Bennet, *Hecla;* W. Bridle, *Hogue.*

SLIGHT CONTUSIONS.—Captain W. Ramsay, *Hogue;* Lieutenant G. F. Burgess, *Blenheim.*

BURNT SLIGHTLY.—J. M'Gregan, J. M'Griffin, *Hogue.*

Well might Admiral Berkeley say, there " was not bloodshed enough to please the people of England ;" though " the Government was highly pleased that there was so little."

One more remark on the capture of Bomarsund is necessary. Upon the great fortress, operations were only commencing when it surrendered. In the opinion of General Jones, it ought not to have surrendered ; for, in his despatch on the subject, he said that the interior of the place showed that the fire of the ships did but trifling injury, and that the Governor of the fortress, with so strong a garrison in a casemated work, and *without a breach being made*, ought not to have surrendered. This expression of General Jones, " without a breach being made," is conclusive that the military breaching batteries had nothing to do with the surrender of the fortress.

The opinions of General Jones have been so prominently brought forward in other cases, that they are fairly open to criticism. If the ships had done no injury, or trifling injury, what induced the Governor to surrender? The military force, by General Jones's account, made no breach in the great fortress, and all the damage done was done by the ships' guns, French field batteries, and French mortars. The answer is evident. The Russian General had seen his western tower surprised by the French Chasseurs, and his eastern tower crumble before the fire of the seamen and marines. The ships themselves had commenced an attack on the great fortress, whilst the breaching batteries were preparing for attack. Hence the Russian General, like a brave man, humanely deemed it useless to waste the lives of his troops to no purpose. In so doing, he was borne out by his own Government, not usually over tolerant to failure of any kind. This is more to his credit than the comment of General Jones to his discredit.

Captain G. R. Munday, R. N., who, whilst waiting for an opportunity to join the *Nile*, had accompanied the force before Bomarsund, was mentioned by the General in his despatch to the Duke of Newcastle, for the zealous and active services which he rendered during the siege.

The following Returns of the operations at Bomarsund have never before been fully made public.

Return of Staff, Royal Engineers, and Sappers and Miners disembarked at Bomarsund on the 9th of August, 1854.

STAFF.
{ Brigadier-General, Harry D. Jones.
Brigade-Major, Captain H. St. George Ord.
Aide-de-Camp to Gen. Jones, Lieut. J. C. Cowell.

ROYAL ENGINEERS.
{ Captain T. W. King.
Lieut. C. B. P. N. H. Nugent.
Lieut. the Hon. Cameron Wrottesley.

ROYAL SAPPERS AND MINERS.
{ 5 Sergeants.
2 Buglers.
90 Rank and File.

ABSTRACT.

Officers	-	-	-	-	-	6
Sergeants	-	-	-	-	-	5
Buglers	-	-	-	-	-	2
Rank and File	-	-	-	-	90
Total	-	-	-	-	103

Return of the Battalion of Royal Marines under the command of Colonel Graham, Aide-de-Camp, landed at Bomarsund, 8th August, 1854.

	Colonels.	Majors.	Captains.	Subalterns.	Sergeants.	Corporals.	Bombardiers.	Drummers.	Gunners.	Privates.	Total.
Staff - -	1	1	2	2	--	--	--	--	--	--	
Eight Parade Companies	--	--	7	15	18	20	1	7	70	541	
Totals -	1	1	9	17	18	20	1	7	70	541	685

Names of Officers attached to the respective Parade Companies of Royal Marine Battalion.

1st COMPANY.

Captain Chas. O. Hamley.
Lieut. H. L. Evans.
Lieut. W. R. Jeffreys.

2ND COMPANY.

Captain R. K. Clarell.
Lieut. W. F. P. S. Dadson.

3RD COMPANY.

Acting Captain, Lieut. Geo. Naylor.
Lieut. I. F. Sanders.

4TH COMPANY.

Captain Wm. L. Sayer.

Lieut. Thos. Bent.

5TH COMPANY.

Captain H. E. Delacombe.
Lieut. Alex. Tait.

6TH COMPANY.

Captain Robt. J. M'Killop.
Lieut. Wm. Sanders.

7TH COMPANY.

Captain Thos. D. Fosbroke.

8TH COMPANY.

Captain Jno. Elliott.
Lieut. R. W. B. Hunt.
Lieut. Jas. P. Murray.

FIELD OFFICERS.

Major P. B. Nolloth.
Captain W. M. Heriot.

Brigade Major - - - - Captain W. C. P. Elliott.
Adjutant - - - - - Lieut. O. F. C. Fraser.
Orderly Officer - - - - Lieut. Jno. M. Lennox.

ARTILLERY COMPANIES.

Lieutenant H. W. Mawbey.
Lieutenant John Poore.
Lieutenant Henry Hewett.
Lieutenant Joshua Brookes.
Lieutenant E. C. L. Durnford, Acting Engineer.

MEDICAL STAFF.

Daniel J. Dingan, Assist. Surgeon - *Duke of Wellington.*
Seaton Wade   „   - *Blenheim.*
Dr. William L. Gordon „   - *Majestic.*
George C. Wilson, Acting Surgeon - *Majestic.*

Return of Officers landed at Bomarsund.

From what ship.	Name.	Rank.	
Hogue - -	William Ramsay, Esq. - -	Captain.	
	Morgan Singer - - -	Lieutenant.	
	Charles Smith - - -	Mate.	
	Abraham R. Bradford - -	Surgeon.	
Duke of Wellington -	George W. Preedy - -	Commander.	
	L. E. H. Somerset -	Gunnery Lieutenant.	Aide-de-camp to General Jones.
	Lewis M. Crake - - -	Mate.	
	Hon. Ernest G. L. Cochrane -	Mate.	
Edinburgh -	George F. Burgess - -	Lieutenant.	
	H. G. H. Prince Victor of Hohenlohe - -	Midshipman.	
	Edward J. Giles - - -	Passed Clerk.	
Ajax - -	Henry L. C. Robinson - -	Mate.	
Blenheim -	The Hon. Frederick J. Pelham	Captain.	At small battery with 10-inch guns.
	Francis A. Close - - -	Lieutenant.	
	John J. Ball - - -	Master.	
	Leveson Wildman - -	Acting Mate.	
	Mr. Green * - - -	Carpenter.	* Re - embarked when battery was constructed.
	Mr. Alton * - - -	Assistant Engineer.	
	Thomas L. Ward - - -	Lieutenant.	
	David Orr - - - -	Acting Mate.	
Driver - -	The Hon. Arthur A. Cochrane	Commander.	Aide-de-camp to General Baraguay d'Hilliers.
	John C. Wells - - -	Acting Mate.	
	C. H. Gibbon - - -	Midshipman.	
Lightning -	Frederick A. Cudlip - -	Lieutenant.	
	F. Rossey - - -	Gunner (3rd class).	
	TOTAL - - - -	25 OFFICERS.	

CHAP. XVI.

On the 17th of August, the day after the surrender of Bomarsund, Sir Charles Napier wrote to the Hon. Arthur Magennis, the British Minister at Stockholm, apprising him of the fall of the fortress, and of the necessity of immediately communicating with the King of Sweden, to know what his intentions were respecting Aland. To this Mr. Magennis replied, that he considered it impossible for His Majesty to give a definitive answer in the present state of the negotiations. The Admiral again wrote to Mr. Magennis, saying that the King of Sweden had no time to lose, as the troops must either stay or be removed, the French orders on this point being imperative, as well as the report of the English and French engineers, which represented that if the place was to be occupied, preparations must be made for the winter; if not, the sooner the troops were removed, the better. All the commanding authorities were of opinion that Bomarsund should be destroyed.

The Admiral had been instructed from home that his proceedings with regard to Bomarsund would depend upon the answer General Baraguay D'Hilliers might receive from the Swedish Government, and that he was to be guided by that. The reply of the King of Sweden was to the effect, that from circumstances, he was not in a position to occupy the Aland Islands, but that he must discounsel their evacuation. This intimation was followed by a letter from our minister, explaining that, as he had anticipated, Sweden had refused to accept Aland. She was in no alliance with France and England, and had not broken with Russia. To take Aland would be an act of hostility to Russia, and therefore she would not do it.

" Notwithstanding this," continued Mr. Magennis, " the hopes of an alliance with Sweden are not abandoned, and we should only weaken our cause if we destroyed the forts." He begged of the Admiral to procure as great a delay as possible.

In the mean time the Admiral wrote home for instructions. He told Sir James Graham, that the works which Russia had been preparing at Bomarsund were on a gigantic scale. The French wished to blow up the forts at once, but he would not consent. Sir James replied on the 25th of August,—

" *I am more than satisfied with your proceedings. I am delighted with the prudence and sound judgment you have evinced. It would have been a miserable want of firmness had you yielded to clamour, and risked your ships, and sacrificed many valuable lives in an attempt to destroy by naval means works which were certain to fall to an attack by land.*

" Your reasoning also in favour of the immediate and entire destruction of Bomarsund is irresistible, and I hope you will take care the destruction is complete, and that not one stone is left upon another.

" I am well pleased also with the promptitude with which you have sent back the line-of-battle ships and steamers. *The work has been well done,* and I gladly give you the utmost credit for it.

" I write in great haste, but that which presses is the order for destroying Bomarsund."

In a previous letter of the 22nd of August, Sir James Graham wrote as follows : —

" We can decide nothing as to the disposal of Bomarsund, until we have ascertained the wishes and intentions of the French Government. If the Swedes refuse to accept it, and if the French are unwilling to garrison it during the winter, it must be blown up and levelled with the ground.

" I shall be anxious to hear what is your next move. Transports for the French troops will be joining you every day, until you will have ample means of moving the whole body. I think you might beat up their quarters somewhere with advantage. Surely either Abo or Revel are open to attack.

" Many thanks for your kindness to my boy. As a father, I rejoice that my son has for the first time been under fire in your presence."

From this it is evident that Sir James Graham expected the French troops to remain, and take part in some fresh operation.

To Lord Clarendon the Admiral wrote that it would be impolitic to give up Bomarsund to Sweden, as she could neither finish the works, nor hold it against Russia. The designs of Russia with regard to Bomarsund had been gigantic; foundations were laid to make it stronger than Sweaborg, and had these been finished, it would have been unassailable. The fortress was evidently intended to domineer over Sweden, as well as to command the Gulfs of Bothnia and Finland, and even when it was destroyed, Russia ought never again to be allowed to fortify Aland. This blow would throw back Russia for years in her designs on Sweden.

The destruction of the fortress being thus determined, no time was lost in carrying it into effect, the task being given to Admiral Martin.

After the fall of Bomarsund, Admiral Martin had been relieved in the command of the Nargen squadron by Admiral Plumridge, who had, by the retirement of Admiral Corry, become second in command. Admiral Plumridge, on taking charge of the Nargen squadron, hoisted his flag on board the *Neptune*. Rear-Admiral Martin was therefore directed to take charge of Admiral Plumridge's squadron in the Gulf of Bothnia, and hoisted his flag on board the *Leopard*. Captain G. R. Munday was appointed to the command of the *Nile*, in succession to Admiral Martin.

The demolition of the works occupied considerable time; and it was not till the 14th of September that Admiral Martin made his final report to Sir Charles Napier. Though out of order as regards time, we shall here give an analysis of his report.

The Presto Tower was blown up by the French on the 30th of August; Fort Nottich on the 31st, and the Great Fort was partially destroyed on the

2nd of September, the French troops embarking on the 3rd, leaving the demolition incomplete.

Admiral Martin therefore proceeded to their entire destruction, which was carried out by Capt. King, of the Engineers, with the aid of the Sappers and Miners, and Marines. The new casemates were thrown down, as well as the foundations of the new towers, and other buildings designed for barracks, &c. The materials were scattered and destroyed. Many hundreds of granite slabs, dressed with great labour, as well as granite blocks prepared for casemates, were split and rendered useless. The mole-head was blown up; the wooden wharfs burned. The stone wharfs were thrown into the sea, so that Sir James Graham's instructions, not to leave one stone on another, were literally complied with.

The mortars which were in the Great Fort were burst, as were all the guns not buried in the ruins, one mortar only being taken on board the *Leopard* as a trophy.

Previous to the entire destruction of Bomarsund, the Admiral was desirous of ascertaining the effect of shot on the fortress; and he ordered Admiral Chads to try the effect of his guns against it. The following is the substance of his report, and the observations of Sir Charles Napier on it, in a letter to Sir James Graham.

Admiral Chads having anchored the *Edinburgh*, at 1060 yards from a portion of the Great Fort, which was untouched, though much shaken by explosions, commenced by trying the force of all descriptions of shot in comparison with each other. Four discharges were made from each gun, and the effect on the fort ascertained by inspection. The guns and charges were as follows : —

Lancaster shells, 12 lb. charge, and 100 lb. shell.

68-pounder, solid shot, with 16 lb. charge, 95 cwt. gun.

10-inch, 85 cwt. gun, 12 lb. charge, 84 lb. hollow shot.

8-inch, 65 cwt. gun, 10 lb. charge, 56 lb. hollow shot.

32-pounder, 56 cwt. gun, 10 lb. charge, solid shot.

8-inch, 53 cwt. gun, 8 lb. charge, 56 lb. hollow shot.

Lancaster, and all the other shells, burst on striking. Shells with percussion and time fuses alike ; but previously striking with the same force and effect as the shot of the same calibre and weight, *the explosions doing no injury whatever.* The Lancaster shells were eccentric in their flight,—no dependence being to be placed upon them for precision at short range. Four only struck out of eleven fired. The two first struck with one and a half degree elevation, and falling short afterwards with two and a quarter degrees. The Lancaster gun with solid shot, and a 16 lb. charge, was found to answer admirably, so that the gun may be considered as available for double purposes — extreme ranges of near 5000 yards with the most destructive shells, and in short distances almost the same as other sixty-eight pounders.

When this practice was completed, broadside firing commenced ; and 390 shot of all descriptions were fired. The fort was again inspected, and the walls were found to be considerably damaged and shaken. Three of the embrasures had fallen in, so that the guns could not be worked.

The *Edinburgh* was then, with difficulty, moved round a reef of rocks into a position not much greater than her own length, at 480 yards from the fort, on which the broadside was again opened. The effect was almost instantaneous. Large masses of wall came down with clouds of dust, so that no aim could have been taken by the enemy, nor could the men have stood to their guns. The whole body was brought down with 250 shots. At this short distance, the 8-inch guns of 53 cwt. told with full force.

From the above practice, it will be seen that shells against stone forts are not more destructive than shot, and therefore should be sparingly used, on the chance of entering an embrasure; and when so used, time fuses of 3 inches are preferable to percussion; as on missing the object, they may strike barracks, storehouses, &c., when the burning fuse may cause fires.

Altogether, the following conclusions may be drawn.

The first shot and shell at 1060 yards made but trifling impression, only starring the stones, unless when striking the embrasures, when the whole frame was generally loosened, and the concussion of the guns afterwards sometimes shook the whole down, particularly in those embrasures where the guns required considerable elevation to return our fire; the embrasures admitting of nine degrees only at extreme elevation.

The repetition of the blows of the shot showed

the instability and weakness of the whole work, and Admiral Chads felt assured that a ship of the line, when once fairly placed, pouring in her broadside to the extent of 1000 shot and shell at 1000 yards, would demolish the front of a work similarly constructed of stone facings and brick inside. If the ship were placed at 500 yards, half that number of shot and shell would have the same effect.

There were, however, says Admiral Chads, advantages to be taken into account in these experiments. The *Edinburgh* had not to pass under a severe raking fire of hot shot and shells, before taking up her position, or after anchoring. The distance was correctly known, and proved by trial shots. There were no interruptions in taking correct aim by casualties from the enemy's shot, and the *Edinburgh* had heavier guns than the other ships of the line.

On the 4th of September, the Admiral thus reported the result of Admiral Chads' experiments to Sir J. Graham : —

" I got the General to leave six embrasures of Bomarsund untouched, and desired Admiral Chads to try his guns upon them at 1000 yards. I then told him to get into the intricate passage within 500 yards, and he knocked it all down in about half an hour. It was only faced with granite, and very badly put together with brick and stone. If all the batteries are like this, there will be no difficulty in knocking them down, if you can get close. Here you will see, by the charts, that it could not be done. A ship going in would have been cut to pieces. Once there, they could not have stood. But then Bomarsund was so constructed that they could not get more than twelve guns to bear on a ship. There was only room for two at a short distance. But then, this was all after knowledge."

On the 29th of August, Sir James Graham again wrote to Sir Charles Napier, to let "the work of destruction" be such, that not a vestige be left, "either of forts, or outworks." This had been done. Sir James Graham further stated that *the fleet must now be withdrawn from the Baltic.* As these instructions are of vital importance to what followed, we must transcribe Sir James Graham's own words. "When we know what arrangement is to be made with respect to the French army, we will concert measures with France *for the gradual withdrawal of the fleet from the Baltic.* You should begin by sending home, *without much delay,* the sailing three-deckers the least weatherly of the sailing line-of-battle ships, and the slowest and worst of the block ships. This will do for a beginning; and by degrees you must withdraw to the southward, leaving the Gulf of Bothnia open, and watching only the Gulf of Finland with a squadron of observation."

Here is a positive order from Sir James Graham, before the demolition of Bomarsund was completed, that the Admiral must prepare to return home, the time depending on what the French Government was going to do with its army in the Baltic. About this order there can be no mistake whatever.

On the same day, Admiral Berkeley, the senior naval Lord of the Admiralty, wrote to Sir Charles as follows: "We wish you, if no other operations are to be undertaken, to reduce your ships of the line, the French in proportion, to as many as you deem sufficient to meet the Russian fleet when joined together from Helsingfors and Cronstadt, sending first the sailing three deckers and the block ships, keeping your steam ships of the line, in preference to others." These instructions were as precise as were those of Sir James Graham.

But the Admiral had no wish to send his ships home. As he was now at Bomarsund, Abo might, he thought, be attacked, and was within easy reach. It was a place of great importance, and there were 10,000 Russian troops there, who had been sent to reinforce Bomarsund, had the thing been practicable. Now Bomarsund had fallen, and as the French troops were there, there would be no great difficulty in attacking Abo.

Accordingly, the Admiral despatched Captain Scott with the *Odin, Alban, Gorgon,* and *Driver,* to the vicinity of Abo, for the purpose of gaining intelligence of the enemy's force and movements there. Captain Scott reported to the Admiral that, after a dangerous voyage, in which all his ships had got ashore, he had not been successful in picking up much useful information; but being unwilling to return without effecting something of importance, he had resolved to effect a passage to Abo, in order to ascertain what was going on there.

Surmounting the difficulties of an intricate navigation, in which the *Gorgon* again grounded, Captain Scott succeeded in reaching the comparatively open track to Abo, closely watched by a Russian steamer.

Approaching within 3000 yards of Abo, the *Alban* stood close in, and found the entrance of the harbour closed by two impediments: first, a chain laid across on a floating platform; secondly, a still more formidable obstruction, consisting of stakes and booms, between which gun-boats were stationed at regular intervals. Several other gun-boats were engaged in moving a body of troops abreast of the chain, the Russians evidently taking the reconnaissance as the precursor of an attack, for which they had made every preparation. Four steamers were sheltered behind a point to act as their services might be required.

The *Alban*, on nearing the booms, fired a shell, which burst over one of the gun-boats. The other vessels then commenced firing, but with little effect, except that of answering Capt. Scott's purpose in drawing a return fire from the masked batteries and gun-boats. He thus ascertained that a concealed battery, at the end of the boom, mounted guns of large calibre and long range; whilst three others, to the westward of the boom, discovered themselves in the same way. A fort, mounting eight or nine long guns, had been constructed to enfilade the passage, and repeatedly fired, the shot, however, invariably falling short.

As Capt. Scott's object was not to attack Abo, but to examine its defences preparatory to an attack by the combined forces, he contented himself with an occasional shot at the gun-boats, or wherever he suspected a masked battery to exist. Commander Otter, of the *Alban*, gallantly pulled in with his gig within range of the gun-boats and batteries, which kept up a constant fire on his tiny boat, but without doing any harm.

Capt. Scott, with the assistance of Commanders Otter, Cracroft, and Hobart, ascertained that the Russian force amounted to seventeen gun-boats, mounting two guns each, four steamers, the same number of masked batteries, and another in course of construction. The channel was very narrow, and capable of being effectually defended by riflemen. The thick woods on either side were full of troops, who had, as Capt. Scott ascertained, on the previous day received a reinforcement of 4000, 5000 more being expected on the following day. He was further informed by the Fins, that the number of steamers at Abo was six, one of very large burden, and that there were eighteen gun-boats manned with eighty men each, besides the troops; so that the Russian naval force was greatly superior to his own little squadron, but nevertheless did not venture to attack it.

Capt. Scott considered that the place might be attacked by sealing up the inner channel with steamers of light draft, so as to prevent the escape of the enemy's steamers and gun-boats, or the arrival of others from Hango to support them. He then proposed to occupy the promontory of Lipsala and the island of Little Beckholm with troops, the landing of which could be effected out of reach of the enemy's guns, and under the fire of our own vessels. Without this, Capt. Scott considered the passage of any channel—the safest of which only contained fifteen feet of water — must be attended with great loss of life from the riflemen on each side, and without a chance of either capturing or destroying the steamers and gun-boats, which could retire out of reach as our own steamers approached.

On receiving Capt. Scott's masterly report, the

Admiral considered it possible to attack Abo, and at once proposed the expedition to his French colleagues, who did not approve of it ; General Baraguay D'Hilliers not being disposed to risk his troops at that season of the year; besides which, he had a great deal of cholera amongst them. The weather was, indeed, getting very changeable, and heavy gales were frequent.

Finding that the French declined to assist him in attacking Abo, he notified this to Sir James Graham on the 22nd of August, adding that the season was too far advanced, and the intricacy of the navigation was such, that we could not hope to do all that might be done there. Half measures ought not to be undertaken, and it would not do to go to Abo and come back without doing something of importance. The Admiral apprised Sir James that he should shortly begin to send home ships, and he was glad that Sir James agreed with him that the ships must begin moving south before the middle of September, but the Baltic must not be left by the combined fleet till the Russian fleet was locked up in the ice. He told the First Lord that he need not alarm himself about the Russians putting to sea in September.

This communication was written in reply to one of Sir James Graham's letters, dated 15th of August, in which the First Lord had expressed himself as follows : " I agree with you in thinking that before the end of September the fleet must begin its movement to the southward. Before this retrograde movement, is there anything that can be done by the fleet and army on the enemy's coast on either side of the Gulf of Finland, which would be permanently injurious to him ? Is Abo or Revel—one or both—unassailable ? The Baltic cannot be left by the combined fleet until the Russian fleet is locked up in ice ; but the anchorage of the squadron of observation must be well considered, and carefully selected, pending the blockade by nature. Kiel would appear to be the harbour for watching the Belts; Wingo for securing the Sound. There is inconvenience in dividing the force, unless, indeed, France would take one, and leave us the other. But *I shall want a large portion of your fleet at home before winter sets in, to make arrangements for reliefs both in the Mediterranean and elsewhere.*"

Here is a distinct intimation from Sir James Graham that he wanted a large portion of the Baltic fleet at home before winter, and that the best places for keeping the Russians within the Baltic were Kiel and Wingo Sound. It must be clear from this that Sir James contemplated the withdrawal of a large portion of the fleet from the Gulf of Finland, leaving sufficient ships to blockade it till the ice set in. The reader is requested to bear in mind the matters which have been just narrated.

The Admiral told Sir James that Revel had a large garrison—"they say 50,000, and the Emperor has been there lately." Nothing then could be done with Revel if the French agreed to attack it, which they were not likely to do, having declined to attack Abo.

All these instructions combined, cannot leave the smallest doubt on the mind of the reader that the

Government was most fully satisfied that all had been done which could be done, and that the withdrawal of the fleet was the next movement contemplated, unless Abo could be attacked, or Revel ; and we have shown why they could not. Sir Charles was repeatedly ordered by Sir James to preserve the greatest cordiality with his French colleagues. He had again reiterated the caution, and Sir Charles replied, "Give yourself no uneasiness about my French colleagues. I am quite aware of the danger of any disagreement." Yet Sir Charles Napier has since been treated by the Government as though the French Admiral and General had been subordinate to him, and he had the supreme command, in place of having only one voice in three. It is quite within our power to make such extracts from Sir James Graham's letters on this head, as few Englishmen would like to read ; and which would show that Sir Charles Napier possessed no superior voice ; of which, in obedience to the command of Sir James Graham himself, he never attempted, nor could have attempted the exercise. The French were jealous of the honour of their country, if Sir James Graham was not. Nothing can be more easy than to prove the correctness of these remarks, should they be called in question.

As the weather was now becoming very unsettled, and as the *Euryalus* had parted her anchor in a heavy gale, the Admiral directed Admiral Plumridge that his look-out ships had better go to Baro Sound, or Nargen, but this he left to his own judgment. The Gulf was narrow and dangerous ; and the

Russian ships at Sweaborg could not come out with a southerly wind.

On the 4th of September, Sir Charles Napier replied to several of the recent letters of the First Lord, as follows : —

" I received your letters of the 25th and 29th of August, and am glad my proceedings have given you so much satisfaction.   I shall never be led into follies by people who talk big, but were they in my position would probably do nothing.   Many of such people are in the fleet.

" Bomarsund is blown up, but the destruction of the new works is neglected.   I wrote to the General on the subject, and send you my letter.   I shall leave the *Ajax* and *Cumberland* there to assist, and Admiral Martin also.   When done, I shall send those two ships home, which I think will meet with your wishes, and shall desire Admiral Martin to withdraw from the Gulf of Bothnia, when dangerous.   Indeed, it can hardly now be considered a blockade, as we were obliged to give it up in order to take charge of the different passages in the Aland Islands.

Sept. 5th, Ledsund.   " I came down here last night in the middle watch.   The wind shifted suddenly to the northwest in a heavy squall.   The French Admiral's ship and two frigates drove with top-gallant yards across.   Before the Admiral brought up, he was in our hawse, with our dolphin-striker thumping on his poop — our cable out to the clinch. Had he come on board us we should have been a wreck and on shore in half an hour, whilst we should probably have taken the *James Watt* with us.   Happily, he brought up, and we shackled the sheet cable to the bower, and were enabled to veer fifty fathoms."

CHAP. XVII.

ON the 27th of August Gen. Jones had transmitted to
the Admiral certain opinions which he had formed
relative to the capture of Sweaborg. The circumstances under which Gen. Jones made this report are
worthy of narration, as the report itself afterwards
became of considerable importance as regarded the
course pursued by the Admiralty.

Gen. Baraguay D'Hilliers, Admiral Parseval, and Sir Charles Napier had decided, and had so told their respective Governments, that nothing could be done with Sweaborg during the present year, both from want of gun and mortar-boats and other materials for a siege, and from the advanced season of the year, which rendered it imperative that the French troops should get away from the Baltic as soon as possible, as, now that Sweden had declined to accept Aland, it was out of the question that the French troops should winter in the Baltic; and therefore no time was to be lost in their return to France.

Both the French and English Governments fully concurred in these views, the French Government ordering their troops back to Cherbourg, and Sir James Graham, as well as Admiral Berkeley, directing Sir Charles Napier to begin to send home his ships, where they were wanted to relieve the ships on other stations. As both the French General and the French Admiral had declined the attack on Abo, and as it was known that there were 50,000 troops at Revel, nothing more could be done there; in this view both the Allied Governments had concurred.

But Gen. Baraguay D'Hilliers, not having seen Sweaborg, was unwilling to leave without having inspected it, and with this view, he himself, in company with Gen. Niel, an Engineer officer who had accompanied him to the Baltic, and Admiral Parseval, went up to Sweaborg for the purpose; Sir Charles Napier, having long before formed his opinions on Sweaborg, — both from his own inspection, from the reports of the inshore squadron, and especially from the reports of Capt. Sulivan, who, in addition to his surveys, had most favourable opportunities of inspecting the fortifications, when twice in with a flag of truce, and who had reported to the Government how it might be taken when means were supplied in the following year — remained in Ledsund with the fleets.

The French Admiral and General were piloted to Sweaborg by the *Lightning*, under the command of Capt. Sulivan, who, from his previous opportunities, as well as his ability as a surveyor, knew most about the Channels. Gen. Jones also went up with Capt. Sulivan in the *Lightning*, and, together with the French authorities, obtained a good general view of the fortifications.

The inspection fully satisfied Gen. Baraguay D'Hilliers and Gen. Niel that there was nothing to be done with Sweaborg with the number of troops present, and particularly at this season of the year; and Admiral Parseval, together with Sir Charles Napier, had long before come to the same conclusion. On returning, however, Gen. Jones made a report to the Admiral of a different tendency, though it must have argued no small confidence in his own abilities, to make a report from casual inspection on what the Admirals had already decided from actual survey, especially as regarded the operations of the fleets; though the recommendations of Gen. Jones are based upon military operations, and rather concerned Gen. Baraguay D'Hilliers than the Allied Admirals. Gen. Jones's report was as follows : —

"H.M.S. *Lightning*, at Sea,
27th August, 1854.

" SWEABORG.

" A VERY erroneous opinion will be formed of the strength of the fortifications of Sweaborg by a mere inspection of the plans only. The works do not present those regular lines as represented on the plans, and moreover the ground in front of them is much broken, and in parts intersected with walls and gardens, which must interfere very much with the efficacy of the fire from the batteries between them and the sea.

" The works appear to be filled with barracks, storehouses, and public buildings, evidently leaving but a small area of ground unoccupied in their interior.

" The defences appear to have been constructed with a view to resist an attack on the town and harbour fronts; evidently not anticipating or considering that an attack would ever be made from the sea. During the present summer several additional works must have been thrown up, particularly on Bak Holmen and islands to the eastward.

" Sweaborg being purely a military and naval establishment, all persons residing or quartered upon the islands must be regarded as non-combatants.

" The usual force stationed in Sweaborg is no doubt at all times considerable, and not to be disregarded. At the same time it must be borne in mind that such a garrison is necessarily much subdivided between the numerous islands they have to garrison.

" Sweaborg, from its insular position, is naturally a very strong one, and not open to a regular attack. Such being the case, it then becomes necessary to ascertain in what way such an important establishment can be injured or destroyed. After a careful reconnaissance, the only mode which appears to present itself with any prospect of success, is by a heavy bombardment from a combined operation by land and sea. *A force of* 5000 *men should be thrown ashore on the Island of Bak Holmen,* on which heavy batteries of guns and *mortars* could be constructed ; and when ready to open their fire, the ships should take up their positions for commencing simultaneously with the land batteries; the fronts of the whole of the line of works facing the sea should be attacked while this was going on; the battery on Bak Holmen would take them in flank, and enfilade the entire of the principal works in Vargon, and dockyard, warehouses, &c. From such a heavy concentrated fire the buildings would soon be laid in ruins and set on fire. *Large rockets* would be found very efficacious. The buildings of Sweaborg no doubt contain a great deal of combustible material, from the general mode of constructing houses, and wood being the cheapest material, and most easily procured.

" Helsingfors has not been taken into consideration, as from its situation the troops quartered in it could take very little, if any, part in the defence of Sweaborg. At the same time it would be proper to occupy their attention by the appearance of an intention to land, and to take possession of the town.

" The above is merely an outline of what is feasible, practicable, and of *easy execution*, should the destruction of the arsenal be considered a desirable object. Should it be determined to make such an attack, a more close and particular reconnaissance would be desirable, in order to ascertain the best points for landing the troops in Bak Holmen, and also the particular stations for the different ships to be engaged. Should everything prove favourable, the operation ought not to occupy more than seven or eight days.

" The close of the summer season may probably be considered the best for bombarding Sweaborg, as the winter following close upon the destruction of the public establishments and buildings would preclude the possibility of repairing or rebuilding them during a northern winter.

(Signed)   " HARRY D. JONES,
" Brigadier General."

If the reader will turn to Sir Charles Napier's plan of attacking Sweaborg, when the Government should send out the means for attack, he will see that

General Jones's plan contained nothing new, except the 5000 troops to be landed on Bak Holmen; though when making this suggestion of "easy execution," General Jones could hardly have been aware of the Admiralty having previously sent out to Sir Charles Napier a communication pointing out that there were 40,000 troops in Sweaborg and its vicinity, or he would not have proposed to operate against such a force, defended by one of the strongest garrisons in existence, with 5000 men only! Since that communication had been made, there was reason to believe that those troops had even been strengthened, which makes General Jones's suggestion the more singular; the military rule being, that the besieging force should be three times the strength of the garrison; so that, in place of 5000, supposing the enemy's troops available, the besieging troops ought to have been 120,000. Sir Charles Napier had said that it would require 50,000; Sir J. Graham, 50,000 Swedes and 200 Swedish gun-boats. General Jones said, " 5000 men."

General Jones also required " mortars and large rockets." The Admiral had not so much as one of either in his fleet, as General Jones knew. The French army had four mortars; but, as will presently be seen, General Baraguay D'Hilliers was too good a general to permit them to be used, at that season of the year, for any such operation, however " easy of execution " it might appear to General Jones.

On receiving the preceding report, the Admiral at once transmitted it to his French colleague and to the Board of Admiralty, with the following remarks:

"I agree with the report of General Jones, as will be seen by a letter which I wrote *some time ago* to Sir James Graham; except that part of the report proposing to land 5000 men at Bak Holmen. The place is of too much importance to be feebly garrisoned; and if you land 5000 men, the Russians will pass 10,000 men over Gustaffs Sward, *and make them all prisoners.*"

To the preceding report General Jones appended another on Revel, but as there was no intention on the part of the Allied forces to attack Revel, it need not be further alluded to.

On the 3rd of September General Baraguay D'Hilliers notified to Sir Charles Napier, that, on the 29th of August, the Minister of War, conformably to the orders of the Emperor, had directed him to evacuate Bomarsund, as Sweden would not take possession of it; and had moreover ordered the *French troops back to Cherbourg.*

Just at this period some sensation was produced by the intelligence that Sweden had ordered all her gun-boats from Gottenburg to Stockholm, and that the order had been executed. The Swedish people took this movement as an indication that something was about to be done, and that the Government would open the port of Carlscrona and other ports as wintering places for the Allies. All this was, however, fallacious, though the movement of the gun-boats appeared to indicate that Sweden was making some preparations for the following spring.

On the 4th of September the Board of Admiralty

directed Sir Charles, that, " *as the season was drawing to a close, during which so large a combined fleet would be able to remain in the Baltic, he should consult with the French General and Admiral, as well as with his own Admirals, as to what further operations remained to be undertaken this year.*"

There was scarcely any need of the injunction to consult his colleagues as to further operations, though, as the French General had sailed, he could not be consulted. Before the departure of the troops, Sir Charles had laid General Jones's plan before the French Commanders-in-Chief, who would have nothing to do with it, and very rightly so; for a more Quixotic plan than that of attacking a large Russian army, sheltered by one of the strongest fortresses in existence, and that with 5000 troops, aided by ships which could not get up to the fortress from danger of sunken rocks, has seldom been broached. The best proof, perhaps, of this is, that in the following year, when supplied with gun and mortar-boats, rockets, &c., Admiral Dundas did not make any attempt on the batteries with his ships, but was alone able, with his mortar-boats and gun-boats, to burn at long range all that was combustible.

How, then, the first Baltic fleet, under Sir Charles Napier and Admiral Parseval, was to effect without either mortar-boats or rockets that which Admiral Dundas could not effect with them, can only be explained by General Jones himself; for, assuredly, neither the Allied Admirals nor the French General could enter into the merits of his plan so as to induce them to adopt it.

As so much was afterwards made of this plan of General Jones, when it suited the purpose of the Admiralty, it is necessary to be very particular in all that relates to it.

General Baraguay D'Hilliers, in a letter to Sir Charles Napier, dated 2nd September, pronounced that General Jones's plan of attacking Sweaborg, as regarded the combined operation of the fleet or army at this dangerous season of the year, appeared to Admiral Parseval and himself *equally impossible.*

As the matter has become one of historical importance far transcending the plan itself, it will be better to give General Baraguay D'Hillier's opinion in his own words.

" Vous m'avez fait l'honneur, Monsieur l'Amiral, de me communiquer un rapport de M. Gen. Jones, sur la forteresse de Sweaborg. M. le Gen. de Division Niel, qui a pris connaissance de ce même rapport, m'a écrit la lettre ci-jointe que j'ai l'honneur de vous transmettre. Nous partagions l'opinion de M. le Gen. Jones, que Sweaborg peut être attaqué et pris par les flottes, si elles veulent faire contre cette forteresse une attaque sérieuse : sans doute, l'action des troupes de terre, débarquées sur Bak Holmen, pourrait contribuer au succès. Mais cette action *qui nécessiterait un débarquement à cette époque dangereuse de l'armée paraît à M. l'Amiral Parseval comme à nous également impossible.*"

" You have done me the honour to communicate to me Gen. Jones's report on Sweaborg. Gen. Niel, who has taken cognisance of the same report, has written me the accompanying letter. We partake of the opinion of General Jones, that Sweaborg can be attacked and taken with the fleets, if it were desirable to make a serious attack. No doubt the co-operation of the troops landed at Bak Holmen would contribute to its success. But this operation, which would necessitate the debarkation of the troops *at this dangerous period of the year, appears both to Admiral Parseval and ourselves equally impossible.*"

From the expression in the above letter " nous partagions l'opinion de M. le Gen. Jones, Sweaborg peut être attaqué par les flottes," it would appear that Gen. Baraguay d'Hilliers had mistaken the purport of Gen. Jones's report, which was not to make the attack by the combined fleets alone, but with the aid of 5000 of Gen. Baraguay D'Hilliers' army. The French General afterwards notices this, but his first expression is ambiguous.

The annexed is a translation of General Niel's letter, referred to as above by General Baraguay D'Hilliers.

" GENERAL,

" I proceed to take cognisance of a report made by Gen. Jones on Sweaborg, which report has been communicated to you by Admiral Napier.

" Gen. Jones thinks the strength of Sweaborg much exaggerated, and that in eight days it could be destroyed, if — taking possession of Bak Holmen with 5000 troops, and constructing on that island several gun and mortar batteries against the Sweaborg fortifications, if these batteries were brought into play at the same time that the two fleets, moored head and stern against the fortified island, should concentrate their fire on the sea fronts, which are incontestably the weakest.

" I have already informed the Minister of War, that I did not think that fortifications on so confined a space as that of the islands of Sweaborg, could long resist the effects of a bombardment. I do not at all doubt that the plan of attack proposed by Gen. Jones may lead to the destruction, if not to the taking possession of the fortifications of Sweaborg;

but here are the reasons which prevent me from proposing a complete adoption of it.

" In the first place it is to be remarked, that as soon as the fortifications of Sweaborg are threatened with destruction, the Russian fleet will go and take refuge at the further extremity of the roadstead, more than 3000 metres distant, and under the protection of the land batteries erected at Helsingfors, in order that the destruction of the fortified island may not bring with it the loss of the fleet.

" But the most important observation I have to make is, that if the fleets really wish to take up a position at easy range of the guns of the fortifications,— say within three or four cables' length, — this would perfectly suffice to destroy and render completely untenable the fortress of Sweaborg, and the island of Bak Holmen, which is but an advanced post, will fall with the same blow, with all the land batteries which have been erected there, whilst the batteries of the Helsingfors roadstead will, in consequence, remain defenceless. If, on the contrary, the fleets do not take up such position, but one twelve or fourteen cables' length off,— to take advantage of the differences of the calibre of guns, much greater in marine artillery than in shore artillery,— they will produce no effect on the fortifications against which they are acting. In this case, there can be only one serious attack, that on the land batteries of Bak Holmen, which I look upon as insufficient with our present means, as I am about to explain.

" The island of Bak Holmen cannot be carried without great loss. The Russians have there constructed three batteries; that of twelve guns, situated on the edge of the channel, is a raking battery. The approaches, moreover, are flanked on one side by the fortifications of Gustavsvard: on the other, by a redoubt established on another island to the right (Kung's Holmen). The force which the Russians maintain in Helsingfors is computed at 15,000 men. These forces would continually be increasing if the fort were attacked. Besides these, there are 10,000 men of the line. The certainty of being able to withdraw their troops from Bak Holmen by the roadstead, without receiving a shot, shows that the Russians would not fail to throw a large number of men into this island to defend it. If we admit that it will be taken from the Russians, we cannot dispute that this occupation will cost us dear. Then again, it will be necessary to occupy beforehand a position for the 5000 men who will be at Bak Holmen, under fire of the batteries of Sweaborg, as well as under that of the fleet firing from the interior of the harbour; and who will not cease to be disturbed by the guns and musketry of the Russians, who will be able to approach well within musket shot by the islands on the right, which islands will not be occupied.

" I certainly do not dispute the advantages of an attack by Bak Holmen, but with other means than those we at present possess, viz. : —By occupying the wooded island to the right ; by having a *good number of heavy mortars, whilst we have but four small ones ; and above all, by operating at a season when the communication between the army and the fleet would be well assured, which does not happen in the month of September,* as we every day experience."

General Niel, as a brother engineer officer, does not dispute General Jones's plan, he only demolishes it thoroughly and completely, both as to means and season ! which General Jones says is the best, and General Niel says is the worst. Were it not that General Jones's plan was afterwards made so much of, these comments of General Niel would scarcely leave room for remark.

General Niel next gives a plan of his own :—

" To resume. If the fleets were to anchor within easy range of Sweaborg, neither depth of water nor space are wanting ; they would be opposed to the weakest fronts, *and in less than* two hours the fortifications would be untenable. A ship of a hundred guns can fire from one side 2500 rounds in an hour. Let us imagine the action of eight or ten ships on masonry heaped together as the works of Sweaborg are, and we must acknowledge that such a shower of balls, scattering stone splinters in all directions, will render the defence impossible, and will leave nothing but ruins. *But ships are very complicated machines; very easy to be set on fire. Such an operation is rash (hardie). It has never been done that I know of, and it does not come within my province to advise it.* I only remark that if it should be tried, it renders useless the attack by way of Bak Holmen; which, even in case of success, would be attended by much greater loss of men than in an attack by sea.

" If the attack by the fleet should be made at a great distance, its effect will be absolutely nothing, and an attack by land will be insufficient. It will be necessary to re-embark in front of the enemy, an operation even otherwise difficult and dangerous, and the landing itself would be very much so.

" I conclude, then, that under the circumstances, the *land attack by way of Bak Holmen, the difficulties of which no one can dispute, is useless in the one case, insufficient and dangerous in the other. I could not therefore advise it.*

" NIEL,
" General of Division."

Thus General Niel completely demolishes the plan of General Jones, and states that he cannot recommend the carrying out of his own plan. General Niel, however, makes a serious mistake, arising from his necessarily incomplete examination of Sweaborg. He says, the sea-fronts are incontestably the weakest (" *les fronts de mer qui sont incontestablement les plus foibles* "). A closer examination would have shown him that they were incontestably the strongest, if strength consists in a range of guns *en barbette*, with casemates cut in the solid rock, against which no bombardment could avail, nor could the guns easily be silenced, as they would have had to be taken in detail where the ships would have been most exposed, and could have operated with least advantage. This is very different to General Niel's expression ("*maçonneries entassés*"), works "heaped on one another." This expression arose from the spot from which General Niel got a view of Sweaborg; from this point the works, though greatly extended, look as though massed together.

General Niel is mistaken in saying that marine artillery is of larger calibre than shore artillery, and has therefore the advantage. In Russia the contrary is the case. One fort alone, in Cronstadt, mounted 128 guns, thirty-two of which were 112-pounders, or, according to some, 120-pounders; thirty-two were 98-pounders; thirty-two 64-pounders; and the other thirty-two 48-pounders. No ship that ever swam has carried such an armament. Even the *Duke of Wellington*, the largest ship of the fleet, had not an armament to compare with this. She had only one 68-pounder pivot-gun; sixteen 8-inch guns (65 cwt.); fifty-six 32-pounders (56 cwt.); thirty-eight 32-pounders (42 cwt.); and twenty 32-pounders (25 cwt.); so that the artillery of the Russian forts, in place of being inferior to the armament of the ships, was incomparably superior to it.

We have now shown the opinion of General Niel on General Jones's plan for attacking Sweaborg, and his disapproval of it, as well as its final rejection by the French Marshal. Let us examine it yet more closely. General Jones's report is dated Aug. 27th, at which period the weather had become very unfavourable, as General Jones had himself experienced.

General Jones says that a very erroneous opinion will be formed of the strength of Sweaborg from the plans, &c. Let us, for the sake of argument, admit this to be true. This admitted, let us proceed to examine his plan of attack, and we shall see that nothing more absurd could well have been devised, because General Jones knew nothing of combining a naval attack with that of his army of 5000 men!

General Jones says, after a careful reconnoissance, the only mode which appears to present itself with any prospect of success, is by a heavy bombardment from a combined operation by land and sea. A force of 5000 men is to be thrown on shore on the island of Bak Holmen, where General Jones admits that the Russians have already erected batteries, but on which, notwithstanding, heavy gun and mortar batteries could be constructed, and when ready to open their fire, the ships should take up their positions simultaneously with the land batteries. While this is going on, the front of the whole of the line of works facing the sea is to be attacked.

All this looks very well on paper; but General Jones has forgotten to say where the fleet is to anchor to make preparation for landing the troops and heavy guns. If it anchored in Miolo Roads, the ships would be within range of Bak Holmen, Kung's Holmen, and Sandhamm, on all of which guns were placed. Let us suppose that there were no guns there. General Jones would have had difficulty in finding an Admiral ignorant enough to take up such an anchorage in the month of September, which, in the Baltic climate, is equivalent to the latter end of November in England.

But setting this aside, let us suppose that the French General *had* placed 5000 of his men under the command of General Jones, and that the allied Admirals *had* consented to embark them, and take them to Miolo Roads. Nay more, we will suppose that the weather was fine, the water as smooth as glass, and there was not a gun or a soldier to oppose him while he landed his 5000 men, guns, stores, mortars, &c., though the latter would have been a difficult operation, seeing that there was not a single mortar in the British fleet. Let us suppose that there was an excellent road from the south of Bak Holmen to the ground opposite Sweaborg, and that the Admirals had landed **heavy** guns, with seamen to drag them into position, as was done at Bomarsund. What would have happened? The Russians, if wise, —and they are quite as great adepts in military service as General Jones,—would no doubt have allowed them to advance to the centre of the island. They would then have crossed over 10,000 men from Sweaborg, — they could have spared even more, — and 4000 or 5000 more from Kung's Holmen and Sandhamm on their flank, and General Jones, with his army of 5000 Frenchmen, would have been obliged to lay down their arms without firing a shot, and in forty-eight hours they would have been conveyed to St. Petersburg, troops and guns together, through the inner navigation, where no ships could have come to their rescue. When there, he would perhaps have received the thanks of the Emperor in the great square of the Russian metropolis, which he would have richly merited; whilst the French General and the Allied Admirals would have been ordered home, tried by a court-martial, and shot, as they, too, would have richly merited.

Let the reader take up a chart of Sweaborg, and we defy him to come to any other conclusion. Nevertheless, Sir James Graham said General Jones's report made a great impression in England. If by that he meant a great impression was produced upon himself, his colleagues, and upon the Board of Admiralty, that General Jones's report would serve their turn at the expense of the Allied Admirals and Generals,— from the presumption that the English public knew no better, — they were perhaps right; but in the estimation of naval and military men, they could only prove themselves unfit for their positions, and that this Sweaborg affair, without going farther, would fully account for all the future failures at Sebastopol.

This is the fair weather view of it. But suppose a heavy gale of wind had come on, — a common circumstance at this season of the year, — and had the fleet, or part of it, been driven on shore, the anchorage being, as Mr. Biddlecombe had described it in his own way, " *loose sand or gravel,*" that would have completed the catastrophe! What would Sir James Graham and his colleagues have said to this? What would the country have said?

It is necessary to be yet more particular about General Jones's report. The best commentator upon General Jones's report is *General Jones himself.* No one will for a moment question his authority or opinion on such a subject.

On the 8th of June previous, Sir James Graham had sent to Sir Charles Napier a report on Sweaborg by General Jones, who states in this report that he had personally visited the Baltic ports, so that he must have been well acquainted with their fortifications, about which he was not therefore likely to make any mistake whatever. The following is his former report *verbatim* : —

"The object to be obtained by an attack upon Sweaborg must be considered that of the destruction of the enemy's men-of-war and Naval Arsenal, which are lying within, or established upon some of the islands forming the group under the denomination of Sweaborg.

" Where works are *so numerous,* and where flanking fire and mutual defences are established, as well as *interior lines of defence* constructed, it must be presumed, of a permanent character, *to attempt to take such fortifications by a naval attack, or by a coup de main, would be contrary to all military principles,* and would be rash in the extreme.

" The islands of Sweaborg are so grouped together, and lying so compactly, that a converging fire from several batteries being brought to bear upon them would be certain to destroy the shipping and storehouses, and greatly injure the fortifications. The point most favourable for the attack, would be upon the island of Bak Holmen, on which cover, it may be assumed, could be easily found for the establishment of batteries, which would fire direct up the channel between "Stwar Oster Swarto" and "Vargon," as well as enfilade many of the faces of the works on those two islands. Other batteries might be established on Sandhamm Island, the fire from which would be very effective at a range of about 2000 yards: and if a battery could be established upon the island of "Kalfholm" there can be no doubt of the result. There appears by the chart a good depth of water to 'Kung's Sound,' by which a secure and safe communication could be kept up with the men-of-war, and where stores and guns could be landed for the operations on Bak Holmen and from 'Kung's Sound' for those on 'Sandhamm.'

" As the coasts of Finland are generally protected by gun-boats, *any operation carried on against any of the Baltic ports by a naval force should be accompanied by a large flotilla of that description.*

" In attacking any fortified post, one of the first operations should be to cut off all communication between the post and the country around it, *and such it would be very desirable to do in the case of Sweaborg, by landing and taking possession of the town*; and if there should be any of the enemy's ships of war lying in the North Harbour, possession of the town might lead to their destruction.

" To offer an opinion upon the attack of such a place as Sweaborg, from plans only, must be done with great diffidence, so much depending on the ground in advance of the works, as well as the manner in which they are defended, not only in respect to each other, but also as to the command they have of the approaches leading up to them. An engineer, with the aid of the plans in possession of the Government, and a careful reconnoissance, would, without difficulty, be able to decide upon the point or points most open to and most favourable for an attack.

" It may be permitted me to state, *what made a great impression on my mind at the time I visited the Baltic ports,* that every expedition operating against them *should be furnished with a large supply of rockets.* Although not very accurate in their flight, they are very destructive in their effects — are easily transported — and can be taken to and fired from many situations where it would not be practicable to take up a gun of large calibre.

(Signed,)   " HARRY D. JONES,

" Colonel, Royal Engineers.

" Royal Engineer Establishment,
      Chatham, 1st May, 1854."

Military and naval men can compare the two reports of General Jones with each other, and with General Niel's report and our own observations. We have now given the whole, so that the information on this point is complete.

General Jones did good service in pointing out to the Government, on the 1st of May, that a large number of gun-boats and rockets was most essential in *any* attack upon the Russian forts. It was afterwards put forth as an excuse for not providing them, that if the Government had known time enough that they were wanted, they could have supplied them. Setting aside Sir Charles Napier's demands for them, here is General Jones urging upon the Government to supply them, even before the British squadron had got beyond Stockholm, and long before it came near Sweaborg! Not a gun-boat or rocket was sent to the fleet!

A report far transcending any of the preceding engineer reports, as being to the purpose, was one from the pen of the Emperor Napoleon himself. His Imperial Majesty was satisfied with what had been done, saw at a glance what could be done, and how it ought to be done, when the English Government could be awakened to a knowledge of what was really requisite for the success of the fleets against such forts as Sweaborg and Cronstadt. But even the remonstrances of the Emperor Napoleon failed to make an impression on the Admiralty, as far as the Baltic fleet was concerned.

The Emperor's opinion was as follows :—

" Les Officiers de Marine en France, comme peut-être en Angleterre, n'ont pas assez réfléchi sur la différence qu'introduit dans la guerre maritime l'usage des canons paixhans ; c'est-à-dire, de canons lançant des obus d'un grand diamètre. En effet, cette innovation doit donner naturellement l'avantage aux batteries de côtes ou aux forts, tirant contre des vaisseaux, car tandis que les batteries de côtes souffrent peu des projectiles creux qu'on lance contre leurs parapets formés de terre ou de gros blocs de granite, les vaisseaux peuvent être presque detruits par quelques gros obus éclatant dans leurs planes. Les batteries de Cronstadt et de Sevastopol ne sont donc surtout formidables que parce qu'elles sont armées d'un grand nombre de canons à la paixhan.

" L'attaque de Cronstadt est en outre rendue très-difficile par la peu d'eau qui se trouve autour les fortifications. Pour surmonter ces obstacles, l'Empereur a donné l'ordre au Ministre de la Marine de faire construire des batteries flottantes, répondant aux conditions suivantes :

1. " Construire des bateaux plats, ayant une petite machine à vapeur de 10 ou 20 chevaux, ne calant tout chargés que 6 pieds d'eau.

2. " Ces bateaux auraient sur chaque bord 3 embrasures, mais en réalité trois ou quatre canons pour tirer à boulets pleins, qui seuls sont efficaces contre la maçonnerie.

3. " Tout le bateau serait entouré d'un large et épais parapet formé de tôle en fer et de bois, il serait couvert d'un toit au blindage pour mettre à l'abri des projectiles creux.

" On peut affirmer qu'un petit nombre de ces bâtiments ferait tomber successivement tous les forts de Cronstadt, car tirant peu d'eau, et ayant des parapets autrement resistants que ceux des vaisseaux ordinaires, ils pourraient arriver tout près des forts, les attaquer à revers par la gorge, là où les défenses manquent, et seconder aussi puissamment l'attaque de front des vaisseaux de ligne.

" Le tout est de savoir si l'on aura le temps, d'ici à deux mois, de construire ces bâtiments.

" *L'Empereur désire que le gouvernement Anglais étudie la question et s'occupe de la resoudre.*"

TRANSLATION.

" Naval officers in France, as perhaps in England, have not sufficiently considered the difference which the use of paixhan guns has brought about in naval warfare ; that is to say, guns throwing shells of great diameter. This innovation, in effect, *ought naturally to give an advantage to coast batteries, or to forts firing against ships; for whilst land batteries suffer little from hollow projectiles discharged against their parapets formed of earth or huge blocks of granite, ships may be almost destroyed by large shells bursting in their sides.* The batteries of Cronstadt and Sebastopol are not then alone formidable because they are armed with paixhan guns : *the attack on Cronstadt is, moreover, rendered very difficult by the small depth of water surrounding the fortifications.* To overcome these obstacles the Emperor has given orders to the Minister of Marine to construct floating batteries answering to the following conditions : —

1. " To construct flat-bottomed boats, having a small engine of ten or twenty horse power, and drawing only six feet of water when fully equipped.

2. " These vessels should have three port-holes on a side, but actually three or four guns to fire solid shot, which alone is effective against masonry.

3. " Every vessel should be surrounded with a strong bulwark formed of iron plate and wood. It should be covered with a roof or blindage, so as to be sheltered from hollow shot or shells.

" It might be confidently expected that a small number of such vessels would cause the whole of the forts of Cronstadt to fall in succession, for drawing little water, and having bulwarks better calculated for resistance than those of ordinary ships ; they could get very close to the forts, attack them by the ' *gorge,*' where the defences are weak, and thus powerfully second the attack on the front by the ships of the line.

" The question is, whether in *two months* there will be

time to construct the vessels. The Emperor wishes the English Government to study the question, and occupy itself in resolving it."

This remarkable plan places the foresight and energy of the Emperor in strong contrast with the want of foresight and apathy of our Government. They had sent out a fleet to the Baltic, without any bombarding vessels at all, and no reserve ammunition ship, as was sent in the following campaign under Admiral Dundas. The Emperor saw the fatal nature of the omission, and urged upon the English Government to remedy the mistake, *if there was time.* The Admiralty received the Emperor's suggestion, on or before the 16th of May, before Sir Charles Napier was in the Gulf of Finland, or a shot had been fired.

It is also remarkable that the Emperor anticipated, what Admiral Chads afterwards found to be the case, that solid shot would alone be effective against masonry. But the most curious part of the Emperor's letter is, its antagonism to the opinion of General Niel, that " marine artillery, from its assumed greater calibre, is stronger than fort artillery," an opinion which, as we showed in its place, is unmistakeably erroneous. The Emperor, who is accounted one of the best artillery officers in Europe, is decidedly of a contrary opinion, and considers that ships have no chance with forts, when the latter are armed, as the Russian forts were, with heavier guns than the ships; in fact, almost exclusively with the heaviest guns known to military and naval science.

The preceding plans of the Emperor were sent to Sir Charles Napier, without drawings or other explanations as to what the batteries proposed were like. He did not, from this imperfect notice, think much of them, but replied, that though they might be serviceable, we had not got them, and they would not be built in time. He was wrong. When these identical batteries were afterwards constructed by the French, and used at Kinburn, not a shot would touch them, all glancing off without scarcely leaving a mark.

We will conclude this dissertation on batteries as against ships, by an extract from Sir Howard Douglas's *Naval Gunnery*, p. 350.

" A battery of ten pieces, served by skilful gunners firing in succession, would soon overpower a ship, *whatever might be her force*, especially if the guns be of high calibre, or if red-hot shot be projected. The shot from ships, the decks of which are six, twelve, and eighteen feet above the water, cannot, in *ricochetting*, rise up to the battery, whilst the latter can employ both a direct and *ricochetting* fire against the whole body of the ship. On the other hand, only those shots from the ship can take effect, which pass eighteen inches above the parapet of the battery, since the guns in the latter are only so far exposed, and the gun itself covers the head of the man who points it; all the rest of the service is performed behind the parapet. Thus, the ship, for every eighteen feet length of gunwale, has no other object to aim at than the muzzle of a gun presenting only about two square feet of surface, while the battery has before it an object presenting 2000 square feet of surface, independently of the masts, ropes, and sails."

When speaking of two months being sufficient for building the floating batteries alluded to by the Emperor Napoleon, we omitted to state that in 1855, Mr. Laird, of Birkenhead, launched a mortar vessel in *three weeks!* He received the order on the 23rd of October; the keel was laid down on the 25th; and on the 13th of November, just *three weeks* from the date of the order being received, she was afloat in the Mersey, *all complete*, with mortar bed, masts, rigging, anchors, cable, sails, shellroom, and accommodation for crew. There not being time, then, to send Sir Charles Napier mortar boats, was a miserable subterfuge on the part of the Admiralty.

Sir James Graham stated in Parliament, that if Sir Charles Napier had asked for gun-boats in May, he could have had them. Sir Charles Napier was not at Sweaborg in May, but on his way only. And Sir James Graham has written, that he did ask for this class of vessels " from the first hour of his appointment." Even if he had not asked for them, here is the letter of the Emperor Napoleon, on the 16th of May, pointing out their immediate urgency. Why then did not Sir James Graham supply these vessels on the Emperor's requisition ? But the Admiralty did not even supply them to Admiral Dundas in the following year. If, in 1855, the energies of the Admiralty could only supply fifteen gun-boats to Admiral Dundas, what becomes of Sir James

Graham's assertion in Parliament, that in 1854 he could have furnished enough had he known in time that they were wanted? Yet in the same space of time, the Russians had built gun-boats by scores. But of this, more hereafter.

CHAP. XVIII.

Now that the French army was gone, the Admiral determined to leave Ledsund and return to the Gulf of Finland, at the same time apprising the authorities at home of his intention. On the same day that he had thus announced his determination, he received a letter from Admiral Parseval, stating, that as the French Minister of Marine, in a letter just come to hand, had advised him that the period had arrived when the combined squadrons should return home, he wished to consult Sir C. Napier on the subject. This letter was dated Sept. 5.

It has already been said that the Board of Admiralty as well as Sir James Graham and Admiral Berkeley had ordered Sir Charles Napier to begin sending his ships home, and this was no doubt done in concert with the French Government, as the French Minister of Marine, in his orders to Admiral Parseval, makes use of the expression, " l'époque à laquelle les *escadres combinées* rentreront dans leurs ports." It is hence clear that both the French and English Governments had fully agreed to withdraw their respective squadrons; and therefore equally clear, that nothing more was expected to be done by them at the now advanced season, which would soon become dangerous to the ships; the orders of both Governments to their Admirals being precise on this subject.

The French army sailed the day before the date of Admiral Parseval's letter, viz., Sept. 4th. On the 31st of August, Gen. Baraguay D'Hilliers had asked Sir. C. Napier for steamers to tow the eleven transports containing the French troops through the Cattegat, as well as to pick up a transport at Faro Sound, with 500 troops on board, which had not been brought to Bomarsund. Though the steamers could ill be spared from the blockading squadron, the request was complied with, and the Admiral detached the

Hecla, Driver, and *Gladiator* for this purpose, Admiral
Parseval adding the *Asmodée, Brandon* and *Cocyte,*
so that six steamers were withdrawn from the combined fleet. One steam transport only, the *Prince,* had
been used in the conveyance of the troops to Bomarsund. On the 3rd, Gen. Baraguay D'Hilliers apprised
the Admiral that as His Swedish Majesty would not
take possession of Bomarsund, it was the Emperor's
order that it should be destroyed, and that when this
was done, he was to take the troops back to Cherbourg.
On the morning of the 4th, the General went on
board the *Duke of Wellington* to take leave of Sir C.
Napier, and in about an hour afterwards sailed for
France.

Heavy gales had now set in, and the *Edinburgh* and
the French ship of the line *Tilsit* left Bomarsund. On
the 7th the *Tilsit* and two French frigates were despatched by Admiral Parseval to Cherbourg. On this
day, from the increasing gales, the *Majestic* parted
her chain cable, and fears were entertained for the
Nimrod, provision transport, which had got on shore
in coming into Ledsund. After long-continued exertions the latter vessel was got off, but not before a
great portion of the cargo had been spoiled, to the
serious inconvenience of the squadron, which was in
want of many articles rendered useless by the accident.

On the 4th of September, the Board of Admiralty
wrote to Sir Charles Napier that as the season was
now drawing to a close during which so large a combined fleet could remain in the Baltic, he must consult
with his French Colleagues and the Admirals on
whom he had reliance, as to what operations remained
to be undertaken this year. He was told to bear in

mind, that any object to be gained must be worth the attempt, and that useless expenditure of life, with destruction of ships, should not be hazarded for any object unworthy the risk and the cause in which he was engaged. The Board trusted the deliberations of the Admirals would be unanimous, and that it had the fullest confidence in the Admirals coming to a decision which would reflect credit on the arms of the Allied forces, and justify before the public the confidence placed in them.

This letter was received on the 12th, and the Admiral at once apprised Admiral Parseval of its purport. As the French General and army were gone, he of course could not be consulted. Sir Charles having "reliance" on his Admirals, summoned the only two available, viz., Admirals Chads and Michael Seymour, and these, together with the French Admirals, held a consultation as directed: unanimously deciding that "in consequence of the advanced season of the year, nothing could be undertaken against Sweaborg, or any other fortified port on the coast of Russia with a chance of success." They were also unanimously of opinion that "with the resources at present at their disposal, nothing more could be done without the loss of a great many men, and seriously compromising the ships."

When transmitting this report, the Admiral told the Board,—

" I dare say there is a great deal of dissatisfaction in England that more was not done by so large an army ; but the fact is, they came too late in the season to carry on any ulterior operations, whilst their departure has been hurried. I wished them to go to Abo, which was a purely military question, but no one seemed to like it, and as a heavy gale of wind came on the night they left Ledsund, there is no knowing what might have happened had we gone there. The French Rear-Admiral's ship drove into our hawse, our dolphin-striker thumping against her stern, and our cable out to the clinch. Had she fallen on board us, and we had both gone ashore, and taken another line-of-battle ship with us, the people of England would perhaps have come to their senses, and seen that operations in these seas are not easy at this season of the year.

"Their Lordships will observe that Gen. Jones proposed landing 5000 men at Sweaborg, and planting batteries against it, and he thought this a good season to do so. Had the French General been unwise enough to have followed this advice, or had the Admirals been indiscreet enough to have countenanced an operation that by his own account required seven or eight days to have brought it to a successful termination, the troops would have been made prisoners, and probably half a dozen of the ships lost. This would rather have made a bad finish to the first campaign in the Baltic.

"If their Lordships will read with attention Admiral Chads' report, my own, and Gen. Jones's (with the exception of what I had stated), they would find us all pretty well agreed as to the proper mode of attacking Sweaborg, a strong fortification, that *either ought to be attacked in a proper manner, or not at all.* I have received many propositions for attacking both Sweaborg and Cronstadt, but I never will lend myself to any absurd project, or be driven to attempt what is not practicable by newspaper writers, who, I am sorry to say, I have reason to believe are in correspondence with officers of the fleet, who ought to know better."

It was clearly not the fault of the Allied Admirals that the French troops had sailed for Cherbourg, nor that they had not come out in sufficient time for ulterior operations after the fall of Bomarsund. As the reader knows, Sir Charles Napier had been most urgent that they should have arrived earlier. The Admiralty, moreover, was cognisant of their immediate return, for the French Minister had applied to them to order steamers to tow the troops, and therefore, could not have supposed otherwise than that they were gone when its order to hold a consultation arrived. The Admiral felt annoyed at this, and therefore wrote the straightforward letter we have just quoted, an offence which the Admiralty never afterwards forgave.

On the 9th of September, the Board of Admiralty acknowledged the receipt of the Admiral's remarks on Gen. Jones's report, and his intimation that the French General and Admiral agreed with him that nothing could be effected against Sweaborg or Revel with the force they then had. Their Lordships ordered Sir Charles Napier immediately to lay the report of Gen. Jones before the French General-in-Chief and Admiral, and in a Council of War to decide whether the opinion of Gen. Jones so far altered that which they had already formed as to induce them to undertake the operation. Similar instructions, continued the Board, have been sent to the French Officers by their Government.

This order was received on the 16th, nearly a fortnight after the French General and army had sailed, so that no council could be held with him; and the plan of Gen. Jones, being a military one, no council could be held on the subject in the absence of the troops which formed the basis of Gen. Jones's proposed attack. The order itself was a singular one. It was written on the 9th of September, four days after the French Minister had applied for steamers to tow the French troops home, so that the Admiralty must have supposed that they were gone, as was the case.

The Admiral at once replied, that he had laid Gen. Jones's report before the French General and Admiral, and on the 2nd of September had forwarded Gen. Baraguay D'Hilliers's reply, together with Gen. Niel's report of the 1st of September. He had already transmitted a report of a consultation of the Admirals agreeably to their Lordships' directions of the 4th of September. The departure of the French General prevented a second council from being called; but, added the Admiral, "I see no reason whatever to alter the opinion I gave to Sir James Graham some time ago; and the state of the weather has been such that had the troops then at our disposal been considered sufficient, an attack on Sweaborg by the ships and troops would have been perfectly impracticable."

On the 12th of September Admiral Berkeley expressed "astonishment that the French troops and their ships should have withdrawn so hurriedly." The French General and his engineer said *eight ships would destroy Sweaborg in two hours!* but "why have we not the opinion of the French Admiral? You are now left with *only thirteen sail of the line, and three block-ships.* I don't see how we are to withdraw any till we withdraw the whole of the ships of the line."

On the same day (September, 12) Sir James Graham wrote as follows to Sir Charles Napier:—

"Our British steamers of war, in fine weather, and in the early part of September, might have been more gloriously and usefully employed than in towing transports back to France from the scene of action, with a French army on board. However, considering the circumstances, you would have acted unwisely if you had withheld the facilities which were eagerly demanded. We know nothing with certainty respecting the return of the French fleet from the Baltic, but we hear from Cherbourg that the whole fleet is expected there early in October.

" I hope when this letter reaches you, the French Admiral with his line-of-battle ships will still be within your power of communicating with him; for Gen. Niel's letter, which you transmitted to us in your despatch of the 5th, renders it necessary that you should distinctly and officially raise the question whether he concurs in the opinion expressed by the French military authorities, that Sweaborg *may be attacked with success by naval means alone.* Gen. Niel speaks of eight or ten sail of the line as sufficient for the purpose. *If the French be disposed to risk one half of this number,* I do not imagine that volunteers to an equal amount would be wanting in the British fleet. On the other hand, if the French Admiral repudiates the suggestions of the French General, he ought, *in writing,* to concur that the operation is too hazardous. If, unhappily, nothing more can be done, it is wise *to send home at once the smallest and least effective of the steamers, and the least weatherly of the large ships.* Should you decide on any further active operations, you are, of course, at full liberty to postpone any diminution of your force. We shall send you no positive orders respecting the withdrawal of the fleet in the Baltic, which must be effected at all events gradually, until we know what is the intention of the French as to remaining there; and whether their whole fleet will winter within the British Channel."

The remark that the French troops had gone home " *in fine weather,*" was incorrect, as Sir James Graham must have known, and is a gratuitous slur on the judgment of Gen. Baraguay D'Hilliers, who had lost no time in getting his army away on account of the *badness of the weather* ; the troops even sailing in a gale of wind, in preference to waiting for worse. How was it possible for Sir James Graham in London to judge of the weather as Gen. Baraguay D'Hilliers could in Ledsund? Had the ex-First Lord consulted his naval colleagues, they ought to have told him that in September the weather in the Baltic was hardly fit for ships, much less for troops; and of this opinion, in the following year, Admiral Dundas gave practical proof by sending his gun-boats home in the middle of August, and confining his ships to blockading only, without attempting further operations. Surely then Baraguay D'Hilliers might have been permitted to take his troops home in September, having decided, and rightly, that nothing farther could, in sound judgment, be done with them. A Marshal of France should be as good a judge of the management of troops as an English Lord of the Admiralty, who could know nothing practically of either naval or military operations. This interference in matters beyond his knowledge constitutes the chief characteristic of Sir James Graham's conduct of the war. A mob might applaud such a course, but professional men must deplore it.

We have already given the Admiral's letter to the Board of Admiralty, when transmitting the report of the Admirals. At the same time the Admiral wrote to Sir James Graham as follows:—

" Admiral Berkeley tells me, that there is a sad commotion about the French army going home. We have had a hard gale of wind for five days, and had we gone to Abo, it is difficult to say what would have happened. Had we gone to Sweaborg and landed 5000 men, as proposed by Gen. Jones, they would all have been prisoners at Helsingfors, and half the ships lost. No man in his senses would, in this season, attempt to land or make an attack upon an enemy's coast which required seven or eight days, as specified in Gen. Jones's report.

" I have sent home the *Belleisle*, and she will be followed by *Ajax* and *Cumberland*. I think also of sending home the four sailing ships, leaving off the mouth of the Gulf of Finland the seven frigates supported by the line-of-battle ships till later in the season.

" But should the Helsingfors ships take it in their heads to go to Cronstadt, I should, of course, be abused ; but it is not possible to stay here till the last moment, so, stay or go, they will find an opportunity of going to Cronstadt, if they wish it. If they were there, it would make the blockade much easier next year, and we should be in a better position to distress the enemy.

" I don't like the roadstead of Nargen. The wind at N. and N.N.E. is right in. At Baro Sound, the S.W. wind is in also ; and here, which is the best of the three, a W.S.W. is in too, without protection, but the ground is good. I don't think the people of England will be satisfied till we lose three or four sail of the line, and if we could save the people, the sooner the better. That, and that alone, would bring them to their senses."

On the 13th Sir Charles apprised the Admiralty that he had sent home the *Belleisle* and *Volcano*, and they would shortly be followed by the sailing ships. He had sent the *Amphion* to reinforce the squadron off the coast of Courland, and to remain there as long as prudent. Several steamers were also in the Gulf of Bothnia, but these must shortly be withdrawn.

On the 17th the French Admiral began to send his ships home, and Rear-Admiral Penaud sailed with five ships. The Admiral requested of Admiral Parseval not to send away his two line-of-battle ships at Nargen, as this would be too sudden a reduction of the fleet. The French Minister, when giving the order, remarked, " the separation of the French fleet is to be regretted." Admiral Parseval asked of Sir Charles Napier what were his intentions as regarded his fleet : to which Sir Charles replied that he had no authority, but that he thought of sending home his sailing ships. Admiral Parseval said, that in that case he would send his, but otherwise he would not do it, notwithstanding his orders.

The French ships sent away with Rear-Admiral Penaud were the *Duperré, Duguesclin, Trident, Poursuivante, Breslau,* and *Algerie.* On the withdrawal of these ships, Sir Charles wrote to Admiral Parseval that the British Admiralty stated they did not know anything of the French ships being ordered home beyond rumours from Cherbourg, and that Sir James Graham, remarking on General Niel's observation as to eight ships being sufficient to attack Sweaborg, suggested that if Admiral Parseval would risk four ships in the attack, we might risk four also. Sir Charles, therefore, proposed to Admiral Parseval that, as he had replied that if he saw the smallest prospect of success he would gratify the Admiralty and the public with a fight, Admiral Parseval, if he agreed with him, had better retain his four ships still here and at Nargen. To this communication Sir Charles received no reply; a pretty conclusive hint that

Admiral Parseval did not choose to suffer himself to be goaded into fighting to no purpose beyond that of fighting's sake, even though his own engineer officer General Niel, had stated that in *two hours* Sweaborg might be destroyed with eight ships. And Admiral Parseval was right. To say nothing of the absurdity of demolishing a fortress as strong as Gibraltar, in two hours, with eight ships, a fight could have resulted in nothing but the folly of the Admirals in having undertaken it.

Just as the French fleet was thus returning home, and all operations for the year were at an end, the Admiralty sent out *one gun-boat!* Much in the same way as in the following year, after Admiral Dundas had sent his gun-boats home for want of mortars, the Admiralty made a great show of sending out mortars to replace those used up, and the *Sanspareil* actually took them as far as Kiel, having met Admiral Dundas's gun-boats coming home! Such proceedings as these could only be intended to throw dust in the eyes of the people, and blame on the Admirals. But the *one gun-boat* sent to Sir Charles Napier after the whole campaign had been paralysed for want of gun-boats, is an affair so supremely ridiculous as to appear like farce rather than reality.

The gun-boat sent out was worthy of the wonderful energy which had occupied a whole campaign in building it. Sir Charles Napier thus wrote to Admiral Berkeley respecting it:—

"I do not think it is exactly what you want in a gunboat; if intended as a despatch vessel you might have a less complicated one. She has *fighting boilers* and *despatch boilers.* You might have got a better despatch vessel than

her, and a more comfortable one, had you not united the
two.

"It appears to me, what you want in a gun-boat in these
seas, is to have a vessel with one gun that you can either get
ahead or astern; the extremities presenting the least space
to the enemy, and the vessel having the least motion.
Whereas, if your guns are fitted as they are in the *Wrangler*,
you present *the full length to the enemy's shot*, and I should
think she would not be so steady. *She has no protection for
the men, who would all be knocked down with rifles.*"

The "*despatch boilers*" and "*fighting boilers*" of
this memorable craft, will, no doubt, remind the
reader of the college story of Sir Isaac Newton, who
cut a large hole in his door to let the cat out, and a
little hole for the egress of the kitten. The *Wrangler*
was no more original than she was of any use when
she was sent out to reduce Sweaborg!

Either on the strength of the *Wrangler*, or something else, the Board of Admiralty, now that the
French army and part of the French ships had gone
home, became enthusiastically warlike. No sooner
had Admiral Penaud set sail, than without waiting
for the result of the order to hold a second council
of war, the Admiral received from the Board of
Admiralty a third despatch, dated 12th of September, ordering him to hold another council of war
on the reports of General Niel, especially as he
declares that Sweaborg can be reduced to ruins in
two hours by ships alone.

The Board added, "But General Niel at the same
time remarks, that *so bold an operation has not to his
knowledge been yet attempted by ships against forts,
and that it is not his province to advise it.* The

question thus left by the French Generals is of a purely naval character, and it does not appear, from your letter, that you reject this suggested attack by naval means only as impracticable, or that you have consulted the French Admiral with respect to it. The French army has been withdrawn, but the French fleet is still present with you, and you must lose no time in conferring with the French Admiral, and in ascertaining whether he is willing to join in a *naval attack* on Sweaborg, such as General Niel regards as certain to lead to success. If at this conference it shall appear, both to you and to him, an attempt too rash to be undertaken, you are hereby directed to cause this joint opinion to be recorded in writing. If one of you be favourable to the undertaking and the other unfavourable, a council of the Admirals present should be called, and their advice and opinion taken. It must be remembered that the destruction of Sweaborg has always been regarded as an object of great importance from the first commencement of the war."

This communication from the Board of Admiralty requires one or two remarks. It had not, from the first commencement of the war, been an object to attack Sweaborg, for the injunctions of Sir James Graham to the Admiral were, up to a late period, constant and emphatic, "not to run his head against stone walls," &c. In place, also, of not adopting General Niel's views, Sir Charles had over and over again told the Admiralty that nothing more could be done, and both Sir James Graham and Admiral Berkeley had long before told him to begin to send his ships home, as the steamers were wanted at home. Sir Charles Napier did not criticise General Niel's report as he had done that of General Jones, because General Niel was a French military officer, with whose opinion he had nothing to do; and as General Niel had, moreover, broadly stated that he considered the operation he had mentioned so bold and novel that "it was not his province to recommend it," criticism on his plan was unnecessary. General Niel's words were, " Mais les vaisseaux sont des machines bien compliquées, bien faciles à incendier. Une telle opération est *hardie*. Elle n'a jamais été faite que je sache, et ce n'est pas à moi de la conseiller." " But ships are very complicated machines, very easy to set on fire. Such an operation is *rash* (hardie). It has never been done that I know of, and it is not for me to advise it."

General Niel had, on the 1st of September, written to General Baraguay D'Hilliers on General Jones's plan, " Je conclus donc, que dans les circonstances actuelles, l'attaque de terre par Bak Holmen—dont personne ne peut contester les difficultés — est inutile dans un cas — insuffisante et dangereuse dans l'autre; je ne saurais donc la conseiller." " I conclude then, that in present circumstances, the land attack by way of Bak Holmen, the difficulties of which no one can dispute, is useless in one case, insufficient and dangerous in the other. I could not therefore advise it."

We have previously given the opinion of General Baraguay D'Hilliers, to which the reader can refer. The whole matter had then been carefully considered by the Allied Generals and Admirals, who had declined embarking in it. The only disingenuousness that appears is on the part of Sir James Graham, who assumed that General Niel's attack by ships alone could be carried out, without noticing the qualified clauses of General Niel's report, that he could not advise the adoption of his own opinion. The Board of Admiralty, in a fairer spirit, admitted General Niel's caution.

On receiving the orders of the Admiralty to hold a second council of war, Sir Charles Napier summoned all his Admirals, and requested Admiral Parseval to join in it, for a reconsideration of the engineer officers' plans. Admiral Parseval refused to participate in the council of war, or in any way to alter his previous determinations. He had already given his opinion that nothing more could be done in the Baltic, and seeing no reason to alter that opinion, he would not sit in judgment on his own previous determinations.

As the French Admiral would not take part in the council of war, Sir Charles Napier, with Admirals Chads, Seymour, and Martin, proceeded to obey the orders of the Admiralty, by reconsidering their previous opinions. The result was the annexed

REPORT OF THE SECOND COUNCIL OF WAR.

" We, the undersigned, have examined the report of Gen. Niel, that Sweaborg can be attacked by ships alone. We have already given a unanimous opinion, that neither the season nor our resources permit such an attack without the loss of a great many men, and seriously compromising the ships; whilst Rear-Admiral Martin having maturely considered our report adopts the same opinion.

"After having read Gen. Niel's report, we see no reason to change the opinion we have already expressed. The French Admiral, having already given his opinion and signed it on the 12th instant, has declined the conference.

"Given under our hands on board the *Duke of Wellington*, in Ledsund, this 18th day of September, 1854.

(Signed)   " CHAS. NAPIER.
             " H. D. CHADS.
             " M. SEYMOUR.
             " H. B. MARTIN."

On the same day (Sept. 18th), Admiral Parseval addressed the following letter to Sir Charles Napier: —

" MONS. L'AMIRAL,

" Je viens de prendre connaissance de la dépêche de l'Amirauté, en date de 12me Septembre, dont votre Excellence m'a fait l'honneur de m'adresser copie. Cette dépêche lui ayant été envoyée avant que les Nobles Lords n'aient eu connaissance de l'avis *unanime* des Amiraux, à la conférence du 12me Septembre, et rien n'ayant pu modifier mon opinion au sujet de l'attaque de Sweaborg, je la prie de me permettre de m'en référer à cet avis, et de m'abstenir d'assister à une nouvelle réunion, *pour y faire la même déclaration.*
         " J'ai l'honneur, &c.
                 " D. PARSEVAL.
" Vice-Amiral Sir C. Napier."

TRANSLATION.
" ADMIRAL,

" I proceed to take cognisance of the Admiralty despatch of the 12th of September, a copy of which your Excellency has done me the honour to address to me.

" This despatch having been sent to you before the Noble Lords had knowledge of the *unanimous opinion* of the Admirals, at their conference of the 12th of September, and not having been able in the least to modify my opinion on the subject of the attack on Sweaborg, I beg you to permit me to refer to that opinion, and to excuse me from assisting at a fresh consultation, only *to make the same declaration.*

" I have the honour, &c.

" D. PARSEVAL.

" Vice-Admiral Sir C. Napier."

This letter from Admiral Parseval bears the character of a protest, and a very proper one, against the right of the Admiralty to order him to reconsider his opinion, whatever control they might assume over their own Admiral. Admiral Parseval was justly indignant at such interference, which virtually asserted the opinions of two engineer officers on naval matters as being superior to those of the Admirals themselves. In fact, no other construction can be placed on the Admiralty despatch, and this, no doubt, was its deliberate intention. The marked phrase, " *pour y faire la même déclaration,*" shows plainly Admiral Parseval's opinion of those plans.

Admiral Parseval saw that the Admiralty was bent on goading on Sir Charles Napier to make a rash attack on Sweaborg, and that if Sir C. Napier made this attack, the French fleet must be drawn into it and lost. At the suggestion of Sir James Graham, Admiral Parseval had been challenged to " risk four of his ships against four British ships," much after the fashion of the same number of cocks in a cockpit. All the Admirals and the French General had no reliance on the engineer officers' plans, and had thus expressed themselves. Finally, the British Admiralty had ordered the French Admiral to reconsider his opinions. The French Admiral, therefore, wisely determined to put a stop to such interference, by immediately sailing to France with his fleet, when he should be out of the reach of further importunity on matters which were not only impossible, but expressly against the orders of his own Government.

This determination was instantly put in execution. On the very same day on which the preceding letter was written, Admiral Parseval set about the return of his fleet; and on the following day, the 19th, he sailed with the remainder of his ships for France, though, previous to this interference, he had intended to remain with Sir C. Napier, with the French steamers, to the last. It is impossible to blame Admiral Parseval; but, on the contrary, the dignity which he displayed in refusing to permit the honour of his flag to be used as a cat's-paw by the British Admiralty to satisfy British clamour, is much to be admired. His own Government was satisfied with him, and afterwards showed its satisfaction by creating him a Marshal of France. Though he would willingly have aided Sir C. Napier to the utmost, he would not do this at the expense of his country's honour being trifled with by the British Admiralty.

The subjoined is a translation of Admiral Parseval's farewell letter to Sir Charles Napier, dated 18th September : —

"ADMIRAL,

" In consequence of the orders which I have received from my Government, the Imperial squadron must immediately return to France, leaving to maintain the blockade, in concert with your Excellency, the number of ships you may point out. The largest number of steamers that I can dispose of will be the *Darien, Phlegeton, La Place,* and *L'Aigle.* The *Phlegeton* proceeds immediately to the anchorage at Nargen, where her Commander will place himself under your flag. The others will make no delay in rejoining you.

" Before quitting these seas, and separating from you, Admiral, allow me to express to your Excellency all the satisfaction which the cordial relations of our two fleets has caused me to feel; the harmony which has never ceased to reign between them, as regards Captains, officers, and crews; as well as the support of your experience.

" Have the goodness to be my interpreter with your Admirals and Captains, and tell them how much I felt myself honoured in associating with the British fleet under your orders, in the accomplishment of our difficult mission, and how much I have been affected by the cordiality with which their important services have been rendered.

" Receive, Admiral, with the expression of these my particular sentiments, assurance of the high consideration with which

" I have the honour, &c.
" D. PARSEVAL."

To this Sir Charles Napier replied on the 19th of September : —

" ADMIRAL,

" I am much obliged to you for placing your steamers under my orders, to assist in maintaining the blockade of the Gulf in the absence of your fleet. I regret the *Austerlitz* is not one of them.

" I beg to express to you my regret that the fleets are

to separate; but as you have received orders to that effect, it could not be helped.

During the time that we have been together, I am happy that both Admirals, Captains, officers, and crews have acted together with so much cordiality, and I beg you will convey to your fleet the very great respect I have for them; and should we be again called upon to act together, I hope that cordiality and friendship will be renewed.

" I have the honour, &c.

" Chas. Napier."

Sir Charles was naturally indignant at the treatment both Admirals had received at the hands of the British authorities, the French authorities relying on the Admirals, and not keeping up a running-fire of instructions as to the slightest movement of the fleets. The reader will no doubt have remarked, throughout the whole of our narrative, this petty interference in every thing. The first portion of those instructions, on the outset of the campaign, as issued by Sir James Graham, counselled great caution. In place of action, every letter was a caution against action. When it was found that this course did not suit the public, though the public was ignorant of the way in which the Admiral had been reined in, Sir James then earnestly endeavoured to goad on both Admirals to a fight, in which they must have lost their ships, to save the Government from the consequences of not having supplied a proper description of force. Sir Charles Napier was unwise enough to suffer himself to be provoked by the urgency of Sir James Graham, to propose to the French Admiral to lose four of his ships against four French ones, as suggested by Sir

James Graham. The French Admiral saw through the device, and did not even reply to the proposition: it was no part of his business to lose his ships to save the British Government from popular clamour, rightly directed against them. It is very remarkable, too, that almost at the very moment Sir James Graham was urging the Admiral thus to lose his ships, the Admiralty was explaining to him why it had not sent mortar-vessels and Lancaster guns to the fleet in the Baltic.

Accordingly, when transmitting to the Board of Admiralty the report of the second council of war, Sir Charles Napier wrote as he felt regarding the way in which he had, together with the French Admiral, been goaded into some desperate act, notwithstanding that Admiral Berkeley had cautioned him against being goaded beyond his own judgment.

The Admiral's remonstrance will long remain a monument to Admiralty imbecility, and anxiety to shift its consequences from their own shoulders:—

"I hope I may be permitted to ask their Lordships what reliance could be placed on the opinion of two military engineers on naval subjects, when one decides that Sweaborg could be destroyed by 5000 men, guns, mortars, and rockets from the island of Bak Holmen, *combined with an attack by the allied fleets in seven or eight days;* whilst the other decides that it can *be laid in ruins in two hours by the fleet alone ?*

"Gen. Jones required 5000 men to be landed, batteries of guns and mortars placed, and a demonstration made against Helsingfors; and with all these means, if everything turned out favourably, it would require seven or eight days to reduce it. *I only required gun-boats, mortars, and the fleet to do so.* I differed, as their Lordships will see, about the troops, and remarked that if troops were landed, *it must be a superior army.* Gen. Jones also thought the season favourable. *I thought no such thing.* Gen. Niel thought the ships alone sufficient. *The Admirals thought differently.* I made no remark on Gen. Niel's suggestion, as I thought that Gen. Niel was not a proper judge of what ships could do, and also that my opinion, as well as the opinion of Admiral Chads, had already been given to Sir James Graham, and that he had submitted it to their Lordships.

"Their Lordships observe, in their letter of the 9th of September, that on the return of the French Admiral and General from reconnoitring Sweaborg and Revel, I stated that they agreed with me that neither one nor the other could be attacked. That was in a conversation which took place before the sailing of the packet. But Gen. Niel's report was made some time after that, and after having considered the report of Gen. Jones, and decided on sending home the troops."

The Admiral enclosed his former report on Sweaborg (July 18th) to Sir J. Graham, which does not appear to have been laid before the Admiralty by the ex-First Lord, for some reasons which he can, no doubt, explain. His not laying it before their Lordships is pretty conclusive proof that he did not expect Sweaborg to be attacked, as, indeed, his letters state clearly enough. It was only when the season had passed away, with neither gun-boats, mortar-boats, nor rockets supplied to the fleet, and when the public had become clamorous, that he urged rash impossibilities, knowing full well that the Admiral would not adopt them. This letter sealed the fate of Sir Charles Napier, though not a word of its plain, solid truth could be taken hold of. It was as guarded as it was unanswerable. For the Admiralty to be told in plain terms that all the Admiral had asked for to destroy Sweaborg was gun-boats, mortar-boats, &c., whilst the Admiralty was catching at the straws thrown to them by two engineer officers, was too true to be palatable. Henceforward it became evident that the only relation in which the Board of Admiralty and Sir Charles Napier could stand towards each other was, who should bear the blame with the public; and for this contest the Admiralty girded up its loins right manfully. The Senior Naval Lord, with a degree of frankness, apprised Sir Charles of the coming storm in the following words: — "We shall have blue-books and parliamentary questions without end. THE ATTACK FAILING AGAINST YOU, WILL BE LEVELLED AT THE BOARD; OR FAILING AGAINST THE BOARD, WILL BE LEVELLED AGAINST YOU."

The only fault to be found with Sir Charles Napier as regards this letter is, that he did not carry it home himself, as he must have known that the Board would never send him out a second time. Well might a member of the Board, when writing to him some time after, say, "We never found fault with your acts, but we *do find fault with your writings!*" Had the Admiral placed his ships, and Gen. Baraguay D'Hilliers his troops, at the disposal of Gen. Jones, they must have been sacrificed to no purpose, and both France and England would have held the allied chiefs responsible. To have been expected to do so was an insult both to the General and the Admirals. The order to reconsider Gen. Niel's plan, though Gen. Niel himself had plainly pronounced against it, was perhaps an act of courtesy to an Ally, though with this act of courtesy the French Admiral would have nothing to do. To be called upon to reconsider Gen. Jones's and Gen. Niel's report, was a virtual order to both French and English Admirals to surrender their naval judgment to that of a military officer, who could have known nothing of Sweaborg beyond his limited examination in the *Lightning*. To rid himself of such groundless importunity, the French Admiral wisely adopted the step of sailing away with his fleet. Sir Charles Napier was obliged to stay to bear the brunt, and the storm soon burst.

CHAP. XIX.

ON the 12th of September (notwithstanding the previous orders of *the same date*), the Board of Admiralty ordered Sir Charles Napier, if he came to the decision that nothing further could be undertaken with a fair prospect of success, to send home the following steamers:—*Porcupine, Zephyr, Cuckoo, Pigmy, Lightning, Otter,* and *Wrangler;* the latter being the *one gun-boat* of which we have before spoken. It is difficult to account for orders so completely contradictory. On the 18th of September, the Admiral wrote to Admiral Berkeley, expressing his surprise that the British Government did not know of the French fleet being ordered home. Admiral Parseval had shown him a telegraphic message from the French Secretary of Legation in London, to the Minister, in which he used the words, " It is to be regretted that the fleets are to separate ;" so that some communication must have been made to the English Government.

The annexed is the substance of another telegraphic message, on the same subject, dated London, 1st September, from the French Minister in London : — " En réponse à l'avis du Gouvernement Français à celui de sa Majesté Britannique du rappel de cet escadre. Cette dépêche est de notre Chargé d'Affaires — interprète *de l'opinion du Cabinet Anglais.*" That the British Government did not know this, is simply, therefore, not fact. There is no escaping this conclusion, and therefore all expressions of ignorance on the part of the Government go for nothing.

Admiral Parseval had, moreover, shown him his orders to go home, and he had apprised Sir James Graham of this, adding that he should begin to send his own ships home, in obedience to the instructions of Sir James Graham of the 29th of August. Sir Charles told Admiral Berkeley that Admiral Parseval had declined attending the second council of war ; because having once recorded his opinion, he saw no occasion to repeat it. Admiral Parseval had intended to have gone himself up the Gulf of Finland again ; but seeing that, if the British squadron attempted anything, he should be bound to assist, he had declined this also; as if anything happened to the fleet, or a failure took place, he would be accused by his Government of acting against his own opinion. For the same reason, Admiral Parseval would not risk his ships, as suggested by Sir James Graham.

The rest of Sir Charles Napier's letter to Admiral Berkeley, must be given in his own words.

"I do not say that if Admiral Parseval had consented to risk his ships, I should have run headlong into such an operation, after the opinion I had given, and in which I was quite justified both by Sir James Graham's letters and the Admiralty's. But if I had seen a chance of success I might have tried it. At present, by the disappearance of the French fleet, and of two of my line-of-battle ships, it is out of the question. I rather feel offended at the Admiralty ordering me to hold a council of war, and before they received our answer ordering another to be held to consider the report of a French engineer officer, who knew nothing about naval affairs, and who tells us Sweaborg *could be laid in ashes in two hours*, when an English officer requires all the fleet, batteries, mortars, and 5000 men to destroy it in eight days.

"I did not require a council of war to make me do my duty, nor, after all the praises which have been heaped on me, *and after the warnings which I had received, to be goaded on to rashness.*

"I suppose I shall be right in sending home our fleet *gradually*, although you say we must *withdraw them all*, except a squadron to blockade the Gulf."

It will be fresh in the recollection of the reader that Admiral Berkeley had cautioned Sir Charles Napier against being "goaded on" against his own judgment. A clear proof that an intention to " goad him on " existed in the minds of some of the Admiralty authorities, and that Admiral Berkeley disapproved of it.

On the same date (September 18th), Sir Charles addressed a similar letter to Sir James Graham. From this we will make the following extract : —

> " I feel hurt that you and the Admiralty should have thought it necessary, on the report of two military engineers, to order me to hold a council of war, particularly as the English engineer *demanded more means* than I thought necessary to accomplish the object in view. As to the French engineer's plan, it is even of less value. Can any man suppose, that such works as those of Sweaborg could be destroyed in two hours ? What opinion must a man have of engineers, when one tells him 5000 men must be landed—batteries raised—mortars brought into play — the ships to lay alongside the walls—and if everything was favourable, it would require seven or eight days to destroy it, whilst the other says that in *two hours* you might knock down the sea-face of Sweaborg ? Were it like Bomarsund, no doubt it might be done, but the plans (furnished by the Admiralty) make it a great deal stronger. If you did knock down the walls, is the job done ? The entrance to the harbour is filled by a three-decked ship, and that ship is more formidable when sunk, than when afloat, as, in the former case she would entirely block up the harbour. When Sweaborg is attacked, *it ought to be attacked properly, or not at all,* and laid in ruins. If my advice is followed, next summer you may do it, and also capture the fleet. It is very well for people to talk big, and say what they will do ; but put a fleet of twenty sail of the line into their hands, and let the fleet be conducted amongst unknown rocks and shoals — *not yet surveyed,* and at this season of the year, when you cannot depend on the weather for two hours—when it would require two days to buoy it off ; and then' suppose a gale of wind

to come on, and suddenly, when you are at anchor, as we have already seen, what would become of your ships? Add to that, a fleet superior to your own, and ready to pounce upon you should you be disabled."

The best comment on this is, that in the second campaign, with every place thoroughly surveyed for him by Sir Charles Napier's fleet, and with means, all of which were wanting to the first fleet, Admiral Dundas could not reduce the fortifications of Sweaborg. So satisfied was he of their impregnability, that he never even assembled his fleet, for the purpose of attacking them. The bulk of his fleet was watching Cronstadt, whilst he was shelling the Sweaborg dockyard with his gun-boats and mortar-boats. Nay more, he found the greatest difficulty even in placing these; for he says in his despatch, " the intricate nature of the ground from rocks awash, and *reefs under water, rendered it difficult to select positions for the mortar-vessels.*" And that " the *Merlin,* under Capt. Sulivan, struck upon an unknown rock, on ground which he himself had repeatedly examined."

What then must have been the difficulty of placing a fleet in the first campaign, in the month of October, which is winter in the Baltic, where Admiral Dundas could hardly place gun-boats in the second campaign, though only at the beginning of August, when the transient summer of the Baltic was already passing away? Admiral Dundas says, that he was to have left Nargen on the 4th of August, but was delayed till the 6th, " *in consequence of bad weather.*" A few days of good weather fortunately intervened, otherwise, Admiral Dundas, with gun and mortar-boats

supplied to him, would not have been able to fire a
shot against Sweaborg; and, taking advantage of
favourable weather, he could only operate with his
gun and mortar-boats, but not with his fleet.

Sir James Graham replied to the Admiral on the
26th of September: —

" When I wrote to you on Saturday, I was not prepared
for the intelligence that Admiral Parseval had left you on the
19th, with all his sailing ships. You say that he had gone
to Kiel, but as far as the blockade of the Gulf of Finland is
concerned, he might as well be at Cherbourg. We shall be
disgraced if we allow a Russian ship of war to pass from the
Gulf into the open sea before winter sets in, and the ice bars
the passage. This matter has become a point of honour,
which affects our naval character and credit, and you must
hold on and not retreat to the southward, till you are sure
that the Russian fleet cannot move to the westward. You
have 12 sail of the line, and three or four large frigates, and
must hold your own to the last moment.

" I know that there is some risk in this, but Lord de
Saumarez, and Sir Byam Martin encountered it in circumstances more difficult; and if we run away from the Baltic
prematurely, leaving the sea open to the enemy, we shall be
covered with abuse. I am sure that you will not allow any
such evil to befal us.

" If the Russians think fit to attack you, because your
own force has been so much diminished, I have no doubt
that they will rue the day, and never return into harbour."

In this letter, Sir James Graham evades all mention
of Sweaborg. Nor need he have been alarmed that
the Admiral would give the Russians a chance of
escape into the North Sea, as when urged to send
his ships home, the Admiral had himself told Sir
James Graham, that enough must be left for the
blockade of the Gulf. However, to make sure of
this, the Admiral, a fortnight before the receipt of

Sir James Graham's letter, had left Ledsund for Nargen with his force, to join the squadron already there under Admiral Plumridge, Admiral Martin having gone to the Gulf of Bothnia.

Sir Charles Napier anchored at Nargen on the 21st of September, the strength of the squadron being now as follows : —

Ships of the Line.—*Duke of Wellington, St. Jean D'Acre, Majestic, James Watt, Royal George, Princess Royal, Nile, Cæsar, Cressy, Neptune, St. George, Monarch,* and *Prince Regent.*

Block-ships. —*Edinburgh, Hogue.* and *Blenheim.*

Frigates.—*Euryalus, Arrogant,* and *Impérieuse.*

Steamers.—*Magicienne, Desperate, Hecla, Cruiser, Basilisk, Driver,* and *Wrangler.*

We have here the Admiral returned with his reduced fleet to Nargen, at an advanced season, when he had been ordered to begin sending his ships home. It will be remembered that Admiral Berkeley, in the House of Commons, stated that Sir Charles Napier had "lost his nerve, was much disinclined to enter the Gulf of Finland, and was always inclined to leave it." Here we find Sir Charles re-entering the Gulf after the French fleet *had* left it, viz., on the 21st of September, from Ledsund. Now let us inquire into the state of Admiral Berkeley's nerves, when sitting by his fire at the Admiralty, more than *a month before*, viz., on the 15th of August, on which day Admiral Berkeley wrote to Sir Charles Napier as follows : —

H H

"I am seriously thinking when it will be time to get you *out of that infernal Gulf.* How long do you think it will be right to permit those big ships to remain? Autumn is getting on fast."

This was before the fall of Bomarsund. Whose nerves were strongest, those of Sir Charles Napier, who returned to that infernal Gulf, after being told to send his ships home, or those of Admiral Berkeley, who a month before wanted to get him out of it?

Again on the 19th of September, when Sir Charles was on his way to the dreaded Gulf, Admiral Berkeley again wrote:—

"Of course you can drop down to the southward to Wingo Sound, or any other harbour, *within the Baltic!* keeping up the blockade as far as it is possible with the steamers!"

But Wingo Sound happens not to be in the Baltic at all! so that, by way of keeping the Russians in check, Admiral Berkeley advises Sir Charles to leave the Baltic! Whose nerve was the greatest? that of Sir Charles Napier who remained, or that of Admiral Berkeley who told him to go? Was it not rather Admiral Berkeley who was disinclined for the ships to re-enter the Gulf of Finland, and Sir Charles Napier who was inclined to re-enter it? Yet Admiral Berkeley could not, when he made his statement, have forgotten writing these orders. It is singular that the gallant Admiral who had the management of the fleet did not know that Wingo Sound was not in the Baltic at all. Had Sir Charles Napier obeyed this demi-official order, would he have been excused because it was conveyed in a " private letter ? "

Bad weather had now set in, in the Gulf of Finland, the ships losing anchors continually. The blockade of the Gulf was nevertheless strictly kept up ; and ships were kept constantly before Sweaborg, the Russians showing no inclination to leave their shelter, even to attack the small force hovering in the vicinity of their harbour — the main body of the squadron being kept at Nargen.

An episode here occurred which must be noticed. On the 17th of September, General Jones wrote a letter to the Admiral, demanding to know whether it was his " intention to undertake any further operations against the enemy, during the present year." As the credentials of General Jones, on his coming out, were to the effect that he was to " assist the Admiral in his communications with the French military authorities," this assumption of a power to ask the Admiral's intentions as to his future operations will no doubt be duly estimated, both by military and naval authorities. When the French army and fleet had gone, even by the tenor of General Jones's instructions, his occupation was gone too, and he was clearly going beyond his province in asking such a thing.

But General Jones went farther. He asked the Admiral to give him a steamer to go to Cronstadt, in order that he might form an opinion about the place. To use General Jones's words, as contained in his requisition, " I need not add that it appears to me very important that I should do so, as no doubt the Government, as well as yourself, will be anxious to have the latest possible information as to the state of the works, before the season closes. It is now, I believe, upwards of *three months* since you visited that part of the Baltic," &c.

If General Jones had known anything of the operations of the fleet, he would have known that Cronstadt had been watched as well as Sweaborg; and that on the fourth of August, Capt. Watson had visited the place by orders of Admiral Martin. As it was no part of the Admiral's business to account to General Jones for the operations of the fleet, it is quite possible that General Jones did not know this; nor did it at all affect the mission upon which he had been sent that he should have known it.

The Admiral replied, that it was not his intention to undertake any further operations against the enemy, and, as he had no orders to that effect, he did not see the necessity of General Jones's visiting Cronstadt. It would be necessary to send a considerable force of steamers with him, and it would be very expensive to get together coals for the purpose.

General Jones then went to England, and wrote a letter to the Duke of Newcastle, enclosing Sir Charles Napier's refusal to send him to Cronstadt. The Duke wrote to the Admiralty, expressing his regret that the Admiral had not enabled General Jones to make a reconnaissance of Cronstadt! thus confirming the course which General Jones had pursued, in considering himself entitled to demand it against the Admiral's judgment, and at a moment when, with his diminished force, every steamer was an object of paramount importance to the fleet, even if the enemy remained inactive ; as the greatest vigilance had to be exercised in the frequent gales which occurred. To send away a squadron of steamers, then, at this season, for the purpose of inspecting Cronstadt, was an operation of which none but a military officer or a minister of war would have dreamed — even had General Jones the right to demand it.

On the 25th of September, the Admiral sent to the Board of Admiralty the following report of his proceedings, since leaving Ledsund : —

" *Duke of Wellington*, Nargen,
25th of September, 1854.

" Sir,

" I arrived here on the 21st inst. We had bad weather in coming up the Gulf. I do not much like the anchorage, as it is exposed to the winds from N. to N. E., and I think it is high time the fleet should leave the Gulf of Finland.

" On the 22nd I reconnoitred Revel, which is very strong ; and, even if there was an object, an attack from the sea I look upon as very dangerous.

" On the west of the town there is a large curved battery, divided into four by flanking towers, mounting 150 guns towards the sea. Immediately under the Domberg, is another battery of 38 guns on one tier. Above this battery is another of 5 guns. Over this again, there is a battery of 10 guns for pointing seaward.

" On the eastern side of the town, between it and the mole-head, there is a strong battery mounting 20 guns.

" The mole has two entrances composed of pile-work, filled in at the back with stones, on which a parapet wall appears to have been built, pierced with embrasures curved, and is flanked with huge circular towers, the whole mounting 66 guns seaward.

" On the bastion part of the bay—to flank ships standing in — there are 5 earthen batteries, mounting 52 guns, and another in progress. Besides which, there is a mortar battery. I enclose a sketch by Lieut Cowell, R. E.

" On the following day, I proceeded to reconnoitre Sweaborg in the *Driver*, piloted by Capt. Sulivan, through an intricate passage of sunken rocks, little more than a quarter of a mile wide, and stopped abreast of Grohara Island, about two miles south of Gustav's Sward.

" The sunken rocks are shown in the small Russian chart only. From this position, the fortress appears like batteries heaped one on the other, pointing towards the sea.

" On the southern face of Gustav's Sward and Vargon 77 guns cover the approach of a fleet from the southward, besides 29 guns on three batteries at Bak Holmen. The three-decker lies on the entrance of the passage between Bak Holmen and Gustav's Sward, and her broadside also covers the approach from the south.

" The best reconnaissance was made by Capt. Sulivan, when twice in with a flag of truce, he being at anchor for seven hours, and having leisure well to examine the southern part of the fortress.

" Their Lordships will observe that we could not get a view of the western defences, and I think Gen. Niel, having only seen the western part of the fortifications for a short time and at a greater distance, is rather hasty in giving an opinion that 8 or 10 sail of the line would lay it in ruins in two hours.

" There was not time to find a passage through the rocks to enable us to see the western face, at the north end of which a line-of-battle ship was placed to cover the entrance by Langhorn, and another at hand to support her.

" In my former report I agreed with Capt. Washington that the fleet could lie in Miolo Roads in the summer. That is now more difficult, as batteries have been built on the south points of Sandhamm Island; but they could be destroyed.

" *If Sweaborg was attacked by a fleet alone,* they would approach from the south in one line, raked by 160 guns. One or two of the leading ships would anchor, and occupy the batteries at Bak Holmen. The next would pass on, fire a broadside into the three-decker and anchor clear of her broadside, against the S.W. angle of Gustav's Sward; she would be followed by the next, pouring a broadside into the three-decker, and anchor ahead of her leader, and so on in succession, as close as the ships could lie. By this time the three-decker would probably be sunk, and the whole western face of Sweaborg engaged.

" A small squadron would be required to anchor south of Langhorn. They would have to contend against it, and two or more line-of-battle ships, and what guns were in Helsingfors.

" All the passages should be buoyed, and small steamers stationed in the narrowest and most dangerous channels. The large steamers should be under weigh in various directions, to assist ships in difficulties, and a reserve squadron ready to take the place of disabled ships.

" *Whether this attack would succeed or not, it is impossible to say*; but we must calculate on ships being set on fire by red-hot shot and shells, of which the Russians would have abundance. Whether successful or not, it is evident *that our ships would be in no condition to meet the Russian fleet afterwards ; and if the attack was made at this season of the year, when you cannot depend upon the weather for two hours, I do not know how many would be lost.*

" I beg their Lordships will not suppose for a moment that Sweaborg cannot be attacked. I think it can; *but it must be with caution and judgment.*

" I have little to add to the report I made to Sir James Graham, a copy of which I sent to the Admiralty. Since that report it has become easier. We have now Lancaster guns ; every ship in the fleet should be furnished with them. *Thirteen-inch mortars should be placed on Laghara Island and Lango Rocks, and gun-boats carrying Lancaster guns should be added to the fleet.* Those ships should be placed at different points, at a proper distance from the fortifications, *well furnished with shot, shells, and rockets*, and a bombardment commenced, and continued till the wooden buildings, of which there are many, were on fire, and an evident impression made on the fortress. The ships should then close in and finish the work. How long this would take I cannot say, but I am quite certain the fortress would be laid in ruins, and most probably an entrance opened to the ships. I have said nothing about troops, but there is no doubt they could be most usefully employed."

In this additional report, the Admiral alludes to his former report of July 18th, addressed to Sir James Graham, for the sake of secrecy. We will again recapitulate it : —

" The only successful manner of attacking Sweaborg that I can see, after the most mature consideration, assisted by Admiral Chads, who is a practical man, and knows more about gunnery than any man in the service, is by *fitting out a great number of gun-boats*, carrying one gun with a long range, and placing them west of Sweaborg, and south of Helsingfors. Every shell from them would tell somewhere, and perhaps not *five per cent.* from the enemy would take effect. Back these by the fleet, to relieve the men, and in the course of the summer Sweaborg would be reduced to ashes, and Helsingfors also, if it was thought proper; and I don't see why we are to be meally-mouthed in time of war. The ships you will see could not be destroyed, because they could move out of the way.

" I was at the siege of Martinique many years ago. We could not batter Port Bourbon, as it lay higher than the ground around it. But fifty mortars plunging their shells into it made it surrender; and whether mortars are placed on shore or in gun-boats, is quite immaterial. Indeed, the latter have the advantage, for when their shells begin to tell and our blood begins to warm, the ships would move up to the batteries, and close quarters would finish what the mortar-boats began.

" I sent you home, I think, copies of all the plans I have, and if you will lay them before the engineer and artillery officers, I will be bound for it they will agree with me that this is the only way to destroy Sweaborg, without an army superior to the Emperor of Russia's, which we are not likely to bring into the field. *It is too late this year ; but be prepared next, now we know the anchorage, and begin early.*

" I forgot to say that the islands within range may all be put in requisition for 13-*inch mortars.* The expense would be very great, no doubt ; but, if we are to bring the war to a conclusion, *expense must not be thought about.*"

Here, on July 18th, the Admiral asks for gun-boats and 13-inch mortars, none of which were supplied ! Even then he tells the Board that " *it is too late this year* ; " but " *begin early next year.*" No man of ordinary intelligence can read this as referring to the present year. Much less could he construe the report on Sweaborg of the 25th of September as referring to the present year ; for not only was the French fleet and army gone, but the Admiralty itself had long before ordered the ships home ! and some had sailed in obedience to this order ; though the Admiral himself, to prevent the possibility of the Russians getting out, had returned to what Admiral Berkeley had graphically termed the "infernal Gulf" of Finland.

When the report of September 25th reached the Admiralty, it was eagerly seized on by the Board, as an intimation that the Admiral could *at once* attack Sweaborg ; though, from the expressions in his letter, it was clear that he only intended it as an appendage to his former report of July 18th. He indeed refers them in words to his former report ; says, " *if* Sweaborg was attacked by a fleet alone," " the fleet could lay in Miolo Roads *in summer.*" " There was not time to find a passage through the rocks." " Whether this attack would succeed or not, it is impossible to say." " It must be done with caution and judgment," &c., &c. Then follows the caution and judgment spoken of, and the first element of this was, not to attack Sweaborg without the means to ensure success. The Admiral expressly tells the Board that " 13-*inch mortars* " must be placed on Laghara Island, Lango Rocks, and elsewhere. He *had not a mortar of any description in his fleet!* He would require " gun-boats and Lancaster guns to every ship." He had only one gun-boat, the *Wrangler*, and one Lancaster gun, the Board of Admiralty telling him that they could not get any more ready for him. The ships must be well furnished with " shot, shells, and *rockets*." The quantity of shot and shell he had was only eighty rounds of shot per gun, and *not a rocket had ever been supplied to him!* To imagine then that he intended to attack Sweaborg with a fleet now reduced to a handful of ships, those not half supplied with ammunition, and at this boisterous season of the year, was a wilful perversion of his letter to a meaning which it was never intended to bear, nor could be made to bear, except by men who, in retaliation for his plain-spoken letters, were determined, if possible, to ruin his reputation, in order to cover their own deficiencies, which the Admiral had so plainly pointed out.

It is necessary to pay attention to this point, as we shall shortly see the shameful use which was made of this letter. In order that the reader may fully comprehend the matter, both as regards the practicability of an attack on Sweaborg with the fleet at the command of Sir Charles Napier at this season of the year, and also of the real opinion of the Admiralty as to the desirableness of such attack, we will just glance at the force of the fleet in the Baltic, in September, 1854, and that of Admiral Dundas, in August, 1855, when Admiral Dundas stated that "no attack was contemplated against the fortifications of Sweaborg;" he having deemed himself competent to shell the dockyard and town with his gun-boats and mortar-boats only, not even assembling his fleet for the purpose of attacking the place.

The whole force under the command of Sir Charles Napier at Nargen, on the date of the above letter, was thirteen ships of the line, three block-ships, four frigates, twenty steamers, amounting, with a few others, to some forty ships. The force of the combined fleet in the Gulf of Finland, under Admirals Dundas and Penaud, when he stated that "no attack was contemplated on the fortifications of Sweaborg," was ten English screw-ships of the line, three French ships of the line, nine block-ships or third-rates, three fourth-rates, two fifth-rates, nine sixth-rates, four French corvettes, five screw sloops, five paddle sloops, seven paddle steamers, twenty-one screw gun-boats, sixteen mortar-boats, eight French gun-boats, five French mortar-boats, the *Volage* powder depôt, and *Belleisle* hospital ship; total one hundred and nine vessels, besides mortars on the islands. For not attacking the fortifications of Sweaborg, with a hundred and nine ships at his command, in the month of August, Admiral Dundas received the thanks of the Admiralty. For not attacking the fortifications of Sweaborg with thirty-one ships, and at the beginning of winter, Sir Charles Napier was bitterly censured by the Admiralty, and finally dismissed from his command. Yet Admiral Dundas, no doubt, judged rightly ; at any rate his judgment was not called in question by the Admiralty. Sir Charles Napier was hunted down by the Admiralty, because, with only a quarter of the force of Admiral Dundas, he did not accomplish what Admiral Dundas declined to undertake. But more of this hereafter in its place.

Independently of the intrinsic evidence that the preceding letter was intended only as an appendage to his former report of July 18th, is coupled the fact that on the very same day, the 25th of September, the Admiral instructed Admiral Martin to return home. In replying to this order on the 9th of October, Admiral Martin remarked that, " in ten days or a fortnight, ships will no longer be able to cruise on these dangerous coasts with prudence or advantage." It was at this period that the Board of Admiralty was urging on Sir Charles Napier to attack Sweaborg! and nearly two months later in the season than Admiral Dundas in the following year had deemed it right to send his gun-boats home. This could not have arisen from ignorance on the part of the Board of Admiralty, for, with the exception of the First Lord and the Junior Lord, all these are naval men, who knew better, or should have known better. What such treatment of Sir Charles Napier did arise from will unfold itself as we proceed.

So far from dreaming of attacking Sweaborg at that season of the year, and with his diminished force, the Admiral wrote to Lord Palmerston on the following day (September 26th) that he was going to move to the south, as the Gulf was no longer safe. The Admiral's words to Lord Palmerston were : " The weather has been so bad the last month, that even had the French fleet and army been here, no operation was practicable. I closely reconnoitred Sweaborg the other day, and nearly got on shore, which would have led probably to my passing the winter at St. Petersburg ; the navigation amongst these islands is very dangerous. You will probably see my report on Sweaborg. I am going to move to the south, as the Gulf is no longer safe."

On the 26th, the Admiral also wrote to Lord Loftus at Berlin : " There is no chance of any further operations here ; all the French troops are gone, and I am sending away my sailing three-deckers and small steamers. This is not the weather for large ships to be cruising in these seas. Our frigates off Helsingfors have had a sad time of it. It is not safe to keep them here much longer."

On the same day, the Admiral wrote to the Duke of Newcastle: " Your Grace will see my opinion about Sweaborg, we had a good look at it, and were very nearly ashore. I have ordered the sailing ships to Kiel, as I do not think them safe here, and I shall proceed there shortly myself, leaving a strong squadron of steamers at the entrance of the Gulf, the blockade of Sweaborg being impossible any longer. The officers who have been there have not had their clothes off for weeks, and deserve the greatest credit."

On the same day the Board of Admiralty wrote to Sir Charles : " The intelligence of Admiral Parseval having left you *has taken us by surprise.* The British Ambassador was informed in Paris on Saturday last by the French Minister of Marine that a letter dated the 13th instant had been received by the French Government from Admiral Parseval, from which it was quite clear that he intended remaining with the greater part of his fleet and all his steamers as long as the British force remained."

This is very probable. We have already said that Admiral Parseval intended to remain to the last; but on the interference of the Admiralty, in ordering him to reconsider his opinions on the engineer officers' plans, and being goaded by Sir James Graham to risk four of his ships with four British ones, Admiral Parseval very wisely did not lose a moment in re· voking his determination to remain, and in putting his fleet out of the reach of further importunity, by sailing away the very day afterwards. The Admiralty had driven him out of the Baltic, and now were surprised that he had gone! Admiral Parseval never did a more prudent thing in the whole course of his career ; and it would have been well if Sir Charles Napier had followed his example.

Were not this order of Sir James Graham to " *risk* four British ships if Admiral Parseval would *risk* four of his " now lying before us, we should hesitate in giving publicity to it. There is something so revolting in an order consigning eight sail of the line and 7000 men to certain destruction, that it is difficult to believe such an order could have emanated from a Lord of the Admiralty. It is no wonder that Admiral Parseval lost not a moment in getting his ships beyond the reach of such influence. It redounds highly to the honour and humanity of Sir Charles Napier that his " moral courage," which had been so highly lauded, alone prevented such a cruel catastrophe. It was not the first hint of the kind he had received. When complaining of the bad state of some of his ships, he had been told on another occasion by Admiral Berkeley to " put them in the front, they would serve to be knocked to pieces in place of better ships."

But the Admiralty, when thus expressing its surprise at the departure of the French fleet, could not but have known that on the 30th of August, Admiral Parseval had received orders from the French Government to return with his fleet to Cherbourg. When he had intended to remain, it was that he would not leave Sir Charles Napier by himself, though contrary to the orders of his Government. It was only when his indignation was roused by the uncalled-for interference of the Board of Admiralty that he saw it was no longer safe for him to remain. That they were determined on goading on Sir Charles Napier to some desperate act he saw not the smallest reason to doubt; and to sail away at once was the only way to keep himself from being dragged into the same mess.

The remainder of the Admiralty despatch was occupied by cautions that the Russian fleet might get out; though of this there was not the smallest danger. No Russian fleet would have ventured out with the weather which now prevailed, even in their own waters.

These Admiralty precautions are so curious, that our narrative would be incomplete without them.

"It appears that you are now left alone in the upper part of the Baltic, no French ships of war being present, with the exception of four or five steamers. We cannot too strongly impress on your mind the imperative duty of keeping the Russian fleet closely confined within the Gulf. They must on no account be permitted to appear outside on the coast of Prussia or of Sweden, or in any part of the Baltic. They must be blockaded until they are confined by ice to their harbours.

"It is an object of primary importance that a triumph on the part of the Russians, such as the appearance of their fleet in the open sea, should be prevented by you, and by the fleet under your command.

"We have already stated, in our former orders, that when by ice and stress of weather you are compelled to withdraw to the southward, it will be still necessary for you to distribute your steam force, so as closely to watch both the Belt and the Sound.

"No Russian ship of war must be allowed to enter the North Sea, by either passage; and the power which steam gives you, and which the Russians do not possess, fully justifies us in the belief, that this expectation will not be disappointed.

"We have approved your orders for sending home the *Cumberland* and *Ajax*, but the withdrawal of the French fleet renders any further immediate diminution of the strength of your line-of-battle ships inexpedient; and the sailing ships and even the three-deckers must be detained till the last moment consistent with their safety.

"An autumn cruise for the Russian fleet in the Baltic when the British fleet had abandoned it, would bring dishonour on our arms. At all hazards, so great an evil must be averted; and you will remember that in former wars, when the power of steam was unknown, a squadron of British line-of-battle ships has maintained the blockade in the Baltic till the end of November."

These querulous fears about the Russians getting out are, to say the least, puerile. The Admiral had not suffered a single Russian ship to pass him, nor was he likely to do so. In every letter he had written about the withdrawal of the ships he had notified the preparations which would be made to keep the Russians in the Gulf. He would only have been too glad had they attempted to come out, and had used not a few stratagems to induce them so to do. It was even bad policy to shut them up in the Gulf of Finland, as was constantly reiterated to him; the true policy would have been to entice them out, if possible, and then secure them. The true secret of the Admiralty fears was the defenceless state of the English coasts from the low state to which the navy had fallen.

On the 26th of September, Sir Charles apprised the Admiralty that, considering it unsafe for the sailing squadron to remain any longer, he had directed Admiral Plumridge to proceed to Kiel with the *Neptune, Prince Regent, Royal George, Monarch,* with the steamers *Hecla* and *Driver,* and the French steamers *La Place* and *Phlégéton.* It must be observed that on taking this step, the Admiral had not got the Board's letter, which was written in London on the same day with his own despatch from Nargen.

*1 1

Admiral Plumridge's squadron left for Kiel on the 27th of September, after a heavy gale which lasted for three days.

The Admiral apprised the Board that he felt it his duty to mark the great exertions made by Capt. Watson, and the officers under his orders, in maintaining the blockade of Sweaborg, and he begged to mention them all to their Lordships as deserving the warmest thanks. They were Capt. Watson, C.B., of the *Impérieuse*, Capt. Ramsay, *Euryalus*, Capt. Yelverton, *Arrogant*, Capt. Fisher, *Magicienne*, Capt. D'Eyncourt, *Desperate*, Capt. Willcox, *Dragon*, and Commander Wodehouse, *Rosamond*.

It may not be amiss here to notice more particularly the contradictory orders which were from time to time sent to Sir C. Napier. Admiral Berkeley on the 15th of August, even before Bomarsund was taken, asked "*when it was time to get those big ships out of that infernal Gulf*." Sir J. Graham, on the 29th of August, instructed him to adopt measures for withdrawing the fleet from the Baltic. On the 5th of September, Admiral Berkeley "did not know what to do about recalling the fleet." On the 12th of September, Admiral Berkeley says, "I don't see how we are to withdraw any, till we withdraw the whole of the ships of the line;" and on the same date, Sir James Graham says, "If, unhappily, nothing more can be done, it is wise to send home at once the smallest and least effective of the steamers, and the least weatherly of the large ships." On the 19th of September, the day Sir Charles sailed to return to the Gulf of Finland, Admiral

Berkeley told him he might drop down to the southward to Wingo Sound, or some other port in the Baltic — Admiral Berkeley appeared not to know that Wingo Sound was *in the Cattegat*, and not in the Baltic at all.

On the 22nd of September, Sir James Graham repeated his orders of the 29th of August. On the 26th of September, came two letters from the Board of Admiralty telling the Admiral that they " approved of his sending home the *Cumberland* and *Ajax*, but the sailing ships, and even the three-deckers, must be detained till the last moment consistent with their safety." The second letter, of the 26th of September, says : " My Lords desire to call your attention to the fact that they had not sanctioned the return of the sailing ships," — notwithstanding that both Sir J. Graham and Admiral Berkeley had ordered them home. These contradictory orders did not arrive till the ships had sailed in obedience to the preceding orders, as will be narrated in the following chapter.

Let the reader compare this jumble of contradictory orders,—and we could cite many more,—and he will comprehend the mode in which orders of the utmost moment are issued from the Board of Admiralty. We shall be surprised, if he be not at the same time of opinion, that it is scarcely less difficult for an admiral to encounter a Board of Admiralty than to encounter an enemy.

CHAP. XX.

TRANSACTIONS AND CORRESPONDENCE PREVIOUS TO THE FLEET RETURNING TO KIEL.

ORDERS OF THE ADMIRALTY ANTICIPATED. — SIR CHARLES ON THE ADMI-
RALTY PRECAUTIONS. — NECESSITY TO QUOTE PUBLIC DOCUMENTS. —
CONTRADICTORY ORDERS OF THE ADMIRALTY, AND LAME EXPLANATION
OF THE FIRST LORD. — HIS ANXIETY FOR AN ATTACK ON SWEABORG. —
HIS PECULIAR TALENT. — HIS MISREPRESENTATIONS. — PERVERSION OF
REPORTS. — DIFFERENCE BETWEEN ORAL AND WRITTEN SOPHISTRY. —
THE "FALL OF SEBASTOPOL" HOAX. — ITS INFLUENCE ON ADMIRALTY
ORDERS AND EXPECTATIONS. — SWEABORG TO BE TAKEN IN OCTOBER.
— THE ADMIRAL TO CHOOSE HIS OWN DAY. — FOLLY OF THE ORDER,
WITH A REDUCED SQUADRON AND NO TROOPS. — EXTRACTS FROM
ADMIRAL BERKELEY'S LETTERS. — REMARKS ON HIS DESPATCH OF OCT.
4TH. — CLUMSY PERVERSION OF SIR C. NAPIER'S PLANS OF ATTACK.—
HIS "CAUTION AND JUDGMENT." — SWEABORG NOT INTENDED TO BE
ATTACKED. — THE ADMIRAL'S WARINESS. — OPINION OF THE RUSSIANS.
—DUNDAS'S ATTACK ; WHY DESISTED FROM : NAPIER'S, WHY OR-
DERED. — WHY AFTERWARDS FORBIDDEN. — EFFECTS OF THE CALUMNIES
ON SIR CHARLES. — HIS REASONS FOR NOT ATTACKING SWEABORG. —
OFFERS TO RESIGN HIS COMMAND. — HEAVY GALES ENDANGER THE
SHIPS. — "FINE WEATHER" FOR AN ATTACK. — HISTORICAL PRECE-
DENTS. — ADMIRAL PLUMRIDGE ORDERED HOME. — "JUSTICE IN THE
LONG RUN."

ON the 2nd of October, Sir Charles apprised the Admiralty that he had obeyed their orders, with respect to the *Neptune* and *St. George*, which ships, together with the *Prince Regent* and *Monarch*, as well as several steamers, had gone to Kiel. Their Lordships directed the blockade of the Russian ports as long as it was safe. If by the Baltic their Lordships meant the Gulf of Finland, the Admiral did not consider the anchorage safe even now, and so he had informed their Lordships. The Admiralty had told him that it was not their intention to fetter his judgment as to anchorage, and that for the safety of the ships he was, as autumn advanced, gradually to withdraw to the southward, and wait the time they might think fit to recal him from the Baltic. Kiel or the Belt were the only places of safety, but he should delay going there as long as he could maintain himself in the Gulf of Finland.

On the following day the Admiral again wrote to the Board : —

"I cannot conceive that a Russian fleet will leave the Baltic at this season ; as for cruising, either on the coast of Sweden or Prussia, I look upon as impossible, or indeed in any other part of the Baltic ; but I will watch the enemy as long as it can be done with safety to the fleet, and shall take care that no Russian ships will get into the North Sea.

"Their Lordships desire me to remember that in former wars, when steam was not known, a squadron of British line-of-battle ships maintained the blockade in the Baltic till the end of November. But there is a great difference *between the Baltic and the Gulf of Finland.* No ships remained in the Gulf after the 1st of October, and the Baltic was blockaded from the Swedish port of Carlscrona—which is interdicted to us — and from the Belt. The journals of Sir James Saumarez are now before me.

"Their Lordships, in their letter of the 23rd of September, do not intend to fetter my judgment as to the port or anchorage I may decide best for the service I am on and for the safety of the ships ; but in their letter of the 26th, their Lordships *throw aside the safety of the ships,* and, *at all hazards,* I am to prevent the Russian fleet coming into the Baltic, because it will bring disgrace on our arms. I do not know where the fleet will be safe, certainly not here with a N. E. wind, nor at Baro Sound with a S. W. wind. They may show themselves out of Sweaborg a few hours, but certainly not to cruise; and I do not see how such a proceeding would bring disgrace on our arms. Their Lordships may rely upon my doing my utmost to comply with their orders, *short of hazarding the fleet.*

" I have now been here twelve days, and it has blown a gale of wind from S. S. E. to N. N. W., with the exception of two days. How we should have fared had the wind been from N. to N. E. I don't know ; but it is certainly far from agreeable to have Revel right astern in a heavy gale of wind depending upon our chains; for should the gale be heavy on a dark night, we could not depend upon our screws taking us to sea; and, in the event of parting the cables, we must go on shore. That is the opinion of many here."

We have hitherto refrained from giving more of public documents and instructions than was absolutely necessary for the comprehension of our narrative, which, by withholding many of importance, has materially suffered. But the extraordinary climax of a campaign in which Sir Charles Napier had been loaded with praises from all parties without exception, up to the present time, and the still more extraordinary abuse which followed those praises from the very men who had so lavishly bestowed them, renders it necessary to give documents more *in extenso*, lest we should be accused of garbling them. The praise we have not inserted to anything like the extent to which it was bestowed, but the abuse forms so admirable an answer to itself, that we will let it speak for itself; and therefore the remaining portion of this history will be much better written by the Admiralty authorities than ourselves.

We have before stated that, on the 26th of September, Sir James Graham, waiving all his previous orders and those of the Admiralty, to send the ships home or to Kiel, had sent an order to hold on to the last moment, even with the sailing three-deckers. Before this contradictory order arrived, the sailing ships had gone to Kiel, in obedience to the orders received. Sir Charles now, on the 2nd of October, addressed Sir James Graham as follows: —

" If I have done wrong in sending the sailing ships to Kiel, I have *been led into it by your letter of the 29th of August.* You say I should begin sending home without much delay the sailing three-deckers, the least weatherly of the sailing line-of-battle ships, and the worst of the blockships. ' This will do for a beginning, and by degrees you must withdraw to the southward, leaving the Gulf of Bothnia open and watching only the Gulf of Finland,' &c.

" Again, in your letter of the 12th of September, you say: ' We shall send you no positive orders respecting the withdrawal of the fleet in the Baltic, which must be effected at all events *gradually,* till we know what is the intention of the French as to remaining there,' &c. The French Admiral showed me his orders dated the 30th of August, and a telegraphic despatch of the 1st of September, showing that the English Government *were aware* of their intention ; so that, in point of fact, they not only got orders to go home, but *had actually sailed,* before I sent our ships to Kiel. You may then judge of my surprise when you tell me you only knew of their withdrawal *on the 25th of September.*

" I have not the least idea that the Russians will move from their ports at this season of the year. They are much too wise to do anything of the sort ; and as for their finding their way into the North Sea, I look upon that as impossible. If they did contemplate anything of the sort, a squadron in the Belt and one at Elsinore would watch them much better than in the Gulf of Finland, which is very dangerous.

" I have the journals of the ships, in 1808 and 1809, and I find Sir James Saumarez withdrew from the Gulf of Finland before the beginning of October. *But there is a great differ-*

ence between the Gulf of Finland and the Baltic, and you may depend I will not leave the Baltic as long as is prudent. But as to the Gulf of Finland, I must use my own discretion; and, when I do leave, I shall keep up a good steam squadron off the entrance of the Gulf, as long as it can be done with safety to the ships.

" We have had heavy gales ever since I came here, and I have been obliged to withdraw the ships from off Helsingfors. It is wonderful how they have been able to remain there so long. The Captains deserve the greatest praise. Such a blockade as they have kept has never been done before.

" I am not at all apprehensive of the Russians attacking me. Should they come in my way with any force, they can send to sea, I dare say I can manage them."

This letter was not to be evaded. The next best thing was to explain it away, if possible; but Sir James Graham appears to shine less in written than in personal debate, and the following lame explanation was on the 17th of October sent in reply : —

" You refer to my letters at the end of August as contemplating then the early termination of active operations in the Baltic for this year. I was not prepared even at that time for the *immediate departure* of the French army after the capture of Bomarsund, and I pointed out to you Abo, Sweaborg, and Revel, as points which, with *military aid,* were open to attack. Much less was I prepared for the withdrawal of the French squadron from the *combined naval operations* almost simultaneously with the departure of the army so soon as Bomarsund had been destroyed. These decisions were taken on the spot, I believe with your consent, but without any reference to the English Government.

" But in August we had not seen the report of Gen. Jones on Sweaborg, which you forwarded to us from Ledsund on the 29th of August, and which was in your hands before either the French army or the French fleet had left the Aland Islands. That report is entitled to respect. It made a great impression here, and raised a strong presumption that, with *the aid of the military force then present with the fleet,* in seven or eight days the works at Sweaborg might be destroyed, and that the month of September afforded ample time for the operation.

"On the 5th of September you sent us the observations of Gen. Baraguay D'Hilliers and of Gen. Niel on the report of Gen. Jones.

"Gen. Baraguay D'Hilliers says expressly, after having reconnoitred Sweaborg himself, together with Gen. Niel, ' We partake of the opinion of Gen. Jones. Sweaborg may be attacked and taken by the fleets, if they think fit to make on that fortress a serious attack.'

"Gen. Niel went further, and said that without any military co-operation, eight or ten sail of the line could lay the works in ruins in two hours, by a bombardment near at hand on the sea front, where the works are weakest, and *he intimated very distinctly an opinion that the attack ought to be made.* In the face of these reports, and within a week after receiving them, the intelligence that the French army and the French fleet had left you without a shot being fired except at Bomarsund, *was both a surprise and disappointment.*

"Then came your own second reconnaissance of Sweaborg, and a plan of naval attack which you considered practicable. We were anxious, if the French and English forces could be *recruited,* that it should have been tried *even this year,* before the immense fleet which had been assembled retreated from the Baltic; but our own sailing ships having gone to Kiel, and the French squadron being on its way home, the opportunity was lost, and nothing now remains to be done but gradually to withdraw the line-of-battle ships, and to await the moment when ice shall enclose the Russian fleet within the Gulf of Finland for the winter."

When thus admitting that nothing further is to be done, now that the French army and fleet are gone, Sir James urges Sir Charles Napier, by an unmistakable *innuendo,* to try his hand on Sweaborg alone, even though his sailing ships, and no small number of steamers were gone too, and though the ships could no longer remain at their anchorage in the Gulf of Finland, from stress of weather.

"No doubt, at the time of the equinox, there are heavy gales of wind in the Baltic. It is a narrow sea, and there is danger to large ships even when at anchor. But war is not conducted without risks and dangers, and prudence consists in weighing them, and firmness in encountering them ; and nothing great by sea or land can be achieved without considerable peril, as your own experience and example have demonstrated."

There is no mistaking the meaning of the latter paragraph, which extended further than "achieving" a blockade. Had Sir Charles Napier been the rash commander represented, such a spur would have gone far to make him "run his head against the stone walls of Sweaborg,"—against which Sir James Graham had, throughout the previous portion of the campaign, so emphatically cautioned him.

As the preceding letter exhibits the peculiar talent of Sir James Graham in a light much clearer than any other of his epistolary productions which have come before us, it is necessary that this light should be rendered equally clear to the reader ; and with this object in view we must search a little closer into its assumptions.

Sir James assumes that the French Admiral went away with "the consent" of Sir Charles Napier. The French Admiral did no such thing. He sailed away, at less than a day's warning, from Admiralty interference with him, merely apprising Sir Charles

Napier that he was going. So far from going with the consent of Sir Charles, the latter, in his farewell letter, " *regretted* " he was going, and asked him to leave him the *Austerlitz* screw line-of-battle ship, which was declined.

Sir James Graham says, that General Baraguay D'Hilliers expressly states that, he and General Niel partake of the opinion of General Jones, that " Sweaborg may be attacked and taken by the fleets if they think fit," &c. Whereas General Jones never said anything of the kind, but that *with* 5000 *of General Baraguay D'Hilliers' army, it might be attacked and taken:* but General Baraguay D'Hilliers very wisely declined letting General Jones have his troops " at that season of the year ; " though the then season of the year was but the middle of August. The plan of attack by General Jones was purely a military one, with the fleet as an adjunct only. Sir James Graham says, and on Baraguay D'Hilliers' opinion, that it was purely a naval one, " *by the fleets,*" without noticing a word about the troops, which the French General expressly declined to lend for the purpose.

Sir James Graham adduces the opinion of General Niel that, " in two hours, the fleets alone would lay Sweaborg in ruins." But he takes no notice of the twice repeated caution of General Niel, that " *such an enterprise had never before been attempted — that it was rash (hardie), and that he could not advise it.*"

Sir James Graham says that he recommended Abo to be attacked amongst other places, but by *military aid only.* He has not the candour to state, *as he well knew*, that Sir Charles Napier had caused Abo to be reconnoitred by Capt. Scott, and had proposed the attack to his French colleagues, who had declined it; and fortunately so, considering the weather which had set in. Sir James Graham insinuates, that from the second reconnaissance of Sweaborg by Sir Charles Napier, he "considered an attack practicable," *i. e.*, at a time when he had sent a part of his diminished fleet and two of his admirals away, when his ships in the Gulf of Finland would scarcely hold at their anchors. Yet no word in Sir Charles Napier's report of his second reconnaissance, bears any such construction; or if it did, it would immediately cease to bear such construction by his requisition for "13-*inch mortars, gun-boats, rockets*," &c., none of which had ever been supplied to him, and on which *alone* he bases his attack *in the following summer*. Is not this a most shameful misconstruction of an Admiral's report.

Relying but little even upon these devices, Sir James Graham is "*anxious that the French and English forces should be reunited!*" when the French army must have been at or near Cherbourg, and the French Admiral, then at Kiel, would take good care to keep for the future out of the way of the British Admiralty.

We have thus seen how all the explanatory specialities of this memorable letter are mere assumptions, without foundation in facts. Nay, more; had the suppressed portion of facts been adduced by Sir James

Graham, they would have shown the exact contrary of what he assumes.

It is marvellous how such sophistry disappears at the point of the pen. Yet, orally delivered in the House of Commons, it was loudly cheered by men who could have known nothing of the real merits of the matter, and who, by refusing a Committee to Sir Charles Napier, took good care that they would know nothing of it; because, forsooth, care must be taken of the fame of General Jones, though General Jones had about as much to do with the conduct of the naval campaign in the Baltic as he had to do with building the fortifications of Sweaborg. Yet few in that House cared to preserve the fame of Sir Charles Napier, notwithstanding that it adorns some of the brightest pages of our naval history. General Jones was but an episode in the naval campaign in the Baltic; Sir Charles Napier is generally, but erroneously, supposed to have been its commander. The commander of the Baltic campaign directed its operations from Whitehall.

One thing is, however, clear from Sir James Graham's letter; and that is, that without a military force he never contemplated an attack on Sweaborg, unless, indeed, Sir Charles Napier would fly in the face of the First Lord's repeated cautions "not to run his head against stone walls." We shall now be in a condition fully to comprehend the following order from the Admiralty.

Before adducing this, we must, however, notice a remarkable incident which bears directly upon the Admiralty order, viz., the fall of Sebastopol to Lord

Raglan after the battle of the Alma, which intelligence arrived in England on the 4th of October.   This event, or rather the miserable hoax which, instead of the Allied army, had somewhat prematurely captured Sebastopol, had arrived in England, and the Admiralty, elated beyond measure at the easily-won victory, but without adopting the common-place precaution of waiting to see whether any victory had been won at Sebastopol, wrote to Sir Charles Napier, that as Lord Raglan, like the Roman conqueror of old, had completed his " *veni, vidi, vici,*" Sir Charles must do the same.   He had been long enough about the " *veni, vidi* " part of the business, and it was high time that he came to the " *vici* "; in other words, he received a hint that *he was forthwith expected to take Sweaborg*, notwithstanding that the French army and fleet, as well as no small portion of his own fleet, were *gone to Kiel*.

It is necessary to give the Admiralty despatch *in extenso*.

" We have received and duly considered your despatch of the 25th of September.   No. 516.

" For reasons stated to you in our order of the 26th of September, No. 713., we are not prepared to sanction the withdrawal of the fleet from the entrance of the Gulf of Finland until ice shall have closed it, or until you shall have received any further orders.

" Baro Sound is in most winds a safe anchorage, and your command of steam power, whilst the Channel is open, will enable you to keep your position.

" Your reconnaissance of Revel, and your report on its defences, are clear and satisfactory, and may be turned to useful account on some future occasion.

" Your reconnaissance of Sweaborg gives rise to more pressing and serious considerations.

" You desire us not for a moment to suppose that Sweaborg cannot be attacked, and you proceed to point out in detail the precise mode in which the operation ought to be conducted according to your deliberate judgment on a careful review of all the difficulties and dangers.

" You say that troops might, in your opinion, be most usefully employed in aid of the ships. But you do not say that military co-operation appears to you indispensable to insure naval success. On the contrary, you express an opinion that if your plan of attack by the ships were adopted, you are quite certain that the fortress would be laid in ruins, and most probably an entrance opened to the ships.

" What then are the obstacles to the immediate attempt? If the diminution of your force be one, *we have reason to believe that the French fleet has been ordered to rejoin you off Sweaborg*, and by telegraph we have directed Rear-Admiral Plumridge to hold himself in readiness at Kiel to return to the Gulf of Finland, if he hears from you that the presence and assistance of his squadron are required.

" You intimate an opinion that the uncertainty of the weather at this advanced period of the year is no objection to the attack. *You may choose your day and your opportunity*, and some risk must always attend every great operation.

" You anticipate an attack by the Russian fleet if many of your ships be crippled or destroyed. We are always reminded that the Russians are most unwilling to navigate the Gulf of Finland in line-of-battle ships, when autumn has commenced ; and Cronstadt is always locked up by ice fourteen days before Sweaborg is closed. The attack therefore on Sweaborg might be made *towards the end of October*, with least danger of attack from the Cronstadt portion of the Russian fleet.

" *Recent events in the Black Sea will not encourage the Russians to attempt any enterprise of more than usual hazard and daring at this precise moment*." (These " recent events," allude to the mock capture of Sebastopol after the battle of the Alma!)

"It is true that additional boats having Lancaster guns and mortar vessels *have not been sent into the Baltic* since we were led to believe that Cronstadt and Sweaborg were unassailable by naval means alone.

"Your second reconnaissance of Sweaborg opens a new view, and the presence or absence of a *few guns* of an improved construction, or *even of mortar vessels*, cannot make the whole difference between a possible and an impossible attack."

Here then is a *positive order* to the Admiral to "*choose a fine day and his own opportunity at the end of October*," and attack Sweaborg, notwithstanding that the Admiralty had long before ordered him to send his ships home. But as the Admiralty well knew that no such attack could be made, nor, as we shall presently show, was even intended by them to be made, their concluding paragraph shifted all the responsibility of an attack from their own shoulders to those of the Admiral, who, it was calculated, *might* be goaded on to an attack by this letter, and would lose his reduced squadron, now consisting of only *nine ships of the line* and three blockships, in an attack upon one of the strongest fortresses of Europe, garrisoned by at least 40,000 men, according to the advices sent by the Admiralty themselves!

The subjoined is the conclusion of the despatch: —

"This *order* is founded on your own last report. The final decision must rest entirely on yourself. If the attack on Sweaborg, in present circumstances, be desperate, it must on no account be undertaken by you. If, calculating the ordinary chances of war, and on a full consideration of the strength of the enemy's fortress and fleets, you shall be of opinion that Sweaborg can be laid in ruins, it will be your duty, with the concurrence of the French Admiral, not to omit the opportunity.

" Given under our hands this 4th day of October, 1854.

(Signed)   " M. F. BERKELEY.

" PETER RICHARDS."

As Admiral Berkeley has thought proper to pass so severe a criticism on Sir C. Napier, he cannot have the smallest possible objection to be in his turn subjected to criticism, and the less so that we will offer not the slightest comment upon him individually, but from his own previous writings.

The following are a few, and only a few, extracts from the semi-official letters of Admiral Berkeley to Sir Charles Napier ; were the whole to be published, the people of England would no longer trust its navy in the hands of a Board of Admiralty. But we refrain from publishing them, as our object is only to show the exact *previous* opinions of the Board, and to contrast these with the despatch just quoted.

The following are Admiral Berkeley's opinions, with the dates annexed : —

" Your survey of Cronstadt, and your judgment and discretion — I don't mean to play upon that word — are highly approved.   You have had a difficult part to play, every tomfool expecting you to eat Cronstadt and the Emperor to boot. I believe the Government are perfectly satisfied with all your proceedings ; and I can only say that I think you deserve every credit for the manner in which you have handled your fleet in such waters." (*July* 11*th*, 1854.)

" Believe me, I fully enter into all your difficulties and all your feelings, and, let the public say what they will, I shall contend that you have acted *wisely and properly in all your proceedings.* It is naval men, and naval men alone, who can fancy the pressure on your nerves, and the fatigue of mind and body, in such a navigation. We serve a public who expect impossibilities, and who would hang us if we fail in anything we undertake." (*July* 31*st.*)

" I am seriously thinking *when it will be time to get you out of that infernal Gulf. How long do you think it will be right to permit those big ships to remain ? Autumn is getting on fast. I am hard up for steamers. When shall you be able to spare any ?* " (*August* 15*th.*)

It is somewhat singular that on the 15th of August, when both the French fleet and army were with Sir Charles Napier, Admiral Berkeley should have been so anxious to get the fleet out of "that infernal Gulf," whilst on the 4th of October, six weeks later, he tells the Admiral that he can remain in the Gulf well enough, and attack Sweaborg into the bargain, though the French fleet and army were gone, as well as a considerable number of the ships of the British squadron ; nine ships of the line being alone left.

Subsequent to the fall of Bomarsund, Admiral Berkeley, after highly praising the Admiral, says :—

" John Bull, never content, expects more than is possible. *I trust you will not be goaded on, or beaten out of your own determinations. I have every confidence that you will attempt all that is feasible, and that you will succeed in all you do attempt.*" (*August* 22*nd.*)

It is nevertheless passing strange that Admiral Berkeley should have goaded on Sir Charles Napier on the 4th of October to do that against which he had cautioned him on the 22nd of August.

" We wish you — if no other operations are to be undertaken this season — to reduce your ships of the line, the
French in proportion, to as many as you deem sufficient to
lick the Russians when joined together from Helsingfors and
Cronstadt." (*August 29th.*)

" John Bull is getting uproarious because nobody is killed
and wounded. Meetings are being called to condemn the
Government, because Cronstadt and Sebastopol have not been
captured." (*September 5th.*)

" I suppose we may now as well begin sending for the ships
home ; but we wait for the positive assurance that nothing
more is to be attempted." (*September 5th.*)

" We shall have blue books and parliamentary questions
without end. *The attacks failing against you, will be levelled
at the Board, or failing against the Board, will be levelled at
you.* The papers yesterday state that the French fleet has
wholly deserted you, thus diminishing your force to thirteen
ships of the line and three blockships. *Should the Russians
pluck up spirit to come out, the odds, numerically, are too
great to be pleasant ;* nevertheless I firmly believe you would
give a good account of them. You have not looked well at
the gun-vessels — they can fire both guns. *Next year*, if
you have to bombard stone walls, I think you will find them
useful." (*September 24th.*)

Here is a plain admission that nothing more was
to be expected *this year*, and that should the Russians
come out, the " *odds were too great to be pleasant.*"
These frank expressions of opinion were most honourable to Admiral Berkeley, who, whatever may be
his other failings, has the true sailor spirit in him.
The difficulty is how, after such expressions, he
could have attached his name to the despatch of
October 4th. The explanation is, however, easy.
Admiral Berkeley did not write that despatch, though
he signed it.

The proof of this is incontrovertible. On the *same day* (October 4th) that Admiral Berkeley signed that despatch he wrote to Sir Charles Napier as follows : —

" *Through good or evil report, you must act with firmness and according to your own judgment. The public will do you justice in the long run, as I firmly believe that you will do all that can be done or attempted with propriety.*" (*October 4th.*)

From the preceding extract, it is perfectly clear that Admiral Berkeley neither wished nor expected Sweaborg to be attacked, and therefore neither wrote the despatch of October 4th nor approved of it, notwithstanding he had signed it. Were it not that Admiral Berkeley — after having approved of Sir Charles Napier's conduct in everything, even, as we have seen, the unfounded insinuations of this unworthy despatch included — had attacked Sir Charles Napier so virulently in Parliament, especially in that wretched debate about Acre, which so signally recoiled on himself, he would have appeared in the whole matter in a light creditable to himself and worthy of his constant and warm approbation of Sir Charles Napier. As the subsequent attacks of Admiral Berkeley upon Sir Charles Napier are foreign to the Baltic Campaign, we shall not enter further into this subject here.

The despatch states, " *You desire us not for a moment to suppose that Sweaborg cannot be attacked.*" Quite true. The Admiral had told them repeatedly how it could be attacked, were the proper means supplied. On the 18th of July, he had most elaborately pointed out how this could be done, and his communication had not even been replied to, it being afterwards ascertained that this, the most important despatch of the whole war, had never been laid before the Board by Sir James Graham, to whom it was addressed. On the 14th of June, when there was time to supply the requisite means, Admiral Chads had pointed out the same thing, and how it might be effected. This, by the admission of Sir James Graham, was laid before the Cabinet. The members of the Board were in private communication with the other admirals and officers of the fleet, according to the admission of Admiral Berkeley himself, and had no doubt been told the same thing over and over again. Sir Hamilton Seymour, on the 4th of February, had urged the great necessity of gun-boats. General Jones had told them, on the 1st of May, exactly what was wanted to attack Sweaborg ; and had, above all, impressed upon them the necessity of " a large supply of rockets," not one of which was ever sent, any more than were mortars, mortar-boats, and gun-boats. The Admiralty table was thus liberally supplied with excellent advice upon the matter, in abundance of time to have taken that advice. On the 25th of September, Sir Charles Napier added two distinct plans of attack in the following year,—one with ships alone, which he considered doubtful; the other with "13-inch mortars placed on shore, gun-boats, mortar-boats, rockets, &c., the success of which he considered *quite certain.*" Let us see what became of all this.

The despatch goes on : "*On the contrary, you express*

an opinion that if your plan of attack by the ships were adopted, you are quite certain that the fortress would be laid in ruins." Sir Charles Napier said nothing of the sort, and the imputation is so clumsy a perversion of what he did say in his despatch of the 25th of September, that it is marvellous to find that men of ordinary judgment would make use of it, even to serve a desperate purpose.

If the reader will refer to the Admiral's despatch of the 25th of September, he will there see that Sir Charles points to *two* distinct plans of attack,— the first by ships alone, which he considers doubtful of success. Of this he says, "*if* it were made at this season of the year, it is impossible to say how many ships would be lost," —both the result and the "*if*" affording a pretty clear indication that he had no intention of making such an attack at this season of the year, even had he the means to do so. Yet the Admiralty chose to pervert his despatch to this meaning, though the perversion says little for their fair-dealing or nautical experience. "The Channels," said the Admiral, "must be buoyed;" though this could hardly have been done in the heavy gales which had compelled him to send home part of his ships in obedience to Admiralty orders. Perhaps the Board thought the buoys would hold on, though the ships could not. "Small steamers," said the Admiral, must be stationed in the most dangerous channels." But, as the Admiralty had taken good care, he had no small steamers to station; they had been ordered home. Therefore no attack, for which these means were requisite, could have been made without them.

This is the common sense view of the matter.   But it was not the Admiralty view, notwithstanding that the Admiral had said in addition, "if the attack were made at this season of the year, he did not know how many ships would be lost."   They chose to read it that he could *at once* make the attack.   It must have been the very wilfulness of perversion which could give to the despatch any such meaning.

In the same despatch, the Admiral then goes on to say that, with "caution and judgment," by a *second* plan of attack, "Sweaborg may be laid in ruins." But how ?   By "13-inch mortars placed on Laghara Island and on Lango rocks," — not with ships alone. "Lancaster guns must be added to the fleet."   These the fleet had not, with the exception of one only, so that it was folly to interpret the despatch as referring to a present attack, and the more so as the Admiralty had long before told the Admiral they could not get any more Lancaster guns ready.   "The ships," said the Admiral, "should be well furnished with *shot, shells, and rockets.*"   There were only eighty rounds of shot per gun on board, as appeared from survey ; the fleet was short of shells ; there was not a single mortar in the fleet to fire shells, and not so much as a single rocket.   For the Admiralty then to pretend that Sir Charles could mean an *immediate* attack, was a discreditable perversion of his plans to serve their own purposes, in order to get out of a scrape with the public for not having supplied those means without which no attack could be made.

The means being still kept in view, the despatch goes on : "A bombardment must be commenced and continued till the wooden buildings of the fortress are on fire, and an evident impression made." Then, but not till then, the "ships must go in and finish the work;" and this being done, said the Admiral, " I am quite certain the fortress would be laid in ruins, and most probably an entrance opened to the ships."

This forms the "caution and judgment" of which the Admiral spoke in his despatch; and it is the judgment of an admiral who has had more to do with battery fighting than most other admirals in the service. It was his opinion that an attack thus cautiously and judiciously made would be *certain* in its results, as will be the opinion of all other naval men who have now that judgment before them. In short, there are no two opinions about its certainty; and had Admiral Dundas been supplied with the means Sir C. Napier asked for to a sufficient extent, the fortress as well as the dockyard must have fallen, as we will show presently. Russia is indebted to the Board of Admiralty for the preservation of her fortress, and, what is more, is fully sensible of the obligation. None knows better than Russia, how to draw the line between the Board of Admiralty and the British Admirals. In very humiliation for the thwarted honour of our country, we will not attempt to trace that line farther.

The misapprehension of the Admiral's despatch by the Admiralty is most amusing. Either from incapacity to comprehend it, or inattention to it, the Admiralty had made a blunder which is now palpable enough to the reader, and had construed two admirably considered plans of attack on Sweaborg,

when means were supplied in the following campaign,
even as the Admiralty authorities themselves had
suggested, into an attempt on the part of Sir C.
Napier to throw the responsibility of not attacking
Sweaborg on themselves. We have said that, notwithstanding the order of the 4th of October to
attack Sweaborg, it was not the intention of the
writers of the Admiralty despatch that Sweaborg
should be attacked. Here is the proof, in the letter
of Admiral Berkeley of the same date before alluded
to : —

"We have written you officially (Oct. 4.) to show you
that — as was originally intended — the *responsibility of attack
or no attack rests entirely with yourself and your French
colleague.* Your letter (25th Sept.) would make all who
read it believe that that responsibility was too heavy for your
shoulders, and *that you would willingly transfer it to the
Board.* This must not be. I have, and am still prepared so
to do, defended you from unjust attacks. But you must not
endeavour to get rid of the responsibility attached to your
position. Through good or evil report, you must act with
firmness and according to your own judgment. *The public
will do you justice in the long run ;* as I firmly believe that you
will do all that can be done, or attempted with propriety."

This letter is most honourable to Admiral Berkeley,
but it clearly shows that the order to attack Sweaborg was not intended to be put in execution, unless
the Admiral was silly enough to run amuck at the
fortress, with a certainty of losing his ships, at his
own risk. There was no necessity for reminding the
Admiral that the responsibility must rest with him.
Neither by word nor deed had he anywhere attempted
to throw it on the Admiralty. Such an accusation is

then puerile in the extreme, and could only have
been resorted to from the desperate circumstances
in which the Government was placed from its own
apathy in neglecting to supply the fleet with proper
means for the kind of warfare in which it was engaged. The Admiral in the course of his whole
service never cared a straw about responsibility. He
always did what he considered to be his duty, and
allowed responsibility to take care of itself. The
order of October 4th, according to Admiral Berkeley,
— one of the signers thereof,— was intended to shift
the responsibility of not making the attack from the
Admiralty to the Admiral. Nevertheless, they appear
to have counted on his impetuosity, and were hardly
prepared for his wariness. Their wish was " father
to the thought," but the Admiral was not silly enough
to become godfather to it.

An influential organ of the British Navy has well
remarked on this subject : —

" Of Napier's conduct in the Baltic, it may be truly said,
that he served the interests of his country, and consulted
more for his fleet than for his own interest or selfish distinction. Well might the gallant old Admiral exclaim — and
yet he has not done so —

> " ' I dare do all that may become a man,
> Who dares do more — is none.'

To have attacked the strongholds of Russia, and lost Britain
a fleet, *without taking a fortress*, would have been the act of a
selfish, fame-seeking madman — and not the act of a Napier."

The Russians have been far more just to the fame
of Sir Charles Napier than has his own Government.
A Russian officer of eminence, taken at Sebastopol,

told his captors that, instead of blaming Sir Charles
Napier, he was entitled to the highest credit. It was
the Russian object, as even Sir James Graham saw,
to get Sir Charles to attack their fortresses, when,
said the Russian officer, "his ships must have been
desperately mauled, and, having begun an attack, we
well knew his impetuosity would never have allowed
him to desist from it, till his ships were so far
disabled that ours could have gone out and given a
good account of them in their crippled condition.
This was our game ; and from the Admiral's previous
reputation for rashness, bets ran high in St. Petersburg, with considerable odds, that he would fall into
the trap. To our surprise, he did not, and his fame
with us stands higher than ever. Instead of blaming
him for not fighting our forts as we wished, *the
English nation ought to thank him for not losing their
fleet.*"

By referring back, the reader will see that Sir
James Graham had said precisely the same thing,
though in different words.

The question is—and it goes into a nutshell—what,
with the previous experience of Sir C. Napier, did
Admiral Dundas do in the next campaign ? He
proved that he could do no more than Sir C. Napier
did, and the press has not hesitated to assert that,
with more means, *he did less.* This is unjust to
Admiral Dundas. It is true he had more means,
but *not enough* to do anything decisive. When at
Cronstadt, he had *three* gun-boats supplied to him.
These were increased by driblets to *fifteen* in place of
a *hundred*, which even then would not have amounted

to half the number of the Russian gun-boats. With this handful of gun-boats, and a few French ones, and sixteen mortar-boats, he tried his shells on Sweaborg, burned the dockyard, but did not destroy the fortress. He carried out the first part of Sir C. Napier's plan, but not the *second*, viz., to " let his fleet get in and finish the work." On the contrary, he never assembled his fleet at all. This lay doing nothing before Cronstadt, whilst he was shelling the Sweaborg dockyard ; a pretty clear proof that Admiral Dundas did not consider himself in a position to attempt a serious attack on Sweaborg. The French, following out Sir C. Napier's plan, placed " 13-inch mortars on the islands and rocks ; " but what mortars Admiral Dundas had were not on the rocks, but in his mortar-boats ; and these burst, so that he was compelled to desist even from shelling the place, *because he had none to replace them.* He had *more* means, it is true ; but so scantily had they been supplied, that he was, in this respect, treated scarcely less scurvily than had been Sir C. Napier. Let the English public bear in mind, that the Government has no more ventured on publishing Admiral Dundas's letters and despatches entire, than it has those of Sir C. Napier. We do not know officially why he desisted from his attack on Sweaborg, though the naval profession well knows the above to be the reason.

But, continues the despatch, " *the presence or absence of a few guns of improved construction, or even of mortar-vessels, cannot make the whole difference between a possible and an impossible attack.*" This is put with all the tact of special pleading. Sir

Charles Napier had not said it would. What he had said was, that so high was his opinion of Lancaster guns, that "they should be furnished to every ship" When his fleet was complete, he had guns enough in all conscience, though greatly inferior in calibre to the Russian guns. But he had never even alluded to this. The expression "*even of mortar-vessels*," is truly a singular one. Sir Charles asked for *mortars* themselves; he had not *one mortar* in his whole fleet! To have sent a fleet to fight granite fortresses without mortars, was, indeed, to equip it on a peace principle. A fleet so wanting in equipment was probably never before sent on such an errand since mortars were invented, and the fact would be incredible were it not beyond the possibility of doubt. That fleet was never intended to attack the great forts of Russia, as Sir James Graham had cautioned the Admiral over and over again, till, as Admiral Berkeley had said, it became a question of who should bear the blame, the Admiral or the Admiralty. Then, but not till then, he was ordered to attack Sweaborg, at a period when "*ice should have closed up Cronstadt!*" but not the slightest effort was made to supply him with *a single mortar*, to say nothing of "a few mortar-vessels," by which alone an attack could have been made.

Sir James Graham had entirely forgotten his former strong desire for the "200 Swedish gun-boats and 50,000 Swedes," without which, nothing "great or decisive" could be effected.

What a spectacle does this exhibit to the country! A Board of Admiralty — some of whom we will

charitably admit, know no better — tells an Admiral
without gun-boats, mortar-boats, or rockets in his
fleet, that " the presence or absence of these, cannot
make the difference between a possible and impossible attack ! " That is, the very essence of naval
warfare is not necessary to naval warfare ! Though
Admirals Berkeley and Richards signed this, as has
been said before, they never could have written it ;
and the country will deem it incumbent on them to
disown the imputed authorship.

With her fleets thus equipped for battle, and with
such desperate despatches as these sent to her
Admirals when the fruits of non-equipment have
been reaped, England need not wonder at being
openly termed by Continental nations, "no longer a
first-rate power." It will be well if, ere long, we do
not descend beneath the rank of a second-rate power.
Yet her energy is as vigorous as ever, and her
means tenfold what they ever were. Her rulers
have shown how they can neutralise both the one
and the other ; and England may yet find that her
very vigour, thus ill directed, may become one of the
first elements of her downfal.

We have thus taken a moderate review of this
despatch, selecting a few of its leading points only.
The naval reader will appreciate many others, but
our object has only been to point out to the unnau-
tical reader, matters which would engage his attention, without being so well able to fathom their
ill-concealed sophistry. We have purposely avoided
defence in any shape, as unworthy — except as it must
naturally arise from explanation.

But the British Government, evidently fearing that Sir Charles Napier would take them at their word, and rashly lose his handful of ships at Sweaborg, lost no time in sending him another order, *not to attack Sweaborg!* The date of the second despatch was only *four days* after the first, viz., the 9th of October; and so fearful was the Admiralty that Admiral Plumridge would at once go back to his chief, that they sent him an order *by telegraph* immediately to return to England! Yet if it was proper to order Sweaborg to be attacked on the 4th of October, the order could not be otherwise than good on the 9th. Why then should the Admiralty have so suddenly disclaimed its fighting propensity in *four days only?*

The reason is clear. On the 9th of October came the news, that the imaginary victory of Sebastopol was a hoax! and instantly Sir Charles Napier was ordered to stop that for which, only a few days before, he had been so bitterly reflected on for not attempting. So great was now the urgency for not fighting, that Admiral Plumridge was *by telegraph* ordered home forthwith, as well as the French squadron, and Sir Charles was told to use his own discretion in leaving the Gulf of Finland. Before giving the Admiralty order of the 9th of October, countermanding the order which only four days before they had given to attack Sweaborg, it is necessary to give Sir Charles Napier's reply to that unworthy despatch, devoting his ships to destruction, had he been foolish enough to have complied with such an order, and that for no better reason than

*K K 8

that the Government had been subjected to a hoax as regarded Sebastopol.

Admiral Berkeley had told Sir Charles that " none but naval men could estimate the pressure upon the nerves" of an Admiral circumstanced as Sir Charles was. What must then have been the effect produced upon him by this despatch, which the Board of Admiralty, four days afterwards, was ashamed of having written ? To use the words of the Admiral, " I was utterly stupified at such a despatch after the praises which had been lavished on me throughout the campaign. I began to ask myself whether I had ever done anything which entitled me to the command of a fleet."

The Admiral saw that his previous reputation was deliberately sacrificed to save an incapable Government, though even this unworthy course would fail to save it, as was afterwards the case. The obloquy he could have borne, and he had no fears of investigation into the most minute circumstances connected with the campaign ; but the faithlessness of those who had praised him throughout, almost to fulsomeness, was more than an honest, straightforward mind, unversed in the wiles of statesmanship, could bear. To use the words of those around him, " he seemed for awhile utterly prostrated "—a feeling into which all who have made a reputation and find it in danger of being destroyed by unfair means, can readily enter. The necessity for meeting the insidious calumnies contained in the despatch, however, strung up his mind to a reply, as dignified as those calumnies were wanting in that quality.

On the 10th of October, he wrote to the Board of Admiralty, as follows:—

" Before I received your letter of the 4th of October, I had written the accompanying letter, No. 558., giving my reasons for withdrawing from this anchorage ; and, notwithstanding their Lordships' letter of the 4th instant, I still think it my duty to persist in my intention.

" I have already given my reasons for withdrawing the sailing ships, and I thought I was following up Sir James's wishes." (Vide his letter of 29th of August.)

" Neither this anchorage nor Baro Sound are fit for a fleet in the winter.   My letter will clearly point out my reasons. Their Lordships will see that we are losing anchors and cables every day; and we shall soon be losing ships.

" Their Lordships ask me, if I think Sweaborg can be laid in ruins, why I do not attack it ?   I reply that before the ships should go alongside the batteries, my plan was to have it first bombarded with ' *mortars, shells, and rockets,*' from the Island, and with ' *gun-boats, Lancaster guns,*' &c., for a day or two ; and then, when well bombarded, the ships should go alongside and finish the work.   The *want of means* is one obstacle, the weather the next, why I do not attack it.

" Their Lordships tell me to ' choose my day.'   There has not been a day since I have been here (Nargen), that it was possible to attack Sweaborg.   It requires many days.   The channels are studded with sunken rocks.   They must be all sounded and buoyed.   If it came on to blow the fleet would inevitably be lost, and I should be unworthy the command I hold if I risked it.   It would be a long operation.   Their Lordships have not the most distant idea of the dangers.   Whether the Russian fleet in Cronstadt would venture out if we were disabled, I know not ; but the Sweaborg fleet would.

" I have never altered my opinion that Sweaborg must first be attacked by ' *mortars, shells, and gun-boats.*'   But I never would have advised them to be sent here at this season.

" My second reconnaissance was never intended to open a new view.   The view I first took and the last were the same.

L L

" Their Lordships say, the final decision must rest with me, and if the attack be desperate, it must on no account be undertaken. I look upon it that no man in his senses would undertake to attack Sweaborg at this season of the year; and, even in a fine season, I doubt much the success, *without the means I have pointed out.*

" A telegraphic message has stopped the French Admiral, which I am glad of, — his presence would be useless; and I have directed Admiral Plumridge not to come here for the same reason.

" When a Council of War composed of five Admirals—viz., Vice-Admiral Parseval and myself, Rear-Admirals Penaud, Chads, and Seymour, and in whose opinions a sixth (Rear-Admiral Martin) concurred — had given their opinions that *' neither our resources nor the season* would permit an attack upon Sweaborg,' I should have thought that both their Lordships and the public would have been satisfied; and I beg further to tell their Lordships that there is not an Admiral in the British service who would have ventured to attack such a fortress at this season of the year. As their Lordships have so frequently returned to this question, it leads me to believe that, notwithstanding the praises they have heaped upon me for my conduct in the Baltic, and judging from the altered tone of their letters, I have reason to think I have lost the confidence of their Lordships. If that is the case, I shall be *perfectly ready to resign my command. But as long as I hold it, I will do what I think is best for the good of Her Majesty's Service and for the safety of the fleet I command,* which I think is greatly endangered by our present position; and we are risking our ships to no adequate purpose."

No notice was taken of this offer of the Admiral to " resign his command." This was not the object; but to make him the scapegoat, whilst holding the command. Neither was the Admiral's order to Admiral Plumridge to stop where he was, in contradiction of the Admiralty order, noticed by their

Lordships, who soon found out the injudiciousness of their own order, and, without waiting for the ordinary means of communication, stopped Admiral Plumridge by telegraph, and ordered him to return to England.

The despatch, No. 558., which had been written previous to the reception of the Admiralty despatch of the 4th of October, and transmitted home with the preceding, bearing the same date, was as follows : —

"Since my last despatch, we have had constant heavy gales ; the last began at S. S. E., veered to N. N. W., and blew a perfect storm. Fortunately, it stopped there: had it come to the eastward of north, a heavy sea would have set in, and I doubt whether the ships would have rode it out.

"I have withdrawn the ships from before Sweaborg, and sent them to the entrance of the Gulf, or they would most probably have been lost.

"These heavy gales will compel me to go south without waiting for the ice, which may not appear till December; but to continue through them till then I look upon as most dangerous.

"I do not believe the Russians will venture out of their harbours at this season of the year. If they do, they will never get back.

"Their Lordships, in one of their letters, observed, that before the power of steam was known, a squadron of British ships of the line maintained a blockade of the Baltic till the end of November ; but a blockade in the Gulf of Finland is quite another thing. Sir James Saumarez always left the Gulf at the end of September, and blockaded it from Carlscrona. His journal is now before me.

"Steam can do a great deal. But steam cannot resist the heavy gales in these northern latitudes. I should be sorry to see this fleet adrift and trusting to steam to drive the ships to sea on a dark night in a snow-storm.

"In my last, I informed their Lordships that the *Austerlitz* had struck on a rock on the coast of Sweden. Since then we have heard of another French ship having been on shore on Gottska Sando. The *Euryalus* struck on a rock off Sweaborg, and it is a miracle she was saved. She lost an anchor and cable, but recovered it. The *Majestic* parted a bower cable in Ledsund. The *Impérieuse* parted her cable and lost it, so did the *Basilisk*. The *Dragon* lost three anchors.

" With all these warnings before me, — though fully sensible of the responsibility I incur in withdrawing the fleet to the south, —yet I should consider myself unfit for, the command I hold, were I much longer to expose them to the violent gales of the north ; more particularly as their Lordships have directed me in their letter of the 23rd of September — confirmed by their letter of the 26th — *to withdraw when, in the opinion of the French Admiral and myself, the presence here of the combined fleet is no longer safe.*

" The French Admiral having gone, it is now left to my judgment ; and though the thermometer has been only down to 32°, the near approach of winter has been sufficiently pronounced by the continual and heavy gales we have had ; and I am satisfied that, were their Lordships here, they would agree with me that it was quite time to leave the Gulf of Finland.

" In addition to the reasons I have given, our provisions begin to get short. There is no knowing how long we may be shut up by violent south-west gales.

" To the losses of anchors above mentioned, I have to add one more lost by the *Cressy*, with twenty-six fathoms of cable, and one broken by the *James Watt*, — demands for which I enclose."

Fine weather this for an attack on one of the strongest fortifications in Europe ! It is difficult to believe that the writers of the despatch of October 4th could have had any just idea of the effect of weather on ships ; the more so when, in such a season, the fleet would have had to sound and buoy its way into

Sweaborg, before any attack could be made. What must be the opinion of those who would have had to sound and buoy the channels, it would be useless to describe. What will be the opinion of our naval posterity on perusing these records, it is not difficult to guess. It is only to be hoped that some great naval blunder will not one day leave us with not a naval posterity to decide on these or any other matters.

But these speculations are almost as idle as are the orders to attack Sweaborg under such circumstances. Toulon never possessed half the strength of Sweaborg. Yet, in fine weather and with no difficulties of navigation, Lord St. Vincent, Lord Keith, Lord Nelson, Admiral Cotton, and Admiral Pellew, afterwards Lord Exmouth, never attacked Toulon, though lying before it. Cadiz has not half the strength of Toulon, yet Lords St. Vincent, Collingwood, Keith, and Nelson, lay long at various times before Cadiz, and never attacked the forts. Lords Howe, St. Vincent, and Bridport never attacked Brest; though the difficulties were few in comparison to Sweaborg or Cronstadt. Even the inferior fortifications of L'Orient, Rochefort, and Rochelle were never attacked by these, our most renowned Admirals; whilst Cherbourg was not so much as looked at by them.

Our history shows that, with the exception of the attacks on Copenhagen, Algiers, and Acre, all our greatest Admirals carefully refrained from attacking strongly fortified places; whilst Sir Charles Napier has been through life a determined battery-fighter;

acting on the principle, that if ships could get near enough, the batteries must get the worst of it.   It is this which has given him a reputation for rashness; but, be it remembered, he always succeeded.   It was because he had no means to get at Sweaborg and Cronstadt, that he did not attack them.   His successor in command, *with means*, took equally good care to keep his ships out of the way.

When Gibraltar withstood, for three years, the combined fleets of France and Spain, it was not to be compared with Sweaborg in point of strength. There were neither rocks nor shoals in the way of the attacking fleets.   Yet the fortress, with a small garrison, burned a great portion of the fleets, and beat the rest off.   Where would have been the judgment of the Admiral, then, had he attacked Sweaborg with his ships alone, opposed to a fortress stronger than Gibraltar then was, and with a garrison of 40,000 men ?

The following are the *two* Admiralty despatches on the subject, both dated 9th of October: —

" 9th October, 1854.

" With reference to former orders, I am commanded by my Lords Commissioners of the Admiralty to acquaint you that the French Government has countermanded the order given to Admiral Parseval to return with the French Fleet to the entrance of the Gulf of Finland, *and that, an attack on Sweaborg being no longer possible,* Rear-Admiral Plumridge has been ordered *by telegraph* to return to England forthwith with the ships under his command from Kiel.

" I am further directed by their Lordships to acquaint you that you are now at liberty to exercise your discretion in withdrawing to the southward with the remainder of the fleet under your orders; taking care to leave a light squadron of observation, so long as weather will permit, off the entrance of the Gulf in order to watch any movement of the Russian fleet, and prevent its entrance unobserved into the Baltic; and also to maintain an effective blockade so long as prudence will permit, and before ice shall have closed the channel."

Who told the Board that "an attack on Sweaborg was no longer possible?" Four days before they said it "*was possible*," and goaded the Admiral to undertake it. He had not in any way contributed to undeceive them, for they could not have got his reply. But the purpose had been answered of throwing the blame upon him, as was most ungenerously done, knowing that, he not being in Parliament, the public could not get at the real facts of the case. It would have been much wiser to have let the facts come out through the medium of a Blue Book, which few could comprehend, and fewer still would have troubled themselves to read, than to let the whole matter first see the light in a volume like the present.

The second despatch related to Admiral Plumridge's squadron.

" Admiralty, 9th October, 1854.

" I am commanded by my Lords Commissioners of the Admiralty to acquaint you that Rear-Admiral Plumridge has been directed *to take advantage of the weather*, in regard to the return to England with the ships under his command, and to cause them to be accompanied by steamers through the Belt, so far as he may deem proper. He has been further directed to order the steamers to return to rejoin you, calling at Kiel for any instructions that may have arrived from you."

So then it was necessary to "*take advantage of the weather*" for Admiral Plumridge to perform the short voyage from Kiel to the Downs; and in doing this the flag-ship, the *Neptune*, got ashore: and yet, four days before, Sir Charles Napier had, though lying in the Gulf of Finland at the commencement of an arctic winter, been told to " choose a fine day " to attack Sweaborg! Is it possible that any Englishman can read these matters and not feel his bosom heave with indignation at the unworthy treatment the Admiral had received? Or can any Englishman read these matters without exclaiming, with Admiral Berkeley when sending that unworthy despatch of October the 4th, " *through evil or good report you must act with firmness and according to your own judgment.* THE PUBLIC WILL DO YOU JUSTICE IN THE LONG RUN"?

CHAP. XXI.

ON the 17th of October, the Admiral replied to the Board of Admiralty, that he was glad they had allowed him to exercise his own discretion in withdrawing the line of battle ships to the southward. He had anticipated their instructions as to establishing a blockade at the mouth of the Gulf of Finland. This had been entrusted to Capt. Watson, to whom discretionary power had been given as to his final withdrawal. In consequence of the severity of the weather, the force was withdrawn from the Gulf of Bothnia, and placed under the orders of Capt. Watson, whose blockading squadron consisted of the *Impérieuse, Euryalus, Arrogant, Magicienne, Dragon,* and *Desperate.* The *Penelope* and *Odin* were left at Ledsund to watch any Russian movements in that quarter; though of this there was now no danger, as the Russian squadron at Sweaborg had commenced dismasting.

On the 19th, the line of battle ships, with the remainder of the squadron left for Kiel, viz., *Duke of Wellington, Hogue, St. Jean D'Acre, Blenheim, Princess Royal, James Watt, Edinburgh, Cressy, Cæsar, Nile, Majestic, Bulldog,* and *Locust.* The *Gorgon,* was despatched direct for England. The rendezvous was appointed at Kiel, to which port the ships were directed to make the best of their way, independent of stations.

On the 20th, three ships only were in sight of the flag-ship, the rest having dispersed. At sunset none were in sight. On the 21st the Admiral anchored off the entrance to Faro Sound, where he found the *Magicienne, Vulture, Archer, Conflict, Bulldog, Cruiser,* and *Gorgon,* the *Edinburgh* soon afterwards arriving. A Swedish man-of-war, lying at Faro, saluted the Admiral, which salute was returned. On this day the blockade of the Russian ports in the Gulf of Bothnia was formally raised.

On the 22nd, the Admiral again weighed and proceeded onwards, falling in with the *Blenheim.* On the 23rd, the *Hogue* and *Vulture* were alone in sight. On the 24th, the flag-ship passed Bornholm Island. On the 25th, she was off Moen Island. And on the 26th, anchored at Kiel, where she found at anchor the *Royal George, St. Jean d'Acre, Princess Royal, Cæsar, Driver,* and *Rosamond.*

On the 27th of October, the Admiral wrote from Kiel, to Sir James Graham :—

" So far back as the 29th of August, I announced to you the intention of the French General to withdraw his troops. I told you that I had examined Abo, and proposed to move on it, which he declined. It could have been done, but with difficulty.

" I agreed with the French General and Admiral that Sweaborg could not be attacked at this season of the year; and I have no hesitation in saying, that had we moved the troops and ships up to Miolo Roads, and landed 5000 men, we should not have brought off one man, and how many ships we should have lost I cannot say.

" After the capture and destruction of Bomarsund, till I left Nargen, there have not been three days fit for operations which required seven or eight, and then the ships and transports must have lain amongst the rocks and shoals of Miolo Roads, a position that might have done for a General, but certainly not for an Admiral.

" Shortly after the troops sailed, I communicated to you that the French Admiral had received orders to go to Cherbourg, that his orders were dated the 30th of August; so that the decision was not taken on the spot, as you suppose. General Jones's report made no change whatever in our opinions.

" You say, the ' French General partook of Gen. Jones's opinions.' Then why did he not carry them out? Surely, Sir James, you could not have read them? they are quite opposite. The French Generals thought the fleet could knock down Sweaborg in two hours. Gen. Jones required a combined movement which would require seven or eight days.

" The French Generals looked at Sweaborg for a short time, and not close.   They then made a report with which the Admirals did not concur ; but they knew nothing abou: the difficulties of the navigation, and did not inquire into them.

" The French General in his letter to me says, ' Nous partagion l'opinion de M. le Gen. Jones. Sweaborg peut être attaqué et pris par les flottes, si elles veulent faire contre cette forteresse une attaque sérieuse.'

" *You will find no such thing in Gen. Jones's report.*   The French General must have meant Gen. Niel's report.

" The opinion General Niel gave in writing after he landed, he certainly did not give to the Admiral on the spot. The more I think, the more I am satisfied that such an attack would end in a signal failure.   Even if we succeeded in knocking down the sea face, the work was only begun.

" You say, Sir James, that Gen. Niel intimates very distinctly, that the attack *ought to be made.*   Your Board and you, Sir James, don't agree upon that point.   In their letter to me they say, ' *But Gen. Niel at the same time remarks that so bold an operation has not, to his knowledge, been yet attempted by ships against forts, and that it is not his province to advise it.'*

" The Board desired me to confer with Admiral Parseval, and ascertain whether he was willing to join in a naval attack, 'and if it appear both to you and him an attempt too rash, you are to cause this joint opinion to be recorded ; but if one agrees and the other does not, the Admirals present should be called on and their advice taken.'   This was done.

" The French Admiral declined attending the conference, as he had before given an opinion against attacking Sweaborg ; and the English Admirals, after having read Gen. Niel's report, said that they had no reason to change the opinion they had already given, in which Admiral Martin concurred.

" The truth is, the troops came too late — too many for Bomarsund, and too few for Sweaborg.   The cholera got amongst them.   Gen. Jones made a proposal which the

Generals themselves declined acting on, and Gen. Niel made a proposal which the Admirals declined acting upon. The people in England were dissatisfied, and as some one must be blamed, the Government want to throw it on me. But I will not accept it.

" I ask you, Sir James, to examine the Chart of Swea-borg, and ask yourself if any man in his senses would, at this season of the year, anchor his ships in Miolo Roads, and commence operations which would require seven or eight days to finish — which was Gen. Jones's proposal? And I ask you whether any Admiral *would attack Swea-borg with his ships alone, contrary to his own judgment and the opinions of the Admirals he was ordered to consult,* because Engineer officers thought it could be done ?

" You were angry with me because I made use of the word ' mad ;' but, on my conscience, I believe it to be the only word applicable to such an operation. You say, ' Gen. Jones's report made a great impression.' I have no doubt it did. It is very easy to make a report. Gen. Jones knew that the French Admiral would not land a man. We all knew it. And I am quite certain that after the continuation of bad weather Gen. Jones saw on board the *Duke of Wellington,* he himself would not have landed a man.

" Had people considered one moment, they would have seen the impracticability of the attempt ; but they thought Sebastopol was taken, and, of course, I must take Sweaborg, Revel, and Cronstadt.

" After the French Generals had reconnoitred Sweaborg, I examined it again, and sent home my opinion how it ought to be attacked,—by ships, batteries, gun-boats, mortar-boats, &c. The Admiralty, as if anxious to get up a case against me, take it into their heads that I meant to attack it with the fleet alone, and were going to send back the French squadron, and Admiral Plumridge's ships ; and though I have remonstrated, they persist in still thinking so, and you, Sir James, seem to have fallen into the same error.

" You say, ' Then came your own second reconnaissance, and a plan of naval attack which you considered practicable.'

Had I seen the smallest chance of success, I should have attacked without the French; but I did not, and surely my opinion is worth more than a French General of Engineers. But the Admiralty seem to think different. The General talked of destroying Sweaborg in two hours. It is much more likely the ships would have been set fire to by red-hot shot and shells, and some of them on shore, by that time. Be assured, it is a most difficult place to attack, and whoever does it will have a hard nut to crack.

" No Admiral has, as yet, ventured to attack such a fortress, defended, as it is, by art and nature. The sunken rocks alone, combined with the smoke from the guns and steamers, are no bad defence.

" You observed, Sir James, that the month of September gave ample time for the operations. All the month of September it was blowing a gale of wind, and it was all that Captain Watson could do to keep his station. I did not wonder at the people of England expecting impossibilities, but I am surprised at the Government countenancing them at my cost.

" I am glad the French ships did not come back. The Admiral had already given his decided opinion that it was not practicable; and it was with that conviction that I decided on complying with *your wishes* in sending away the sailing ships, of which the Admiralty disapproved.

" I do not wonder at your surprise and disappointment when you heard the French fleet and army had returned. The Government ought to have informed you of it. I always warned you, even before the arrival of the troops, that nothing more than Bomarsund could be done. They came too late: and I think they were fortunate in getting home safe. It is more than I expected.

" I am quite aware that the Baltic is a dangerous sea; and that even blockading at anchor, at this season, is dangerous. I know that war is not conducted without risks and dangers, and am as ready to encounter them as any man; but I will not be driven by clamour to act contrary to my judgment.

" All the summer, Sir James, you were cautioning me, and so was the Government, not to risk my ships against stone walls, for which you had a great respect; and you praised me for the manner in which I had conducted the fleet. Now winter is come, you are dissatisfied at my not doing impossibilities. As the people are not satisfied, the Government are preparing to abandon me, because I will not follow the advice of a French General, contrary to that of my own Admirals, and diametrically opposite to the opinion of their own General of Engineers, and attack a fortress at a season of the year when, it is more than probable, I should have lost half my fleet.

" I have gone into this explanation at great length. It has given me much pain. I am conscious of having done my duty ; and if you are dissatisfied, you can bring me to a Court-Martial, or remove me — as I have before mentioned to the Admiralty.

" I am very far from well, and I assure you this correspondence has not improved my health."

To this Sir James Graham replied, on the 31st of October, as follows :—

" I am very unwilling to be involved in any personal controversy with you, *but you have brought it all on yourself, by your report of the 25th of September*, after your second reconnaissance of Sweaborg. That report appeared to me to be entirely at variance with the opinions previously expressed by you, and I certainly understood you then to say, that if you had mortars, rockets, and Lancaster guns, you considered Sweaborg assailable by sea. In May you declared it to be unassailable by sea or land, and the Admiralty did not send you the appliances which, in September, you declared to be wanting, because they believed, from your account, they would be useless against a place which in the first instance you pronounced to be impregnable. I could not bring myself to believe the want of Lancaster guns, or *even of mortars,* rendered a sea attack, on your plan of the 25th of September, impossible, if you had had twenty-five sail of the line reassembled before the place, *with all their means of vertical fire!*"

What is there in Sir Charles Napier's letter of 27th of October that should render the First Lord unwilling to " enter into a controversy " on the subject? It was merely a calm, though dignified statement of facts which ought to be met, and that on the question of *fact*, not " controversy." Sir James understood the Admiral to say that "if he had *mortars, rockets, and Lancaster guns,* he considered Sweaborg assailable by sea." Of course he did, and, beyond doubt, had these been supplied it would have been so assailable. But the reason why these were not supplied was that, in May, he considered it impregnable. This is not fact, inasmuch as there is a *suppressio veri.* In May, Sweaborg had not been examined, and therefore could not be judged of from the plans which had been supplied to him, and on these Gen. Jones had come to precisely the same conclusion in his report of the 1st of May—when even he pointed out the means required for an attack on the fortress; so that the subterfuge of not having time to supply them, as was asserted, is not tenable. We must be very particular on these points.

On the 27th of February, a fortnight before the fleet left Spithead for the Baltic, Sir John Ross informed the Government that the Russians were fitting out gun-boats in the Gulf, each carrying an 8-inch gun, with a cylindrical percussion shell containing 28 lbs. of powder, which shell bursts on striking; and, adds Sir John Ross, "in 1844, I saw a shell of this sort tried against the side of a line-of-battle ship at 600 yards. It burst on striking, and *made an opening through which I walked.*" The Admiralty gave this information to Sir Charles Napier, so that they must have known that gun-boats and small steamers were most requisite, in order to protect the large ships, if for nothing else; yet none were even attempted to be supplied.

On the 4th of February, three weeks before the appointment of Sir C. Napier to the command of the Baltic fleet, Sir Hamilton Seymour wrote that "light steamers drawing as little water as possible, would be required for clearing the Gulf of gun-boats." There was surely plenty of time to comply with the warning, which, at the period, Sir Hamilton Seymour was the most competent person to give.

In addition to the above, the Government received information of twenty-one small steamers having been organised for service in the Gulf of Finland, the whole of these being mentioned by name, together with the names of the commanders. None were supplied to the British fleet. As has been before mentioned, Sir Hamilton Seymour enumerated 180 gun-boats in the Gulf. The British fleet had none.

On the 28th of March, the Admiralty was advised that this enormous fleet of gun-boats was divided between Cronstadt and Sweaborg, and that at the former place were two floating batteries, each with four 98-pounder shell guns.

As the above advices, and many more which could be particularised, if necessary, arrived *before war was declared,* is it not then idle to say that these were

M M

not supplied because they were " thought to be useless ?"—which is Sir James Graham's expression! In
the House of Commons, in 1856, Sir James Graham
expressly stated that if he had been apprised in May
that gun and mortar-boats were wanted, they could
have been supplied. Evidence is given above that not
only in May, but in February, before the fleet had been
even assembled, the necessity for them was pointed out
by those most competent to judge. To talk of the
ability to supply them in time is so much nonsense.
They were not even supplied to Admiral Dundas in
the following year in numbers to produce a decisive
effect. His bombardment of Sweaborg showed that,
had he been supplied with more, Sweaborg must have
been untenable from the shower of shells that could
have been directed on it. Who, before Sir C. Napier's
fleet, ever heard of a fleet sent to war without mortars?
In Admiral Dundas's bombardment those that had
been supplied burst and became useless, whilst he had
no others to replace them, and was compelled to discontinue his bombardment in consequence, and, as we
have before shown, almost at the moment of victory.

Sir James Graham continues " I could not bring
myself to believe that the want of Lancaster guns, or
even of mortars, rendered a sea attack on your plan
on the 25th of September impossible." If the reader
will be good enough to compare this extract with the
corresponding expressions in the despatch of October
4th, he will be at no loss to know who wrote that
despatch, notwithstanding Admirals Berkeley and
Richards signed it. There can be no mistake on this
point. Sir James, in the letter of 31st of October,

does not think "even mortars" necessary, as, "if he had twenty-five ships *re-assembled* before the place," (Sir James knew he had only *nine* ships of the line, and the "re-assembling" will not now deceive the reader,) "with all their means of *vertical fire!*" an attack was not impossible. A "vertical fire" from long guns will no doubt highly amuse naval men, to whom, however, this display of nautical erudition will be no novelty. They will, however, be somewhat surprised to learn that "*even mortars*" are not essential to bombarding! though how a bombardment can be effectually made without mortars would rather puzzle even a First Lord of the Admiralty to explain.

But we will not pursue this subject farther. It is undignified, even in a naval work, to criticise such palpable ignorance as this. It is sufficient to record it for the amazement of naval posterity. We may nevertheless ask, how it is possible for our fleets to be victorious where ignorance of the very first element of a fleet's power is made to take the place of the power itself. "God bless Sultan Hassan!" cried the owl; "we shall never want ruined buildings while he lives." "God bless Sultan Graham!" may our foes exclaim; "we need care little for English fleets whilst he directs them."

To this remarkable effusion of Sir James Graham the Admiral replied on the 6th of November :—

"I can assure you, Sir James, it is far from my wish to enter into a controversy with you, but I will not admit that I have brought it on myself. There is not a word in either my public or private letters that justifies the construction you and the Admiralty have thought proper to put on them. My letter in answer to their Lordships' last despatch is plain enough; but if their Lordships think proper to deliberate on one part of my letter and ignore another part, I can only protest against it, and am quite prepared to defend myself against any unjust attacks that are made against me.

" I have documents enough in my possession to justify my conduct. Enough has *not been done* to satisfy " an impatient public," as you called them. Some one must be blamed, and I am the *chosen one.* But I will not allow myself to be crushed because I could not do impossibilities.

" All this stir has been caused by the reports of two engineers, the one French and the other English, because they suited the public taste. In addition to these was the report of the capture of Sebastopol, *not yet taken,* though the fleet there is assisted by an army of 70,000 men—in a fine climate. I have been expected to take places much stronger *with a fleet alone ; and the same people who so often warned me against risking my fleet, are now dissatisfied because I did not expose it to certain destruction.*

" I have gone through the world with honour and credit to myself; and just as I am about to leave it, unworthy attempts are made to ruin my reputation. *But they will fail, and recoil on themselves."*

To his cousin, Lieut.-General Sir W. Napier, the Admiral wrote as follows : —

" MY DEAR WILLIAM,

" Things have turned out *just as you warned me.* After Bomarsund was taken, the French General sent home his troops — I think wisely, as the weather got so bad that nothing more could be attempted with the least prospect of success. The people became dissatisfied, and I believe the Government fanned the flame. I got an order to hold a council of war, and the Admirals all decided that nothing more could be done at this season of the year. Gen. Jones made a report that, by landing 5000 men on Bak Holmen, and raising batteries, combined with an attack from the ships,

Sweaborg could be taken in seven or eight days, and this was the proper time. Had he done so, not a man could have got off. They would all have been made prisoners by the garrison of Sweaborg, where the Russians could collect at least 20,000 men, and the ships would probably have been lost amongst the sunken rocks of the place.

" This report I believe the Government made known, and, to serve their own purposes, set it going. I was ordered to bring it before the French General and Admiral. They had already rejected it, and the French General had sailed. Then the French General of Engineers reported that the ships alone could knock down Sweaborg in two hours.

" I was ordered to call another council of war to examine this. The French Admiral declined attending, as he had already given his opinion, and the English Admirals decided against it. There I thought it would have ended. But Sebastopol was said to be taken, and the press flew out against me, egged on, I have no doubt, by Graham. Then I made another reconnaissance, and showed what was necessary to take Sweaborg *in the ensuing summer*. The Admiralty *pretended* to think I meant *now*, threw aside my plan, and pretended t o believe I was to do it with ships alone, and, *for effect*, stopped the French and English ships that were ordered home, and then *cancelled their orders*.

" Then a letter came from Berkeley of a dubious character, showing me that I should be thrown overboard; and finally a jesuitical letter from Graham. These I have answered, and told them, if they were not satisfied, *they had better try me by a Court-martial, or remove me*. It was necessary to blame some one, and so they chose me, and there it rests.

" The weather has been so bad that it was impossible to do anything, even if we had the means. The fact is, the troops came too late. There were too many for Bomarsund and too few for Sweaborg. This the public knew nothing about, and the Government are afraid to say so; so a whisper is quite enough to ruin me, and that whisper they have taken care to give; so that I hear the greater part of the press is abusing me for not having taken Sweaborg,

Revel, and Cronstadt without troops, though Sebastopol is not yet taken, both with ships and troops.

> " I am, my dear William,
>
> "Your affectionate Cousin,
>
> " CHAS. NAPIER.

" Lieut.-Gen. Sir W. Napier."

A word of explanation, as regards this letter, is necessary. Sir Charles Napier tells Sir William that " things have turned out just as Sir William warned him." This refers to the dispute on the appointment of Sir C. Napier, as narrated in the first chapter of this book. On consulting Sir William about accepting the command under such circumstances, Sir William counselled him to " mind what he was about, as some scurvy trick would be served him." The great error of Sir Charles Napier was in accepting the command under circumstances so inauspicious, as he must have foreseen that it could scarcely have ended satisfactorily.

Sir Charles, at the end of his letter to Sir William, refers to Sebastopol. It is not pretended that, before of it the genius of Todtleben made Sebastopol what it afterwards became, Sebastopol possessed anything like the strength of Sweaborg, either by nature or art. Neither Admiral Dundas, Lord Raglan, nor Marshal St. Arnaud were dismissed from their command for not capturing it with their vast fleet and 70,000 men. Sir Charles Napier *was* dismissed from his command for not attacking Sweaborg without troops, and with twelve ships of the line only — for the shallow pretence of ordering back the French squadron and

Admiral Plumridge's ships is too transparent to impose even on a child. A pretext for dismissing him was wanted, and here it was. There stand, side by side, the historical facts: Lord Raglan was made a Field-Marshal for not capturing Sebastopol; Sir Charles Napier was dismissed from his command for not capturing Sweaborg!

Even with the genius of Todtleben, Sebastopol was an inferior fortress to Cronstadt. Yet a quarter of a million of men, with a loss of at least 50,000 lives, and with the aid of an enormous fleet, only succeeded in capturing a part of it after two campaigns. Nay more, there is good reason to believe that the Russian version of their having determined to abandon the south side of Sebastopol from the fearful slaughter of their troops — 1000 per day — is the correct one; at any rate, they had everything in preparation for this retreat to the north side, which was effected without loss. Yet a Lord of the Admiralty was found to declare, that had Sir Charles Napier not been " deficient in energy and spirit," Cronstadt must have " been crumbled in the dust;" that is, a stronger place than had baffled a quarter of a million of men and two fleets, ought to have been taken by Sir Charles Napier without troops, gun-boats, mortar-boats, or rockets!

When Englishmen read these pages, it must be with a blush of shame at the unworthy treatment experienced by Sir Charles Napier. This treatment can be repaired; but there is another matter which concerns Englishmen yet more deeply. Is the Board of Admiralty the best bulwark to fall back upon in case of a fresh emergency?

Were we to answer this weighty question, perhaps the English public might not be inclined to listen to us. Therefore we will not reply to it. A Lord of the Admiralty, of seventeen years' experience at the Board, and of still greater experience as a seaman, shall do so in our stead.

After the death of Admiral of the Fleet Sir George Cockburn, there was found in his secret drawer, and *under his will*, the following opinions on the Board of Admiralty as at present constituted. If Englishmen will accept it, a more valuable legacy was never bequeathed to them:—

" Having filled the station of confidential or principal Sea Lord of the Admiralty for more than seventeen years, I feel that my opinion regarding the constitution of that Board may, sooner or later, be deemed worthy of consideration and attention ; I therefore am induced to place in writing the decision to which my experience has brought me on this point.

" I have, then, no hesitation in stating, that I consider the present establishment of that Board to be the most unsatisfactory and least efficient for its purpose that could have been devised.

" In the first place, it is most inconsistent and inconvenient that one member of the Board should without any communication with his colleagues, issue orders at Somerset House, in the name of the Board, for the governance of the whole fleet, dockyards, &c., provided it relates to the branch of the Admiralty business he is selected to superintend, such orders being issued in the name and under the authority of the Board, without any other member thereof being aware of such order, and often only learning its promulgation from the newspapers, or from questions asked about it in Parliament.

" It is true the 'principal officer' (as he is termed) of that department is, or ought to be, able to give all requisite infor-

mation or advice to such Lord of the Admiralty; but such
' principal officer ' has no responsibility ; yet such course naturally places the greater portion of the real management in his
hands as relates to such department ; the Board — the really
responsible parties — remaining wholly ignorant (with the exception of the single member of it before alluded to) of such
general orders, or of the grounds thereof, unless the particular
Lord of the department mentions the matter to his colleagues,
which, in the latter part of my being at the Board, was very
rarely done, especially by one of my colleagues ; and consequently the business could not but be carried forward in an
unconnected and disjointed manner, the fault being with a
system admitting of, and, indeed, leading to such evil result.

" Secondly, as regards the proceedings of the Board when
united for general business, I must premise that nothing can
well be more contrary to reason, and, I may say, common
sense, than for a person to be selected to preside at such professional Board, who is totally unable and admits his inability
to understand three-fourths of the professional statements or
even expressions contained in the various documents read on
such occasions to the Board, and which, therefore, the professional members of the Board become obliged to occupy time in
explaining and endeavouring to make him comprehend, which,
nevertheless, cannot be always sufficiently effected.

" Then, again, the Board consisting of six persons, and the
professional members, or a portion of them, being selected
with reference to political considerations and their having
seats in Parliament, and without any regard to their knowledge of each other or how far they might be likely to act
cordially together, much valuable time becomes consumed in
fruitless and sometimes irritable and unsatisfactory discussions,
interfering greatly with the necessary advancement of the numerous professional and other matters almost daily brought
for decision before the Admiralty ; and the evil of such check
to business may be well conceived when it is considered that
matters of almost every possible description, from the building
of ships of war and ordering the movements and discipline of
our fleets, down to the deciding on the details and eligibility

of railroads, are now brought either for decision or opinion, before the Board of Admiralty.

" It will not then be deemed surprising that, with the want of concert and the difficulties above alluded to, I experienced frequent annoying checks and obstructions in carrying forward those objects which appeared to me essentially required and called for, and some of which I was obliged to abandon from the opposition of one or other of such disjointed ruling body, and such opposition, in some instances, springing from parties having no real knowledge on the professional matters under consideration, but objecting to them in consequence of something that may have been said to them by some irresponsible person out of doors.

" Indeed, during my last seat at the Admiralty Board the annoyances I was subjected to from the last-mentioned causes kept me in a continual state of anxiety and difficulty, and required from me the strongest exertion of *forbearance* to enable me to remain in a situation so truly unsatisfactory to my view of efficient management of so important and multifarious a department, to advance which cordial union of decision must be urgently necessary, rather than the existing cause of impediments from unworthy jealousies and debates.

" The remedies I would recommend are : —

" 1. That the Admiralty Board should be abolished, and that the management of the Navy should be transferred to a flag-officer, as Naval Commander-in-Chief, to be assisted by two naval officers, either as Vice and Rear Admirals of England, or as Council. That a leading member of Parliament be appointed by the Government (to be in the Cabinet or not, as may be deemed best), to be styled ' Controller of Naval Expenditure,' to be in constant and cordial co-operation with the Naval Commander-in-Chief, to arrange with him the proposed expenditure for each year, to be submitted to the Treasury for approval, the said civilian Controller to be charged with submitting the yearly estimates to the House of Commons, and answering there all financial questions relating to the navy ; the said officer to have the patronage and control of all the clerks and others in the accountant and in the

store departments; all other appointments, as well in the dockyards as at Somerset House and elsewhere attaching to the
naval administration, to rest with the Naval Commander-in-
Chief, whose directions, relative to the number of ships to be
built, or repaired, or fitted for service, and the quantity of
stores required, should be deemed sufficient for the Controller
of Naval Expenditure to provide for the payment thereof,
though he is to be at liberty to make any observation he may
deem necessary thereon to the Commander-in-Chief; and, in
the event of any irreconcilable difference of opinion upon
any such or other points between the said two high officers,
the matter or matters at issue between them to be referred to
the First Lord of the Treasury for his decision, which must,
of course, be adopted.

" So much of the accountant detail being removed from
the Admiralty branch, the Naval Commander-in-Chief and his
two councillors, or assistants, will be more at liberty to give
full attention to the more professional objects of maintaining
and improving the efficiency and discipline of our fleets, as
also the efficiency and works of the dockyards ; though, as regards the latter, I would recommend the appointment of a flag-
officer under the Admiralty, to be continually visiting the
yards in succession, to insure uniformity of practice and
working in all, with such a general superintending officer
under the Admiralty, and a scientific board of construction,
as lately established, to advise and offer suggestions on all
points relating to shipbuilding. This would, in my opinion,
form a most efficient and satisfactory working system ; and of
course the appointment of ' Surveyor of the Navy' (the ob-
jections to such an officer, whether himself a shipbuilder or
not, have been often experienced) would be entirely abolished.

" The Naval Commander-in-Chief and his two councillors
may or may not be in Parliament, as deemed best by the Government ; but I am of opinion they (especially the former)
should not be in Parliament, to render it unnecessary to
change the governing system of our navy with every change
of Ministers, which keeps the naval service in a constant
state of unsteadiness and uncertainty, very detrimental to its

complete and unvarying efficiency — an evil which would be remedied by the Commander-in-Chief and his colleagues being relieved from all political character.

" In the foregoing observations I have mentioned the two assistants to the proposed Naval Commander-in-Chief in union with him, but, although he will have the benefit of their advice and experience on the various points under his control and management, it is to be clearly understood that he alone will be responsible for whatever is done by his authority, and all orders and directions signed by him alone are to be deemed complete, and to be obeyed as such by all subject to his control. But he may, if he think proper, authorise the members of his council to sign conjointly such documents as he may not deem necessary to be signed by himself; and, after he shall have officially notified his authority to such effect, all such directions, signed by the members of his council, to the extent so authorised, are to be deemed of full force, and to be obeyed accordingly.

" The principal objection I have heard advanced to placing a naval officer at the head of the naval service, is that he would be likely to show undue favour to those of the profession who had served with him; but I see no reason why this should be the case more with the navy than with the army, and such has not been found a sufficient objection as regards the Commander-in-Chief of the army. And even supposing, for the sake of argument, such favourable feelings towards any particular officers to be entertained by a Commander-in-Chief, it can only be supposed to arise from such favoured officers having given him full proof of their zeal and abilities while serving with him; and admitting such an impression to have, therefore, any reasonable foundation, it would have a tendency to render officers in general when on active service anxious to secure by their attention and zealous conduct the good opinion and future protective friendship of their superior officers, and might, therefore, have a generally beneficial result rather than otherwise. My conviction, however, is, that a naval officer, placed in the high and honourable post of Commander-in-Chief of the Navy, would evince as much

real impartiality as any other individual of any other class or
rank whatever.

" The only other objection that has been advanced against
placing a naval officer at the head of the navy is, that a naval
officer is not likely, from his earlier habits and education, to
be efficient for the many other than naval matters continually
under consideration of the Cabinet; my answer to which is,
that he need not be in the Cabinet any more than the Commander-in-Chief of the army, though I firmly believe very
many superior naval officers would prove as efficient Cabinet
Ministers as many of those gentlemen I have known there
during my connection with government business."

Has the Board of Admiralty improved since this
was written? Let the late war answer. Fleets were
fitted out such as Howe, St. Vincent, Hood, Keith,
Nelson, Collingwood, and a host of other naval heroes
never dreamed of. What have those fleets done?
Absolutely nothing. The only two operations of importance, viz., Odessa and the bombardment of Sweaborg, Russia has by public proclamation claimed as
victories of her own, and the Board of Admiralty has
" eaten the leek" without question. Were all our
Admirals, then, " deficient in energy and spirit," as
Sir R. Peel said of Sir C. Napier? This is very improbable. The cause of our humiliation, then, must
lie deeper. Sir George Cockburn tells us plainly
enough where it lies; and this volume is only a confirmation of his opinion. Englishmen may depend
upon it, it will be too late to apply the remedy when
the nation is in its death-throe.

This legacy of Sir George Cockburn is, however,
only another version of what Sir Charles Napier
wrote to Sir Robert Peel in 1841. It has been the

lot of Sir Charles Napier to make more suggestions
for the improvement of the navy than most men;
and it has also been his lot to see his suggestions
attended to beyond those of most men. But he has
not succeeded in getting the Board of Admiralty to
recommend his suggestions for the abolition of the
Board of Admiralty, as the one grand obstacle to
naval reformation. Power and place are in this
superior to public utility. Yet the legacy of Sir
George Cockburn had its origin in a letter of
Sir Charles Napier to Sir Robert Peel, in 1841.
From this letter the following are extracts : —

"I am of opinion that the navy should be ruled by a naval
officer,— not a Cabinet Minister,—with the title of ' Admiral
of Great Britain ;' the title of ' Lord High Admiral ' being
perhaps too high for any person under royalty. The whole
of the patronage and responsibility should be vested in him.
He should be assisted by two flag-officers, with the title of
Vice and Rear Admiral of Great Britain — doing away with
the two sinecures of that name ; a flag-officer, or a captain, with the title of Captain of the Fleet ; a civilian, and
two secretaries, one a naval officer and the other a civilian.

"The Vice-Admiral should superintend the dockyard department, the Rear-Admiral the victualling and medical
branch, and the civilian the Accountant-General's department. All correspondence with either of these departments
should go direct to them, and they should give their orders
to the Surveyor, Storekeeper-General, Physician of the Fleet,
and Comptroller of Victualling.

"The Admiral of Great Britain would, of course, consult
with them when he thought it necessary, and give what directions he thought proper. But his attention would be particularly directed to the stationing of the ships, the promotion
and appointment of officers, in which he would be assisted by
the Captain of the Fleet and his Naval Secretary.

" The Civil Secretary should attend to the political part of the business, which should only be known to the Admiral and himself; whereas, at present, there are many transactions which ought to be secret, with which the whole Board are acquainted, and in addition to them, perhaps, one half of the clerks in the Admiralty.

" The inspections at the different ports should be made by the Admiral, the Vice or Rear Admiral. They should hoist their flags and examine minutely into their departments, and *most particularly into the discipline of the ships,* which can never be done by a Board in plain clothes, with a secretary tacked to their tail, running hastily through the departments in the manner they have hitherto done.

" No apprehension could be entertained of any difficulties between the Ministry and an Admiral who could be removed at pleasure, but who ought not to be removed with every change of Ministry. At present, not only the First Lord, but all the Board, *are political partisans ;* and just as they begin to know their business they are replaced by a fresh set, who have their lessons to learn, *and invariably entertain different notions to their predecessors.* Hence arise the constant changes that take place, ruinous to the discipline and the well-being of the service, and expensive to the country.

" It may be thought great presumption in so humble an individual as myself in making suggestions to a Prime Minister how to form his Administration; but I do it from a conviction that, if things are allowed to continue in their present state, *a great catastrophe will befall this country.*

" I know, sir, a Minister may hesitate to adopt my views, fearing to *lose the patronage of the navy.* He may also have difficulties with his political friends, who aspire to the place of First Lord of the Admiralty ; but, sir, Mr. Canning broke through all these difficulties, and I see no reason why Sir Robert Peel should not follow his example."

True, Canning did break through those difficulties, but the aristocracy, who profited by the difficulties,

broke Canning's heart; and Sir Robert Peel had no
mind to become his fellow-martyr, and therefore
did not follow the advice of Sir Charles Napier,
which, says Sir George Cockburn, after seventeen
years' experience at the Admiralty, ought to be
followed even now. The "*great catastrophe*" pre-
dicted by Sir Charles Napier has "befallen this
country;" for surely it is a great catastrophe to the
country that, for want of means, our fleets should
have been paralysed, and a peace patched up in
consequence, which is felt by the country to be a
humiliation. To conceal the real meaning of Sir
Charles Napier, the organs of the Government cry
out that he is "traducing the navy," "fouling his
own nest," he is a "Russian Admiral," &c. His
true meaning, that our undisciplined fleet was owing
to the constitution of the Board of Admiralty, is
overlooked, or purposely concealed in the cry against
him. Yet the First Lord, in a letter before quoted,
tells him that " he thought the means asked for by
the Admiral, viz., gun-boats, mortar-boats, mortars,
rockets, &c., *were useless !*" — this being Sir James
Graham's expression, and the Naval Lords, no doubt
awed by the Civil Lord, durst not say anything to
the contrary. It is not an undisciplined navy that
will one day destroy this country, but the Board of
Admiralty, on whose shoulders that want of discipline
rests. It is not inexperienced officers who are to
blame, but the Board of Admiralty, which, for
political purposes, promotes inexperience and over-
looks experience, — even admitting this, as has been
seen, by setting the Admiral against his officers. If,

when the reader meets with the word "inexperience," as relates to the fleet, he will read "Board of Admiralty," he will then have the key to all Sir Charles Napier has ever said or written on the subject; and what is more, will not be likely to disagree with the Admiral.

One thing is quite clear, viz., that if England will not reform her Board of Admiralty, other nations will reform theirs; and what will be the result of effective Boards of Admiralty against an ineffective Board it is not difficult to guess. If we persist in the delusion that one English seaman can fight half a dozen French or Russian seamen, we can hardly be so blind as to assert that one inefficient Board of Admiralty can fight half a dozen efficient Boards belonging to other nations. However these very matters, of which we are now writing, may be despised by Whitehall place-hunters, they will be cherished by Russia, France, and America, and the result does not require a prophet to foretell. Every nation which in the whole range of history has fallen at all, has fallen from its own blind security in inadequate means, coupled with the acute vision of those who destroyed or supplanted it. England holds no charter from Divine providence which shall shield her from the consequences of ordinary cause and effect.

N N

CHAP XXII.

THE SQUADRON AT KIEL. — VOYAGE TO SPITHEAD. — ADMIRAL ORDERED TO STRIKE HIS FLAG. — CORRESPONDENCE WITH THE ADMIRALTY.

CONCEALMENT BY THE ADMIRALTY OF ITS KNOWLEDGE OF SIR CHARLES NAPIER'S FIRST PLAN OF ATTACK ON SWEABORG. — THE ADMIRAL'S VERACITY DOUBTED. — WHY A COMMITTEE OF INVESTIGATION WAS RE-FUSED. — ADMIRAL DINES WITH THE KING OF DENMARK. — CAPTAIN OF THE FLEET ORDERED HOME. — COMPLIMENT PAID TO CAPTAIN WATSON AND HIS SQUADRON. — LEAVE OF ABSENCE REFUSED TO SIR CHARLES. — A MASTERSTROKE OF ADMIRALTY DIPLOMACY. — ADMIRAL'S LETTER TO PROFESSOR KEY. — SAILS FOR ENGLAND. — ORDERED TO STRIKE HIS FLAG. — COMPARISON OF THE TREATMENT RECEIVED BY ADMIRALS NAPIER AND DUNDAS. — TARDY THANKS TO THE FORMER. — SIR CHARLES'S REPLY TO THE ORDER TO STRIKE HIS FLAG. — REJOINDER OF THE AD-MIRALTY. — LETTER TO THE DUKE OF NEWCASTLE. — THE DUKE'S REPLY. — HER MAJESTY'S COMMAND TO THE ADMIRAL TO DINE AT WINDSOR. — ADMIRAL'S RECEPTION BY SIR JAMES GRAHAM. — SIR CHARLES AGAIN ADDRESSES THE BOARD OF ADMIRALTY. — CORRESPONDENCE THEREON. — THE ADMIRALTY'S FINAL ÆGIS. — ALL INVESTIGATION AVOIDED. — SIR CHARLES OFFERED THE GRAND CROSS. — HE DECLINES THE HONOUR. — HIS LETTER TO PRINCE ALBERT.

IT has been seen, in the previous portion of this work, that frequent reference has been made to the Admiral's plan of attacking Sweaborg in the following year, when gun-boats, mortar-boats, and the other requisite *matériel* of war, should have been supplied. The report containing these plans was, as the reader is aware, dated July 18th, and to this the subsequent report of September 25th bore distinct reference, the reference being even admitted by Sir James Graham, who calls it his "second reconnaissance," thereby clearly intimating that he was in possession of the result of the "first reconnaissance," which he never laid before the Admiralty. On the 10th of November, the Board of Admiralty wrote to Sir Charles, *that it had never received any plan of attack on Sweaborg, except that of the 25th of September!* or, to use their own words, "prior to the 24th of July," at which time the Admiral considered any attack on Sweaborg as entirely out of the question.

This reference to the Admiral's letter of the 24th of July was a trick which should scarcely have been adopted by so dignified a body as the Board of Admiralty. It will have been seen, in a former portion of this work, that, previous to the arrival of the French troops in the Baltic, the Admiralty did not know what fortress the French General and the Allied Admirals, when in consultation together, would decide to attack, though it well knew, from the Admiral's previous letters, that Sweaborg was not likely to be decided on, as the troops came to attack Bomarsund, and the Admiral had told the Board that the French troops were "too many for Bomarsund, and too few for Sweaborg."

In this light, therefore, the Admiral on the 24th of July, wrote as follows:—

"As an attack on Sweaborg is entirely out of the question, the *rendezvous* (for the French troops) must not be at Baro Sound, as Bomarsund is the most likely place to be attacked.

I have already directed the line-of-battle ships, with troops, to meet me at Ledsund, which is the outer roadstead of Bomarsund, and where I now am."

The despatch of the Board professes to construe this into an assertion that Sweaborg *cannot* be attacked, though the Admiral had sent home two distinct reports, each containing plans whereby Sweaborg might be attacked, and with a *certainty* of success, when means were supplied, and at a proper season of the year, in the next campaign. To pervert this to another sense was perhaps necessary, to support the previous perversions of the Admiral's letters. So true is it that the perpetration of wrong requires a persistence in wrong.

Not relying on this, which was too transparent to deceive any one, the Board tells the Admiral that, on the 30th of May, he told them that " Sweaborg was unassailable by sea or land." The Admiral did say so; but this was before it had been examined, and on the strength of the Admiralty plans only. The Admiral was then at Hango, on his way to Swea-borg, and could have known nothing of the place itself; neither he nor the Admiralty, therefore, could have considered his opinion decisive before the place was examined. The favourite military authority of the Admiralty, General Jones, on the 1st of May, had given them the same opinion, pointing out, how-ever, what additional means he thought necessary to attack it with success. These means, as the reader knows, were never supplied. When Sweaborg had been examined, Sir Charles said it could be attacked, even without troops, and showed how. When General Jones *saw Sweaborg*, he said the same thing, but *with troops*, which the French General would not let him have. To fling in Sir Charles Napier's teeth, then, his opinion on the imperfect plans supplied to him before he had seen Sweaborg, and to ignore his plans of attack *after* he had seen it, was unworthy of the Board of Admiralty, which had taken good care to recognise General Jones's plans of attack with troops, though neither the French General nor the Allied Admirals would recognise them.

The Admiralty despatch of the 10th of November is, however, doubtful whether these reminiscences will hold good, as we have shown they will not; and it proceeds to throw doubt upon the Admiral's *veracity*, by asking " to be informed when the forts and works of Sweaborg were inspected by him previous to the 18th of July? — in what ship the inspection was made, and at what distance from the forts and wôrks ?"

The reader who has paid attention to the former portion of this book, can answer the question for himself; viz., that when, on the 12th of June, the Admiral at once proceeded to examine Sweaborg, as near as he could get, Mr. Biddlecombe, the Master of the Fleet was sent in to make a regular survey, and reported that the channel used by the Russians was difficult, unless buoyed, which was impracticable; but that he had found a channel to the eastward of Storo Miolo which he thought would prove practicable, as was afterwards found to be the case. In this survey,

Mr. Biddlecombe took with him three steamers, the *Basilisk*, *Bulldog*, and *Driver*, all of which were engaged in the survey. Captain Sulivan had alone, on the 11th of July, been into Sweaborg with a flag of truce, and got a full and close inspection of the works.

Surely this was a sufficiently close reconnaissance. The Admiralty, when thus covertly attacking the veracity of Sir Charles Napier, had forgotten that they considered the view of Sweaborg obtained by Generals Jones and Niel sufficient warranty for the soundness of their plans, which happened to suit the public taste, as would have done the plans of Sir Charles Napier, had these been laid before the public. But they were never laid before the public, as the Admiralty had not supplied the means to carry them out, and must have borne the odium of this, as they will now have to bear it. It is not now difficult to understand why no Committee was granted to Sir Charles Napier for an investigation, though it is difficult to see how the Government can yet avoid it, but this time themselves suppliants for it, in place of the Admiral.

Little confident in any of these resources to get out of the scrape, the Board, in the conclusion of its despatch, had recourse to open quarrel with the Admiral, by telling him that, " with reference to his letter, he supposed a determination on the part of their Lordships *to deliberate on one part of his statement, and to ignore others.* My Lords desire me to inform you, that they cannot permit any officer under their orders to suppose that they can deliberately misinterpret explanations on which they still require further information."

But they did so misinterpret his despatches, and they could not require further information, for the information alluded to had not only been reported by the Admiral, but by the Master of the Fleet. The information was then most full and complete.

The Admiralty despatch has been honestly and minutely canvassed, and nothing can be *more easy than for the Admiralty themselves to make it public*, should they deem it desirable. Were all their despatches made public, the nation would draw from them deductions, from which we have refrained, out of sheer regard for the honour of our country.

The Admiral's reply to this despatch of November 10th necessarily and entirely consists of recapitulations now familiar to the reader, so that we need not again reinsert them.

Whilst at Kiel, and during the period that the fleet was engaged in provisioning and other necessary operations, the Admiral paid a visit to Hamburg. When there he received an invitation from his Majesty the King of Denmark, then at Altona, to dine with him. The Admiral was graciously received, and told His Majesty that next spring he hoped to see the Danish squadron united with the British fleet. His Majesty said he should be neutral as long as he could, war was an expensive thing; but if compelled to go to war, he certainly should not be against us.

On the 20th of November, the Admiralty took the unusual step of ordering home Rear-Admiral Seymour, the Captain of the Fleet. It is not difficult to guess at the object of the Board in thus ordering home the Captain of the Fleet before the Commander-in-Chief, but it may be imprudent to allude further to that object. Admiral Seymour must have felt himself placed in a somewhat invidious position, though, of course, he could only obey orders.

On the 22nd of November, the *Impérieuse* and *Euryalus* were ordered to England, in consequence of damages which had been sustained from a collision which had taken place on the 12th; the *Euryalus* lost the whole of her cutwater and her bowsprit, the *Impérieuse* lost her main chains and nearly all her main shrouds, besides receiving other damage in her upper works, the *Euryalus* having run stem on to her whilst wearing.

On the 25th of November, the *St. Jean d'Acre* and *Princess Royal* sailed for Devonport ; Admiral Seymour hoisting his flag in the *Princess Royal* in obedience to Admiralty orders, and proceeding home in her. On the 26th, orders were received for the *James Watt* and the *Cæsar* to proceed to England.

On the 27th, the Admiral despatched the *Vulture* to the Gulf of Finland, with orders to Captain Watson to withdraw from the blockade ; the Admiralty having instructed Sir Charles Napier that he was at liberty to withdraw the steamers from the Gulf when he was satisfied that the Russian fleet was sufficiently secured by ice, and that the presence of British ships of war, for the purposes of blockade, or for the protection of British shipping, was no longer useful.

The blockade of the Gulf to so late a period reflected the highest honour on Captain Watson and the officers and men under his command. The weather had been fearful, with constant heavy gales and snow-storms. These, with the current setting towards Sweden, made it difficult for the ships to keep their stations, whilst from the absence of the sun the difficulty was greatly increased. When reporting the blockade to the Board, the Admiral paid the following well-merited compliment to Captain Watson and those under his command.

" I have not words to express my approval of the persevering conduct of Captain Watson and all his squadron ; and I do hope their Lordships will note their approval of his conduct by the promotion of his First Lieutenant (Cockcraft), or in any other manner they may think fit. Capt. Watson began the blockade of Sweaborg early in spring, and has continued there ever since, with little intermission ; and I do not believe, in the height of the last war, a stricter or more dangerous blockade was ever kept up."

The ships comprised in the blockading squadron off the Gulf were *Impérieuse*, Captain Watson ; *Euryalus*, Captain Ramsay ; *Arrogant*, Captain Yelverton ; *Penelope*, Captain Coffin ; *Amphion*, Captain Key (on the Courland Coast) ; *Magicienne*, Captain Fisher ; *Conflict*, Captain Cumming ; *Desperate*, Captain D'Eyncourt ; *Odin*, Captain Scott ; *Dragon*, Captain Willcox ; *Archer*, Captain Heathcote (on the Courland Coast) ; and *Cruiser*, Commander Douglas.

On the 28th, the *James Watt* and *Cæsar* sailed for Spithead. On the 1st of December the *Magicienne* sailed for Elsinore, to convey British or French traders bound for Memel and the southern part of the Baltic; Mr. Buchanan, the Minister at Copenhagen, considering such protection desirable.

On the 2nd of December, the *Cressy* and *Majestic* were ordered to proceed to Sheerness. The *Driver* arrived from cruising between Bornholm and Memel, having gained no intelligence of Russian steamers having been seen at sea, as had been reported.

On the 4th, the Admiral received orders to return with the remainder of the fleet to England, leaving Admiral Chads to bring home Captain Watson's blockading squadron, on their arrival at Kiel. Receiving this order, the Admiral, by telegraph, asked permission of the Board to be allowed to return home overland to Hamburg, and thence to England; as the fleet was now reduced to six sail of the line, and urgent private affairs required his presence at home.

This request was ungraciously refused by the Board of Admiralty, who told him that " leave of absence could not be given to him. If he was obliged to *vacate his command*, Admiral Chads must shift his flag to the *Duke of Wellington*, and execute the orders of the Admiralty." The Admiral was further instructed to announce his intention forthwith.

The Admiral, however, saw through the device, and replied by telegraph : " I do not intend to *vacate my command*. I shall carry out their Lordships' instructions."

The reader will perhaps smile at this eagerness of the Admiralty to get Sir Charles Napier to vacate his command, by refusing him leave of absence after so long a campaign, and when his presence with the remnant of the fleet could be of no further use; he will be still more amused when initiated into the mystery of this masterstroke of Admiralty diplomacy.

On the 1st of December Mr. Thomas D'Iffanger, Hon. Secretary to the Committee for conducting the Marylebone Election to provide a successor to Lord Dudley Stuart, wrote to Sir Charles Napier at Kiel that his name had been selected amongst others at a public meeting to represent the borough of Marylebone; he therefore solicited him to attend a public meeting at the St. Pancras Vestry Hall, in pursuance of the object of the Committee.

All this was, of course, well known to the Government, who shrewdly guessed what were the "urgent private affairs" of the Admiral. At that moment the appearance of a live bombshell in Parliament would have been about as desirable as that of Sir Charles Napier, and the "leave of absence" asked for was promptly refused. It was, however, supposed that the Admiral's love of electioneering would induce him to vacate his command, and thus relieve the Admiralty of the difficulty of displacing him. This the Admiral saw through, and did not choose to fall into the trap laid for him.

On the 6th of December he therefore wrote to Mr. D'Iffanger as follows :—

" I always have and always will support a large and comprehensive Reform in Parliament, vote by ballot, shortening Parliaments, and the cause of education throughout the land. I should have attended your public meeting, *but their Lordships did not think proper to grant me leave of absence, and I did not choose to take the alternative of resigning my command.*"

To Professor Key, who had also written to the Admiral on the same subject, the latter replied : —

"6th December, 1854.

" MY DEAR PROFESSOR,

"I enclose you a letter which only came to hand this morning. I send you the answer I should have given to it had I received it in time, and I should have attended the meeting, *had their Lordships given me leave ; but they refused, and told me I might vacate my command.* This I did not choose to do. They don't want to see me in Parliament. They have treated me too ill, and fear an *exposé.* I sail the moment it moderates.

" Yours very truly,

" CHAS. NAPIER."

The public can judge for itself of this Admiralty electioneering trick. It however carries a moral with it, viz., that as long as the Board of Admiralty exists in its present shape and power, all admirals who have acquired such a reputation as to induce their fellow-citizens to elect them members of Parliament, will do well to decline accepting commands under a body which condescends to turn even popular elections by the adoption of such a course as this. It is a fit finale to the way in which the Baltic campaign was conducted at Whitehall.

On the 7th of December, the Admiral sailed for England with the *Duke of Wellington, Royal George, Nile, Hogue, Blenheim, Bulldog, Driver,* and *Locust;* leaving at Kiel, Rear-Admiral Chads in the *Edinburgh,* with the *Vulture* and *Euryalus,* to bring home the remainder of Capt. Watson's squadron on its arrival from the Gulf of Finland.

On the 8th the squadron anchored off Sprogo. On the 9th it reached Reefness. On the 10th the *Royal George* was directed to rendezvous at Sheerness, the *Hogue* and *Blenheim* at Devonport, the *Driver* at Harwich, and the *Bulldog* in the Tyne, agreeably to the stations which had been assigned them by the Admiralty.

On the 16th, at midnight, after a succession of strong gales, the *Duke of Wellington* was off the North Foreland, and at 8.50 p. m. the next day anchored at Spithead.

On the 22nd the Admiral was ordered to strike his flag.

The following is the order :—

" The Baltic fleet, on its return from port, being now dispersed in different harbours of Great Britain, and several of the ships which composed this fleet being under orders for service in the Black Sea and Mediterranean, you are hereby required and directed to strike your flag, and come on shore."

In this curt order, not a word is said of the services for which the Admiral had been praised to fulsomeness before it became convenient to the Admiralty to make him their scapegoat. An insult so deliberate can only recoil on those who perpetrated it, when it becomes known. When, in 1849, the Admiral retired from the command of the Channel squadron, Sir Francis Baring, then First Lord of the Admiralty, directed Sir Charles to be thanked for his services in the following terms.

" The Lords Commissioners of the Admiralty express their sense of the valuable services which you have rendered during the period that you have commanded the Channel Squadron. The reports of the evolutions that have been carried on under your directions, and the efficiency and high discipline attained by the crews of those ships which have been placed under your command, have been most creditable to the service, and highly satisfactory to their Lordships."

Though not a ship had been lost in this pioneer voyage to the Baltic, beset as it was with dangers which it had now made known, not a word of thanks was uttered to the Admiral, his officers, or men. Yet in the following year, Admiral Dundas, who had the experience of Sir Charles Napier's campaign to fall back upon, was warmly thanked for not losing any of his ships, this circumstance being attributed to the "judgment shown in the arrangements, and the skill with which the various services have been effected by the officers and men of the respective ships." The officers and men of Sir C. Napier's fleet, who had pioneered the way for Admiral Dundas, received not a word of thanks, any more than did their Admiral.

Sir C. Napier's fleet, together with the Allied forces had captured Bomarsund, had destroyed or captured a large portion of the Russian merchant navy, had destroyed immense stores of naval material. The French Government had made their commanders-in-chief Marshals of France, whilst their British ally had not a word of thanks given to him any more than his officers and men. In the following year, Admiral

Dundas was thanked warmly "for the skill and gallantry of his officers and men in harassing the enemy's forces on shore, and for destroying the forts, defences, and public storehouses within reach." He was highly praised, as he deserved, for "destroying the arsenal and storehouses in the dockyard of Sweaborg." And when doing this the Admiralty might have highly blamed themselves for not supplying him with the means of finishing his work. Admiral Dundas and his fleet were also highly praised for "maintaining the blockade till the last moment, when our cruisers were driven away by the *early severity* of the weather." Sir Charles Napier's blockading squadron was not even mentioned for maintaining the blockade till the "*late severity* of the weather" drove them away.

The Admiral was thus not only unceremoniously dismissed from his command, but negatively condemned for all he had done in the Baltic, notwithstanding that praise had all along been showered upon him! To make sure of the position in which he really was considered by the Admiralty to stand, he wrote to the Board to know if his command was at an end, and to Admiral Berkeley to know why the services of his officers and men had been ignored. Admiral Berkeley's reply we cannot give, as he now positively interdicted his letters from being used, marking them "most private and confidential."

The Admiral's letter to the Board was as follows:—

"25th December, 1854.

"I have the honour to acknowledge the receipt of their Lordships' orders, directing me to strike my flag; and with reference to the same, I request their Lordships will inform me whether I am to consider that my command is at an end ? "

In the meantime their Lordships had discovered, or it had been pointed out to them, that they had committed an error in not having thanked Sir Charles Napier for his services, especially after the superabundant praise which they had all along lavished on him. The whole thing bore so palpably the aspect of personal malice, that they hastened to correct the error, and on the 26th wrote to the Admiral as follows :—

" With reference to yours of yesterday's date, I am commanded by my Lords Commissioners of the Admiralty to acquaint you that the order which you have received, agreeably to custom, to strike your flag and come on shore, is always the termination of a Flag Officer's command ; and I am directed by my Lords to take this opportunity to express to you the sense their Lordships entertain of your exertions during the period of your service in command of the Baltic fleet."

Still the Admiralty refused to thank Sir Charles for his services, though up to the despatch of Oct. 4th, and when in the Baltic, he had been thanked by them, publicly and privately, and that in the warmest manner, dozens of times over. He was now thanked for " *his exertions,*"—whilst, contrary to all precedent, his officers and men were not thanked at all, notwithstanding their, in some cases, almost superhuman efforts, in a sea unknown to a British fleet.

To this communication the Admiral replied on the 2nd of January, 1855, as follows—taking no notice of the thanks for his exertions, beyond the mere recapitulation of the Admiralty despatch : —

" I have to acknowledge your letter of the 26th of December, acquainting me that ' the order which I have received, agreeably to custom, to strike my flag and come on shore, is always the termination of an officer's command '—and adding that you are directed by my Lords to take this opportunity to express to me the sense they entertain of my exertions during the period of my service in command of the Baltic fleet.

" I regret that their Lordships should not have taken the opportunity of the dispersion of the Baltic fleet to recognise, in any manner, the services of the several *Admirals, Officers, and Ships' Companies* lately under my command. I am not aware that their services were inferior to those of the Admirals, Officers, and Ships' Companies of the French fleet, during the period of our acting together : and they were extended over a much longer period of time ; for their Lordships know that the British fleet was sent to the Baltic at a very inclement season, long before it was joined by the French squadron, and that it remained in the Baltic far into another very inclement season, long after the French squadron had gone home. Yet the French Emperor, in his speech to the Chambers, pays a just tribute of praise to his fleet, as well as to his army, for their devotion and discipline in the North, as well as in the South ; and records a success in the Baltic, in which the fleet under my command participated. The Queen was not advised to advert in her speech to Parliament to the services of Her Baltic fleet, nor do their Lordships now notice them. It would have been gratifying, certainly, to have been directed, on hauling down my flag, to communicate to all those lately under my command their Lordships' satisfaction with their conduct.

" I took to the Baltic a fleet splendid and magnificent, no doubt, in the size of the vessels of which it was composed ; but their Lordships cannot be ignorant of the defects in the composition and quality of the crews hastily put on board. That fleet was not manned like the fleets of Lord Nelson and Lord St. Vincent ; nor, with the exception of a few ships which had been off Lisbon, was it then fit to go into action ;

but I brought back a fleet really magnificent, not in vessels only, but in the crews (without which vessels are nothing), perfect in gunnery, in seamanship, and discipline. These results were obtained by the unremitting exertions of the officers, and through the willing obedience of the seamen, many of whom had necessarily been compelled to serve on their return from foreign stations, when they had expected their discharge or a long run on shore on leave.

"I consider the country to be greatly indebted to those officers, and to those seamen, and it would, indeed, be a subject of regret to me to think, that on account of any dissatisfaction their Lordships may entertain with respect to any part of my conduct, they should abstain from signifying to the admirals, officers, and seamen of the late Baltic fleet their grateful sense of their services.

"As regards my own conduct, it would be most gratifying to me if their Lordships would afford me the opportunity of justifying every part of it before any tribunal of officers competent to form a judgment upon naval questions; but I cannot but feel that, in the consideration of my conduct, more than naval questions are involved.

"As long as we have a superior fleet in the Baltic, we protect the shores of England from insult and desolation, our commerce from ruin : we retain Sweden and Denmark in their neutrality.

"Behind that fleet there is nothing—no naval, no military reserve at home, to defend our coasts ; no fortifications adequate to protect our ports. If at any time—through any disaster arising out of a most dangerous and little known navigation, or out of the accidents of treacherous and tempestuous weather, or out of an attack on forts which, with whatever caution and judgment it might be conducted, and whatever more or less of success might attend it, must be expected to result in the crippling of many of the ships engaged —our Baltic fleet should, under circumstances of great temporary disadvantage, be brought into action with the very powerful fleet of the enemy, and in that action should sustain defeat, in three weeks from that time, a Russian fleet, full of troops, might be on our coasts, and even, as the Dutch once were, on the Thames.

"I did not think, and I do not think, that for any chances of success which were ever within my reach, I should have been justified in incurring that risk. I afforded the enemy frequent opportunities of engaging the fleet in open sea. There I knew that the chances of war were equal, and that even if not fully successful (but I justly expected full success), I must so cripple the enemy's fleet as to make it incapable of further enterprise. These opportunities of equal battle the enemy declined, and many I gave them of unequal battle they declined also. I did not think myself justified in engaging, with such means as I had at my disposal, forts first, and a fleet afterwards ; and it was not so easy, as their Lordships seemed to think, to choose a fine day at the end of October, when the Cronstadt fleet would be frozen up, and Sweaborg open. And I say deliberately, that I do not think that any thing short of a reasonable expectation of complete success, not against the forts only, but against the fleet within them, would justify an attack by ships upon such forts as those at Sweaborg ; and so thought the French Admiral, whom their Lordships have necessarily included in their censure. And had the Marshal of France not sailed with his army, he also must have been included in their dissatisfaction that Sweaborg was not attacked before he sailed. I never would, under pressure from without, and against my own better judgment, advise an attack upon forts like that *which lately failed at Sebastopol.*

"If their Lordships should be of opinion that, with the means at our disposal, we ought to have made an attack on Sweaborg, it is for them to test the correctness of their opinion, by submitting my conduct, for not advising it, to the judgment of a Court-martial. I repeat, that it would be most gratifying to me there to explain and justify all my proceedings ; and I can truly say that, on reflection, I am more satisfied with myself for having resisted the instigations I received, to do what I felt to be wrong, than for the various measures in which I succeeded, and for which I had their Lordships' approbation.

> " I have the honour to be, Sir,
> " Your obedient, humble servant,
> " CHAS. NAPIER, Vice-Admiral.

" To the Secretary of the Admiralty."

The Admiralty in their reply took no notice of the Admiral's demand for a Court-martial on his conduct, and stated that as regarded the officers, such had been promoted as he seemed to think worthy, and Capt. Watson and his officers had already received the approbation of the Board. This reply distinctly intimates to the other officers and seamen of the fleet, that their services were not worth mentioning! The subjoined is the Admiralty reply.

> " Admiralty, Jan. 8, 1855.

" SIR,

" I am commanded by my Lords Commissioners of the Admiralty, to acknowledge the receipt of your letter of the 5th instant.

" Their Lordships awarded to the officers and men serving under your command at the capture of Bomarsund, such promotion and rewards as your statement of their services seemed to merit, considering that the operation was a combined one, in which the French army, as well as the French fleet, bore a conspicuous part.

" The approbation of the Board has been notified to Captain Watson, and to the officers and seamen under his immediate command, for the bold and successful manner in which they maintained the blockade of the Gulf of Finland, in the presence of a superior force of the enemy, long after the commencement of severe frost, when the fleet under your orders had retired to Kiel.

"I am to add that their Lordships have already expressed to you their sense of your exertions during your late command in the Baltic, and no censure has been conveyed on any point requiring further investigation.

"I am, Sir, your most obedient servant,

"W. A. B. HAMILTON.

"Vice-Admiral Sir Charles Napier, K.C.B."

Finding that the Admiralty would not grant the Court-martial which was demanded, Sir Charles applied to the Duke of Newcastle, then Minister of War, asking his Grace for that which the Admiralty had denied, though they had so unceremoniously dismissed him from his command, and that under circumstances of insult which had never before been offered to an Admiral without inquiry. The subjoined is the Admiral's letter to the Duke.

"Merchistoun, Horndean, Jan. 5. 1855.

"MY LORD DUKE,—When I went to the Baltic I was under your Grace's orders, and I carried them out, in conjunction with my colleagues, to the best of my ability, and my conduct was much approved of by the Government up to the fall of Bomarsund.

"I concurred with the French Admiral, the Marshal of France, and the French General of Engineers, in repudiating the plan of General Jones for attacking Sweaborg, which, if carried into execution, would have ended in inevitable disaster, worse even than Sebastopol.

"The French General was made a Marshal of France; the French Vice-Admiral, a full Admiral; Brigadier Jones, a Major-General; and I have been censured, deprived of my command, and obliged to ask for a Court-martial to justify my conduct. Is this justice, my Lord Duke?

"I have the honour to remain,

"Your Grace's obedient servant,

"CHAS. NAPIER, Vice-Admiral.

"To His Grace the Duke of Newcastle."

To this letter the Duke of Newcastle replied as follows:—

"War Department, Jan. 12., 1855.

"SIR,

"I have the honour to acknowledge the receipt of your letter of the 5th instant.

"When you left this country last year to assume the command of Her Majesty's fleet in the Baltic, Her Majesty's commands relating to the duties to be discharged by you, were signified by me to the Lords Commissioners of the Admiralty, and communicated by their Lordships to yourself.

"But although the general instructions for the conduct of operations of war, whether by land or sea, are issued by the Sovereign, through one of her principal Secretaries of State, all specific orders for the guidance of the Admirals and other officers of Her Majesty's Navy emanate from the Board of Admiralty alone; with whom also rest all questions, affecting the discipline of the naval service, and upon whose recommendation alone to the Secretary of State all honorary rewards for naval services are conferred by the Sovereign.

"Such being the case, it is out of my power to interfere, or even to express an opinion on the question with which your letter to me concluded.

"I have the honour, &c.

"NEWCASTLE.

"Vice-Admiral Sir C. Napier."

A matter must here be noticed which has given rise to remarks on the Admiral, as being wanting in respect to Her Majesty. On the 26th of December Her Majesty had honoured the Admiral with a command to dine at Windsor Castle. It not being known at the palace where the Admiral was, the card of invitation was endorsed " Enquire at the

Admiralty." It was then sent to Sir Thomas Cochrane, the Commander-in-Chief, at Portsmouth. By Sir Thomas Cochrane it was forwarded to Mr. William Grant, the Admiral's banker at Portsmouth. Mr. Grant transmitted it to Mr. Ozzard, the Admiral's Secretary, at Southsea, and by Mr. Ozzard it was forwarded to the Admiral, who was then at his seat at Horndean. It will readily be comprehended that an invitation at so short a notice, which had, moreover, run the gauntlet through so many complications, could hardly reach the Admiral in time to prepare for a banquet at Windsor Castle, and then to travel to London and back to Windsor, a distance of more than a hundred miles, in time for Her Majesty's dinner-hour. This was the case, and Sir Charles did not attend Her Majesty's dinner.

It was asserted by the papers, that Sir James Graham was also commanded by Her Majesty to dine at Windsor, and the use made of the Admiral's not having attended was a disinclination to meet Sir James Graham, who had received Sir Charles somewhat uncourteously on his reporting in person his return from the Baltic. It was not very probable that, had the First Lord and the Admiral met at Her Majesty's table, any altercation would have there arisen.

We have said that the Admiral was somewhat uncourteously received by Sir James Graham on the return of the former from the Baltic. Sir Charles gave the following account of his reception by the First Lord, in the newspapers of September 17. 1855: —

" On the *Wellington's* arrival at Spithead, I obtained the Commander-in-Chief's leave to proceed to town, and was certainly not received in a very gracious manner by the First Lord of the Admiralty.   I was asked to sit down with that insolent sneer on his countenance so well known in Parliament, which did not presage any change of opinion; he told me *he would hear what I should say, but would make no reply.* He did hear what I had to say, and I spoke to him as plainly as an officer before his chief could do ; and I only regretted that respect, not for him, but for his office, prevented me using the language his conduct deserved. After having spoken my mind, I retired, and proceeded to Portsmouth, where *I found an order to haul down my flag.*"

This reception by the First Lord ill accorded with the uniform praise which he himself had bestowed upon the Admiral when in the Baltic.   Nothing was said to him about striking his flag, this was evidently reserved as an " agreeable surprise " to him on arriving at his ship at Portsmouth.   This, at any rate, was not in accordance with the custom of the service, however the striking of an Admiral's flag may be so.

The Admiral was not likely to remain satisfied with these replies from the Admiralty, which exerted no small amount of ingenuity to evade his homethrusts. Accordingly, on the 12th of January, he again addressed the Board :—

" 18. Albemarle-street, 12th Jan., 1855.

" SIR, — I have received your letter of the 8th January, and I beg respectfully to observe that their Lordships have *evaded,* but not *replied* to my letter.   I did not complain that my officers had not been promoted, and I knew very well that the French army and navy bore a conspicuous part in the capture of Bomarsund.

" I knew also that their chiefs were promoted, and the army and navy thanked by the Chambers, while the only chief on our side promoted has been Brigadier Jones, who proposed a plan of attack on Sweaborg, which was condemned and rejected by the French Marshal, the French General of Engineers, the French Admiral, and myself, as impracticable and dangerous, whereas I have been deprived of my command, and her Majesty has not been advised to express her approbation.

" I did not complain of any neglect of Captain Watson or his officers and men, and I am glad their Lordships have at last promoted his First Lieutenant, and no reward is too great for his bold and successful blockade of the Gulf of Finland after I retired with the fleet to Kiel ; and it is most providential that some of his ships were not lost : it is probable that such would have been the fate of my fleet had I remained at Nargen, as ordered by their Lordships, until the ice came, and at all hazards ; and it is singular also, the dates of my letter, announcing my intended retirement, and the date of their Lordships' letter withdrawing the order to remain at all hazards, were the same.

" Their Lordships conclude their letter by saying, they had already expressed their sense of my exertions during my command of the Baltic fleet, but they forgot to do so when they ordered me to haul down my flag ; and they also forgot to promote my Flag Lieutenant, agreeably to the custom of the service.*

" I was not desired to thank the junior Admirals, the officers, and men, without whose exertions and willing obedience, under the most trying circumstances, the wretchedly manned and inefficient fleet could not have been brought into the state of discipline it was in when I brought it home, after having for nine months conducted them through all the dangers of the Baltic and Gulf of Finland — conducted them safely into anchorages that no fleet had visited before, without pilots, without lights, and without buoys or beacons, except those placed to mislead us, — and all this with a fleet of such

* He was afterwards promoted.

a size and magnitude as had never been before seen ; and after being repeatedly offered battle, with only one-third of the Russian force, and blockaded Bomarsund amidst a labyrinth of sunken rocks and islands, and finally, in conjunction with a French army and fleet, took it.

"Their Lordships say no censure has been conveyed on any point requiring further investigation. I beg to differ from their Lordships : I will not enter on the fact of Sir James Graham having, in his capacity of First Lord, written to me to begin to withdraw the fleet, and then, in his capacity of one of the Board, reproving me for so doing. The points on which an investigation of my conduct is necessary are, whether I was right or wrong in agreeing with a Marshal of France, a General of Engineers, and a French Admiral in rejecting the impracticable plan of an English Brigadier-General of Engineers for attacking Sweaborg, with which decision the Admiralty have expressed their discontent ; whether the report of my second reconnaissance of Sweaborg deserves the construction their Lordships thought fit to give it ; *and, indeed, changed the sense and meaning of it altogether, to make out a case against me, at the same time using language to goad me to attack Sweaborg, contrary to my judgment, contrary to the judgment of the French Admiral, and contrary to the judgment of my own Admirals,* whom I was ordered to consult; *this was to the imminent risk of Her Majesty's fleet, either from the fire of a fortress of the first order, or from tempestuous weather, or from both ; unless, indeed, I could hit on a fine day in the latter end of October, when the Cronstadt fleet should be frozen, and that of Sweaborg open. These were their Lordships' instructions, and they showed that they were totally ignorant of the state of the Baltic.**

" Had their Lordships consulted Sir Byam Martin, who was then alive, or, indeed, any Captain of a Baltic trader, they would have told them whether a fine day was likely to be found at that season of the year, and whether any sane man would push a fleet amongst sunken rocks, without beacons or buoys,

---

* The Italics are my own.

to attack one of the strongest fortresses in Europe, when he could not depend on the weather for two hours.

" Notwithstanding all the explanations I gave to their Lordships in public letters, and to Sir J. Graham in private letters, they persisted in writing to me in a style that might have done for a man who either did not know his duty, or was afraid to do it; but not to a man of my character and services.

" If enough was not done in the Baltic to satisfy the pub-lic, and if blame was to attach to any one, it should attach to the Government, for not sending out a sufficient number of troops at a proper season of the year, and if that was not practicable, for not sending out the appliances pointed out in my report of the 14th of June, and which differed little from my report of the 25th of September. Their Lordships thought proper to interpret the last as an assurance that I could attack Sweaborg with ships alone, and that I meant to do so, though I most distinctly said, after giving a detailed account of how it should be attacked, if by ships alone — ' *Whether this attack would succeed or not, it is impossible to say; but we must calculate on ships being set on fire by red-hot shot and shells, of which they would have abundance; and whether successful or not, it is evident the ships would be in no state to meet the Russian fleet afterwards; and if the attack was made at this season of the year, when you cannot depend on the weather for two hours, I do not know how many would be lost.*'

" I then proceeded to say : ' I beg their Lordships will not suppose for a moment that Sweaborg cannot be attacked; I think it can, but it must be done with *caution* and *judg-ment.*' Then followed a complete detail of the manner it should be attacked to ensure success, and I should have thought that their Lordships really misunderstood my letters had they not persisted in addressing me in the same style after my explanations.

" During the whole of the summer Sir James Graham was cautioning me against risking the fleet against stone walls, and complimenting me for having proved myself a consummate Commander-in-Chief — praised me for all my arrangements—for the capture of Bomarsund, with which he was more than pleased; but then, because two engineers proposed plans diametrically opposite to each other, he forgot his former cautions and all his former praises—forgot his consummate Commander-in-Chief — and urged me to attack Sweaborg, contrary to my own judgment and that of my colleagues, and risk Her Majesty's fleet amongst sunken rocks, against heavy batteries, and at a season of the year which any man who knew his business would have positively forbidden, instead of goading to attempt.

" In Sir James Graham's letter to me, of the 17th of October, he makes use of the following expression—it is the French General who writes: — ' We partake of the opinion of General Jones. Sweaborg may be attacked and taken by the fleets, if they think fit to make on that fortress a serious attack.'

" Now, there is no such thing in General Jones's report; —the French General meant General Niel's report, and Sir James Graham either never read General Jones's report or thought proper to forget it. General Niel, after stating that he thought the fleets could lay Sweaborg in ruins, added, ' Mais les vaisseaux sont des machines bien compliquées, bien faciles à incendier ; une telle opération est hardie — elle n'a jamais été faite que je sache, et ce n'est pas à moi qu'il appartient de la conseiller.'* This Sir James thinks proper to interpret, in the letter to me, ' General Niel intimated very distinctly an opinion, that the attack ought to be made ;' and then goes on to say, alluding, I suppose, to General Jones's report, ' that report made a great impression here, and raised a strong presumption that, with the aid of the military force then present with the fleet, in seven or eight days the works at Sweaborg might be destroyed, and that the month of September was the proper time for the operation.' Whatever impression it made on Sir James Graham (who I do not think a good judge) that report made none on the French Marshal,

---

* General Niel acted like a man of sense and honour, in qualifying his opinion.

none on the French Admiral, the French Engineer, or myself. We all considered it impracticable, and as the weather turned out, had it been put in course of execution, the communication with the fleet would have been cut off, and the troops and stores in possession of the enemy before sunset; a portion of the fleet would most probably also have been lost — it would have been worse than Sebastopol! Sir James then continues thus: ' Then came your second *reconnaissance* of Sweaborg and plan of naval attack, which you considered practicable.'

" I gave two plans, one with the fleet alone, the success of which I doubted, and thought dangerous; the second I thought certain of success. Their Lordships thought proper to deliberate on one and to ignore the other, which differed, however, little from the one I gave on the 14th of June; and then Sir James Graham tells me an opportunity was lost; adding words about risks and dangers, and telling me that prudence consists in weighing them, and firmness in encountering them. Had their Lordships weighed these things, they would not have written me such letters.

" Sir James, in another letter, tells me he is unwilling to be involved in a written controversy with me; but that I had brought it on myself by my report of the 25th of September — that report appeared to him to be entirely at variance with the opinions previously expressed by me; and he certainly understood me to say, that if I had mortars, rockets, and Lancaster guns, I considered Sweaborg assailable by sea.

" Now, in May, I declared it to be unassailable by sea or land, and the Admiralty did not send to me the appliances which, in September, I declared to be wanting, because they believed, from my account, they would be useless against a place, which, in the first instance, I pronounced to be impregnable.

" Sir James then continues thus: ' I could not bring myself to believe that the want of Lancaster guns, or even of mortars, rendered a sea attack, on your plan of the 25th of September, impossible, if you had 25 sail of the line reassembled before the place, with all their means of vertical fire.'* But Sir James forgot that my report in May was made before I had seen Sweaborg; but the report of the 12th of June was after I had seen it; and it differs little from that of the 25th September!

"I wonder whether Sir James Graham, when he wrote this, had forgotten his great respect for stone walls, and his warnings to avoid them; and had he forgot his consummate Commander-in-Chief?

"I have now again well weighed and considered this painful subject. I have consulted friends, and I am of opinion, and so are they, that my character has been attacked by the First Lord of the Admiralty, and by the Board; and coupling that with my dismissal from command, *I have nothing left but to demand that my conduct be investigated before a Court-martial.*

"I can quite understand that their Lordships wish to avoid an investigation; for they are quite aware that my conduct will be proved creditable to me, and very different to their Lordships.

"I have the honour to remain

"Your obedient humble servant,

(Signed)   "CHAS. NAPIER."

The insult offered to the French was even greater than had been offered to the Admiral himself, for throughout the whole campaign Sir James Graham had been nervously anxious that Sir Charles Napier should agree with them in everything, as a point of the deepest political importance; yet when the Emperor Napoleon had rewarded his officers in every possible way, the Board of Admiralty dismissed Sir Charles Napier from his command for having, as Sir James

---

* Where was the vertical fire to come from? We had no mortars. Did he mean the ships to be heeled over, and act with the ports caulked over?

Graham over and over again testified, so well co-operated with his French colleagues! They could not have told the Emperor in plainer language that he was altogether mistaken in rewarding his officers; he ought to have dismissed them on anchoring at Cherbourg. No man possessed of a sane mind can contend for a moment, that if Sir Charles Napier was deserving of censure, the French Commander-in-Chief and the French Admiral must be equally so, inasmuch as they were consenting parties to the very acts for which Sir Charles Napier was dismissed from his command. Thanks to the tact of Sir C. Napier, this Admiralty blunder produced no ill consequences.

When Sir Charles Napier had thus pointed out to the Board the blunder they had committed, they evidently became alarmed, and without, as usual, waiting for days to intervene, they replied, next day, that they had not censured him for his acts, *but his writings!* — a new accusation altogether.

The following was the Board's reply. The marginal notes are Sir Charles Napier's.

[Copy.]

Admiralty, Jan. 13. 1855.

Having laid before my Lords Commissioners of the Admiralty your letter of *yesterday's* date, I am commanded by their Lordships to acquaint you that although my Lords upon some occasions have not been enabled to express the same satisfaction at receiving your reports, which they have directed to be conveyed to you upon others, they have only to repeat that no censure has been passed upon your conduct in reference to the operations of the fleet under your orders, and their Lordships have already expressed their sense of your exertions in a manner customary upon intimation that the flag of an officer of your rank has been struck in pursuance of their Lordships' orders. They had also, in accordance with your recommendation, promoted the Flag Lieutenant who was the bearer of your despatches, announcing the fall of Bomarsund, and since your flag has been struck the name of no other officer has been submitted by you.

I submitted a name, and he was promoted.

My Lords do not feel themselves called upon now to enter a second time into discussion of reports on which they have already stated their opinions, and still less to take cognisance of other informal documents which have never been laid before them, and which they decline to recognise.

These, I suppose, are Sir J. Graham's, that are called informal; a pretty way of carrying on business.

They consider that no inquiry into your conduct is necessary, and they entirely decline to submit a controversy raised by an officer under their orders, to the decision of a Court-martial.

My Lords further direct me to inform you, that while they have been *unwilling to pass censure upon any part of your conduct,* they have not failed to observe, from the moment of your first quitting *Wingo Sound* without orders, and down to the present time, you have repeatedly *thought fit to adopt a tone, in your correspondence with their Lordships, which is not respectful to their authority.* Such a course, if generally adopted by other officers, would be destructive to the discipline and injurious to the best interests of the service, and is not calculated to inspire confidence in an officer entrusted with an important command.

Why did they not produce them?

I defy the Admiralty to produce one instance in the British Navy where an officer's letters were falsified.

I am further directed to add that this decision is to be considered by you as final.

I am, sir, your most obedient, humble servant,

W. A. B. HAMILTON.

Vice-Admiral Sir Charles Napier, K.C.B.

The correspondence had now assumed a somewhat undignified aspect, resembling nothing so much as a hare-hunt. The more the Admiralty doubled to get clear of their pursuer, the more perseveringly did he follow them at every turn, and into every corner, adopting, in fact, the tactics by which he had run to earth more wily enemies than a Board of Admiralty. However Sir James Graham may shine in debate, no man could possibly exhibit a more helpless spectacle on paper. The gift of oratory is, indeed, generally accompanied by the gift of practical incapacity, and in this respect the First Lord appears to have formed no exception to the general rule, possessing both gifts in high perfection. However much he may have been an overmatch for the Admiral in the House, he was no match for him in the art of letter-writing ; and if the Admiral had stuck to his gift, instead of trenching on Sir James Graham's gift, in Parliamentary debate, it would have been none the worse for him. However, posterity has now both combatants before it, and can weigh their respective gifts as it pleases, there being little doubt as to the way towards which the judgment of posterity will incline, or even that of the present generation, now that the *facts*—not the *oratory*—are before them.

The rejoinder of the Admiral was a collection of facts of a most unpleasant nature, rendered infinitely more unpleasant from being placed side by side with ignorant assumptions.

"Merchistoun Hall, Horndean,
Jan. 20, 1855.

"Sir,—I have received your letter of the 13th instant, in which you state that although my Lords, upon some occasions,

P P

have not been enabled to express the same satisfaction on receiving my reports which they have done on others, that they never passed censure on me in reference to the operation of the fleet under my command. This communication leaves me at a loss to understand why their Lordships' letter of the 4th October, No. 774., was written ; and I shall therefore take that letter paragraph by paragragh, and reply to it.

LETTER.

REPLY.

1. Your renewed reconnaissance of Sweaborg gives rise to more pressing and serious considerations.

1. My opinion since I first saw Sweaborg has never changed.

2. You desire us not for a minute to suppose that Sweaborg cannot be attacked, and you proceed to point out in detail the precise mode in which the operation ought to be conducted.

2. Certainly. I pointed out the precise mode of attack. *One with ships alone,* but saying success would be doubtful and many ships would be lost. *Another with ships, guns, gun-boats, Lancaster guns, rockets, 13-inch mortars on the islands, and a vast supply of shot, shells, and rockets, in addition to the ships.* This mode I thought certain, and do still think so, notwithstanding the disaster at Sebastopol.

3. You express your opinion, that if your plan of attack by the ships were adopted, you are quite certain the fortress would be laid in ruins, and most probably an entrance opened to the ships.

3. I never said anything of the sort. I said, if attacked by the ships alone, success would be very doubtful. The ships would be set on fire by red-hot shot and shells, and be left in no condition to meet the Russian fleet afterwards : and if attempted at that season of the year, I did not know how many would be lost.

4. What, then, are the obstacles to the immediate attempt? Admiral Plumridge and the French Admiral are ordered to rejoin you.

4. The want of the means I pointed out to insure success. Had Admiral Plumridge and the French squadron rejoined with the month's provisions he was

5. Recent events in the Black Sea will not encourage the Russians to attempt any enterprise of more than usual hazard and daring at this precise moment.

ordered to take in, it would have been nearly expended before he got back, and could have done us no good without the appliances I asked for. Neither could he have come until the end of October. The period their Lordships *thought most favourable for attack, but which I knew to be most unfavourable.*

5. Recent events in the Black Sea were a miserable deception ; more recent events showed that the British fleet was nearly destroyed. And had that been known at the Admiralty, Sir J. Graham's cautions to me would have been repeated instead of his goadings.

6. Your second reconnaissance of Sweaborg opens a new view, and the presence or absence of a few guns of an improved construction, or even of mortar-vessels, cannot make the whole difference between a *possible* and an *impossible* attack.

6. My second reconnaissance opened no new view *to me :* and the presence or absence of a "*few guns,*" as their Lordships are pleased to call what I asked for, just makes all the difference between the *possible* and the *impossible.*

" Any man reading the foregoing letter would say that nothing more goading could have been written to one in my position — nothing short of a positive order more urgent and imperative ; it was to say, If you don't act it will be a disgraceful backwardness ! It is a letter which will remain at the Admiralty on record ; and if hereafter my life should be written, posterity will perhaps take it as a proof that Sir Charles Napier was a cowardly commander !

" This injurious letter was followed up by another from their Lordships, October 17., No. 779., which I will now dissect as I have done the first.

1. Their Lordships *might* also have been satisfied with the decision adopted by you, on the joint report of the flag-officers referred to, if the reports of the French and English military officers had not contained adverse opinions, and if your own letter of Sept. 25th had not afterwards expressly informed their Lordships that they were not to suppose for a moment that Sweaborg could not be attacked.

1. If this is not censure is it?

It might be thought the opinions of the naval flag-officers were of more worth than those of the French and English military officers on naval affairs. It is probably the first time that soldiers were considered better judges of naval warfare than sailors! And those soldiers announced opinions directly at variance with each other.

But how was it to be attacked? *Not by ships alone!* And that was well known to their Lordships, though they thought fit to ignore it.

" In their next letter, October 31., No. 796., their Lordships told me plainly they could not express satisfaction with the decision come to, not to attack Sweaborg, after the fall of Bomarsund. That was not only a censure on me, but on a Marshal of France, a French Admiral, and on my own Admirals. The French Chamber, however, did not agree with their Lordships; they gave thanks to their officers, and the Emperor promoted them; but I have been removed from my command by the English Admiralty.

"Their Lordships speak of *informal documents*, which they will not recognise. Are, then, the letters of the First Lord of the Admiralty, official and momentous of meaning, informal? Were they to be of force for stimulating, goading an Admiral, against his judgment, to risk the destruction of a noble fleet, amidst fogs, sunken rocks, stone fortresses, and ice and fire, and yet to be of no authenticity or weight in justification of an injured and insulted man?

" Their Lordships say no inquiry into my conduct is necessary, and decline submitting to a controversy, raised by an officer under their orders, to the decision of a Court-martial.

But it was not I who raised the controversy. It was their Lordships, by misinterpreting my letters.

" But they further direct you to inform me, that while they are unwilling to pass censure on any part of my conduct, they have not failed to observe that, from the moment 'I first quitted Wingo Sound *without orders*,' down to the present time, I have repeatedly thought fit to adopt a tone in my correspondence which is not respectful to their authority.

" This passage is to me surprising. For, first, *I did not quit Wingo Sound without orders.* Their Lordships, by letter of the 8th of March, ordered me to proceed to Wingo Sound. On the 10th of March, they sent me Lord Clarendon's instructions to dispose my fleet so as to prevent the Russian ships passing out of the Baltic.

" Acting on those instructions, I left Wingo Sound, proceeding to Kioge Bay, as a better station for effecting the object of Lord Clarendon's communication. I arrived there on the 1st of April, and was immediately *reproved by the Admiralty for obeying Lord Clarendon's orders, transmitted to me by the Admiralty!*

" On the 2nd of April I received orders from the Duke of Newcastle, also forwarded by the Admiralty, to proceed to the entrance of the Gulf of Finland, from Kiel, as soon as possible.

" On the 3rd of May I received a letter from their Lordships, dated 8th April, *approving of my proceedings in leaving Wingo Sound!* Also came a letter from Sir James Graham, dated 10th of April, from which the following is an extract:—

" ' *I am entirely satisfied with your proceedings.* Neither Lord Clarendon nor I anticipated your movement inside the Belt, and believed that you would watch in the Cattegat, the entrance to the Sound, and of the Belt, until you received orders to enter the Baltic. You judged, however, very wisely, and the time which you have gained has been very precious ; and the passage of the Belt in fine weather, and in safety, has been a most successful exploit.

" ' You will also have been enabled to exercise your officers

and men to great advantage, with the certainty that the
enemy is in front of you, blocked up in ice for some time to
come ; and that your reinforcements will arrive, and that your
discipline will be improved before he can move, even if he
were so disposed.'

"On the 5th of April, Sir J. Graham wrote thus, also :—

"' I am highly satisfied with your movements, and with the
position which you have taken up for the present. Mr.
Buchanan and Mr. Grey can readily communicate with you
where you are now, and most useful information from Stockholm reaches you without loss of time.

"' Considering the state of the ice in front of you, I rejoice
in the belief that you are on the ground in time, and that you
will be strong and well prepared before the critical moment
arrives.'

"Now, on the 14th Jan., 1855, I received a letter from
their Lordships, again accusing me of leaving Wingo Sound
without orders, and also remarking that down to the present
time, from that period, I have repeatedly thought fit to
adopt a tone in my correspondence which is not respectful to
their Lordships' authority.

"I believe in one instance only, up to the 4th of October, I
did write hastily to their Lordships ; and I afterwards expressed my regret to Admiral Berkeley for having done so.
Up to that date, also, I received nothing but praise from their
Lordships. Since then, I admit the use of strong language,
but I was goaded to it by their Lordships' public letters, and
by Sir J. Graham's private letters, which were almost past
endurance.

"Their Lordships have directed you to add, that this, their
decision, is to be considered by me as final. It may be final
for their Lordships, but certainly will not be final for me,
until I receive complete satisfaction for the injurious imputations on my character and conduct.

"Her Majesty was certainly not displeased with my conduct
in the Baltic, for she invited me to Windsor on my return.
The invitation reached me too late to obey Her Majesty's command ; and as it has not been repeated, my hope is that Sir

James Graham's misrepresentations to myself of my opinions and conduct, have not been extended so as to affect Her Majesty's sentiments. But I have been deprived of my command — an unusual act, save where an officer has misconducted himself.

"I have the honour to be, Sir,
"Your most obedient Servant,
"Chas. Napier.
"The Secretary of the Admiralty, &c., &c., &c."

This was unanswerable, and the Board of Admiralty fairly ran to cover, sheltering themselves under the *ægis* of power, instead of that of truth, justice, or argument. They had dismissed the Admiral from his command, and beyond question they had the power to do it, even had their own shortcomings, placed on his shoulders, been tenfold as great as they were. It was the only valid argument they had used throughout, and, unhappily for the cause of justice, this argument, under the despotic system in vogue in the navy, is as unanswerable as it is valid.

The following was the reply of the Board: —

"Admiralty, Jan. 22. 1855.
"I have received and laid before my Lords Commissioners of the Admiralty your letter of the 20th instant, in reply to their Lordships' letter of the 13th instant.
"I am, Sir, your most obedient, humble servant,
"W. A. B. Hamilton.
"Vice-Admiral Sir Charles Napier, K.C.B."

A higher compliment could not have been paid, either to the acts or the letters of the Admiral. Both were unimpeachable and unanswerable. There must be an end to everything, and therefore to this dis-

P P 4

pute amongst others. But there are two kinds of end—noble and ignoble. Under which of the two the Admiralty " end " will be classed, there is very little doubt. But the power which brought about that end could not command it to remain in obscurity. It will take its place upon the pages of English history as a blot on the fair face of the book ; and it will be well if that blot do not deface some of the last pages. When our naval men of renown are thus treated, they must, ere long, become scarce.

Failing to obtain a hearing from the Admiralty, Sir Charles addressed Lord Aberdeen on the subject, demanding an investigation into the conduct of the campaign. To this communication Lord Aberdeen replied, that as he had placed his resignation in the hands of Her Majesty, no more meetings of his Cabinet would take place, so that it was out of his power to grant the request. A similar communication to the Duke of Newcastle, as Secretary at War, produced the reply, that as the conduct of fleets was solely under the control of the Board of Admiralty, it was not in his power to interfere.

On the accession of Lord Palmerston to the Premiership, Sir Charles reiterated his demand for investigation, but in this case received no reply. It was clear that the Government was unwilling or afraid to grant the investigation demanded; and in Lord Palmerston's case, it is equally clear that the Government was rather afraid than unwilling so to do, for before Lord Palmerston's accession to the Premiership, he had warmly eulogised the whole conduct of the Baltic campaign, and has since repeated his eulogies in a manner highly honourable to himself, and in direct contradiction to the course pursued by the Board of Admiralty, which, up to the present time, pursues a system of unrelenting hostility to the Admiral, notwithstanding the previous warmth of its eulogies upon his conduct, as adduced in this volume.

The worst feature in the case is yet to come. Though censured, degraded, and dismissed from his command, in July, 1855, the Board of Admiralty, nevertheless, intimated that it had recommended the Admiral to the honour of the *highest class of the Order of the Bath*, thereby annulling all their previous imputations against him, on account of which he had been deprived of his command. To have accepted the honour without investigation would have been impossible. The deprivation of command had been conveyed to the Admiral under circumstances of marked insult, and this unexplained, rendered honour out of the question.

The following correspondence between Sir Charles Wood and Sir C. Napier, will best explain the course which the latter deemed it incumbent on him to pursue.

[PRIVATE.]
" Admiralty, July 4th.

" DEAR SIR,

" I have recommended to Her Majesty to promote you to the highest class of the Bath, G.C.B., and Her Majesty has been graciously pleased to approve of this recommendation.

" I have the honour to be, dear Sir,

" Yours faithfully,

" CHARLES WOOD.

" Vice-Admiral Sir Charles Napier, K.C.B."

[REPLY.]

" DEAR SIR,

" Lord Collingwood, on the battle of the 1st of June, did not receive the medal. On the 14th of February he was offered one, which he declined, as he had done his duty as well on the 1st of June as he did on the 14th of February.

" During the time I served in the Baltic I did my duty, and did not deserve the treatment I met with, and must therefore decline the Grand Cross.

" I am, however, much obliged to you for having brought my name before the Queen.

" I have been expecting every day to hear of Sweaborg being attacked. But I suppose Admiral Dundas, who was one of the Board who gave me such sage advice, is waiting till the end of October to choose his day, when Cronstadt is frozen up, and Sweaborg is open.

" Together with your letter, I received one from the Usher of the Order, desiring me to be at Buckingham Palace to-morrow, to be invested. I have written to Prince Albert, as Grand Master of the Order, to state my reasons for declining it, and requesting him to lay them before the Queen.

" Yours truly,

" CHAS. NAPIER."

" Admiralty, July 7th, 1855.

" DEAR SIR,

" I had the honour of receiving your letter this morning, and I have, with Her Majesty's sanction, directed the omission of your name from the list of Officers which will appear in the Gazette, as receiving the honour of G.C.B.

" Yours faithfully,

" CHARLES WOOD."

LETTER TO H. R. H. PRINCE ALBERT.

" SIR,

" I have received your Royal Highness's commands to attend Her Majesty on the 7th of July, to be invested with the insignia of a Knight Grand Cross of the Order of the Bath. I beg your Royal Highness will convey to Her Majesty my humble duty and sincere thanks for the honour Her Majesty contemplated conferring on me, and I beg most respectfully your Royal Highness will convey to Her Majesty my regret that I do not think I can, consistent with my own honour, accept it. I beg to assure your Royal Highness that I mean no disrespect to Her Majesty; she has not a more devoted subject than myself, and I am ready to lay down my life in her service.

" I have served Her Majesty's family with honour and credit for fifty-five years, and at the end of my career have been grossly insulted, and false interpretations put upon my despatches, by the Admiralty, and been degraded and dismissed because I resented, as became a man of honour, injuries wounding to my character. Her Majesty last year confided to me the command of the finest fleet that ever left these shores, as far as ships were concerned, but badly manned and totally unorganised. I led that fleet to the Baltic and the Gulf of Finland much earlier than usual, with imperfect charts and ignorant pilots, and conducted them safely through all the dangers and intricacies of that little known sea; and in conjunction with Her Majesty's Allies, took and destroyed the western bulwark of the Emperor of Russia's dominions, and because I would not attempt impossibilities suggested by an English Brigadier-General and recommended by the Admiralty, though disapproved of by myself, by my Admirals, by the French Marshal, and by the French Admirals in Councils of War, I received insulting letters, and was deprived of my command because I resisted, as a British Admiral ought to do, such unworthy treatment.

" I have no hesitation in saying, had I followed the insane suggestions of Sir James Graham and his Admiralty, the

Allied Army would have been made prisoners, and the greater part of Her Majesty's fleet lost. I stated this to the Admiralty, and I demanded a Court-martial to investigate my conduct, which was refused, and I do not think I can accept an honour until my character is cleared.

" Your Royal Highness is a soldier, and you know what is due to a soldier's honour, and I feel satisfied your Royal Highness will pardon the unusual course I have taken to convey my feelings to Her Majesty.

" I am, &c.,

" CHARLES NAPIER."

CHAP. XXIII.

SIR C. NAPIER'S NOTES ON RUSSIA.

RESOURCES OF RUSSIA.—A GREAT FALLACY TO SUPPOSE THAT THEY CAN BE CRIPPLED.—THE PAPER-MONEY OF RUSSIA.—ST. PETERSBURG THE WONDER OF MODERN TIMES. — NO FAILURE DURING THE RECENT WAR OF THE CZAR'S RESOURCES. — THE GREATEST LIVING SOVEREIGN. — ADMIRAL'S DESCRIPTION OF CRONSTADT AND ITS FORTS.—ITS DOCKS AND ARSENALS, BARRIERS AND BATTERIES, INFERNAL MACHINES, REDOUBTS, AND NEW DEFENCES.—GUNS MOUNTED IN THE SEA FORTS.

As this volume has of necessity extended to a somewhat unreasonable length, we must perforce comprise the Admiral's "Notes on Russia" within a small compass, selecting such only as bear more immediately on the subject of our narrative.

During the war much was said in this country about "crippling the resources of Russia," "reducing her to distress for want of money," &c., &c. There can be no greater fallacy than this. It is impossible for Russia to want money, so long as her people are satisfied with her monetary system, as was the case in the war, is at present, and in all probability will be for the future. So long as Russia possesses a paper-making machine and a printing press, she cannot want money. The paper rouble issued by the Government has precisely the same value as the silver rouble ; i. e., no tradesman will give you more for a silver rouble than he will for a paper rouble. Nor can this affect her foreign commerce, since, as every one knows, foreign commerce is carried on by paper also, viz., bills of exchange. Whenever gold appears in the transaction, it is when the exports of a country exceed the imports, so that the balance is in favour of the exporting country, which, instead of sending gold out, gets gold in. Whatever may be the crotchets of currency-mongers upon these points, and we neither profess to understand them, nor to have any inclination to study them — there stands the fact, that the monetary system of Russia is a paper one — that the people are not only satisfied with it, but even prefer it in their ordinary transactions to a metallic one — that no depreciation takes place in the value of the paper medium — and that all the practical operations of the country are carried on by it, the value of the paper depending alone on the stability of the Government; a pretty secure basis, as compared with the insecurity of the paper issued by English banks, some one or other of which is generally occupying the attention of the Bankruptcy Courts. If Russia have not arrived at the secret of a true paper currency, most assuredly England has not, and is therefore the less qualified to judge of that of Russia.

One fact, or rather series of facts, stares us in the face, viz., that on the banks of the Neva stands a city, the wonder of modern times; the approaches to this city are defended by fortresses, the most gigantic the world ever saw; armies are supported beyond modern precedent in number; a navy has

been created which we may one day learn not to
think lightly of; a whole nation is placed in a degree
of comfort quite equal to our own; whilst in the
higher classes an amount of wealth and luxury is
apparent, even surpassing our own. All this is more
or less the result of a paper medium. Not that Russia
does not possess gold, and in abundance; but her
paper has paid the workmen who have created all
this, and the armies who defend it when created.
Russia has then acquired the secret of using paper-
money to advantage, and of keeping it within those
bounds which prevent disadvantage. The military
chest was captured at Bomarsund. It consisted of
paper roubles — just as valuable to the garrison as
silver roubles; but, of course, worthless to the captors—unless they had gone to St. Petersburg to
spend them.

Whilst at St. Petersburg, the Russian Government
had politely requested one of its nobles, Count ——,
to accompany Sir Charles Napier, to show him
everything he wished to see, and explain anything
he wished to know; thus showing a marked courtesy
to an honourable foe, which contrasts strangely with
the unworthy treatment which Sir Charles Napier
had received at the hands of his own country. When
alluding to the mistake which England had committed in supposing that the resources of Russia had
been crippled, Count —— pointed out what had been
done during the war, and asked the Admiral if he
saw any signs of distress amongst the population, or
anything else which showed that the resources of
Russia had at all failed. The reply could only be in

the negative. There were no signs of distress on the surface, and there was nothing to prevent him from looking beneath the surface if he chose. It is folly for the English public to shut its eyes to these things. The true way to comprehend a fact is to look it boldly in the face, however unpleasant the view may be; and considering the intolerable burden which the war has laid on the English public, and the more so from mismanagement of our resources, the view presented is by no means a pleasant one. It must, nevertheless, be seriously scrutinised; the necessity for this being the greater, the less importance may be attached to it by the Government. As the "*Times*" newspaper remarked, on the late coronation of the Emperor, that "he was the greatest living sovereign, for whom his people were willing to lay down their lives if necessary;" there is no blinking the fact; and in case of another collision with Russia, it will be quite as well to take an accurate measure of her power, both as to her capabilities for war, and her means to carry on war.

We will next adduce the Admiral's description of Cronstadt and its forts in his own words : —

"I left St. Petersburg at ten in the morning of the 27th of July, in a Government steamer, and landed at the Mole to the east of Cronstadt, where I found the Governor's carriage, which conducted me to his house. An officer was appointed to show me everything worth seeing. We first went to the Menschikoff Fort, which is a granite 4-decker, mounting forty-eight heavy guns, enfilading the approach to the inner roads, about a gun-shot inside of the Alexander Battery.

"From Fort Menschikoff, the sea-wall extends nearly a mile, thickly studded with heavy guns, and joining the land-wall at right angles, extending entirely across the island. From the end of the sea-wall we returned to Fort Menschikoff, and passed outside of the Merchant Basin, which is very extensive, and so full of ships, that a considerable number were admitted into the Government Basin, which is very large, capable of containing all the navy. We entered the basin by an entrance sufficient for the reception of any sized ship, and went on board a very large screw frigate, like the *Impérieuse*, and I was quite surprised to find her in the highest order and neatness. The greater part of the ship's company were on shore, but everything appeared in its place, both above and below ; the ship was well rigged, and sails beautifully furled. From the frigate we rowed to the landing place, where several hundred sailors were bathing. They all appeared strong, muscular men. I tasted their dinner, which was composed of soup, with vegetables, and a pound of meat chopped up, to each man. They have no stools or tables, but eat out of a large bucket triced up to the deck, the men standing round it.

"On landing we found the Governor's carriage, which conducted me to the Club, a large building for the reception of naval officers and the Emperor's suite, when he comes to Cronstadt. I found rooms prepared for me, and very comfortable. After dressing I was conducted to the Governor's, where I met the chief of the staff and a party of officers and ladies, and we dined very well according to the Russian style, and found the ladies, who talked French, very agreeable. After dinner and wine, we all rose from table, smoked a cigar, and the carriage was at the door. The same officer conducted me outside the town to the place we had left off in the morning, at the corner of the sea-wall. We drove out to the country, which is covered with field-works, to obstruct the approach of an enemy, should he succeed in effecting a landing. These redoubts are not strong, nor could the land defences stand a long siege, but the facility of bringing any number of troops from St. Petersburg, renders any attack on Cronstadt from the land hopeless, even if a landing could be effected. Indeed, it would be impossible to land in face of an enemy, and if landed, even with a sufficient force, there would not be time before the winter sets in to take the town.

"On the 23rd of July, we went to the docks, which are very inconvenient. A long canal leads to five docks at the head of it, so that the nearest ship must be taken out first, and so in succession, for there is no room to pass in; but as they are now widening and deepening the canal, it might be better arranged. There are also other docks at another part of the yard, having the same fault. They were originally built by Peter the Great.

"From the factory we went to the storehouse for arms, which is beautifully arranged, and well supplied with guns of all sizes and dimensions. There I saw the gun taken at Old Carbury, and a flag that looked very much like a Union Jack. From the Arsenal we went, in the Governor's carriage to the Mole, where we first landed, and where we found a steamer, which carried us all round the steam gun-boats, 75 in number, mounting two 68-pounders, and one 36; very fine vessels, and well adapted for defensive purposes. They steam eight or nine knots, and were all planned by the Grand Duke. I saw three building in floating-docks. They appear to be too sharp. They have, besides the gun-boats, 14 floating batteries, mounting four 68-pounders, well adapted for defence. They are constructed with one bulwark only, cased with iron four inches thick. Outside the ports they slant down to the water. That is cased with iron also. A shot striking the bulwark will not penetrate, and striking the sloping part, it bounds over. Behind the bulwark is a platform, on which are mounted the guns. A shell falling on the magazine would, I presume, go through. This floating battery is mounted on ten flat coffers, filled with empty casks, so that, should a shot or shell go through one, she could not fill, as there would not be much room for the water. They can be towed three or four knots, and can be placed where wanted. I was anxious to go to the north of Cronstadt, but no one is permitted to do so.

"When I was there in 1854 the passage was piled right across. Behind the piles lay four block-ships of the line, and four frigates; behind them again were 140 row gun-boats, large and unwieldy, mounting two heavy guns, and in a calm not rowing more than three knots. Seventy of these gun-boats were begun in March, 1854, and were ready when I appeared off. Mortar-vessels, however, could have thrown their shells into Cronstadt to the north, and might have reached the dockyard, and would have done great mischief, which I mentioned in my report.

" Before Admiral Dundas came out, they had put other obstructions to the north, to hinder the approach of mortar-vessels within range ; but not content with that, they have now run a barrier right across from Cronstadt, several hundred feet wide, at which they employed all last winter 20,000 men. The piles are several feet under water ; at the end of each pile, are iron bars, so low down that a circular saw could not be employed to saw them off under water. Behind these piles there are five batteries, not yet finished, but which would have been ready had the war continued. To support these batteries, there are seventy-five steam gun-vessels, and about 120 row gun-boats, and as many block-ships as they choose to place. After this, Russia is not to be despised. Such tremendous exertions cannot be excelled. Against such defences Admiral Dundas, had he come out in the beginning or middle of July, would not have accomplished a single thing, even had he brought double the number of mortars. As the weather was bad, the probability is, that many of his mortar-vessels would have been swamped.

" So much for the north : I now turn to the south. The Russians have now in the Roads eleven sail of the line, all good ships — one a screw, and two more without their engines ; with four fine frigates, ten large paddle-steamers, and twenty small ones, with a great many merchant steamers that they could hire, of different sizes. They have also several corvettes and brigs, and two razee frigates, not ready.

" In the basin there are two three-deckers, and five two-deckers, good ships ; and four sail of the line and four frigates not good for much, and three in dock ; one three-decker building at St. Petersburg, and eight or nine corvettes. They had seventeen sail of the line here ready for sea in 1854, besides their block-ships, and seven sail at Cronstadt.

" After seeing the gun-boats, we went to Fort Alexander, a stone four-decker, mounting 130 heavy guns, many of them 68-pounders, and others upwards of 100-pounders. It is situated on the left hand going in, and is supported by Fort Peter, which is considerably inside, but bears on you on entering before you get abreast of Fort Alexander, and then opens as you pass it. It mounts 60 heavy guns. Opposite it is the Risbank, mounting 190 guns, of heavy calibre. Inside of it is Cronslott, mounting 170 guns (opposite Menschikoff), and now about to be raised to a four-decker; but how many guns it is to mount is not known. All those batteries are of solid granite, and beautifully built. They enfilade the whole of the entrance of the harbour, which is narrow ; and the inside ship, which now lays nearly out of range, is in 27 feet water. The ships look remarkably well. I visited the Admiral in a steamer, where his flag was flying — a heavy paddle-steamer ; and I visited, also, the only screw line-of-battle ship, a 74, and everything appeared in good order — there was no preparation. The crew appeared very fair. In 1854, they were all inside of Menschikoff, in a line from it. The two three-deckers moored across the harbour, protected by strong booms ; and I believe had an attempt been made to force the harbour, our fleet would have been destroyed. There was first the shallow water ; then the smoke, which would have covered everything ; and after passing the batteries (if that was possible) there were seventeen sail of the line to fight, and lots of infernal machines.

" If fifty sail of the line, and 50,000 men in steamers, were to attempt an attack, it might just be possible to succeed, provided they did not sink ships between Menschikoff and Cronslott, and our ships did not take the ground in going in.

" It would be necessary for the leading ships to anchor against the batteries. Those following should go in and break the boom. If they succeeded, we would probably overpower the fleet, and the steamers would land the troops on the sea-wall. If we failed in breaking the boom, there would be great confusion, and there is no knowing what would happen. It would also be necessary to have a strong reserve to take the place of the ships against the batteries, if

they failed in silencing them, which is more than probable.
If all went right, Cronstadt would be taken; and if all went
wrong, the fleet would be lost.

"No one I think, *except* the *Times,* would have tried
Cronstadt. They said it was not necessary to see how one
was to get out; it was only necessary to get in.

"I have shown that the north passage is double—I may
say triple piled, and four new batteries built; so that passage
is sealed.

"There are no guns on the north wall; but outside there
are redoubts well armed.

"On the south side, between Risbank and the main land,
there are two new batteries, which render it unassailable, and
the passage up towards Peterhoff is piled also.

"On the ramparts there are about 120 guns, many of them
pointing seaward. The carriages are not in good order.

"Fort Menschikoff is now fitted with platforms like a ship's
decks, with 32-pounders, where the seamen are exercised in
the winter. It is well ventilated, having no guns on the sides
or rear.

"On the shore, inside Peter the Great, there is a heavy
earthen redoubt which points to the sea. There are redoubts
all over the island, and on the western part of it a new fortification is begun right across, and between it and the town a
chain of redoubts. The line wall is of small stones, like
Bomarsund, which could be easily knocked down. There is
a ditch, but no glacis. I forgot to say the screw line-of-
battle ship has 830 men, excluding engineers and stokers.

Names of Forts.				Number of Guns.
Menschikoff	-	-	-	- 48
Risbank	-	-	-	- 190
Alexander	-	-	-	- 130
Peter the Great -	-	-	-	- 60
The Mole	-	-	-	- 140
No. 1. Redoubt -	-	-	-	- 20
Cronslott	-	-	-	- 80
On the Inner Mole	-	-	-	- 20
				688

After Sir C. Napier had returned from Cronstadt, Sir Robert Peel—who had accompanied Lord Granville's embassy to Russia, and therefore perhaps considered himself a sufficient judge of what ships could do against forts, or probably thinking that, in virtue of his position as a Lord of the Admiralty, he possessed the requisite knowledge *ex officio*—avowed at a public meeting at Stafford that if Sir C. Napier had done his duty at Cronstadt that fortress would have been " crumbled in the dust;" and that, from " the Grand Duke Constantine to the youngest midshipman on board the *Vladimir*," this was the general opinion in Russia. At another public meeting at Tamworth, Sir R. Peel further stated, that " the highest authority in the realm" was of the same opinion.

As Sir R. Peel was a member of the Government and a Lord of the Admiralty, Sir C. Napier deemed it incumbent on him to address Lord Palmerston on the subject; the Admiral, on this renewed accusation repeating his demand for an inquiry into his conduct. It was not without considerable perseverance that Sir Charles obtained a reply to his letters. At length, however, Lord Palmerston did reply, completely vindicating the Admiral from the aspersions of his colleague as regarded the Baltic Campaign, but strangely enough, evading all mention of Sir Robert, and accusing Sir Charles of having needlessly fallen out with the Board of Admiralty and Sir James Graham —the parties by whom he had been so pertinaciously attacked for the very acts which drew forth the otherwise unqualified praise of Lord Palmerston. The subjoined is the correspondence which took place on the occasion.

Sir Charles Napier to Lord Palmerston.

"Merchistoun, Horndean, 29th October, 1856.

" My Lord,

" You have no doubt seen or heard of the attack made on me by Sir Robert Peel, at the Staffordshire banquet.

" To prevent any mistakes, I send your Lordship the printed speech as reported in the ' Times,' of the 27th of October. (Enclosure A.)

" I have judged it expedient to write a letter to Sir Robert Peel, a copy of which I also forward to your Lordship. (Enclosure B.)

" But, my Lord, that is not sufficient; Sir Robert Peel, a member of the Board of Admiralty, and of your Lordship's Government, has publicly accused me of not doing my duty before Cronstadt, and distinctly stated that if I had done it ' Cronstadt would have been crumbled in the dust.'

" Your Lordship is aware that on my return from the Baltic, in 1854, and conceiving the Admiralty had reflected on me, I repeatedly asked for an investigation into my conduct, which was refused.

" I submitted my case to Lord Aberdeen, and requested it might be laid before the Cabinet; the following was his answer :—

" ' Downing Street, February 2nd, 1855.

" ' DEAR SIR CHARLES,

" ' As the Queen has accepted my resignation, as well as that of all my colleagues, no further meeting of the Cabinet will take place. I am therefore unable to comply with your request to lay your statement before them.

" ' I am, dear Sir Charles,

" ' Very truly yours,

" ' ABERDEEN.

" ' Vice-Admiral Sir Charles Napier.'

" When your Lordship came to the head of the Government I submitted it to you, but received no reply. It was in consequence brought before the House of Commons by Mr. Malins, and papers were asked for, which were refused on the plea that it would be injurious to the public service.

" When I came into Parliament, I applied for a Committee to

investigate the conduct of the war in the Baltic, which demand was opposed by the Government, and in consequence failed, to which decision I was obliged to submit.

"But, my Lord, things have now assumed a different aspect.

"Sir Robert Peel, a Lord of the Admiralty, and a member of your Government, has publicly accused me of not doing my duty, and I may say of cowardice.

"I hence consider it a duty I owe to myself and to my family, to demand of your Lordship a full investigation of the whole of my conduct during the time I commanded the Baltic Fleet; it cannot now be alleged that there is any danger to the public service; — we are at peace.

"If I have not done my duty, I ought to be punished; if I have done my duty, my character as an officer ought to be cleared and my honour allowed to go down to posterity untarnished.

"No man is better acquainted with my career than your Lordship. I have repeatedly served under your office, and you have frequently termed my services 'most brilliant.' Even Sir Robert Peel, the father of my accuser, stated in the House of Commons that 'by my brilliant courage I had changed a dynasty in two minutes, and performed other brilliant services.'

"I call upon you, my Lord, as a gentleman and as a man of honour, to enable me to clear up my reputation, which has been so cruelly and unjustly aspersed for upwards of two years.

"Your Lordship granted a Commission of Inquiry into the conduct of Lords Lucan and Cardigan and other officers who had served in the Crimea: they thought that they had been reflected on in the report of the Crimean Commissioners; but, my Lord, my case is stronger; a member of your Government accuses me of little short of cowardice, and your Lordship cannot, and ought not, with justice, to refuse the investigation I demand.

"I think the assertion of Sir Robert Peel as to the belief of the Grand Duke Constantine is, my Lord, not true.

"I asked the Grand Duke if he thought I should have led the fleet into Cronstadt; his reply was 'perhaps.' The Grand Duke then produced the plan of Cronstadt, and pointed out to me the preparations he had made to meet me, and his conviction that had I made an attack I should have been defeated.

"His Highness's preparations were judicious and irresistible. In addition to the numerous granite batteries, he had moored two three-deckers between Forts Menschikoff and Cronslott: they were defended by strong booms outside of them; and should they fail, they were prepared to be sunk. Inside the three-deckers there were eighteen line-of-battle ships, moored in line, in close order, and a garrison of many thousand troops.

" In addition to these and the forts, infernal machines were laid so thick in the channel, that it was with some difficulty their own vessels could avoid them in going in and out.

" With regard to the north side of Cronstadt, he thought I would have attacked it; but when I told him I had no means of doing so — that I had neither gun-boats, mortar-vessels or rockets — his surprise ceased.

" I then asked his Highness if he would allow me to speak plainly to him — to which he assented. I told him, had he met me at Kiel with his whole fleet, we were so ill-manned and so ill-disciplined that I did not know what would have been the consequence. He said he was not aware of our state till too late, and added — holding out his hand in the most frank and sailor-like manner — ' Had I had screws I should have had the honour of meeting you.'

" I have, my Lord, a great respect for the Grand Duke Constantine, — not merely from his civility to me, but because I believe him to have been a generous foe and a man of great ability; and I am satisfied he is incapable of telling me one story and a Lord of the Admiralty another.

" It is lamentable, my Lord, to see a member of Her Majesty's Government, who does not and cannot know anything of naval affairs, pursuing a course so unworthy; and it is still more lamentable to see an organ of the press, which is generally believed by the nation to be all-powerful, ' patting him on the back ' for so doing. With such a combination no man's honour or reputation is safe. Ever since the Sebastopol hoax the Admiralty and the ' Times ' have been leagued to crush me, and my repeated demands for an investigation have been constantly refused.

" Years of faithful service and actions which have become history are flung to the winds by such an unholy alliance.

" On these considerations, my Lord, I demand an investigation of my conduct, which your Lordship cannot in justice refuse, as a member of your Lordship's Government is now my accuser.

" I have the honour to be, my Lord,
" Your Lordship's most obedient Servant,
" CHARLES NAPIER, Vice-Admiral.
" The Right Honorable Viscount Palmerston, &c. &c."

Sir Charles Napier to Lord Palmerston.

(No. 2.)

"Merchistoun, Nov. 5th, 1856.

" My Lord,

" Under date of the 29th of October I wrote to your Lordship on the subject of an attack made on me by Sir Robert Peel, a member of your Lordship's Government.

" That letter your Lordship must have received, and I cannot conceal my disappointment that I have not had a reply.

" Lord Harrowby, one of your Lordship's colleagues, was at the dinner; it was his place to return thanks for Her Majesty's Ministers.

" His Lordship appears to have put forward Sir Robert Peel, saying, ' that he would tell them something more of the Emperor of Russia.'

" Sir Robert Peel then accused me of not doing my duty.

" My Lord, an officer's character is dear to him. In this country he is nothing without it.

" After a long and honourable career, my conduct in the Baltic has been called in question. I have done everything to obtain an investigation, but in vain.

" Now that I am accused by a member of your Lordship's Government, in the presence of one of your colleagues, your Lordship cannot, in common justice, refuse me an inquiry.

" There are no State reasons against it; there are no secrets injurious to the country to divulge. The question is a simple one : ' Did Sir Charles Napier do his duty or not ?'

" I have the intimate conviction that I did, and I know that no officer in the service could have done more.

" Had Lord Nelson himself been raised from the dead to command the Baltic fleet, he neither would have touched Cronstadt nor Sweaborg. He was long before Toulon and Cadiz, and never attacked either the one or the other ; and now I am abused for not attacking an impregnable fortress.

" If I did wrong, surely the French Admiral was as much to blame as myself; but he received praise and honour from his Emperor.

" Justice, my Lord, is the privilege of an Englishman. I demand it of your Lordship as a gentleman and a man of honour. I ask of your Lordship to give me an opportunity of clearing my reputation.

" No member of my family was ever before accused of not doing his duty.

" I wish to preserve the name *sans tâche.*

" I have the honour to be, my Lord,

" Your Lordship's obedient Servant,

" CHARLES NAPIER, Vice-Admiral.

" The Right Hon. Viscount Palmerston,
      &c. &c. &c."

Sir Charles Napier to the Grand Duke Constantine.

" Merchistoun, 29th October, 1856.

" SIR,

" I beg to send your Imperial Highness a speech of Sir Robert Peel — a Lord of the Admiralty — in which he accuses me of not doing my duty before Cronstadt.

" I also send your Highness my letter to him, and two to Lord Palmerston.

" I think I have distinctly stated what passed between your Imperial Highness and myself relative to Cronstadt, which certainly does not agree with what Sir Robert states.

" I shall make no apology to your Imperial Highness for writing to you. Your Highness is a frank, open-hearted sailor.

" I therefore request you will be pleased to inform me whether I have correctly stated what passed between your Highness and myself when you honoured me with an interview, and whether, as stated by Sir Robert Peel, if I had attacked Cronstadt, I would have have crumbled it into dust?

" I have the honour to remain,

" Your Imperial Highness's devoted and

humble Servant,

" CHARLES NAPIER, Vice-Admiral.

" His Imperial Highness the Grand Duke Constantine,
    " St. Petersburg."

Sir Charles Napier to Lord Palmerston.

(No. 3.)

"Merchistoun, November 24th, 1856.

"My Lord,

"When one gentleman writes to another, even should one be the Prime Minister and the other an Admiral, he has a right to a reply.

"I have twice written to your Lordship on public service, demanding an investigation into my conduct, in consequence of an unjustifiable attack made upon me by Sir Robert Peel, a Lord of the Admiralty and a member of your Lordship's Government.

"You have had several Cabinet Councils and ample time to consult your colleagues on the subject.

"What I ask for, my Lord, is just and reasonable ; the humblest man in the land is entitled to a reply ; your Lordship has not vouchsafed me one.

"I have been given to understand that your Lordship could not reply to me till you had seen Sir Robert Peel, who was laid up with the hooping cough ; but, my lord, it appears he is recovered, as he has been exhibiting at Tamworth in a more unjustifiable manner than he did at Stafford, and has stated that 'the highest authority' in the country had approved of what he had said. He, moreover, accused me of lowering the character of the British sailor.

"It is impossible, my Lord, that you can refuse an investigation into my conduct, now that 'the highest authority' in the land approves of what Sir Robert Peel has said.

"I do not fear investigation, my Lord. There are no State secrets to divulge that can injure the country. My character ought to be cleared, and my conduct either approved or condemned.

"Is the Government, my Lord, afraid that things may come out injurious to the late Administration ?

"Is the Government afraid that I will show that the Administration did not furnish me with the means necessary to satisfy the expectations of the people of England ?

"Is the Government afraid that it will appear that Admiral Chads' report of the 14th of June, relative to Sweaborg, sent to Sir James Graham by me, and my report of the 18th of July, pointing out the proper means of attacking Sweaborg, were never laid before the Government ?

"Is the Government afraid that, notwithstanding my report on Cronstadt—(which the Admiralty characterised as a very able one)—Admiral Dundas, in 1855, was only furnished with three gun-boats in the first instance, and fifteen afterwards, to attack Cronstadt, when the Russians had two hundred?

"Is the Government afraid that I will show that, though I was accused by Admiral Berkeley of a disinclination to enter the Gulf of Finland, he had written to me to ask 'when it was time to leave that infernal Gulf,' and authorised me to leave the Baltic altogether, and go to Wingo Sound ; instead of doing so, I actually sailed the day of the date of his letter, and proceeded to Nargen, where I remained till the 19th of October?

"Is the Government afraid that I will show that although no means were furnished me for attacking Cronstadt Admiral Berkeley stated in the House that it was my fault Cronstadt was not attacked in 1854 ; and Sir Robert Peel, since, in his speech at Stafford and Tamworth, stated that it was my fault it was not crumbled to the dust?

"Is the Government afraid that I will show that at the time I was accused by Admiral Berkeley of a disinclination to enter the Gulf of Finland, I was publicly and privately applauded by the Admiralty for acting as I did?

" Is the Government afraid that I will show that I received the greatest praise from the Admiralty for my conduct in command of Her Majesty's fleet till the hoax about Sebastopol, received on the 4th of October, 1854, and that I was then goaded to attempt impossibilities at a season of the year when the fleet would, in all probability, have been lost, and by the men who were advising me not to allow myself to be goaded to attempt impossibilities?

"Is the Admiralty afraid that I will show that on the 9th of October, when they discovered the hoax, they forgot their order of the 4th of October ; and the French and English sailing ships were directed by telegraph to return to France and England forthwith, and I was ordered to use my own discretion and retire on Keil when I judged fit?

"I beg your Lordship to believe that I mean nothing disrespectful to your Lordship in thus pressing for a reply ; and I am satisfied that, had your Lordship been at the head of the Government in 1854, and acted with the same vigour you did in 1856, you would have given me means, and I would have used them with the same energy and success I have before done when under your orders.

"I have the honour to be, &c.

"CHARLES NAPIER.

"The Right Honourable Viscount Palmerston."

Lord Palmerston to Sir Charles Napier.

"94. Piccadilly, December 1st, 1856.

"My dear Sir Charles,

"I can assure you, with the greatest truth, that the various discussions which have taken place out of Parliament and in Parliament between you and the Board of Admiralty, in regard to the Naval operations in the Baltic while you commanded in that sea, have been witnessed by me with very great pain.

"I have deeply regretted those discussions, both from my personal regard for you, and from the interest which I take in the good of the public service.

"But I should not be dealing candidly and frankly with you if I were not to say, on this occasion, that if those discussions have been attended with circumstances unpleasant to your personal feelings, you have for this yourself to blame. It was you who first began the controversy, by what I must be allowed to characterise as a very unseemly and improper attack, made by you, on a public occasion, on Sir James Graham, then First Lord of the Admiralty.

"You have often complained that you have been, without just foundation, accused of want of discretion. I have always maintained that on all occasions on which you have been professionally employed, in executing instructions on matters connected with the departmemt of the Government which was under my charge, I had full reason to be satisfied with your judgment and discretion. I wish I could say as much for your conduct on shore, and when you have been acting upon your own impulses. But I am bound to say that, estimating highly, as I do, the great services which professionally you have performed ; and respecting, as I do, the noble qualities of which, in your professional career, you have given such frequent proofs, I have seen, with sincere grief, in your conduct on shore, things which your best friends (and I claim to be one of that number) could not witness without deep regret.

"I do not wish, however, to rake up the past ; my present purpose is to answer your application for a public investigation of your conduct in not having attacked Cronstadt. That application being founded upon observations which have lately been made on that subject at some public meetings.

"My answer is plain and simple : I think no such investigation necessary, because I consider your conduct in refraining from attacking Cronstadt to have been judicious and proper, and to have been founded upon a correct sense of your public duty in the very responsible situation in which you were placed as Commander-in-Chief of the Baltic Fleet.

" The fleet which you commanded in the Baltic was a very fine fleet, and the Board of Admiralty of the day deserve great praise for having equipped and sent to sea in so short a time so powerful an armament. That fleet was perfectly sufficient—especially when reinforced by the French squadron—to have enabled you to give a good account of the Russian fleet if it had come out to give you battle. But the fleet under your command was not sufficient for the double purpose of attacking the stone batteries of Cronstadt and of afterwards encountering with success the Russian fleet.

" If you had attacked the batteries of Cronstadt, whatever the result of your attack might have been as to the Russian batteries, your ships must have been seriously damaged, and your fleet, after such an action with the batteries, would probably not have been in a condition successfully to encounter the Russian fleet. The consequence of such a state of things might have been a naval disaster, or the temporary ascendancy of the Russian fleet not only in the Baltic but in the North Sea and on the coasts of England.

" I consider, therefore, that in the then existing state of things you acted with sound judgment in refraining from attacking the batteries of Cronstadt with the fleet under your command, and that in pursuing that course you best performed the important and very responsible duty which you had undertaken.

" This is my opinion now ; this was my opinion at the time ; and I think you would find it expressed in a private letter which I wrote to you while you were still in command in the Baltic. And this is the opinion which I have invariably expressed to all with whom I have at any time communicated upon this subject.

" My dear Sir Charles, yours sincerely,
" PALMERSTON.

" Vice-Admiral Sir Charles Napier."

Sir Charles Napier to Lord Palmerston.

(No. 4.)

" Merchistoun, December 5th, 1856.

" MY LORD,

" Your Lordship tells me that 'you have witnessed with great pain the discussions that have taken place between me and the Board of Admiralty, both in and out of Parliament, and the attack made by me on Sir James Graham on a public occasion ;'

but, my Lord, if you have felt pain on that occasion, provoked as I was by Sir James Graham and his Board, how much more pained must you have been to witness the unprovoked attacks made upon me by a member of your Lordship's Government on two public occasions?

"Your Lordship tells me that 'you have always maintained, when professionally employed in executing instructions under your department, that you had full reason to be satisfied with my judgment and discretion; and you are bound to say that you estimate the great services which professionally I have performed. You highly respect the noble qualities of which in my professional career I have given such frequent proofs; but you have seen, with sincere regret, in my conduct on shore things which my best friends (and you claim to be one of them) could not witness without deep regret.'

"How much more poignant, then, my Lord, must have been your 'grief,' and how much more deep your 'regret,' to witness the conduct of Sir Robert Peel, a Lord of the Admiralty, a member of your Government, in attacking an old officer, double his age, who had served his country honourably for upwards of fifty years, had several times received the thanks of Parliament, and had even been highly lauded in Parliament by the honourable Baronet's own father?

"Your Lordship must also remember that in attacking me he attacked the French Admiral, my colleague; and in so doing must have given offence to the French nation—our Ally.

"Your Lordship will permit me to observe that you do not put the case sufficiently strong. The attacks were made at public meetings it is true, but they were made by Sir Robert Peel, a Lord of the Admiralty, a member of your Lordship's Government, and in the presence of one of your colleagues.

"Your Lordship thinks no investigation ' necessary, because you consider my conduct to have been judicious and proper, and to have been founded on a correct sense of my public duty in the very responsible situation in which I was placed as Commander-in-Chief of the Baltic Fleet.'

"The fleet I commanded, your Lordship observes, 'was perfectly sufficient, when reinforced by the French squadron, to have enabled me to give a good account of the Russian fleet if it had come out to give me battle. But the fleet under my command was not sufficient for the double purpose of attacking the stone batteries of Cronstadt and afterwards encountering with success the Russian fleet.'

"Your Lordship further observes, 'that if I had attacked

Cronstadt, whatever the result might have been to the Russian batteries, my ships would have been so seriously damaged, and my fleet after such an action with the batteries would probably not have been in a situation to encounter the Russian fleet. The consequence of such a state of things might have been a naval disaster, or the temporary ascendancy of the Russian fleet, not only in the Baltic, but in the North Sea and on the coasts of England.'

" You therefore think ' that, in the then existing state of things, I acted with sound judgment in refraining from attacking the batteries of Cronstadt with the fleet under my command, and that in pursuing this course I best performed the important and responsible duty which I had undertaken.'

" This, your Lordship says, is your opinion now, was your opinion at the time — and it was so expressed in a private letter to me when I was still in command of the Baltic fleet, — and that this is the opinion you have invariably expressed to all with whom you have communicated at any time on the subject.

" I feel highly gratified that you entertain so high an opinion of my public services in general, and particularly of my conduct before Cronstadt. But I do not think, after what has passed, that even your good opinion will clear me in the eyes of the world.

" It was stated by Admiral Berkeley in the House of Commons, in 1856, that it was my fault Cronstadt was not attacked.

"·It has been stated at one public meeting, in presence of one of your colleagues, by Sir Robert Peel, another Lord of the Admiralty, that, ' had I done my duty, Cronstadt would have been crumbled to dust.'

" This was confirmed at another public meeting; and it was stated by Sir Robert Peel, that ' what he had said at Stafford was approved by the "highest authority."' This has gone forth to the remotest corners of the earth.

" The ' highest authority' could not have been your Lordship, after what you have written to me. It could not have been Her Majesty. Therefore, I think the country has a right to know who this ' highest authority' is.

" Sir Robert Peel's opinion, my Lord, on naval matters is not worth much; nor, indeed, on any other. His want of judgment is proverbial; but his position gives him weight.

" The course he has pursued reflects little credit on your Lordship's Government; and be assured, my Lord, that he is not the Samson to pull down the pillars of the State and crush the Administration beneath its ruins.

R R

" I therefore trust your Lordship will reconsider your decision, and grant me the investigation I request.

" I have the honour, &c.

" CHARLES NAPIER.

" The Right Honourable Viscount Palmerston."

Sir Charles Napier to Lord Palmerston.

(No. 5.)

" Merchistoun, Dec. 7th, 1856.

" MY LORD,

" Since writing to your Lordship on the 5th of December, I beg to send you a copy of the Grand Duke's reply to me, just received.

" It is for your Lordship to judge whether a member of your Lordship's Government, who has endeavoured to ruin the reputation of an old officer, is fit to be one of his masters; and your Lordship may perhaps be able to ascertain who the ' highest authority' is to whom Sir Robert Peel alluded in his speech.

" I have the honour, &c.

" CHARLES NAPIER.

" The Right Honourable Viscount Palmerston."

The Grand Duke Constantine to Sir Charles Napier.

" St. Petersburg, $\frac{13}{25}$ Nov., 1856.

" MY DEAR ADMIRAL,

" In answer to your letter of the 29th of October, I willingly affirm that you have quite exactly reported the conversation I had with you concerning Cronstadt.

" With regard to Sir R. Peel's statement, I consider it necessary to say that I spoke with him but once, viz., at his official presentation in Moscow; and that not a word concerning Cronstadt—not even the name itself—was mentioned by either of us.

" Yours, affectionately,

" CONSTANTINE.

" Sir Charles Napier, Vice-Admiral."

INDEX.

THE END.

Printed in the United Kingdom
by Lightning Source UK Ltd.
135919UK00001B/180/A